Children's Drawings
as Measures
of Intellectual Maturity

CHILDREN'S DRAWINGS AS MEASURES OF INTELLECTUAL MATURITY

A Revision and Extension of the Goodenough Draw-a-Man Test

DALE B. HARRIS

The Pennsylvania State University

HARCOURT, BRACE & WORLD, INC.
New York · Chicago · San Francisco · Atlanta

To the memory of Florence L. Goodenough

Preface

A PREFACE OFTEN SERVES the author better than the reader. It gives the author an opportunity to explain those circumstances that facilitated, or limited, his project. Thus it serves a valuable personal function by giving "closure" to the author. One also has, of course, the pleasant satisfaction of acknowledging publicly the assistance of colleagues and friends.

This project originally was undertaken collaboratively with Dr. Florence L. Goodenough, as a revision of her well-known scale. Her illness prevented active collaboration, but her interest was always keen.

The present book has sought to accomplish several goals: to put in order certain uncompleted aspects of the Goodenough research, and to extend the knowledge of the psychology of children's drawings through certain original researches. In the process of these researches, including the revision and attempted extension of the original scale, the author's respect for this brief test of intellectual maturity steadily increased, as did the author's respect for the validity of Dr. Goodenough's original ideas. Dr. Goodenough outlined the true scope of the problem and delineated essential dimensions in 1926, in her short but insightful book. The present work has built onto, but not substantively changed, the insights of that work.

Another goal the author sought was to present a comprehensive survey of the literature on children's drawings in this country and abroad. The major theoretical positions reflected in this literature have been outlined. Such an encyclopedic review assembles so many contradictory findings that generalizations are necessarily broad. Much contemporary psychology rather vigorously disowns eclectic empiricism. As a result, reviews of the literature are sometimes made in terms of one theoretical position. The danger in this approach is that materials failing to support the chosen position are overlooked, ignored, or discarded outright. The oversimplified position presented may mislead several generations of students by its easy, persuasive statement, based on what is in fact a selected body of evidence.

Despite the acknowledged dangers of eclecticism, the author has tried faithfully to set forth the contending and contrasting points of view. He believes that in a field as amorphous and as theoretically undeveloped as the psychology of children's drawings, a comprehensive survey is essential to reveal where theory may profitably be constructed.

As must be the case, the author's expressions of appreciation list only a few of the many persons who have contributed significantly to his work. More than he can express he regrets the fact that Florence Goodenough herself did not live to see this work brought to conclusion. To John E. Anderson, former teacher and, later, colleague, he expresses his gratitude for many stimulating and insightful discussions of the psychology of art and drawing, for critical reading of parts of the manuscript, and for many valuable suggestions which have been incorporated. Professors John Hall and Arthur Brayfield of The Pennsylvania State University also contributed critical readings of the manuscript. Dr. Pramila Phatak of the University of Baroda, India, made helpful suggestions on the final scoring instructions, growing out of her extensive work with children's drawings in India and in the United States. To art educators, Clifton Gayne of the University of Minnesota and Kenneth Beittel of The Pennsylvania State University, the author owes an appreciative statement for their helpfulness with respect to children's art. Dr. Beittel also contributed critical readings which were most valuable. Professor Robert Spencer, anthropologist at the University of Minnesota, was instrumental in obtaining the sample of drawings from Eskimo children at schools in Alaska.

To students and other colleagues and to his research assistants who supplied so many valuable hours, the author owes a particular debt of gratitude. He only hopes that these people gained in some proportion as they gave to his work.

Elizabeth S. Harris made considerable contributions to the research and to the preparation of the manuscript. At a time when the author's professional duties were particularly pressing, she relieved him of work with the proofs. This assistance is gratefully acknowledged. Appreciation is also expressed to Miss Mariette de Groot of the Netherlands, who helped with the translation of Dutch sources.

Substantial contributions to the project were made from the Graduate Research Fund of the University of Minnesota, by the Institute of Child Development and Welfare of that University in research facilities, and by the Psychology Department of The Pennsylvania State University, also in time and facilities.

DALE B. HARRIS

Contents

List of Tables

List of Plates

Part One

Chapter One

Introduction

OF THE MANY tests of intelligence, the Goodenough Draw-a-Man Test (1926) is perhaps the most unusual in basic conception, brevity, and general convenience. It has been widely used to survey the intellectual status of young children, and to study children with hearing handicaps and suspected neurological deficiencies. It has been used to study personality and adjustment problems, delinquency, and character defects. Several modifications of the Draw-a-Man technique have been introduced as "projective tests." As the idea of testing engaged the cultural anthropologist, this device and modifications of it quickly appeared in his repertoire.

Writing in the *Fourth Mental Measurements Yearbook* (1953, p. 292), Naomi Stewart affirms that the Draw-a-Man Test measures intelligence primarily and should be evaluated as such a device. Pointing out that the norms for many tests have shown changes after twenty-five or thirty years, she suggests that the Goodenough scoring points be re-evaluated and the test be restandardized.

Such considerations, among others, have led to the present text, which reports a series of studies covering a decade of work. In brief, this program of research has re-evaluated Goodenough's method, extended it to older groups, and developed an "alternate form" of the test by adding to the drawing of a man a drawing of a woman and a drawing of the self. Work has been done to restandardize the instrument, to derive a somewhat more defensible quantitative expression of the child's performance, and to establish a convenient approximation to full-scale scoring. In addition, studies have also thrown further light on the variety of abilities tapped by the drawing test, and rationalized its place as a measure of ability.

Two generations of evaluating one of psychology's firmest achievements, the measurement of intelligence, have produced at least three major changes of position. A concept long defined empirically and statistically as "general intelligence" no longer is considered unitary or monolithic. The measurement of this ability (or abilities) no longer seeks to divert itself of cultural or social encumbrances in an effort to get at a residual "pure" or "native" ability. The age scale method of expressing the development of this ability has been discarded in many instruments for more sophisticated and presumably more accurate measures of exceptionality.

1

Changes in the Meaning of Intelligence

A significant change has taken place in what is understood as "intelligence." Binet replaced the notion of many separable mental functions with the idea of "general intelligence." This idea, somewhat akin to a "faculty," was in line with an older psychology still influential in his day. Subsequent researches showed that the concept of a general ability arose from the substantial intercorrelations among the work samples comprising intelligence tests. Further studies with larger varieties of items and appropriate statistical techniques suggested that the varying patterns of intercorrelation really expressed the presence of a *number* of rather distinct abilities, often defined in terms of the mental operations required by the work sample.

To determine how many such abilities exist has been something of a task. Spearman (e.g., 1927) argued for a general factor (g) plus a specific factor (s) that was peculiar to each different task sampled. Thurstone (e.g., 1938) held for a number of separate factors, of which 10 or 12 could be measured reliably. Guilford (e.g., 1959) felt that the number of factors is much larger than this, perhaps as great as 120. Others, notably British psychologists (e.g., Vernon, 1950), argued for a hierarchy of abilities, extending from one general to many specific abilities by way of major and minor group factors of differing degrees of generality.

However these differing viewpoints may finally be resolved, it is not likely that psychology will return to the notion of a monolithic "general intelligence," except possibly for predicting school achievement. The abilities most involved in academic work seem to be verbal and abstract, and are sufficiently intercorrelated to permit the practical use of the general ability concept, even though separate abilities such as number concept and verbal fluency may even here be discerned. It is becoming common practice to refer to such achievement tests as tests of "general mental ability," or "general scholastic ability." The term "general intelligence," although widely known popularly, no longer has the standing it once had in technical psychology.

The Assessment of Abilities

In technical usage, the idea of a pure measure of potentiality or intelligence has been abandoned as impossible. It has long been accepted that abilities or potentialities can be estimated only after their development. Such development is now seen not as a simple unfolding of inborn or native capacities, but as growth in richness of response, the result of learning processes in which the stimulation afforded by growth and special experience plays an important part. Abilities are not, however, to be equated with learned performances; attempts to equalize opportunities to practice, and to learn, often result in *increased* rather than decreased individual differences. The notion of structure or quality of the organism as setting certain limits on the effect of practice and learning opportunities persists, at least implicitly.

The richness of the person's responses increases with the passage of time. His performances become more complex. As Thorndike showed (1926), mental performances move up in *altitude* or level, and broaden in *range* or scope. The mental performances that involve symbolization and problem solving increase in complexity as a result of associative processes, both simple and elaborate. So complex do these become that some psychologists prefer to speak of them as cognitive processes, and their contents as concepts or abstract ideas.

Whether the components of so-called general mental ability become more numerous with development, and their organization more elaborate and complex, has been the subject of debate. It is easy, by analogy to anatomical growth, to hypothesize an early differentiation and elaboration from rather simple beginnings (e.g., Garrett, 1946). Not all investigators have agreed on this, however. There is general recognition that the development of mental abilities is best described by a negatively accelerated (though not uniformly so) growth curve. Increments of change are undeniably greater in the younger organism. Rapidity of growth in the early years gives the appearance of a high intercorrelation of abilities simply because the increments are large for units of time, and accumulate substantially. As rate of growth decreases, increments becoming smaller, the spurious correlation contributed solely by the sweep of rapid growth over time falls away, and abilities are less substantially interrelated. There is good evidence for this in the motor abilities of children (e.g., Wellman, 1937), though less so, perhaps, in mental abilities.

Bayley (1957) believes that the principal components of the complex we call "general mental ability" do change with age, increasing in number as well as changing in their relative contribution to the total variance. A factor analysis of Bayley's data (Hofstaetter, 1954) suggested that a "Sensory-Motor Alertness" factor is relatively more important in the first two years of life, a "Persistence" factor from age two to four, and a "Manipulating Symbols" factor after age four. Bayley also found evidence in her data for a growth spurt in mental development around age nine; other data (Freeman and Flory, 1937) showed this spurt occurring about two years later. Such data suggest an underlying control on the growth process; demonstrated changes in individual growth curves undeniably reflect also the differential effect of stimulation on growth. Having said that growth may be facilitated or retarded is not to say that it is known how such changes are accomplished. Indeed, growth factors and situational variables that might allow experimental manipulation of mental development are far from being identified.

Piaget has studied children's mental growth by clinical interrogation (1950, 1952) rather than by tests and growth curves. He concluded that there are four major stages of mental development: The first, up to age two, is primarily a sensorimotor stage, when the child comes to know that objects exist, even apart from his perception of them, and that these objects can be viewed from different perspectives. The next phase reaches from the development of language (age two) to age five or six. In this phase the child comes to represent objects and events by symbols, but he is essentially "preoperational" in that he seldom distinguishes between himself as agent and his goals as the effect of action. From five or six to ten or eleven, Piaget sees the child as acquiring the ability to carry out *concrete operations*. From eleven or twelve to fifteen or so, the child shifts from concrete operations to *formal operations*. Operations are defined as actions, overt or covert (as in thinking out a problem). These operations mentally transform data about the real world in terms of functions, so that they can be used in the solution of problems. Piaget associates these operations with the formal operations of logic, such as class inclusion operations, serial ordering operations, and the like.

It is interesting to note that Piaget's "stages" break at roughly the ages noted by Bayley as transitional periods. These periods acquire significance for the present studies when it is noted that the drawing test is most effective in the years between four or five and twelve or so, approximately Bayley's "manipulating symbols" period and Piaget's "concrete operations" stage.

The Index of Measured Abilities

The final major shift since the early days of intelligence testing has been in the index of performance adopted. Binet's great contribution, the age-scale method, has only recently yielded ground. There is much to be said for an age-scale concept, with its implicit reference to normal or typical growth, when studying children; so many aspects of development are age-related. Yet the mental age concept has always presented difficulties as the fact of decreasing increments makes itself felt on the growth curve. The assumed straight line mental age function simply does not agree with the facts of development. As the process of development is more completely understood, age, or time, seems to be only a crude index. Cumulative changes that occur through accretion or association seem to depend on repetition or reinforcement, not merely lapse of time.

Convenient statistical methods for describing variation and for scaling in reference to such normal variation have been devised. These scales accurately place the individual in comparison with a known or defined group. Unfortunately, these methods do not readily supply growth measures; they are purely *relative*. But they do permit ready comparison with indices of other performances or variables, which either have never been or cannot be scaled on an age basis. Consequently, percentile and standard score conversions are more and more preferred to the mental age concept and its derivation, the IQ.

As the concept of many mental abilities has replaced the concept of a unitary intelligence, the notion of a multiple score test has come into use. Today one frequently meets the graphic "profile," or other representations of multiple scores, representing different "factors" or functions measured by a test. As has been pointed out, the single score measure of mental ability is becoming more and more restricted to measures of academic or scholastic ability. (Even in this area, however, recently developed tests tend to follow the multiple ability concept.[1])

The score on the Goodenough Drawing Test is a single score; how, then, can one justify continuing its use, as has been done in the present research? Three reasons may be offered: (1) The score, in the age range of four or five to fourteen or fifteen, where increments can be measured, correlates substantially (often in the .70's and .80's) with measures of general mental or scholastic ability;[2] (2) the components of the score, in the form of scoring points, appear to separate criterion groups selected both according to other measures of mental ability and to total score on the drawing test itself;[3] (3) the concepts or ideas tapped by the drawing test seem to relate theoretically; i.e., the concrete operations reflect elemental cognitive concepts that in turn logically make up more complex concepts. These more complex concepts are thus genetically related to the simpler order concepts, and it seems reasonable to use the simpler order concepts as an index to the more complex.[4] This point is expanded in the section that follows.

Intellectual Maturity and Concept Formation

In discussing the abilities tapped by the drawing test, it has seemed desirable to replace the notion of intelligence with the idea of *intellectual maturity*, and perhaps more specifically, *conceptual maturity*. This change gets away from the notion of unitary intelligence, and it permits consideration of children's concepts of the human figure as an index or sample of their concepts generally.

By intellectual maturity is meant the ability to form concepts of increasingly abstract character. Intellectual activity requires: (1) the ability to *perceive*, i.e., to discriminate likenesses and differences; (2) the ability to *abstract*, i.e., to classify objects according to such likenesses and differences; and (3) the ability to *generalize*, i.e., to assign an object newly experienced to a correct class, according to discriminated features, properties, or attributes. These three functions, taken together, comprise the process of *concept formation*.

For example, a child early learns to discriminate the features that set dogs apart from other animals. He does this in terms of the properties of dogs— noises emitted, number of legs, general size, selected behaviors (e.g., tail-

---

[1] For example, the Differential Aptitude Tests, published by the Psychological Corporation, or Holzinger-Crowder Uni-Factor Tests, published by Harcourt, Brace & World, Inc.

[2] See Chapter II.

[3] See Chapter IV.

[4] See Chapters X and XII.

wagging), type of skin or coat, and the like. Sounds, legs, size, coat or fur, and behavior are also properties of cats, cows, and horses, but in different kind and degree. The discrimination of likenesses and differences for a number of specific examples in each of these classes of quadrupeds permits a child to *abstract* the elements characteristic of, indeed essential to, "dogginess" (as separate from "horsiness"), and to *generalize* the concept appropriately when he first sees, for example, a Mexican hairless dog.

The very young child may on first sight refer to a horse as a "big doggie." He is both right and wrong in his conceptualization; right in discerning, abstracting, and generalizing certain features as coat and four-leggedness; wrong in failing to discern, abstract, and generalize certain other essential features, such as sound, relative size, and tail-wagging.

A concept is usually defined in psychology as the product of a mental or thought process whereby the qualities, aspects, and relations of objects are identified, compared, abstracted, and generalized. When the process covers different individuals or items it is called a class concept; when the process represents a common aspect of the class it is an abstract idea.[5] The processes which include perception, conceptualizing, and knowing, as well as judging and reasoning, are called *cognition*.

As contrasted with the less mature child, the older child discerns and can specify properties in greater detail. He can also recognize more readily the characteristic and essential properties of a class and thus can form more precise and specific concepts.

Age or experience alone is not the only factor, however. Some quality of psychological organization seems to permit one child to form more precise and effective concepts than another child with roughly similar background and experience. In an earlier period of psychology this difference was attributed to a hypothetical "general intelligence," which was said to be an intrinsic property of the organism. More recently, as has been pointed out, psychologists have become less sure about the intrinsic nature of this property. It is believed that this property may be extremely complex and subject to learning or modification in ways that at present cannot be fully stated.

The evidence of the accumulated literature and of certain studies reported in this volume suggests that a child's drawing of an object is an index to his conception of that object; that is, of his grasp of the essential features which permit him to form a class concept including that object as a member. The child learns to group "horses" and "dogs" as distinct and separate classes within the larger class of animals; he does this in terms of a progressive differentiation and specification of details in the objects he perceives and classifies. Presumably, then, as he draws familiar objects, or describes them in words, he includes the elements he finds essential to his class concepts. As he can express the common aspects of a class, he forms an abstract idea.

[5] So defined in Warren, H. C., *Dictionary of Psychology*, N.Y., Houghton Mifflin, 1934.

The Hypothesis of This Book

The review of the literature and the experimental studies reported in this volume have led to the following hypothesis: The child's drawing of any object will reveal the discriminations he has made about that object as belonging to a class, i.e., as a *concept*. In particular, it is hypothesized that his concept of a frequently experienced object, such as a human being, becomes a useful index to the growing complexity of his concepts generally.

The fact that Goodenough test scores cease to show increments soon after Bayley's "manipulating symbols" period of mental development terminates, and during Piaget's shift from "concrete operations" to "formal operations," suggests that the drawing test evaluates primarily the ability to form concepts. For the young child these are primarily concepts of concrete objects, experienced directly. Very possibly the child's conceptualization of the human person is not greatly different, in process, from his conceptualization of other animate or inanimate objects in his experience. Because the human being is so basically important to him, affectively as well as cognitively, it is probable that the human figure is a better index than, for example, a house, or an automobile. The concept of a person as a concrete object undoubtedly undergoes a more elaborate differentiation with age. The human figure both in its parts and as a whole must come to include a richer store of associations, or "meaning," than most other complex objects.

When the child's intellectual processes become sufficiently advanced and complex for him to conceptualize relationships as well as objects, he moves into Piaget's "formal operations" period. Now his thinking characteristically involves higher order abstractions, governed by the rules of logic. At this time the drawing test, tapping more concrete concepts, ceases to show increments and therefore ceases to be an index to the child's further growth in intellectual maturity.

It has been pointed out that psychological study of concept formation involves perception, a process which has increasingly engaged the research efforts of psychologists in recent years. The analysis of children's earliest drawings must take into account the psychology of perception as well as the organization of perceptual responses into the systematic patterns called concepts. Because vision is the primary distance receptor, it is plausible that visual perception increasingly comes to dominate the child's conceptual processes as he matures and learns. A review of studies will show that the drawings of young children reflect several perceptual modalities, tactual and kinesthetic as well as visual. Increasingly with age, which in childhood is a simple measure of learning and experience, the visual modality does come to dominate his drawings. This review will also show that with maturity comes increasing ability in drawing to specify relevant and significant features of concepts, both ideas of specific objects and class concepts.

Contributions of This Book

The contributions of this text may be briefly summarized as follows:

1. This revision of the Goodenough Draw-a-man Test attempted (a) to extend the Goodenough scale to include adolescent years, and (b) to develop an "alternate form" to the Man scale by deriving an analogous point scale for the figure of a woman. The second objective was successful, although the first was not.

2. A drawing of the Self was included as (a) a potential "third" form, (b) a possible avenue for studying the emerging self-concept, and (c) a possibly more valid "projective" device for the study of affect and interest than impersonal figures. Certain possible lines for further work with this drawing are indicated.

3. The Man and Woman Point scales have been standardized on more representative samples than were available to Goodenough in the early 1920's. The restandardization (a) shows a greater percentage of children now than then passing the majority of scale points, (b) confirms Goodenough's finding of a sex difference in mean score, and explores these differences more fully, and (c) confirms only in part Goodenough's guess that the woman figure would not be so good a device as the male figure. The drawing of the female figure shows a clearly defined progression.

4. Quality scales for quick approximation to point scores have been developed. For children from five to nine or ten years of age, Quality scales discriminate conceptual development about as adequately as the Point scales. These scales, however, only reflect the general conceptual development recorded in total score; they are therefore useful as descriptive rather than as analytic or research devices.

5. The accumulated empirical and theoretical literature is rather completely reviewed, and from this and the present researches it is concluded that for children from about four to fourteen years this drawing test assesses intellectual or conceptual maturity, and is of much less value as a "projective" device for studying affect or personality.

6. A basis is established for relating the drawing act to current theoretical developments in the study of perception and conceptual processes.

Organization of This Book

The plan of this book is as follows: Chapter II undertakes a comprehensive review of the early research literature on children's drawings, including a detailed review of the studies of Goodenough's method and its reliability and validity. This chapter seeks to summarize what is known about the psychology of drawing as a motor and cognitive act. Chapter III summarizes the significant studies that have viewed children's drawings as reflecting affect, or personality. This chapter includes a review and evaluation of drawing as a "projective" device and of various clinical applications.

Chapter IV presents the methodology of a point scale for scoring drawings of a man and of a woman as indices to general intellectual maturity. These two drawings are presented with some qualification as "alternate forms" of the test. This chapter describes the original Goodenough scale and the modifications attempted in the revision and extension of the scale, and discusses certain scoring and scaling problems with the solutions adopted. A modified standard score rather than a "mental age" is used for summarizing test performance. General qualitative features in the conceptual development of the female figure are described.

Chapter V presents evidence for the reliability of scoring the revised scales, certain evidences for validity, and the relationship of the old and new scales. Chapter VI describes how norms for the revised point scales were derived, presents sex differences in mean score on each of the drawings, proposes separate norms for boys and girls because of these differences, and reports data on the intercorrelation of the Man and Woman scales.

Chapter VII describes the construction and standardization of Quality scales for the man and woman figures and presents these as "short forms," more conveniently scored. Chapter VIII offers additional indirect evidence on the validity of the drawing test as a measure of conceptual maturity by discussing more fully the sex differences found in boys' and girls' drawings of the male and female figures, certain cultural differences noted in the drawings of the human figure by Eskimo children, and differences reflected in children's performances on the items of the revised scale as contrasted with Goodenough's data on the same items. Chapter VIII also discusses unsuccessful attempts to relate aspects of children's drawings to personality data. Some suggestions for further research on the drawing of the Self conclude the chapter.

Chapters IX and X present summaries of principal "theories" of children's drawings, including Goodenough's, and through the reconsideration of new information offer an extension of her viewpoint concerning the psychology of children's drawings. Chapter XI relates this point of view to more general studies of children's art.

Chapter XII recapitulates the major findings of the literature reviews and of the present research program.

The Test Manual in Part II is also published separately for the psychologist's convenience, but must be used in conjunction with the data and interpretations of the present volume. It contains instructions for administration and a general orientation toward scoring the test, detailed scoring requirements for the Man and Woman Point scales, and plates for the Man and Woman Quality scales, together with information for relating Quality scale scores to their Point scale equivalents.

Chapter Two

Historical Survey
of the Study
# of Children's Drawings[1]

THE IDEA THAT the spontaneous drawings of young children may throw light upon the psychology of child development is not new. While psychology was still a youthful science, Ebenezer Cooke (1885) published an article on children's drawings in which he described the successive stages of development as he had observed them, and urged that art instruction in the schools be made to conform more nearly to the mentality and interests of the child. Corrado Ricci (1887) published an account of the drawings of a group of Italian children. His collection of children's drawings is probably the earliest of which we have a record.[2]

Overview

As the child study movement grew during the last decade of the nineteenth century, many investigations of children's drawings were undertaken. Interest has continued to the present day.

For convenience, the psychological study of children's drawings may be considered as falling into several periods, each following its own principal lines of inquiry. The early period of descriptive investigation fell between 1885 and 1920, with greatest interest between 1890 and 1910, when a substantial literature grew up on the Continent and in America. This period established the developmental character of children's drawings, and culminated in the excellent and psychologically perceptive account of developmental stages pub-

[1] More extensive reviews of the scientific literature on children's drawings may be found in Goodenough (1926, 1928, and 1931), Goodenough and Harris (1950), Graewe (1936), Naville (1950), and Schringer (1957), Baumstein-Heissler (1955) has surveyed work in Russia. Rioux (1951) lists a comprehensive bibliography with cross references to the annotations of Naville (1950).

[2] The English translation of the main part of Ricci's article may be found in Volume 3 of the *Pedogogical Seminary.*

lished by Cyril Burt (1921). During this time there were few serious attempts to establish a *theory* of drawing behavior; there were several unsuccessful attempts to parallel the child mind with the so-called primitive mind, inspired by the oversimplified concept of societal evolution in vogue at the turn of the century.

With Goodenough's (1926) successful demonstration that a large intellectual component existed in the development of children's drawings of a man, the study of children's drawings took a new direction, one closely linked theoretically to the psychometric study of intelligence. This emphasis, particularly heavy in the literature up to 1940, has continued to the present time, especially in America, England, and Japan where the testing movement has flourished. The Goodenough test has been extensively investigated in India and in South Africa, where convenient nonverbal measures were needed to classify large numbers of nonreading children for educational purposes. The chief contribution of this period, and of this direction of research, was to demonstrate the intellectual aspects of children's drawings and to make a beginning at analytical studies.

With the advent of the so-called "projective methods" of personality study in about 1940, a new interest in the drawing of the human figure appeared. Particularly prevalent in the American psychological literature of 1940 to about 1955, this research on the projective use of drawings has receded somewhat in recent years in America. In terms of theory, this field of research has been quite diffuse. Rather than scientifically analytical, its proponents have tended toward intuitive impressionism. Goodenough anticipated that drawings could be used interpretatively in the study of personality. An interest in art as revealing the unconscious symbolically, and as a diagnostic technique, goes back much further. Some of the more recent studies relate to body-image concepts; others to sex-role identification. Many investigators assume an isomorphic relationship between details of the human figure drawing and the adjustment mechanisms adopted by the ego. This area represents a particular emphasis rather than a coherent body of theory.

The experimental study of children's drawings dates from the mid-twenties of the present century. While early results were promising, this approach has not attracted a large group of investigators. The few studies done proceeded descriptively and atheoretically, trying various stimuli and collecting drawings under different sets of instructions and from groups differing psychologically on known dimensions. Some studies were initiated by an interest in children's drawings as art. Many exploratory studies published since the 1920's do not at first seem to yield coherent generalizations. Yet some order may be discernible in the apparent empiricistic chaos.

The growth of psychology toward theory and experiment since the 1930's and 1940's has stimulated new interest in perception and in cognitive processes, especially since 1945. It is the author's hypothesis that this contemporary interest in psychology affords a basis for organizing much of the observed phenomena of children's drawings. It is one of the purposes of the present book to review the literature that falls readily into the three categories described above, i.e., (1) descriptive, developmental studies; (2) the Draw-a-Man technique; and (3) projective studies of children's drawings. Further, an attempt will be made to organize the remaining empirical studies in terms of the contemporary interest in perception and cognition. It is hoped that this effort will provide a basis for an experimental approach to children's drawings that will link with the perceptual and cognitive theories now being shaped in laboratories. The first two categories will be treated in this chapter; the third in the next chapter. The remaining literature on the psychology of drawing will be discussed later, following presentation of the author's researches with the Goodenough method.

Early Developmental Studies

Among the best known of the earlier writers are: Perez (1888), Barnes (1893), Herrick (1893), Baldwin (1894), O'Shea (1894, 1897), Maitland (1895), Lukens (1896), Brown (1897), Shinn (1893), Götze (1898), Clark (1902), Sully (1907, 1908), and Luquet (1913). Their reports were chiefly descriptive although in some cases a few statistical figures were included. Nevertheless, their findings were very instructive, throwing much light on individual differences and on mental development in children. The discussion that follows, to page 17, is taken from Goodenough's summary (1926, pp. 1–7).

Early Systematic Studies

Between 1900 and 1915, two great international research undertakings were carried out. The first of these was conducted according to a plan proposed by Lamprecht (1906) and was based largely upon the method used by Earl Barnes in this country. Drawings were to be made by children from all parts of the world and from all levels of civilization, from primitive to advanced, according to standardized directions. These drawings were to be sent to a central bureau at Leipzig for examination and comparison. Lamprecht's proposal was received with much enthusiasm, and many thousands of drawings were sent to him, examples coming from almost every nation in the world. The collection also included drawings made by several primitive African races. It is greatly to be regretted that this investigation, which held such possibilities for psychology, anthropology, and ethnology as well as for practical education, was not carried through to completion. Levinstein (1905), who collaborated with Lamprecht, published a summary of certain parts of the material, but no adequate comparative study of the entire collection ever appeared.

Claparéde (1907) outlined a plan for the study of children's drawings that was quite similar to Lamprecht's, but that had a somewhat different end in view. Lamprecht was interested primarily in the question of racial similarities and differences, with special reference to the theory of recapitulation. Claparéde proposed a careful study of the developmental stages in drawing, with the idea of ascertaining what relationship, if any, exists between aptitude in drawing and general intellectual ability as indicated by schoolwork. From Claparéde's plan Ivanoff (1909) worked out a method of scoring the drawings according to a six-point scale including: (1) sense of proportion, (2) imaginative conception, and (3) technical and artistic value—equal weight being given to each of the three criteria. He then compared the obtained values with teachers' ratings for general ability, standing in each of the school subjects, and certain moral and social traits. He found a positive correlation in nearly all instances.

The material that Ivanoff collected from four Swiss cantons was used by Katzaroff (1910) in a study of the subjects most frequently drawn by children. Katzaroff's results for children aged six to fourteen showed fair agreement with those obtained by Maitland (1895) in this country, although it is impossible to make more than a rough comparison, since Katzaroff did not treat the different ages separately. Maitland found the human figure the most popular subject at all ages up to ten years. In Katzaroff's table it ranked third, with "miscellaneous objects" and "houses" taking first and second places.

Schuyten (1901, 1904, 1907), in a study extending over a period of several years, made use of a method that differed greatly from those employed by other investigators of his time. His object was to establish, if possible, a standard of excellence for each age—that is, a series of age norms. He used the human figure as the subject. Drawings were made from memory; the children were simply told to draw a man "in whatever way you are accustomed to draw it." By means of very minute measurements of each of the separate parts of the body and by comparison with classic standards, Schuyten hoped to be able to devise an objective method for his ratings. The plan was not successful, but the idea is worthy of note as one of the earliest attempts to devise a purely objective measuring scale based on age standards.[3]

Schuyten's method was used by Lobsien (1905) in a study of drawings made by public school children at Kiel. Although no precise norms were established, he found, as did Schuyten, that with increasing age the proportions of the different parts of the body as drawn by children approach more nearly the realistic standards. Lobsien also compared the drawings of imbeciles with those of normal children and found that, age for age, the sense of proportion displayed by imbeciles is decidedly inferior to that of normal children.

Subjects Drawn Spontaneously by Children

The early literature frequently comments that children draw the human figure by preference (e.g., Maitland, 1895; Lukens, 1896; Ballard, 1912; Luquet, 1913). Later studies generally confirm this, although McCarty (1924) found that houses, trees, furniture, boats, vehicles, parts of houses, and ani-

---

[3] Schuyten's original article is written in Dutch and has never been translated, but an excellent review and criticism can be found in Rouma's *Le Langage Graphique de l'Enfant*, pages 14–16 and 80–83.

mals were also drawn by five to ten per cent of all children. Indeed, when topics were grouped broadly, the per cents drawing "aspects of nature," or "buildings," slightly exceeded the proportion drawing "persons." Adolescents' spontaneous drawings (collected from high school and college wastebaskets, notebooks and similar sources), investigated by Hurlock (1943), show that the human form is a favorite subject, exceeded only by printed and decorated words and by caricatures. When caricatures and faithful reproductions of persons are combined, the human figure is by far the most popular single subject. Animals and houses each constituted less than three or four per cent of Hurlock's total collection. A great many other subjects, including vehicles, ships, and scenes, also appeared in this collection, but each topic was represented by a very small per cent of the cases.

In more recent years, animal drawings have been specifically studied by several investigators. Graewe (1935) found evidence of clear-cut developmental progressions in children's attempts to draw animals. For the preschool child the same general schema serves for both animal and human figures. Later, by orientation of the figures to the horizontal plane, rather than the vertical, and by appendages such as a tail or leg, there is some deliberate attempt to differentiate the animal form from the human. Still later, as the child gains more technical control, he attempts to portray the animal as animal from the start. In an unpublished paper filed at the University of Baroda, Miss Kunjlata Desai (1958) has attempted to scale the drawing of a cow in much the same fashion Goodenough (1926) has used with the human figure. Desai discerned thirteen clear-cut stages that reflect the development described in more general terms by Graewe. As in human drawings, body parts of animals are discerned and included before the problems of proportion are attempted or mastered. DuBois (1939) reported the standardization of a sixty-point Goodenough-type scale for the drawing of a horse. For Pueblo Indian children of the Southwest, he concluded that the horse-drawing test is a more valid measure of mental ability than the Goodenough.

Anastasi and Foley (1938) found that animal drawings by Pacific north coast Indian children were predominantly realistic. Some of the drawings, however, were highly stylized, especially those in which children chose animals frequently used in the traditional legends and art of the tribe. These drawings reflected the techniques of representation found in traditional tribal art. The authors minimized age-level differences, finding sex differences in subject matter more striking. Boys were more likely to use stylized themes and to draw naturalistic horses and hunting scenes. The lack of age changes is not surprising in view of the fact that over half the children were more than twelve years old.

Bender and Rapoport (1944) and Schwartz and Rosenberg (1955) obtained drawings of animals to throw light on patterns of personal and social maladjustment in children. Generalizations concerning the meaning of various species reflect the particular dynamic personality theories of the authors rather than empirical findings.

Bender and Wolfson (1943) studied nautical themes, assuming the ship as a feminine sexual symbol. They noted that as contrasted with younger children, older subjects make more differentiated and detailed ships and are more likely to put in a sky line, or detailed background. We have seen that ships are not an uncommon subject in children's spontaneous drawings; Ballard (1913) found the ship in about one-third to one-half the drawings of elementary school children in seaport towns of England.

Kerr (1937) and Markham (1954) have studied children's drawings of houses; both found few consistent qualitative changes with age, but did find a general improvement in symmetry and in the neatness of lines and angles. The absence of marked qualitative differences is probably attributable to the wide variance in the type of houses with which children are familiar.

The Nature of Developmental Sequences

One of the most extensive and carefully controlled studies ever made in this field was made by Kerschensteiner (1905) at Munich during the years 1903–1905. Kerschensteiner was given the task of reorganizing the course of study in drawing for the folk schools of that city. In order to establish a scientific basis for his work, he spent about two years collecting and studying almost 100,000 drawings made under standardized conditions by children in Munich and surrounding areas. He classified these drawings under three main heads, with certain intermediate types. The main heads were as follows, and represent a rough age sequence:

1. Purely schematic drawings. These correspond to what Verworn (1907) has called the "ideoplastic stage" in drawing.

2. Drawings in terms of visual appearance—Verworn's "physioplastic stage."

3. Drawings in which the child attempts to give an impression of three-dimensional space.

The Kerschensteiner book was profusely illustrated and contained many tables showing, by grades and sexes separately, the percentages of children whose drawings fell within each of the three classes mentioned above. The author also devoted several pages to discussing the drawings of three especially gifted boys. He analyzed the differences between the drawings made by the feeble-minded and those made by normal children, and demonstrated that differences are qualitative as well as quantitative. Not only do the feeble-minded tend to produce drawings that are more primitive than those made by normal children, but their drawings also show lack of coherence—"*Zusammenhangenlosigkeit.*" This latter difference has been remarked upon by several other writers as well—for example by Cyril Burt (1921), who believed that it is possible in most instances to differentiate between the drawings of normal and backward children by that characteristic alone.

Kerschensteiner found very marked differences between the performance of the two sexes. The boys exceeded the girls in all types of drawings except certain kinds of decorative design, in which the girls did better than the boys.

At about this time, also, Stern called attention to the differences in imaginative conception displayed by children, and to the age development in the manner of indicating space (1907, 1908, 1909, 1910, 1914).

The Analysis of Developmental Stages

A most extensive and valuable study of children's drawings was that by Rouma (1913). This study included: (1) all drawings made by eight children, seven to eleven years of age, during a nine-month period, (2) drawings produced during a ten-month term by all members of several elementary schools, including one for retarded children under Rouma's direct supervision, and (3) free drawings made weekly for a long period by children in the six- to eleven-year age range. In addition to these direct observations, drawings from several kindergartens and primary schools were collected for Rouma by the teachers, on the basis of which he selected children for individual study.

Rouma did not employ statistical methods in the treatment of his data, but he based his conclusions upon unusually careful observations, and gave numerous case studies in support of his statements. The book was profusely illustrated.

In studying drawings of the human figure, Rouma distinguished the following stages:

I. The preliminary stage.

   1. The child adapts his hand to the instrument.

   2. The child gives a definite name to the incoherent lines which he traces.

   3. The child announces in advance what he intends to represent.

   4. The child sees a resemblance between the lines obtained by chance and certain objects.

II. Evolution of the representation of the human figure.

   1. First attempts at representation, similar to the preliminary stage.

   2. The "tadpole" stage.

   3. Transitional stage.

   4. Complete representation of the human figure as seen in full face.

   5. Transitional stage between full face and profile.

   6. The profile.

Rouma also stated that the drawings of subnormal children resemble those of younger normal children. He noted, however (1913, p. 199), the following special differences between the two types of drawings:

> The spontaneous drawings of subnormal children show: (1) a marked tendency to automatism, (2) slowness in the evolution from stage to stage, and (3) frequent retrogression to an inferior stage. (4) There are numerous

manifestations of the flight of ideas. The drawings which cover a sheet of paper are not finished, and they have to do with a number of very disparate subjects. (5) Certain drawings by subnormal children, taken singly, are very complete; but when we examine them more closely we find that the child has confined himself to a series of sketches which have evolved slowly, and by slight modifications have gradually reached a certain degree of perfection. The conservative tendency of the child has favored the development of the drawing. It occasionally happens that a subnormal child possesses an unusual power of visual memory and is thus capable of producing very remarkable drawings. These cases are analogous to those of other inferiors who display a great superiority of one of their faculties, of whom Inaudi and Diamondi are celebrated types. (6) Many subnormal children show a great anxiety to represent an idea in its totality, or to reproduce all the details in a given sketch. It is this tendency, above all others, which favors the perfection of the drawings mentioned in the preceding paragraph. (7) Subnormal children prefer those drawings in which the same movement frequently recurs, and (8) they do meticulous work.

General studies of large collections of children's drawings are reported from Brazil by Rabello (1932) and by Barcellos (1952–53), by Marino from Uruguay (1956), and by a number of French authors in a 1950 issue of *Enfance*. None of these studies contributes any new insights to the developmental principles developed forty years earlier.

Possibly the most important single contribution of the early period of research on children's drawings was this classification into sequences or stages, and thus the delineation of children's drawings as developmental in character. Burt's early analysis and description (1921), based upon his own observations and those of earlier investigators, remain a lucid and psychologically perceptive account. For him, drawing was a mode of self-revelation, particularly useful when speech and writing are inadequate. Because drawings are neither linguistic nor arithmetical, they give a valuable access to the child's power of imagination and construction. Says Burt:

> Progress in drawing shows successive changes in kind as well as in degree. It resembles, not so much the uniform accretions of the inanimate crystal as the spasmodic growth of some lowly organism, one whose life-history is a fantastic cycle of unexpected metamorphoses. Each advance follows a different line from the last (1921, p. 318).

In the progression several distinct steps may be noted. These stages, with discernible subdivisions, are here paraphrased from the essential features described by Burt (1921, pp. 319–327):

1. *Scribble* (ages two to three)

   a. Purposeless pencillings, enjoyed principally as motor expression.

   b. More purposive pencillings, the results themselves becoming the focus of attention.

    c. Imitative pencillings, modelled on an adult's movements rather than his production.

    d. Localized scribbling; child seeks to reproduce specific parts of an object.

2. *Line* (age four). Single movements of the pencil replace oscillations of massive scribbling. In the man drawing, parts are juxtaposed rather than organized.

3. *Descriptive symbolism* (five to six). In the man drawing a crude scheme becomes apparent, with little attention to shape or proportion, involving principally head, body, arms, legs, and facial features. "Laid horizontally, with limbs appropriately rearranged, it serves, with equal felicity, drawn large, for a horse or a cow; drawn small, for a cat or a dog" (p. 320).

4. *Realism* (seven to nine or ten). Emphasis is on the descriptive rather than the depictive. The drawing still symbolizes rather than represents, though the scheme is more true to detail and to fact. Clothing and decorative detail appear.

5. *Visual realism* (ten to eleven, or so). Technique has improved, and child is inclined to copy or to trace the work of others, or to draw from nature; he attempts visual representation.

    a. Two-dimensional drawing, chiefly in outline and silhouette.

    b. Three-dimensional drawing. The three-quarter view may be attempted, particular persons are depicted, action is introduced. The child begins to compare and contrast his own several efforts at a subject and consciously to improve his rendition. Landscapes may be attempted, with some concern for overlapping and perspective.

6. *Repression* (occurs prepubertally, eleven to fourteen years). Drawings show a deterioration or regression. Progress becomes laborious and slow. Some of this deterioration may be ascribed, perhaps, to emotional conflicts, but cognitive and intellective factors are also assuredly involved. There is increased self-criticism, increased power of observation, and increased capacity for esthetic appreciation. Growing ability to self-expression through language plays a large part. The human figure becomes rare in spontaneous drawings, but geometrical, ornamental, and decorative drawing becomes very common, when drawing of any kind is attempted.

7. *Artistic revival* (early adolescence, though many children never achieve this stage). Drawings are now made to tell a story; they approximate more to the methods of the professional (e.g., use of portraits or bust). Definite esthetic elements appear, notably interest in color, form, and

line as such. Boys may become interested in technical drafting. Artistic talents can rarely if ever be discerned before a child enters this stage, and special artistic powers are rarely discernible before age eleven, even in the most precocious.

There has been a tendency in some recent writing to decry this emphasis on sequence of stages as artificial, obscuring the continuities which in fact exist throughout development. It is important to understand that these investigators do not think of such steps as discontinuous with each other. Stages are merely convenient ways of describing perceptibly different orientations and organizations of the drawing act as the child moves from his first pencil strokes to quite elaborate productions. That different investigators have located similar stages, that these stages can be established against an age scale, and that the succession is notably similar for most children, has been sufficiently well validated to establish the usefulness of the concept of stages or phases in describing the *course* of development. Most investigators, certainly, have noted that the aspects which set off one phase from the next can be discerned only by looking at the "middle" of the period covered by the phase, or by constructing an artificial or idealized example that contains the several most common or characteristic features a child might include at this stage. Most have explicitly stated that when one examines samples of work arranged between these modal or typical examples, he notes that the samples blend into each other by very small changes.

Direction of More Recent Analytical Studies

The major early studies were rich in insights into the psychology of children's drawing and art, and they have furnished a picture of developmental aspects of drawing that in general outline has been unaltered to this day. The more analytical temper of the last four or five decades, and the amount of attention given in research to techniques of sampling and control have, however, helped us fill in detail. Not the least important discovery of recent years is the discovery that children's drawings have great psychological complexity. The art of drawing delineates perceptual experience and conceptual formation; it represents fact and projects fancy; it shows clear developmental trends and permits innumerable idiosyncratic expressions. Another major step ahead has been the growing recognition that a knowledge of the usual is essential for the recognition of the unusual. Many reputedly abnormal or unusual features in the drawings of individual children or of small, selected groups lose their apparent significance when the age and sex of the subjects and the conditions under which the drawings were made become known. All this serves to emphasize how valuable were these early descriptive studies of drawings by large groups of school children as a basis for more recent work. Certainly the demonstration of developmental process in drawing laid the basis for the use of drawings as a test of intelligence, the next major emphasis in research to be reviewed.

The Draw-a-Man Technique

With the publication of the Goodenough test in 1926, a new method for evaluating children's drawings was available,[4] and the response of the scientific world of psychology has been gratifying. Using a point-scale method, Goodenough demonstrated that drawing, for children, had a more cognitive than esthetic meaning. She discussed briefly two possible applications that have since been explored at considerable length: the use of drawings in the study of children's personalities, their affect life and conflicts, and their interests; and the use of drawings to study children limited by lack of language or by linguistic barriers.

Psychological Development Portrayed in the Human Figure

By far the most extensive research has used the Goodenough method to evaluate the psychological development of children, and to understand the developing concepts and ideas that their drawings reveal. This discussion will review the literature that bears principally on Goodenough's method and its value as a test of intelligence, reserving for a concluding discussion research findings pertaining to the broader consideration of the psychology of children's drawings and the relationship of drawing to the development of cognitive processes generally.

Goodenough's finding that the drawing test ceases to show age increments by early adolescence differed from the results of all other measures of intelligence, and early attracted attention. Oakley (1940) proposed to extend Goodenough's method to drawings by adolescents, and suggested a number of promising leads. A number of master's theses done at Columbia University (Cohen, 1933; Dyett, 1931; Eggers, 1931; Gitlitz, 1933; Levy, 1931) were devoted to the general topic of ascertaining the usefulness of the Goodenough test for subjects older than those for whom it was originally designed. In general, Goodenough's original contention that the test ceases to discriminate intellectual differences at about age eleven or twelve was borne out. Berdie (1945) reported a correlation of +.62 between Goodenough and Wechsler IQ's with older adolescents of average and below-average ability, and Birch (1949) found that the Draw-a-Man discriminates adequately among adolescents of Binet IQ 70 or lower.

[4] Apparently Fay (1923, 1934), in France, developed a method of drawing analysis somewhat similar to Goodenough's at about this time but it was never published widely. The Fay test consists of asking a child to illustrate the situation, "A lady takes a walk and it rains." The subject has five minutes to complete the drawing. Scoring is in terms of details included by the child. Wintsch (1935) reported an extensive study of children's drawings of the human figure and gave norms for French-Swiss children. He also used the Fay test with various European children, as have Fontes and others (1944) and André Rey (1946). Rey does not find the measure useful after age twelve; Wintsch suggests the age of nine. Weil (1950 a, b) prefers the Goodenough method and gives some normative data for French children.

Israelite (1936) compared the relative difficulty of the items on the Goodenough scale for normal and mentally defective children of the same mental age. In general, the defectives surpassed the normals in respect to the number of details shown, while the normal children excelled on items involving the correct organization and proportion of the parts. Earl (1933), who compared the drawings of adult defectives with those of normal children, found much the same thing to be true. Spoerl (1940 a,b), likewise, found that retarded children showed more details in their drawings than did normals who earned comparable total scores, but their sense of proportion was very poor. McElwee (1934), who compared the profile drawings of normal and subnormal children, found that although the latter depicted more detail than the former, the number of incongruities resulting from confusion between the full-face and the profile position was much greater in the drawings made by the subnormal than in those made by the normal children.

Statistical Evaluations of the Scale

The reliability and validity of the Draw-a-Man technique have been the subject of a number of investigations. The most thoroughly controlled was carried out by McCarthy (1944), who gave the test to 386 third- and fourth-grade children on two occasions, with an interval of one week between the two administrations. Scoring was done by graduate students who had been given a period of preliminary training. Each drawing was scored three times, twice by the same person and once by a different person. The correlation between self-scoring was +.94; between scorings by different persons, +.90. Reliability by the split-half method was +.89; by the retest method, +.68. Williams (1935), who had one hundred drawings scored independently by five examiners, found intercorrelations between scores ranging from +.80 to +.96.

Smith's (1937) test-retest reliabilities for 100 subjects at each age from six to fifteen yielded values above +.91 in all but the oldest children. Yepsen (1929) found a retest correlation of +.90 for feeble-minded subjects. Brill (1935) found that upon repetition of the test within two to six weeks the likelihood of a decrease in score was twice as great as an increase. The correlation between two tests separated by two and one-half weeks was +.77; for six weeks, the value was +.68. An abbreviated scale correlated in excess of +.90 with the full-length scale. Of interest is a report by Naville (1948) on the Fay test used in France; three independent scorings of "a woman walking in the rain" by forty children, six to fourteen years old, yielded values of +.92, +.80 and +.79.[5]

McCurdy (1947) obtained drawings of a man from fifty-six first-grade children on two occasions, separated by about three months. The two sets of scores derived by the Goodenough technique correlated +.69, and the mean IQ equivalents differed by a very small amount, statistically insignificant. Of

---

[5] The average of the three scorings was used as the basis.

particular interest in this study is the report of a collection of over one thousand drawings made by a boy between the ages of two and one-half and seven years. Fifty-six drawings of men were selected from this collection, the majority of the complete human figures available, excluding a number "because they were obviously intended as comic distortions or were obviously not done with the usual amount of care." The IQ scores for these drawings averaged 171 with an SD of 22. Two drawings made by this boy at school differ somewhat in IQ score but correspond roughly with values obtained from drawings made at home at about the same time. Likewise, two Binet tests show a direction of IQ difference paralleling Goodenough IQ's obtained from drawings made at home at about the same periods.

McCurdy concludes that variation in Goodenough scores shows fluctuations of ability exceeding "error of measurement," and that, in this instance, variability of the individual and variability of the group are of about the same magnitude. Unfortunately, individual and group variability are not comparable when mean performance differs so greatly. Only one of the fifty-eight IQ determinations for the boy fell below the 97th percentile of general norms.

Williams (1930) constructed a series of growth curves showing progress on the Draw-a-Man scale when the counted items or "points" were reduced to equally spaced units according to the Thurstone method of scaling. He showed that the growth of children whose school progress has been rapid, average, or slow was very similar in pattern, though proceeding at different rates. All three curves showed fairly marked negative acceleration.

McHugh (1945 a,b) made an item analysis of the Goodenough scale with a view to shortening it. He discovered that thirty of the fifty-one points in the scale correlated significantly with his criterion, which was the Stanford-Binet. His findings with respect to the abbreviated scale, however, are questionable, inasmuch as he used the same group of subjects to validate the new scale as were used for the original derivation. He also found that significant IQ gains were registered on a second drawing of a man after an interval of a few months and concluded that the drawing of a man is not free from the influence of experience.

Influence of Specific Drawing Instructions

A number of investigations, some of them truly experimental studies, cast light on the conceptual aspects of drawing the human figure. Ames (1943, 1945) found that children under the age of five depicted more details when adding to an incomplete figure than they did when told merely to draw a man, but that the reverse was true with children over five. However, the Gesell Incomplete Man, which was the model used, does not suggest the need of many details for its completion. A more sophisticated drawing might have yielded different results. The *number* of parts added to the incomplete man (1943) shows a more consistent and steady age relationship than do the specific parts added. This conclusion is in agreement with the basis of the Goodenough test.

Gridley (1938), with four-year-olds as subjects, compared the results of nine prescribed drawing situations. The children were instructed to: (1) "Draw a man," (2) "Draw a little man," and (3) "Draw a big man." They were asked to repeat (1), (2), and (3) in that order. Next, they were asked to make a schematic drawing of a man from copy, and then to draw a man from dictated instructions given one at a time while drawing the different parts. Finally, they were asked to draw a man according to instructions given in advance of the drawing. When scored by the Goodenough method, the averages for most of the drawing situations were similar. As might be expected, the dictation of what was to be drawn brought about an appreciable increase in the score, although neither the provision of a copy nor previous instruction had much effect.

Mott (1939) used the Goodenough scale to compare the drawings made by fifty-eight children between the ages of four and seven years when the instructions given were simply to "Draw a man," with drawings made when the instructions were to "Draw a policeman," "a farmer," or "a cowboy." The majority of the children did best under the first instruction. This may be because in drawing the more specific figures the children's attention was diverted to features of the costume instead of centering on essential aspects of the human subject as such. In another study (1945), Mott investigated the effect upon drawing scores of previous movement of specified parts of the body. Drawings were first made with only the general instruction to "Draw a man." Later, the children were put through a series of exercises involving certain parts of the body, verbalizing as they did so, e.g., "This is my head, I nod it." Drawings made immediately afterward showed that the exercised part was not only more likely to be shown but was drawn with more care for details. Two previous studies by the same author (1936 a,b) utilized drawings of the human figure done on three successive days with slightly different instructions on each day. The drawings were rated for five characteristics. The most interesting feature of these studies is that in each a fairly high correlation is found between ratings on the amount of activity shown in the drawings and those obtained on the Marston Scale for introversion-extroversion. Because of insufficient data concerning the character of the ratings and the age-range of the subjects, corroboration of the findings is needed.

The Draw-a-Man Test in Diagnosis of Behavior Disorders

Goodenough has quite correctly been credited for pointing the way to the use of drawings in the study of personality. Noting that in the early literature there were observations concerning peculiar art forms in the work of mental patients, she also demonstrated that bizarre features in children's drawings appeared to be associated with behavior idiosyncrasies. She states (1926, pp. 62–63):

> In the course of the present study it was found that in a small proportion of drawings, qualitative differences may be observed of a type which cannot

readily be accounted for. These differences are often of so subtle a nature as to render description very difficult, but they may be classified roughly as follows:

1. "Verbalist" type. Drawings containing a large amount of detail but comparatively few ideas. Figure . . . [1] is an example. See Mateer . . . [1924].

2. "Individual response" type. Drawings containing features which are inexplicable to any one except the child himself. See Figure . . . [2]. Compare Kent and Rosanoff . . . [1910].

3. Drawings showing evidence of the flight of ideas, as when hair is shown only on one side of head, or when one ear but not the other has been drawn. See Rouma . . . [1908].

4. Uneven mental development, as indicated by unusual combination of primitive and mature characteristics in a single drawing. (Analogous to "scatter" on the Stanford-Binet.)

Nine children whose work showed one or more of the above characteristics were rated on a simple fifty-item adjective check list containing twenty-five words descriptive of psychopathic tendencies and their opposites. A slightly greater number of words was checked for the "clinical" subjects, and the differences on adjectives suggesting peculiarities were more marked. Goodenough's conclusion was conservatively phrased as a research suggestion rather than proof that drawings can be used to index personality disturbances.

FIG. 1. Man, by boy, 9-9

FIG. 2. Man, by boy, 11-1

In the last twenty years, clinical psychologists have increasingly used human figure drawings to study personality. This trend has been a part of the movement in the use of "projective techniques" and has greatly outstripped the research evidence, as the following chapter will show in some detail. Increasingly it appears that Goodenough's early conservatism has been justified, though one must freely admit that drawings *do* reflect a child's idiosyncratic view of his world and experience. The problem appears to be essentially that of the "nomothetic" vs. the "idiographic" approaches in personality evaluation. If we use the child's drawing as a normative psychometric instrument in the study of personality, we find that validity coefficients are so low as to make individual prediction impossible. On the other hand, intimate knowledge of a child's experience and attitudes makes many of the details and special features of his drawing quite meaningful. However, the great variety of ways in which possible drawing elements can be (and are, in fact), combined by children makes it virtually impossible for one to read predictively from the drawing to the child, despite the seeming success of occasional "blind interpretations." These cases, it should be noted, are usually of quite disturbed children, and the predictions are cast in such graphic language that they cannot help but give a general "fit" to the phenomena observed. Drawings many times confirm or throw light on suspected trends in the detailed clinical study of cases; they are not psychometric instruments.

That the Goodenough score is somewhat sensitive to the child's affect is shown in one experimental study. Reichenberg-Hackett (1953), working with 106 nine- to eleven-year-old children, and 100 controls, has shown that positively toned affective states, experimentally induced, influence children's drawings toward higher scores. This improvement was attributed to an increased ability to apply knowledge and skill acquired in previous learning situations, and to improved ability to perform concrete tasks requiring simple mental organization.

In an "experiment of nature," Ochs (1950) compared fifty-two children diagnosed as primary behavior disorders who improved in social adjustment after a period of hospitalization, with seventy-two children similarly diagnosed who failed to improve in the same period. The former group lost 4.89 IQ points whereas the latter group increased their Goodenough IQ's 3.14 points. Starting at almost the same IQ, this final difference of seven IQ points is statistically significant.

The Goodenough scale has been used specifically as a qualitative aid in clinical diagnosis of specific disorders. Springer (1941) made an item analysis of the Draw-a-Man scale to ascertain which items differentiated between maladjusted and well-adjusted boys as classified by the Haggerty-Olson-Wickman Scale. Of the fifty-one items included in the Goodenough scale, fifteen showed critical ratios of 3.00 or higher. It is interesting to note that the pattern of the differences is the same as that found by those who have compared normal and retarded children; this, in spite of the fact that the two groups were equated for total score on the drawing test.

Berrien's (1935) study attempted an item analysis to obtain a diagnostic measure of different types of behavior disorders in children. The drawings of three groups of abnormal children were compared, including twenty-four post-encephalitics, thirteen diagnosed as "psychopathic personality," and fifteen borderline mental defectives. The post-encephalitic cases showed a number of the characteristics noted by Goodenough as possible indicators of neurotic or psychotic states; most notably, reversal of sex characteristics and combinations of mature and primitive characteristics in the same drawing. The small number of cases and wide spread of ages made the item analysis inconclusive.

In the work of schizophrenic children, DesLauriers and Halpern (1947) found relatively lower IQ scores by the Draw-a-Man technique; this was related theoretically to the psychotic child's "body-image disturbance"—a point to be considered more fully in the next chapter.

Like Berrien, Bender (1940) used the Draw-a-Man Test with a small group of children suffering from post-encephalitic behavior disorders. In each of six reported cases, the IQ obtained from the drawing was far below that obtained on the Binet. Bender's interpretation is that the cerebral damage had caused a considerable disruption of the body image, and suggests that so marked a discrepancy between the two scales may afford a useful hint as to the possibility of brain injury. In another approach to this problem, Hanvik (1953) examined discrepancies between Goodenough and WISC IQ's in children five to twelve years. The rank order correlation for twenty-five youngsters was only +.18 and the Goodenough values were significantly lower, on the average, than mean WISC IQ. Of interest in this connection is Gunzburg's (1955) finding that IQ scores on drawings of a man correlate higher with individual examination IQ's among familial mental defectives than among pathological mental defectives of the same general intelligence range.

While not particularly productive when used with adults, except possibly the mentally retarded, the Draw-a-Man method has yielded a few noteworthy results with other forms of intellectual deterioration. Chase (1941) noted Goodenough test differences between small samples of adult paranoids and normals, and adult hebephrenics and normals, the latter remaining statistically different after being matched for Binet M.A.'s. Chase comments especially on the deterioration to be observed in the drawings by hebephrenics, and their tendency to use geometric forms. That the Goodenough test is not suitable for testing the intellectual level of normal adults is obvious from Goodenough's (1926) standardization data and from Murphy's (1956) attempt to separate three groups of young adult males—applicants for staff positions at a state hospital, alcoholics, and mental defectives. Only in the latter group was there a significant correlation with Wechsler-Bellevue IQ; there were no differences among the three samples in mean Goodenough score. On the other hand, the Goodenough test appears to discriminate to some extent intelligence levels among very old men. Possibly senile deterioration returns the individual to the more concrete processes measured by the drawing test. Jones and Rich (1957) reported correlations of +.47 to +.65 with the several measures supplied by the Wechsler-Bellevue, though the *height* of the drawing alone correlated about as well with intelligence as did the drawing score! The more deteriorated patients produced small drawings, devoid of detail. Darke and Geil (1948) observed that adult male homosexuals drew men with more of Goodenough's "feminine" traits than males whose homosexuality was infrequent or minor, or males who took the active male role in homosexuality.

The possibility of using the Draw-a-Man Test as an indicator of maladjustment was also studied by Brill (1937), who found that his group of maladjusted boys typically scored lower on the scale than they did on the Binet, while the reverse was more often true of his well-adjusted group. His attempt to devise a short form of the drawing test for the purpose of predicting maladjustment commits the too-familiar statistical error of using the same data for validating as for deriving the scale.

In an unpublished master's study Palmer (1953) examined thirty-six normal fourth-grade children, and discovered that Goodenough–Stanford-Binet IQ discrepancies were not correlated with measures of personal-social adjustment as assessed by the California Test of Personality. In another master's dissertation using the same fourth-grade children, Fowler (1953) correlated Goodenough–Stanford-Binet IQ discrepancies with sociometric measures, both measures of how a child is accepted by others and of how he accepts others. He found no tendency for a discrepancy between the two measures of intelligence to be significantly associated with low social acceptance. However, each measure of intelligence, taken by itself, correlated significantly with acceptance. The two intelligence measures themselves correlated +.41.

One of the best studies of the comparative performance of delinquent and nondelinquent subjects on the Goodenough test was made by Hinrichs (1935). Unfortunately, his subjects (ages nine to eighteen years) were for the most part older than those for whom the scale was intended. Hinrichs attempted to remedy this difficulty by devising an upward extension of the scale but found, as have others, that the added section was neither as reliable nor as valid as the part designed for younger children. His subjects were eighty-one institutionalized delinquent boys, none with IQ's below 80. Several control groups from various types of environment were matched with the delinquents. In general, the study is well controlled and the statistical treatment adequate. Hinrichs' chief findings are as follows: The delinquent boys showed (1) somewhat lower mean IQ's on the Goodenough than on the Stanford; (2) more "incongruities" in their drawings than in those made by the controls; (3) greater juvenility in choice of subjects to draw, and more "blood and thunder" characters than in those of controls; and (4) more stereotyped drawings with fewer indications of activity.

Starke (1950), also working with delinquents, examined the relation of dominance behavior, measured by an adaptation of the Pintner-Forlano schedule for the study of dominance feeling, a teacher-rating schedule composed of five linear scales, and a twenty-item "Guess-Who" type instrument based on dominance behavior. For carefully matched (age, grade, socioeconomic status) groups of delinquent and nondelinquent boys and girls, he found no significant differences between his delinquent and nondelinquent measures. Furthermore, the three criteria of dominance failed to intercorrelate significantly. His matched groups of boys differed significantly on those pairs of items on which both Springer (1941) and Berrien (1935) agreed that deviant children were more likely to show discrepancies, but the overlap was great. The girls did not differ to any degree. Delinquent girls were less successful on items that both Springer (1941) and Brill (1937) found to distinguish maladjusted from adjusted children; this was not true for boys, however. On a composite list of points drawn from Machover (1949), Anastasi and Foley (1944), and Springer (1941), no differences appeared in either sex group.

Starke, however, found marked differences between deviant and normal groups on items noted by Goodenough as treated differently by boys and girls. (See p. 32, following.) On features more commonly included by boys, both nondelinquent boys and girls exceed delinquent boys and girls. On features preferred by girls, delinquent boys scored much more often than nondelinquents; as between comparable groups of girls, no such difference appeared. Empirically derived scoring keys based on the observed differences in figure drawings made by delinquent and nondelinquent children of both sexes maintained their discriminating power on similarly selected, new, cross-validation groups. The overlap of the samples was extensive, however.

Using a free-drawing technique, Vogelsang (1934) found that incarcerated delinquent adolescent boys heavily favored erotic themes (especially sketches of the female figure), and these themes increased with the length of time in the reformatory. Unlike the Hurlock (1943) study of adolescent free drawings, the caricature theme was relatively infrequent and the majority of human figure drawings were of the same sex as the artist. Environmental factors undoubtedly account for these differences.

When the evidence from these studies is put together, it appears that a Goodenough IQ markedly lower than that earned on the Binet may afford some indication of emotional or nervous instability or, possibly, of brain damage. However, inasmuch as the self-correlation of the Goodenough test is not high enough to warrant its use for exact comparisons, a finding of this kind cannot be regarded as more than one of the signs comprised in the total syndrome. If, in addition to the difference between the two test results, there are many incongruities or other unusual features in the drawing, the likelihood of personality disturbance is increased, especially if the Binet test shows the child to be of normal or near-normal intelligence.

Drawings by Sensory Deviates

On the assumption that the loss of one sensory receptor may give rise to a compensatory superiority in other receptors, a number of persons have examined the drawings of the deaf. Several of these studies have utilized the Draw-a-Man technique, assuming that this test may provide more objective evidence of compensatory mechanisms than derived by subjective judgment, and assuming that it also offers a better index to the intellectual level of the deaf than is given by verbal tests.

Three principal studies agree in finding mean IQ's for the deaf that fall somewhat below the mean for the hearing. The averages are as follows: Peterson and Williams (1930), 80; Shirley and Goodenough (1932), 88; Springer (1938), 96. The first two studies utilized institutional cases. The last study included day school children enrolled in special classes for the deaf in New York City. This group probably represents a higher socioeconomic level, on the average, than the institutionalized groups. On the other hand, Glowatsky (1953) found that deaf children, while distinctly inferior on verbal tests, were not so deficient on performance measures, including the Draw-a-Man (mean IQ was 98).

The Clarke School for the Deaf has reported (1953) that the Draw-a-Man Test proved better than the Leiter or the WISC for differentiating between good and poor learners. Thiel (1927), on the basis of an examination of approximately two thousand drawings made by children in schools for the deaf, came to the conclusion that the development of drawing among the deaf parallels that found for the hearing, but that progress is slower. Working with a number of tests, including the Goodenough Draw-a-Man, Myklebust and Brutten (1953) found a distinct perceptual inferiority of deaf children. Using the *McAdory Art Appreciation Test*, Pintner (1941) discovered that deaf subjects between the ages of eleven and twenty-one years performed as well, but no better, than hearing subjects of corresponding age. Although the deaf girls did slightly better than the boys, they showed no superiority over hearing subjects.

For obvious reasons, the Draw-a-Man Test has not been used with blind children. Lowenfeld's (1939) important study, however, did incorporate drawings and paintings by children severely limited in vision, as well as clay models by the blind and partially sighted. His assumption was that in the art of subjects from whom the visual appearance of the external world is largely or wholly hidden one might study fruitfully the nature of creative experience. He questioned his subjects extensively about their mental processes while drawing, and inquired into the reasons determining their manner of drawing. From his studies, Lowenfeld concludes that there are two sources of experience, leading to two types of creative expression. The first has its origin in visual or other types of perception and in the esthetic pleasure directly experienced thereby; the artist attempts to reproduce the object as it appears, and thus to convey a similar pleasure to others. This type of art work Lowenfeld designates as the "optic or visual type." The other type of experience is personal. It consists of the feelings and emotions aroused by the total situation; the artist primarily attempts to convey these feelings in his work. In Lowenfeld's terminology, such products are classed as "haptic." They differ from the type previously described in their lessened fidelity to objective reality and their greater fidelity to some core of affective meaning. This meaning is frequently, though not always, discernible to an outsider. There is a centralization of attention upon those features that convey the meaning, with corresponding neglect of other parts that are equally open to visual perception. Lowenfeld's discussion of these factors and his exposition of them in the many remarkably fine color prints contained in the Appendix is highly stimulating, and should be read by all who are interested either in projective theory or in the psychology of art. Revesz (1950) has also treated the haptic, especially in relation to plastic art.

In a later paper, Lowenfeld (1945) reports a number of ingenious tests to detect haptical and visual dispositions. He conceives these dispositions as broadly organized and differing ways of approaching experiences controlling artistic expression. On the basis of these tests applied to more than 1,000 students, Lowenfeld reports that 47 per cent are clearly visual and 23 per cent clearly haptic; 30 per cent are mixed types. Presumably, the predominance of the "visuals" and the large proportion of mixed types reflects the influence of a highly visual culture. In a more recent work designed as a textbook for teachers, Lowenfeld (1952, 1957) has placed more emphasis upon the developmental aspects of drawing together with extensive notes on the possible significance of color, line, and form at the various stages.

The Draw-a-Man Test and Artistic Talent

Goodenough (1926) reported several studies of her method in relation to art training; they indirectly supported the test's validity. She attempted to ascertain whether children who possessed special artistic talent made higher scores on the test than children of equal general ability; in general such did not occur.

An exhibition of the art work of Pamela Bianca (Manson, 1919), classified according to her age when she did the work, was studied. Many of the sketches included drawings of the human figure; for these Goodenough found a mean IQ of 125, which she stated was "not out of proportion to the reported facts concerning her (Pamela's) school progress and general ability" (Goodenough, 1926, p. 52). Much of the work showed immaturity of thought despite its really remarkable artistic qualities. These observations led Goodenough to an intense search for talented child artists. She discovered that while child musicians are not at all uncommon, the child artist is indeed a *rara avis*. Goodenough's statement is:

> In spite of careful research, both in connection with this study and during a year spent as a field worker in the Stanford University Gifted Children Survey, the writer has been unable to locate a single child under the age of twelve years whose drawings appeared to possess artistic merit of a degree at all comparable to the musical genius occasionally shown by children of this age. Examination of drawings which make unusually high scores on the test

leads to the opinion that keen powers of analytic observation, coupled with a good memory for details, are more potent factors in producing high scores than is artistic ability in the ordinary sense of the term (1926, p. 53).

Observing that varying viewpoints exist concerning the art instruction that should be accorded children, and that classroom teachers vary extensively in the emphasis given art and in their own abilities to teach the subject, Goodenough projected two short experiments. In one, direct coaching according to the method used for scoring the test was given to a first-grade class after a control drawing had been obtained from each child. The coaching consisted of half-hour periods of teaching and practice on two successive days. The teacher, who was familiar with the scoring method and had actually scored a good many drawings, dictated instructions to the children as they made their drawings, drew illustrations on the blackboard, pointed out errors in individual drawings, and asked the children to correct them. After such various ways of trying to improve scores, she obtained a second drawing on the second day of coaching. One week later she obtained a third drawing. She states:

> Thirty-seven children were present on all five occasions. The median score made on the first or control drawing was 16.7 points; on the first drawing where coaching was given, 19.2 points; on the second drawing with coaching, 23.7 points. The median score on the drawings made four hours after the second coaching period was 22.5 points; a week later it had dropped to 20.7 points, which is a gain equivalent to one year of mental age above the control drawing. A comparison of the control with the final drawings showed that 70 per cent of the children had gained at least one point, while 8 per cent showed neither gain nor loss, and 22 per cent showed a slight loss. The standard error of estimate of a true score at this age is approximately 2 points. Fifty-four per cent of the children gained more than this amount; 40 per cent did not change their score by more than one standard error; and 6 per cent (2 cases) lost—one 3, the other 4 points.
>   These data show that, at least in the majority of cases, specific training in drawing the human figure does affect the score made on the test. There is no evidence that the kind of art training which is most commonly given in the primary grades, and which does not include formal instruction on the human figure, has any appreciable effect upon the score (1926, p. 55).

Goodenough also observed that children who had little or no previous experience with a pencil should have some practice with drawing before being given the test. She believed that some experience with the pencil quickly removes any initial handicap that might result from unfamiliarity with the medium. She also remarked on the debilitating effect self-consciousness has on drawing, which becomes increasingly noticeable as children grow older.

Sex Differences on the Draw-a-Man Test

In the original standardization Goodenough noted a rather noticeable superiority of girls on the drawing test at every age except twelve, with a tendency for somewhat greater variability among the boys. This difference she attributed to the method employed for standardization of the items. She believed that the school's tendency to promote girls through the grades more rapidly than boys and to hold back boys, made for a disproportionate number of girls among the accelerated children, with a large percentage of boys among the retarded children. This situation favored the selection of items in which girls might exceed boys. Goodenough suggested the hypothesis that girls may be somewhat more docile and of more studious habits than boys, and that the test may tend to favor those children willing to persevere in the face of difficulties and those who give careful attention to details.

Goodenough noted, in addition, certain items that girls are more likely to include than boys, and some items that boys are more likely to include than girls. The accompanying list reports Goodenough's findings with regard to 100 children of each sex scoring between 22 and 26 points:

	NUMBER OF DRAWINGS SHOWING CHARACTERISTIC	
	BOYS	GIRLS
Masculine characteristics:		
At least head and feet shown in profile, and in same direction	58	36
Some accessory characteristic present, as pipe, cane, umbrella, house, or scenery	21	9
Trousers transparent	12	3
Heel present	53	37
Figure represented as walking or running	20	7
Arms reaching below knee	11	3
Necktie shown	25	14
Feminine characteristics:		
Nose represented only by two dots	7	28
Feet less than $\frac{1}{20}$ total body length	4	16
Eyes showing two or more of the following details: brow, lashes, pupil, iris	1	11
Hair very smooth or neatly parted	13	34
"Cupid's bow" mouth	1	7
Cheeks shown	1	7
Trousers flaring at base	6	21
Head larger than trunk	9	17
Arm length not greater than head length	11	26
Curly hair	2	7
Legs not more than $\frac{1}{4}$ trunk length	2	12

These children were selected at random from ten different localities, and represented a wide range of social status and ethnic background. She states:

> For example, a difference in the interest taken in physical activity may be the reason for the greater tendency of the boys to exaggerate the size of the feet and the length of the arms and legs, as compared with the girls' tendency to minimize these parts. [Compare Fig. 5 with Fig. 7.] This is in line with the fact that the drawings of the boys more often show the figure in action. [See Fig. 8.] It is quite possible that it is this desire to express movement which leads to the characteristic change from the full-face to the profile position which has been so universally noted by students of children's drawings. In my collection, this change takes place appreciably earlier and more generally with boys than with girls.
>
> The girls are inclined to exaggerate the size of the head and the trunk, and, more especially, of the eyes [Figs. 3 and 4 compared with 6 and 7]. It is not a very uncommon circumstance for a girl to draw the eyes larger than the feet [Fig. 4], while boys are likely to make the feet larger than the entire head [Fig. 8]. In general, however, the sense of proportion displayed by the boys is decidedly better than that shown by the girls, while girls excel in the number of items and the amount of detail with which they are shown (1926, pp. 60–62).

Fɪɢ. 3. Man, by girl, 12-0   Fɪɢ. 4. Man, by girl, 8-0

Fig. 5. Man, by girl, 8-2

Fig. 6. Man, by boy, 12-10

Fig. 7. Man, by boy, 9-6

Fig. 8. Man, by boy, 12-9

Relation of the Draw-a-Man Test to Other Tests of Intelligence

At several points this review has mentioned the correlation of the drawing scale with the Stanford-Binet scale. Generally, the values are comparable with the values Goodenough has reported (1926). For example, values reported by Williams (1935), Yepsen (1929), and McElwee (1932) are +.65, +.60, and +.72, respectively. In the last few decades there has been a great deal of experimentation with human figure drawings used as a clinical tool. Unfortunately, these investigators have seldom correlated results attained by the Goodenough method with other modes of evaluation.

Smith's (1937) report does not give specific correlations with the several group tests used in his study of 2600 children, but he does state: "Certain significant deviations from Goodenough IQ's were revealed which indicate that the drawing test probably measures somewhat specialized abilities rather than general intelligence of the conventional linguistic type" (1937, p. 761). Pechoux and others (1947) report that for 100 abnormal and delinquent boys and girls between ages five and eighteen, the Goodenough M.A. correlates to only a slight extent with Porteus Maze results (r's of +.27 for the girls and +.25 for the boys) and only slightly more with the Stanford-Binet mental age (+.26 for the girls and +.38 for the boys). Rottersman, in an unpublished master's thesis (1950), reports the following correlations of the Draw-a-Man Test with the WISC, using fifty six-year-old children: Verbal Scale, r = +.38, Performance Scale, r = +.43; Full Scale, r = +.47. In the same group the Draw-a-Man results correlated +.36 with the Stanford-Binet.

Ansbacher (1952) studied the relationship between the Draw-a-Man scale and the Thurstone Primary Mental Abilities Test and with tests of tracing, tapping, and dotting, taken from the McQuarrie Test for Mechanical Ability. He used 100 ten-year-old youngsters as subjects. The Goodenough test was most highly correlated with factors of Reasoning (r = +.40), Space (r = +.38), and Perception (r = +.37), and less correlated with the McQuarrie Tapping (r = +.23), and Dotting (r = +.16). Correlations with the Primary Mental Abilities Verbal Meaning and Number tests were negligible. The Goodenough method correlated somewhat higher with the Tracing test (r = +.34). Ansbacher believed the Tracing test made heavy demands on "youthful willingness to follow directions," which he considered an attribute of personality. Ansbacher took this higher correlation as new evidence that the Goodenough test performance may be related to personality.

Hanvik (1953) reported for twenty-five psychiatric patients, aged five to twelve, significantly lower mean IQ's on the Goodenough than on the WISC. The rank order correlation between IQ's on the two scales was only +.18. Gunzburg (1955) found that Draw-a-Man IQ's of adult mental defectives correlated higher with the nonverbal (r = .73) than with the verbal (r = .43) Wechsler-Bellevue scale; this correlation pattern was higher for familial (r's of .79 and .54, respectively) than for organic cases (r's of .64 and .35, respectively). For seventy normal ten-year-olds, Havighurst and Janke (1944) report correlations with the Draw-a-Man as follows: Stanford-Binet, $r = .50$; Cornell-Coxe, $r = .63$; Minnesota Paper Formboard, $r = .48$.

The objectivity and reliability of the Goodenough scoring method for studying children's drawings of a man have been firmly established. Its value as an index of intelligence is perhaps not quite so firm. Validity coefficients are uniformly positive but range from very modest (the low 20's) to quite substantial (the 70's and 80's) depending on the age of the subjects, the age range included in the sample, and the measure used as a criterion. The correlation values show that the test measures intellectual more successfully than esthetic or personality factors.

Summary

When psychology focused interest on the study of the human mind during the late nineteenth century, children's drawings, as a means of understanding the child mind, came to prominence. Early observers quickly established that young children like to draw familiar objects, such as people, houses, trees, boats, and animals; the human figure being one of the commonest subjects. These early students also established the fact that there is a describable evolution in the child's portrayal of the human figure from simple schematic presentation of general features to detailed delineation.

Those students of children's drawings most interested in the understanding of thought processes adopted an analytical method, the essential method of science. The measurement of drawings by millimeter scales soon, however, gave way to analytical study based on elements—details. This method has been important in the study of drawings to the present time.

Florence Goodenough's scale of points for assessing intellectual maturity has been shown to be reliable; i.e., different scorers agree to a high degree in their results, and children show a high consistency in score from drawing to drawing. The psychological processes evaluated by the scale show considerable resistance to special influence introduced by instructions or "sets" supplied by the examiner.

This analytical method of scoring has been rather thoroughly investigated to see whether socially atypical children perform differently from "normal" or average children. It has been established that socially and emotionally maladjusted children do somewhat more poorly on the drawing test than well-adjusted children of the same general age and mental level. Their drawings tend to resemble those of retarded children. However, this scoring method fails to yield predictions of delinquency, neurosis, or severe disturbance sufficiently high to warrant its use for this purpose. It has some value for the analysis of abilities of deaf children. The method is clearly unrelated to artistic talent, as it is generally appraised in the elementary grades. Girls tend to earn somewhat higher scores than boys, and show certain characteristic qualitative differences not included in the scale.

Chapter Three

The Clinical
and Projective Uses
of Children's Drawings

ALTHOUGH SOME psychologists examine the content of graphic art for symbols to interpret (following Freud and Jung's approach), it is more common for clinicians and research workers to seek evidence of psychological traits, qualities, or states in the formal attributes or the stylistic features of drawings and paintings. The general hypothesis behind this approach is that unverbalized feeling states are projected into the procedure by which one manipulates and arranges a medium that can be formed and patterned. The pencil and paintbrush are devices for giving permanent record to the organization of visual space, and lend themselves particularly well to creative, organizational activity.

Other psychologists are less interested in the general features of a drawing than in the specific treatment of parts or features, particularly in the graphically portrayed human figure. For these psychologists the hypothesis relates to the projected ego or self-image that the subject presumably portrays. A voluminous and ingenious literature, highly theoretical and speculative, has been advanced in support of this hypothesis.

Projection of Affect in Line, Form, and Color

Goodenough's work noted her early interest in drawings as evidence for interests and personality traits (1926, p. 80). Luquet (1927, 1929), in discussions that foreshadow the "projective hypothesis," pointed out that children move from a stage of "emotional unrealism" to a stage of "intellectual realism." Malrieu (1950) in a lucid discussion, emphasized this same point of view. Lembke (1930), who also anticipated projective use of drawings, noted that the boldest and shyest children in each of seventeen elementary school classes differed markedly in their use of color and form in crayon drawings. The bold children outlined their objects much less distinctly, and used darker, noncomplementary color combinations, especially violet and brown.

Lowenfeld (1947, 1952) analyzed the progressive stages in the development of drawings in much the same terms as Luquet. He pointed out that the young child's drawings reflect his own desires, feelings, beliefs, and fancies rather than objective reality. Proportions, for example, represent values as the child conceives them rather than his perceptions of absolute size. As the child moves into what Luquet called the period of "realistic representation," his self-confidence is shaken by the contrast between his internal and external worlds. He may then give up all forms of creative activity, or he may express his conflicts and confusions in his art products.

Charlotte Buhler and colleagues (1952), in a book designed to enable teachers to analyze and understand child personality, affirm that children's drawings reveal much about their motivation. Because knowledge about children's motivations is essential to understand their needs and to judge their maturity or readiness for learning, teachers are urged to study children's artwork. The present author, however, cautions against the use of an elaborate symbolism in the interpretation of children's drawings.

Empirical evidence has accumulated to suggest that drawings by children reflect more than sheer developmental or conceptual maturity. Schliebe (1934), for example, was interested in determining how children depict states of feelings in their drawings. Six drawings were secured from each of 478 children between the ages of four and eighteen years. First they were told to draw a tree. This was used as the standard with which other drawings were to be compared. The children were then asked to draw a cold tree, a happy tree, a frightened tree, a sad tree, and a dying tree. Comparisons were made in terms of height and width, the direction in which the branches typically pointed and a number of other features. Schliebe believed he found characteristic patterns of such emotional expression. Children gave, as their chief reason for making the kind of drawings they did, either recalled or imagined kinesthetic sensations under similar conditions.

Harms (1941) proposed three methods that he considered useful in the study of neurotic children: (1) single lines drawn to denote words having affective value, (2) a picture drawn to illustrate a word chosen from a list of strongly affective terms, and (3) one picture drawn to illustrate the thing the child artist likes best and another to illustrate the thing he most strongly dislikes. These devices are not offered as confirmed techniques but as suggestions that have appeared promising.

In a later article Harms (1946) elaborated the first of his three suggested techniques. Approximately ten thousand subjects ranging in age from kindergarten to the adult level were asked to draw lines representing certain words, chiefly verbs and adjectives such as "walking," "cry," "silent." Harms' immediate task was to reduce the material to a series of objectively defined types that could be used as a basis for further work. Six forms were eventually delimited: (1) *monographical*, (2) *cursive*, in which the same figure was repeated several times in a running line, (3) *pictographical*, (4) *script*, in which a long line was drawn with undulations or circles such as to suggest writing, (5) *spatial*, in which the subject attempted to convey the quality by a change in the direction or form of the line, and (6) *final*, in which the only guiding principle seemed to be that of bringing the line to an end. Whether or not the method will prove useful in the differentiation of personality types remains to be seen, but the study is one of the most carefully worked out in the field.

This work had its precursor in experimental esthetics. Lundholm (1921) showed that artistically unsophisticated subjects, asked to illustrate certain adjectives by pencil line, produced discernibly similar patterns to particular classes of words. Using the stylized patterns that Lundholm described as prototypes, Poffenberger and Barrow (1924) demonstrated overwhelming agreement (from 50 to 90 per cent agreeing on each of eighteen possible choices of patterns), by a large sample of young adults in matching particular patterns with groups of adjectives.

Early work done with adolescents by Hevner (1935) and with children by Walton (1936) showed that lines and forms may express feelings as stated in adjectives. Also, they found considerable agreement as to the feeling states attributed, even among young children. Hevner found that both colors and forms express feeling tone, and that when colors and forms showing similar trends are combined as stimuli, the agreement on the feelings attributed disintegrates. This finding could well be studied developmentally. Walton's work (1936) suggests that young children's attribution of feelings involves principally the pleasant-unpleasant dimension. However, as they learn more words and concepts, children make finer distinctions and discriminate more polar dimensions. His observations agree with developmental thinking concerning both emotional and cognitive processes.

Krauss (1930) also found that when lines drawn by one set of students to depict various emotional states were shown to a second group, correct identification was made in 72.5 per cent of the cases. Scheerer and Lyons (1957) report consistent and meaningful choices in matching "physiognomic" and "neutral" words with patterns of lines. More recently Peters and Merrifield (1958) proposed a list of adjectives and described typical, or "normative," lines drawn to illustrate them. They comment that enough general agreement occurs in response to the stimulus words to warrant further exploration.

Also studying the graphic expression of complex feelings and impressions, England (1943) asked a group of ten- to fourteen-year-old children to "draw the most important event in your life." Twenty-seven per cent of all the drawings were of fears, and the great majority of the fear situations reflected traumatic episodes. On the basis of this, England concludes that fears of older children (between the ages of ten and fourteen) are preponderantly concrete and based on trauma. This finding is contrary to most child psychology textbook teaching, which tends to hold that fears in older children are principally imaginative and based on associative learning. It apparently did not occur to England that simple situations are more readily illustrated than complex events. Williams (1940), who was also interested in questions of methodology, found that drawings made by maladjusted children when alone in a room without distracting influences were more revealing than those made in the presence of the examiner. However, this finding should be checked; it may vary with the interpersonal relations between examiner and child. Furthermore, most clinical psychologists hold that the drawing behavior itself must be observed.

Following the example of Freud on Leonardo, Zilahi-Beke (1931) studied Michelangelo's works to learn how childhood experiences may influence the character of the artist's future work. He interprets the gigantic size of the young David (with whom the artist presumably identifies) as showing Michelangelo's jealousy and resentment of his older brother's favored family position. Shock and grief at the loss of his mother at the age of six is suggested as an explanation for the loving care with which he depicted the figure of the Virgin in the Pietà group, as well as for her very youthful appearance, which would correspond to his memories of his own mother at the time of her death. These speculations are interesting and, to some extent, plausible; but there is, of course, no way to verify them.

Excursions into the artwork of children from many theoretical positions, then, have affirmed that such products reveal psychologically important aspects about their creators. One of the most elaborate studies of preschool children's art and its meaning is the richly illustrated two-volume report by Alschuler and Hattwick (1947). Volume II presents the statistics on which the conclusions of Volume I presumably are based, together with biographical data for each child. There is evidence of considerable confusion between what may be true for an individual and what is characteristic of the group to which he belongs. An example is a case described in Volume I. A little girl designated as Aileen, who was shuttled back and forth between the homes of her divorced parents with occasional side trips to the home of a grandparent or other relative, repeatedly painted an ovular red mass which she said was a "house." Actually, 133 of the 187 paintings made during her first year in nursery school were of this type. The authors state, without giving figures, that these paintings were more likely to be made during periods when the child was unusually depressed and upset, and that in subsequent years when her paintings had advanced to the pictorial stage, she not infrequently reverted to the old pattern at times when her home life was more than usually unhappy. Although one would wish some figures, the following explanation is at least plausible:

> It is not difficult to understand Aileen's unhappiness and her constant anxiety about "home." . . . In her persistent paintings of the ovular red mass, as the full data substantiate, Aileen was expressing her need and deep craving for a home which would give her adequate protection and love (Vol. I, p. 12).

The present writer believes that in view of the very large amount of material available for each of the 150 children studied by Alschuler and Hattwick, the authors might have used statistical methods appropriate for the study of individual cases, together with some interchild comparisons. The attempt to report findings for the group as described in Volume II may, in fact, be misleading. There is no good reason to suppose that the symbolic language of children is universal; it may well differ from one child to another. If this is true, the only generalizations possible are in terms of principles, not of specific symbols. In an attempt to confirm Alschuler and Hattwick's work, Windsor (1949) came to much the same conservative conclusion.

Because of its direct character and primitive method, finger painting has appealed to a number of persons as offering unusual opportunities for emotional expression. A bibliography on this topic has been prepared by Napoli (1946, 1947). Blum and Dragositz (1947) attempted to study the developmental aspects of finger painting comparing first-grade and sixth-grade children's work. Unfamiliarity of both groups with the medium may perhaps account for the fact that so few differences were found. The older children obtained somewhat neater results with less smearing of the colors at points of junction, and better coverage of the paper. Even these differences, however, were so small that two art teachers who served as judges were able to separate the work of the two groups with only slightly better than chance success.

Figure Drawings and the Study of Personality

On the basis of studies and observations such as those cited above, many present-day psychologists have come to believe that drawings and paintings, being spontaneous behaviors, reveal children's feelings and desires. Such free activity, they hold, expresses not only the needs and emotions dominant at the time but also the more deep-seated and lasting characteristics known as "personality."

The use of children's drawings as a projective device was especially promoted by Bell's summary (1948), and there are now many proposals for interpreting the psychological significance of such drawing. Most of these systems examine drawings in terms of signs having psychological significance. Several writers who have worked extensively with the language of signs in drawings cite Goodenough's study with psychopathic children as their inspiration—for example, Despert (1937), and Bender (1940). But all too many investigators appear to have neglected Goodenough's warning:

> The facts herein reported are by no means intended to convey the impression that the writer is able to diagnose psychopathic tendencies in children by means of a drawing. Certainly no such claim is justified. It is believed, however, that by an investigation carried out along the lines which have been indicated a method of scoring might be derived which would throw new light upon eccentricities of mental functioning during childhood (1926, p. 66).

The Goodenough scale as a device for studying behavior disorders has already been reviewed and evaluated (pp. 23–28). The method essentially relies on noting the presence or absence of body parts, detail of body or garb, and the like, all quite carefully defined.

In contrast, the figure-drawing approach and its several variations that have come into favor with clinicians in recent years rely on more loosely defined aspects of the drawing. The subject is asked to draw a person, and, having done that, to draw a person of the opposite sex. The psychological interpretation may rest on the presence or absence of specific parts, but more commonly uses qualitative features of the drawing, for examples, the general way a part is depicted, relative proportions of different parts, mode of treatment of line, contour, shading, etc., apparent expression or mood depicted, and "physiognomic" aspects of the sketch. Such a basis for evaluation introduces both clinical flexibility and statistical unreliability into the interpretation. Evaluations are not based on the accumulation of points, as in a scale; rather, they are based on impressions of "gestalt" effects produced by the arrangement and interrelationships (often only vaguely and very subjectively appraised), of the elements proposed. Although a large number of studies have applied the Goodenough scoring method to drawings obtained in this way, Bliss and Berger (1954) found that such drawings yield significantly lower mental age equivalents than drawings obtained according to Goodenough's instructions, which specify ". . . make a picture of a man. Make the very best picture that you can" (1926, p. 85).

The psychological study of drawings began with analyzing the artwork of normal children and of a few adult psychotics. As clinical psychologists increased their contacts with noninstitutional adults, through the growth of clinics, the collections of adult drawings also increased. Consequently, some reference will be made to this literature, but the focus will continue to be on children's artwork and on developmental studies.

The Theoretical Basis for Figure Drawing as a Projection of the Self

The concept that drawings of the human figure are useful for the study of personality, or as diagnostic tools in clinical assessment, finds its theoretical justification in self-image psychology as well as in the psychoanalytic theory of projection. The physiological and psychoanalytical basis for the "body image" as the person's self-concept has been given by Schilder (1935). He noted that the body image is a configuration, or gestalt, composed of many physical, organic, and physiological sensations and experiences with one's body; these include seeing one's image in a mirror, as well as noting the reactions of others to one's appearance and behavior. Accordingly, when an individual draws a person he may reflect the many impressions he has of his own body.

Schilder treated drawings as equivalent to dream material in reflecting the unconscious. Thus, whether one unconsciously portrays his "self" when he is asked to draw a "person" is scarcely open to direct verification. The vast majority of children asked to draw a man doubtless portray an adult figure; the writer has found that, when specifically asked to draw "a picture of yourself," the majority of children depict juvenile features more or less successfully, and sometimes clearly idiosyncratic features.

One of the more systematic presentations of psychological self-image theory is that by Snygg and Combs (1949), who argue for the significance of the world as perceived, contrasted with so-called "objective reality." It is the world as it is presented to the psychological self (sometimes called the phenomenological world) that is of value to psychology; it is only this subjective world that has psychological meaning and relevance. Rogers (1942) earlier developed a similar point of view in connection with a theory for psychological counseling and therapy. When perceptions can be changed, adjustment may be effected, even though no change is produced in the external situation.

If the human figure drawing can be considered the self-image, consciously or unconsciously projected, then analysis of drawings could have great importance. Distortions in the drawing may be literal or symbolic representations of inadequacies or distortions in the artist's self-image. Such is the theoretical assumption of Machover's Draw-a-Person technique (1949), Buck's House-Tree-Person test (1948), and similar drawing procedures. Machover's hypothesis is that the self-image is projected into the drawing of the human figure, and that interpretation can be based on analogy. She states:

> When an individual attempts to solve the problem of the directive to "draw a person," he is compelled to draw from some sources. External figures are too varied in their body attributes to lend themselves to a spontaneous, composite, objective representation of a person. Some process of selection involving identification through projection and introjection enters at some point. The individual must draw consciously, and no doubt unconsciously, upon his whole system of psychic values. The body, or the self, is the most intimate point of reference in any activity. We have, in the course of growth, come to associate various sensations, perceptions, and emotions with certain body organs. This investment in body organs, or the perception of the body image as it has developed out of personal experience, must somehow guide the individual who is drawing in the specific structure and content which constitutes his offering of a "person." Consequently, the drawing of a person, in involving a projection of the body image, provides a natural vehicle for the expression of one's body needs and conflicts. Successful drawing interpretation has proceeded on the hypothesis that the figure drawn is related to the individual who is drawing with the same intimacy characterizing that individual's gait, his handwriting, or any other of his expressive movements. The technique of personality analysis that is described in this book attempts to reconstruct the major features of this self-projection (1949, p. 5).*

* From Machover, Karen, *Personality Projection in the Human Figure*, 1st Ed., 1949. Courtesy of Charles C. Thomas, Publisher, Springfield, Illinois.

Buck accepts the human figure drawing as a projection of the self-image, and suggests further that the drawing of a tree is the projection of the self's adjustment to the natural world, and the drawing of a house, its adjustment to the human or social world. Both "theories" make many specific statements about the meaning of particular "signs"—the ways in which parts of the figure are drawn. There are other investigators (e.g., Silver, 1950), however, who deny that any such check list of characteristics can be given. They advocate a more intuitive approach; "If the observer tries to understand what is the body image concept represented in each drawing, what are its outstanding features, he will understand more of the patient's problems" (Silver, 1950, p. 136). Unfortunately no well-developed rationale for this theory exists, though some beginnings have been made by Machover (1949, 1951, 1953) and Levy (1950).

Several lines of investigation bearing on this general theory may be summarized: the study of (1) the differentiation of sex in figure drawings; (2) preferred sex in figure drawings; (3) drawings made by persons who are physically atypical, and (4) drawings done by subjects with known neurological damage that interferes with cognitive processes.

The Differentiation of Sex in Drawings

Children's concepts of sex are undoubtedly reflected in the features they select to mark a drawing as one of a boy or of a girl. Bried (1950) has shown that preschool children make only the crudest attempts to differentiate sex in drawing human figures, even when requested to draw "papa" and "mama." Mott (1954) used drawings of preschool children in exploring the meaning of the concept "mother." She notes that prior to age five there is virtually no symbolization of sex; kindergarten children, however, use curly hair surrounding the head and a triangular body to designate femaleness. Knopf and Richards (1952) studied the figure drawings of forty six- and eight-year-old children, concluding that girls exceed boys in the complexity of their drawings of both sexes. This superiority may reflect cognitive and skill factors as well as greater sex awareness or more adequate sex identification.

Swensen (1955) and Swensen and Newton (1955) studied pairs of human figure drawings produced by 163 elementary school children and a small group of young adults. The pairs of drawings were rated on a nine-point scale for adequacy of sex differentiation. Up to the seventh grade, the girls excelled the boys; after the seventh grade there was no difference between boys and girls in adequacy of differentiation. The sharpest rate of improvement was observed from the first to the third grades. Among adults, Murphy (1957), however, found women scoring above men in adequacy of sexual differentiation of drawing. Cutter (1956) applied Swensen's method of rating drawings to the work of adult sexual psychopaths in three classifications, finding that degree of differentiation achieved by a subject in his figure drawings was related to his type of disorder; the better sex differentiation was achieved by the better integrated patients. Social or intellectual aspects of the subjects in relation to their type of disorder were not studied. Evaluation of the foregoing studies is, perhaps, aided by Sherman's (1958) demonstration that scores on Swensen's scale correlate significantly and substantially with a simple rating of artistic quality; it is probable that the ability to depict the sexes in drawings is itself a product of psychological development and correlates substantially with mental level.

Preferred Sex in Figure Drawings

It has been asserted that the figure drawn first in the "draw-a-person" procedure designates the sex identification of the drawer. Weider and Noller (1950, 1953) found that only 70 per cent of primary school boys, but 90 per cent of the girls, drew their own sex first. While the tendency to draw one's own sex first was unrelated to socioeconomic status, the number of sex-specific details depicted (hair, hat, garb, etc.) was definitely related to socioeconomic status. This trend probably reflects factors also reflected in intelligence test performance.

Jolles (1952 b) has shown that children of ages five to eight, when asked to draw a person, draw their own sex first in about 80 per cent of the cases. After age eight, the percentage of boys drawing the male first rises, and the percentage of girls drawing the female first falls. Granick and Smith (1953), Mainord (1953), and Schubert and Wagner (1954) agree that a smaller proportion of adult women draw the female figure first than the corresponding proportion of men who draw the male figure first. The operation of a social stereotype seems to be as plausible an explanation for this discrepancy as that of unconscious sex-role conflicts. Finding no correlation with a measure of attitudinal masculinity or femininity orientation (the MMPI), Granick and Smith doubt that the human figure drawn is an unconscious self-portrait. Children probably draw the figure of the sex group with which they have had more contact, and thus are more closely identified. Deviates from this pattern may reflect psychological deviation; they may also reflect social and cultural factors, or merely incidental and situational influences. Brown and Tolor's (1957) review of the literature found no convincing evidence that choice of sex in figure drawing reflects adequacy of psychosexual identification or adjustment.

Berman and Laffal (1953), in an indirect test of the self- or body-image hypothesis also based on drawings by adults, found a correlation of .35 between Sheldon body-type ratings of drawings, and the Sheldon ratings of their respective drawers' physiques.

Drawings by Physically Atypical Persons

It might be expected that physically atypical subjects would handle the drawing of the human figure somewhat differently than do normals. Kotkov and Goodman (1953) identified seven significant points of difference $(P = .05)$ [1] between the human figure drawings made by obese women and

---

[1] These seven points survived from 129 examined and thus these values, too, could have arisen by chance.

those by women of normal weight matched in age and general intellectual level. Six of these seven "signs" referred to the sketch of the female figure; four of these involved measures of area.

Silverstein and Robinson (1956) were unable to distinguish human figure drawings made by orthopedically disabled children from drawings made by matched control subjects, either by a point-scoring system of "signs," or by a global rating method. Martorana (1954) found that 94 per cent of a group of crippled children drew men as normal. When asked to make self-portraits, however, 72 per cent of the crippled children made drawings in keeping with their true body structure; while 94 per cent of normal children produced self-portraits in keeping with their bodily features. The presentation was uniformly realistic, and approached fantasy or symbolism in only one case in sixty-four. Using ten features of drawings declared by Buck (1948) to characterize the self-image of the physically handicapped, Wawrzaszek, Johnson, and Sciera (1958) failed to confirm a single one of the features in a group of severely handicapped children as contrasted with a carefully matched control group.

Thus, the case for unconscious representation of the "self" in human figure drawings has not been firmly established. But the very nature of the concept defies objective validation. The weight of evidence strongly suggests that children put into their drawings their cognitive concepts, especially the visual ones, and that distortions in size and proportion represent psychological and conceptual inadequacies and immaturities as much as they do affective conditions or unconscious dynamics. Goldworth (1950), coming to a similar conclusion, has suggested that the body-image hypothesis may be valid only for those persons who are not highly "visual," who depend primarily on other modalities (e.g., kinesthetic) for their perceptions. Such persons, however, are probably in a very small minority. Lowenfeld (1939, 1945) has steadily affirmed that the visual mode of perception is the dominant one, especially in a culture that places much emphasis on reading and on pictures.

Furthermore, child self-portraits, when such are explicitly requested, *do* portray the drawer's appearance as it is visibly given to the world, within the capacities of the child to represent. A child's symbolism is a logical one, quite explicable in terms of his understandings and concepts. Too few clinical studies have carefully controlled the psychological and social variables operating selectively in their samples, which are known to affect art productions. Until this has been done the "evidence" adduced from drawings in favor of the self-image theory (in the projective sense) must be regarded with caution.

Drawings by Patients with Known Neurological Damage

Drawings by persons sustaining known neurological damage reflect their condition; but it takes no elaborate dynamic theory to explain why a person suffering serious impairment of motor control produces distorted figures (thus, Sharp, 1949, and Silver, 1950). When no specific motor coordination factor is involved, the distortion of the figure usually reflects cognitive deficits occurring centrally. A literature far too extensive to summarize here has grown up around the Bender-Gestalt test (Bender, 1938) in which the ability to copy visually presented, patterned line drawings presumably reveals these central disorders of perception. Mira's Myokinetic Psychodiagnosis (1940), although promising for work in this area, has apparently not been tried out with children. The Ellis visual designs, similar to Bender's figures, have been used with children by Wood and Shulman (1940) and by Lord and Wood (1942). Sharp (1949) proposed the drawing of geometric designs from memory as a differential test for various psychoses, the differing conditions distorting the reproductions in different ways.

The work of Engerth (1933), of Vedder (1940), of Berrien (1935) and of Bender (1937, 1940), and of Reznikoff and Tomblen (1956) suggests that brain damage in children as well as adults may be indicated by distortions in drawing and copying. Bender (1940) affirmed that the inability to draw the human figure sometimes does not extend to other objects. She believes that this peculiar condition signifies disturbance not only in the perception of visual gestalts but also, possibly, in all other sensory impressions and memory images of earlier body experiences. Freed and Pastor (1951) found that thalamotomy disturbed drawings produced in the weeks following the operation, but that six months later, figure drawings were indistinguishable from preoperative samples made by the same subjects. From a collection of drawings completed before and after shock therapy, Fingert, Kagan, and Schilder (1939) noted a steady quantitative improvement in Goodenough score, and the disappearance of bizarre features in the drawings.

Michal-Smith (1953), examining the diagnostic value of the H–T–P in a group of adult patients with abnormal cerebral electrical function (EEG), found that of the several elements designated by Buck (1948), only "line quality" distinguished his clinical from his normal subjects. Bieliauskas and Kirkham (1958) in an even more carefully controlled study failed to confirm a single "sign" of organic impairment proposed by Buck (1948) or by Jolles (1952 a). These results are in keeping with the hypothesis that inconsistencies and uncertainties in execution rather than in content or in subject representation are more likely to appear in central nervous system deficit.

In a study of emotionally disturbed children age six and under, Owen (1955) claimed to have observed disorders of the body image. Considering how limited are the drawings of young children in concept of the human figure and in execution of detail and proportion, this claim is difficult to accept. Cohn (1953) described how, in normal children of ages three to six, when multiple simultaneous cutaneous stimuli are applied to various regions of the body, stimulation on the face dominates (extinguishes response to) all caudal stimuli. Noting that this pattern occurs also in adults in states of dissolution of normal brain function as a result of structural lesions of the brain, Cohn argues that the body-image concept held by a person reflects the adequacy of neurological functioning. He buttresses his position by noting that in human figure drawings by three- to six-year-old children, the head dominates all other members, which often are even absent. Cohn also found that figure drawings by brain-damaged adults are grossly malformed, or are very simple in form. But it should be pointed out that drawings by normal preschool children are quite different from those by damaged or regressed adults in conception, in general quality, detail, and execution.

A similar conclusion and probably equally erroneous, is inferred by Modell (1951), who reports that during recovery regressed adult patients show changes in figure drawings that can be summarized as body-image maturation and sexual maturation, because aspects of the drawing become increasingly more detailed, complete, and better organized. The inference is that drawings made in the regressed state are similar to those produced by much younger subjects. Such is not the case, as has been also shown in the work of hypnotically regressed subjects (Orne, 1951). It is true that the human figure drawings are simplified under hypnosis, but they do not resemble, qualitatively, the work of normal younger subjects. Likewise, Lakin (1956) as well as Lorge, Tuckman and Dunn (1958), note that elderly persons produce drawings different both from younger adults and from children. The differences appear to lie in the greater constriction, less detail, and less adequately represented concepts of the body shown in the drawings of the aged.

Thus, it appears that neurological deficit may interfere with the production of human figure drawings. It is not clear that the hypothesis of a mediating "body-image" concept, which is subject to age regression, is particularly helpful. Some such idea apparently lies behind the notion that when the IQ estimate obtained from drawing falls considerably below that obtained from verbal test assessments, there is evidence of "brain damage" (Bender, 1937, 1938, 1940). This hypothesis is not yet firmly established but certainly warrants further research. It is clear that suitable statistical criteria must be used to determine the limits of such a discrepancy when quantitatively expressed, in order to assure that the observed discrepancy lies beyond the limits of chance variation. This consideration has been generally lacking in the discussions reported in the literature.

Bender and Schilder (1951) have developed a plausible hypothesis from a study of children's reading disability and graphic art expression. While tachistoscopic studies show poor readers equal to good readers in the mechanics of optic perception, poor readers appear to have difficulty in patterning such perceptions, in differentiating the foreground from the background, and in right-left discriminations. Drawings produced by poor readers may provide a clue to their problem. They have difficulty with the sign function of visual materials; that is, with the attribution of meaning. They can copy a word readily but "it is not a specific object for them to which they can have a specific attitude" (1951, p. 148). Consequently, they may prefer to work with other than verbal symbols—art, craft work, numbers—and may come to excel in these activities. That such a condition, however, constitutes an "aphasia," as some have suggested (Reitman, 1951), certainly needs more demonstration.

Proposals for the Qualitative Analysis of Drawings

Machover's (1948) publication synthesizes her work of many years with disturbed children. She states (1953) that she came to see the projective significance of human figure drawing by noting that some children similar in IQ on other tests of intelligence differed markedly on the Goodenough scores. This could be explained statistically, in terms of the observed correlations between the Draw-a-Man and other estimates of intelligence, but Machover notes that if the drawing fails to express the IQ, it probably expresses something else, presumably personality (1953, p. 85). She also states:

> Although there exists a vast body of literature on the subject of the projective significance of drawing and painting, specific study of the projection of the body with its infinitely subtle language, is relatively unfamiliar to the non-clinician. Publication concerning the technique has not kept up to the increasing verification and support which it has received in its application to clinical problems for more than twenty years (Frank, et al., 1953, p. 89).

It is a great pity that these clinical systems have become available so slowly to research workers for investigation and validation. Systematic review of the scattered clinical reports suggests inconsistencies and gaps, even contradictions, which should be cleared up if such systems are to be helpful, even to their proponents. Indeed, Machover's own suggestions, interesting and ingenious as they are, are presented so unsystematically that it is difficult to use them in research.

Vernier says, ". . . the current absence of any standardized scoring system, of an integrated set of validated principles of interpretation, makes the use of the test hazardous except as one part of a total test battery in the hands of an experienced clinician" (1952, p. 1). The very fact of this acknowledged intuitive approach probably accounts for the inconsistencies among the principal writers on the subject.

Buck's hypothesis concerning the self-image has already been mentioned. The mode or style of treating the human figure in comparison with the subject's treatment of a house and a tree is Buck's (1948) basis for analyzing the person's adjustment as a self, in comparison with his adjustment to the human and social environment and to the natural world. Buck offers a series of conceptual headings for evaluating drawings, and some general principles for scoring. Buck's manual is not clear as to procedure of evaluation, or wholly satisfactory as a guide to interpretation. Two additional manuals have appeared for the H–T–P system (Jolles, 1952 a; Hammer, 1954), differing in a number of respects. Thus, no firm basis for quantitative study is afforded. Buck's own statistical criteria for denoting certain characteristics as unusual, while consistently applied, appear to have no basis in statistical logic (e.g., satisfying a particular level of significance). In Buck's monograph an appendix by Payne makes some suggestions concerning the use of color. Discussed also by Landisburg (1947), this method has generated a large body of studies. Buck's own work, as well as the general findings of an extensive literature on his H–T–P, confirm that drawing behavior exposes the individual's psychological maturity (by which is meant intellectual and conceptual aspects of maturity), somewhat more successfully than it does inner affective states (e.g., Rubin, 1954).

One of the most specific methods proposed for analyzing child personality through drawings is given by Wolff in a table of Graphic Elements (1946, pp. 233–236). Although the table is preceded by a few precautionary remarks, the list is presented as if it were wholly factual. Some seventy characteristics of children's drawings are arranged in columns, with the personality attribute supposedly indicated thereby placed in a parallel column. Examples are:

> Preference for circular movements—Balance, changing moods, evading any decision, manic-depressive.
> Preference for shadings—Tactile sensitivity.
> Interruptions in strokes—Stubbornness, negativism.

It is noted that most of the drawing characteristics named represent continuous rather than discrete variables, though they are not so indicated. Wolff also hypothesizes that proportions in the figure drawn have significance for balance and rhythm in the personality adjustments of the artist. Apart from descriptive accounts of individual cases, objective evidence for the validity of these relationships is wholly lacking. Unfortunately, in the years since the publication of this system virtually no evaluations of, or research on, his suggestions have appeared.

Some systems have been nonanalytic, in that they have relied on ratings of general qualities to be observed in artistic productions. Such a plan has been proposed by Elkisch (1945), and is chiefly applicable to more complex productions than human figure drawings. Elkisch used the following criteria in evaluating paintings: rhythm vs. rule; complexity vs. simplexity; expansion vs. compression; integration vs. disintegration. Each of these terms was defined in some detail. In a second article, Elkisch (1947) reiterated her position that a single production is insufficient evidence for sound diagnosis, and that form rather than content should be the basis for judgment.

This latter view, that formal elements are more significant for personality than content *per se*, is reminiscent of the theory underlying the Rorschach test. A similar view concerning formal elements is held by Schilder and Levine (1942). They apply Freudian symbolism to the formal elements of line, color, angles, borders, contours, balance, and the like, rather than to interpretations of content, as do the majority of psychoanalytically inclined psychologists.

Waehner (1946) also used formal "scoring elements" to evaluate drawings of human faces and figures. Her scoring sheet suggests the Rorschach even more strongly than does the scheme of Elkisch. The statistical treatment is crude but so far as the data go they suggest that the method has some value in differentiating personality types. Munroe, Levinson, and Waehner (1944), with college students as subjects, found that the Waehner system of interpreting drawings predicted Rorschach diagnosis with a degree of accuracy that exceeded the one per cent level of confidence (chi-square method).

Neither the Elkisch nor the Waehner technique has been used widely, possibly because their criteria require the examiner to learn a special set of symbols, terminology and judgments. The "figure drawing" approach, as loosely described by Machover, Buck, Jolles, and others, appears more simple and direct, but permits the interpreter to "project" as much as his subject!

Other techniques have been suggested. The Hares (1956) have suggested and evaluated a Draw-a-Group Test for identifying the social structure of the group and the individual's adjustment to it. Reznikoff and Reznikoff (1956) have offered an analysis of the Family Drawing Test, first suggested by Appel (1931), and also by Wolff (1942). All these psychologists use a form of self-concept theory in their interpretative systems.

Caligor (1957) has his subject redraw, on an onion skin overlay, his original human figure drawing, to add to it or change it in any way he chooses. Then, masking the original figure, the subject redraws his first tracing, and continues thus for seven trials. Caligor offers a conceptual scheme for classifying the modifications, and a manual to aid in clinical interpretation. The latter appears to be based on a "logical" analysis of projective theory rather than on data. This method might well be studied in relation to such intellectual characteristics as creativity, imagination and modification of set, as well as in relation to personality dynamics.

Brown and Goitein (1943) believe that distortions in a subject's self-portrait, drawn while blindfolded, will reveal certain characteristic personality "needs." Spielrein (1931), Wolff (1946), and Mira (1940) have also noted the clinical significance of drawings made without visual inspection of the results. Hellersberg (1945, 1950) and Krout (1950), like Wartegg (1939), offer a child a few lines to incorporate into a picture; the former's analytical system is particularly systematic and elaborate. This approach deserves more study than it has thus far received, though Ames and Hellersberg (1949) have given some attention to developmental trends.

Thus, many psychologists believe that children's drawings provide significant cues for personality diagnosis; however, no complete characterological system based on this evidence has appeared. Wartegg (1939) offers the only characterology based on drawings that has come to the writer's attention. As many of the German characterological systems developed during the 'thirties, Wartegg's study is politically oriented. In this country Alschuler and Hattwick, and Wolff come closest to a characterological system. The work of Buck and of Machover have possibilities of being enlarged into complete theories in which a psychology of drawings is integrated with a psychology of personality. All this material needs more extensive validation.

Generalizations Concerning the Use of Drawings in the Study of Personality

The belief that the art of children is primarily a language, a form of expression, is by no means new, but its emphasis has shifted. Earlier studies were for the most part based on the oft-repeated statement: "A child draws what he knows, rather than what he sees." At the present time many students of child art would revise this hypothesis to read: "A child draws what he feels, rather than what he sees or knows to be true." In spite of those with poor scientific training who have used the method unwisely, evidence has accumulated to indicate that through his drawings the child frequently gives outward expression to his inner thoughts and feelings.

From an extensive acquaintance with studies, observations, reports of cases, and the like, which have used children's drawings as a tool in clinical diagnosis, one may make several generalizations concerning the psychological study of drawings. These generalizations represent in part the crystallization of experience, and in part wide acceptance of speculative "theory"; much less often do they have a basis in research data. They are stated here as eight affirmations that represent the widest practice or opinion as that practice or opinion is revealed in the literature, not as proved scientific generalizations. An attempt has been made to evaluate each affirmation in terms of the scientific evidence available.

1. *Drawing interpretation is more valid when based on a series of a subject's protocols than when based on one drawing.* Alschuler and Hattwick (1947) emphasize this principle as do Naumberg (1947) and many others who use drawings diagnostically. The Goodenough method uses one drawing to estimate intelligence; some evidence exists, for example, Seashore and Bavelas (1942), to show that estimates obtained from children's successive drawings of the man do not change significantly, unless the drawing situation itself is changed by instruction or through boredom or fatigue. It should be clear, however, that the Goodenough method assesses cognitive elements in an assigned task, and might well be more stable from drawing to drawing than more "open," impressionistic assignments. The Goodenough method, being a measurement device, would be expected to yield a more stable estimate from the average of several scores by the same child than from any single component of that average. Likewise, it is undoubtedly true, when *content* or meaning of a drawing is being used as the significant datum, that any one protocol alone might lead to a quite different clinical deduction than would a collection of drawings or paintings. This generalization, then, seems justified on logical if not empirical grounds.

2. *Drawings are most useful for psychological analysis when teamed with other available information about the child.* This principle, too, seems well supported in logic, although instances of great success in "blind analysis" of drawings could be cited. Children are so varied in their productions, even

on assigned topics, that details, symbols, and other aspects of drawings can have quite unique meanings. Highly individual treatments are illuminated as we know more about the child's background, his art training and experience, his interests, and the like. Vernier, for example, affirms that it is her opinion "shared by many other workers in the field, that projective drawings are not primarily a diagnostic test and should be used only as one test in the psychological battery" (1952, p. 1). This principle seems sound, especially when it is the content of drawings alone that is being used for psychological interpretation.

3. *Free drawings are more meaningful psychologically than drawings of assigned topics.* This principle, also growing out of clinical practice, reflects the particular use of the clinician. He wishes to get a different, suggestive, and, perhaps, illuminating view of the psychological dynamics of a single case; he believes he can get this by giving his client freedom of subject. On the other hand, when a *measure* of drawing ability, or an estimate of cognitive powers is required, an assigned subject permits the systematic, controlled comparisons necessary. The anthropologist seeking to understand children's interests, the effect of culture on art styles, or the use of drawings as devices for communicating meanings requires a large collection of drawings obtained under various circumstances; he may want a sample of controlled drawings also, if he wishes to compare children's drawing performance quite specifically and systematically.

Thus, if one seeks new ideas and insights about the individual, or if one explores the range of ideas and techniques of which children are capable, he will want free drawings—many of them. If one seeks to compare children systematically as to abilities, stylistic trends, use of symbols, and the like, he will want to control the production by setting the task or assigning the subject.

4. *When a human figure drawing is assigned, the sex of the figure first drawn relates to the image the drawer holds of his own sex role.* While this principle is stated or implied in many clinical reports, and appears to be the *raison d'être* for use of the "figure drawing" as opposed to "draw-a-man" rationale (see the discussion of the "body image," pp. 42–44), the principle probably does not have universal validity. The majority of children draw their own sex first when asked to "draw a person." Among girls, the tendency to draw a man increases with age, this trend probably reflecting the cultural preference given to the male role as well as an increasing dissatisfaction with sex role;[2] the male figure may be culturally more stereotyped and hence easier to draw than the female figure. The *deviates* from this cultural norm may be psychologically different. If this is true, the deviation might have a quite different meaning for the two sexes. Certainly, there would be meanings unique to the individual also. Hence, the principle is probably not valid *universally*.

[2] Over several studies which include a spread of ages, the percentage figures are surprisingly stable; about 85 per cent of boys and 65 per cent of girls draw own sex first.

5. *A child adopts a schema or style of drawing which is peculiar to him and which becomes highly significant psychologically.* Several studies, for example, Rouma (1913), Burt (1921), Goodenough (1926), have shown that a developmental pattern emerges in children's drawings. That this pattern permits one to appraise the level of cognitive processes is now well established.

That many individuals also adopt a unique expressive style or schema of drawing is also undoubtedly true, but the psychological meaning of such a schema for personality study is less clear. Certainly some children's work can be readily identified by a person only casually acquainted with the child's "style." But is the child who always draws the same subject in the same manner psychologically rigid, while the child who draws many subjects in quite different ways psychologically adaptable, imaginative, or creative? We cannot be sure scientifically, though such conclusions have been offered from time to time. However, no well-controlled studies exist, and those few studies that have tried to test particular hypotheses are generally negative (e.g., W. E. Martin [1955], Rawn [1957]).

6. *The manner in which certain elements are portrayed in drawings may be used as signs of certain psychological states or conditions in the artist.* The identification of elements in a drawing to be treated as clinical "signs" follows from the study of drawings produced by selected individuals representing contrasted psychological conditions. Or, the identification of signs may follow deductively from personality theory. An example would be the notion that a person who is over-controlled, psychologically cramped and inhibited, will reflect this condition in motor behavior of all sorts, including pencil drawings. Hence, a tiny figure might be taken to signify psychological constriction. In a sense, this is reasoning by analogy, and many assertions in the literature reflect this approach, inferring a one-to-one, or isomorphic, relation between the condition and its symbol in the drawing protocol.

Whether or not "signs" are selected by an empirical or deductive procedure, there is still the question of whether form or content will provide the cues. Size, quality or texture of line, degree of angularity, pattern or shape, and placement on the page are often thought to be highly significant avenues for "projecting" unconscious motives or needs.

Another approach is that employed by psychoanalytic theory, which hypothesizes a classic symbolism used for the expression of repressed drives and for the symbolic representation of sexual organs. Indeed, drawings are held to be analogous to dream work. Thus, phallic elements in drawings have been discussed (Jolles, 1952 c) and, as we have already seen, the "mandala" is believed to have a primitive and fundamental character (Jung, 1950). Precker (1950), however, believes that the expressive movements involved in painting and drawing may have quite as much, if not more, psychological significance than the symbolic content of drawings. Hence, he would examine the more formal elements—use of line, form, space, balance, and arrangement. Liss (1938), a psychoanalyst, and Schilder and Levine (1942), also analysts, join Precker in discarding content symbolism for a symbolism found in the formal aspects of drawings. We have already noted that Waehner (1946) similarly abandoned a symbolism of content for elements similar to those of the whole, detail, shading and the like.

Useful and valid signs leading to dependable conclusions are, for the most part, still to be ascertained. We have already cited the systems advanced by Buck (1948), Machover (1949), and Wolff (1946), all of which are based on the presence or absence of elements, which can be treated as signs.

Bell's (1948) extensive compilation of elements in drawings that have been given psychological meaning shows that there is little uniformity with respect to their character and reputed meaning. That some agreement in interpretation of signs occurs, apart from the convergence of empirical evidence, is not surprising. Some agreement would be expected due to the common acceptance of certain symbols by psychologists who share a particular theory.

Common adult associations would account for the fact that smearing of colors should be accepted as a sign of "untidiness," that a preference for red should be thought to indicate feelings of aggression, or that excessive use of dark brown or black should denote depression. But that absence of hands should indicate masturbation, that placing the drawing of a man against one side of the page, or drawing a line under the figure should indicate "need for support," or that a profile drawing indicates "reluctance to face the world" suggests analogical reasoning akin to the "sympathetic magic" of the primitive who sticks pins into an image of his enemy to give that person discomfort. Of all the clinicians who have written about the figure drawing method, only Raven (1951, p. 17) makes explicit the assumption of isomorphy. As will be shown later in this chapter, attempts to validate such isomorphic signs have resulted in almost wholly negative findings. There is little evidence for the validity of signs beyond that of selected case studies using small clinical groups. The drawings made by these selected cases may or may not be representative of those made by others whose behavior is similar. Drawings similar in style or symbolism may be common among persons who show no indications at all of the behavior such drawings have been assumed to symbolize! All this has been said many times before, but so much of the work with projective methods has ignored the caution that it seems well to repeat it here.

Few clinical studies have clearly recognized the great many ways in which children can represent a particular body part or detail. Despite the clear-cut developmental patterns which have been found repeatedly, there are many, many ways in which children can depict a particular concept. This fact militates against a too-detailed schedule of specific forms with corresponding interpretations. In his detailed analysis of how children age three to ten treat parts of the body and face, Djukić (1953) emphasized this point particularly.

7. *Drawings must be interpreted as wholes rather than segmentally or analytically.* Many writers, especially those who hold for the clinical significance of drawings, stress that drawings must be interpreted as entities. Thus Bell (1948), Buck (1948), Bender (1940), Machover (1949), and Windsor

(1949), among others, emphasize the gestalt or total pattern of effects produced by the drawing as vital to its interpretation. In view of her stress on the importance of particular body parts, Machover's position on this point might seem to be incongruous. However, her interpretation of details, although phrased as the treatment of specified features, invariably cites concomitance of two or three such features as evidence for her interpretations.

Undoubtedly, the generalization that drawings be interpreted as wholes grows out of the impression, very common among those who work extensively with drawings, that any analytical or measurement approach fails decisively to convey *all* the researcher's impressions from the product. A similar position is frequently taken in art education; that the very nature of "art" is such as to defy identification by analytical procedures but may be apprehended directly, by intuition. For this reason, Elkisch (1945) chose to evaluate such criteria as complexity vs. simplicity, and expansion vs. compression. (See p. 50 of the present volume.)

The most extensive studies of the component qualities of children's drawings have been made by Martin and Damrin (1951), and by Stewart (1955). Both studies evaluated qualities expressed in drawings, whether these qualities appeared in the drawing as a whole, or in the use of elements, such as form and line. These extensive, analytical studies suggest that drawings are actually appraised in terms of a few general dimensions, although they may be rated on a number of specifically defined elements or qualities. These studies lend credence to the belief that global, rather than highly particularistic, evaluations are more readily and reliably made, and suggest the direction that these global ratings may take. Their findings in relation to personality qualities, however, are not of such magnitude as to support the use of drawings in diagnosing individual cases.

8. *The use of color in drawings can be significant for studying personality.* There is considerable agreement among clinicians on this general point. The popularity of the idea probably reflects the widespread influence of Rorschach theory, though workers with the art of hospitalized patients have long believed that color has expressive value.[3] Certainly Alschuler and Hattwick (1947) and Napoli (1946, 1947), already referred to, make much of the psychological significance of color. Unfortunately, these writers, although claiming the empirical origin of their statements, often disagree.[4] For example, Napoli affirms that black is used more than any other color by the very young, and that it refers to intellectual values, or to life's mysteries, death, fear, and depression. Alschuler and Hattwick affirm that black is very infrequently used by young children but indicates a dearth of emotional behavior induced by repression. Purple, declares Napoli, is widely used by children,

[3] See Fortier (1953) for a comprehensive review of the clinical psychological significance of color.

[4] It should be noted that Napoli worked with finger paints while Alschuler and Hattwick used poster paints. However, both affirm the universality of color symbolism for children.

especially by successful and dominant child leaders; whereas Alschuler and Hattwick say purple is used by few children, and then mainly to express moods of dejection and unhappiness, or feelings of having been rejected by other children.

Such studies seem to assume that deeply embedded intrinsic associations between colors and feeling states express a universal symbolism of feeling states. From many contradictions similar to the examples cited, one is led to wonder whether culturally created and widely held adult color symbolism is not being imposed on the work of children. Much more adequately controlled observations must be made before firm generalizations concerning the psychological meaning of color can be drawn. It may well be that situational factors are the crucial ones; Biehler (1953), for example, found that in easel painting young children worked systematically through the jars of color supplied them. The use and predominance of color in the child's work appeared to be quite as much a function of the arrangement of the jars in relation to the child's right-to-left or left-to-right work habits as of the child's color preferences, *per se.*

Evaluation of the Projective Hypothesis

Fundamental to the use of an instrument for assessment or research purposes are questions of validity and reliability. These questions also apply to the projective use of drawings.

Consistency of Drawing and Its Assessment

Before examining the diagnostic possibilities of drawing assessment, one may well ask whether the systems are applied similarly by different users. When judges or scorers agree reasonably well, we know that the criteria proposed have some objectivity; elements or aspects of drawings can be "seen" similarly by different judges. If criteria prove to be so subjective that they cannot be used consistently by different persons after suitable instruction or training, we must discard the criteria for practical as well as scientific purposes, or redefine them. This fact became painfully evident to one group of clinicians (Cassell, Johnson, and Burns, 1958), who reported that they were jarred by an inter-judge correlation of only .33, using appraisal methods with which they were familiar and which they had been using with confidence in the same hospital. More careful definition of the criteria increased the correlation to .71.

In general, there seems to be fair to good agreement among judges as to the presence or absence of selected features or qualities in collections of drawing protocols. Likewise, in general, subjects show some similarity in the way they draw on different occasions. Lehner and Gunderson (1952), for example, re-rated after one week a series of ninety-one figure drawings made by adult psychology students on twenty-one graphic traits or variables, such as shading, erasures, position on page, detail. Percentages of agreement [5] on several points varied from 70 to 99, with a mean at 90. The authors' ratings, compared with the ratings of three other judges (each judge doing only thirty drawings), varied from 52 per cent agreement to 96, with a mean of 83 per cent agreement. The authors' ratings of a second set of drawings made by the original subjects four months later compared to ratings of their original sketches varied from 42 to 93 per cent agreement, with a mean percentage value of 64. This latter comparison examines artist consistency as well as rater consistency and was interpreted as showing a "tendency for many of the traits to remain constant over a period of months." Lehner and Gunderson also remarked on the stylistic consistency observed in many of the drawings over this period of time. The item "detail" (a "content" aspect) is one of the highly consistent items by all three approaches, which fact, say the authors, supports Goodenough's contention of reliability for the Draw-a-Man method. Other such "content" elements appeared—e.g., treatment of eyes, mouth, hair, etc.—among the more consistent or reliable traits as well as more formal aspects of drawing—e.g., symmetry, position on page, shading, etc. Grams and Rinder (1958), using fifteen "signs" proposed by Machover plus two of their own, obtained 76 per cent agreement between judges on clinical protocols and 83 per cent on normal controls. Korner and Westwood (1955) have shown that inter-judge consistency may be considerably higher for drawing analyses than for Rorschach protocols.

In a carefully controlled experiment, Holtzman (1952) demonstrated that figure drawings produced by subjects of both sexes were not affected by the examiner's sex, physical appearance, or personality (examiners with strikingly different social and temperamental qualities were used). Graham (1956) found that drawings made by students before and after a two hour lecture on the interpretations of human figure drawings in which "drawings were represented as an infinitely revealing device which appeared to expose the worst aspects of any individual's personality" were quite comparable when assessed by clinical standards. Presumably the projective aspects of the drawing experience successfully "resisted" any attempt to modify or to be concealed. Fisher and Fisher (1952) found complete agreement between raters in 86 per cent of all their judgments using four-point scales on selected elements in figure drawings. With the H–T–P method specifically, Bieliauskas (1956) found that IQ determinations by different raters correlated from .68 to .90, depending on the particular IQ score used. Generally, these values were considered "lower than necessary for individual prediction by a single judge," but "sufficient for group prediction." His results also suggested that judges tended to be more unreliable on certain features than on others; this finding argues for more careful definition of certain scoring points.

---

[5] Swensen (1957) has properly criticized this technique of ascertaining "reliability" in terms of the "base rate" or frequency of occurrence in a population of a trait on which judges happen to agree. The more frequently a trait or quality occurs in drawings generally, the higher must the per cent of agreement be in order to be significant.

Albee and Hamlin (1949, 1950) evaluated a rating of "adjustment" applied to drawings made by ten subjects drawn to cover a range of normal, neurotic, hallucinated and delusional psychotic conditions. Fifteen psychologists applied the paired comparison technique to the ten drawings. When divided into two groups, the mean ratings of the judges correlated .96. Correlation of these ratings with ratings of the patient's case record was .62, which is significant at the 5 per cent probability level; the correlation with Wechsler intelligence test results was not significantly greater than zero.

Possibly the most detailed and complete study of the "reliability" aspects of figure drawings is that by Gasorek (1951). Her 400 fifth- and sixth-grade subjects drew four assigned objects (motifs), and made one free drawing, using both crayons and pencil. The subjects repeated their drawings one month later. Forty-three elements mentioned in the literature were carefully defined and scored for each of the five motifs by two judges working independently. Twenty of the elements occurred so infrequently that they were discarded from further statistical work. Inter-judge correlations (phi coefficients) for the remaining twenty-three elements (five motifs considered separately) ranged from .72 to .94. Thus, inter-judge consistency was found to be reasonably high.

Child consistency over one month, however, was much lower, correlations being generally about .30 to .60; but values were somewhat higher when averaged for the five motifs on each occasion (about .30 to .75). Although the results seemed to be unrelated to motif drawn, Gasorek found that such mechanical aspects as size, pressure, and line, as well as appearance of "rigidity" (a stylistic element), and amount of detail, were much more consistent over time than such features as erasures, bizarre features, sketchiness, omissions, shadings, use of color, reinforcement, etc. It is interesting to note that elements of this type are usually prominent among those used by clinical interpreters of drawings. Furthermore, the characteristics or elements do *not* appear similarly in the various motifs, either in the same or on different occasions. The correlations (phi values) run very low, in the .20's, and few exceed the fiducial limits of a hypothesized zero relationship. In most cases, however, the consistency for all characteristics between any two motifs is *lower* than the reliability over a period of time for the same characteristic on any one of the five motifs.

Validity of the Projective Hypothesis in Drawings

Judges may consistently apply definite or objective criteria in their assessments of drawings, and thus consistently locate certain elements or features, and children may use these same features in subsequent drawings. But are affective states of the "artist" carried into his graphic productions? Great art often profoundly stirs the viewer; the artist who produced the work presumably worked from an emotional state. Something of the artist's feeling is conveyed to his public; but whether it is always the *same* feeling state is a point of debate even among art theorists. But whether untrained artists, particularly

children, convey their personalities to their audience or represent them to
the psychologically skilled interpreter, is the question considered in this section. The Reichenberg-Hackett study (1953), already mentioned, showed that
experimentally induced positively toned emotional states influenced children
toward improved drawing performance. Harris (1950) found no detectable
projection of enjoyable and vigorous kinesthetic experience into drawings of
a man made immediately subsequent to an exercise period.

One of the better designed studies (Shapiro, 1957) attempted to evaluate
the projection of aggression and withdrawal, considered phenomenologically,
into children's figure drawings, including a self-portrait. Samples of thirty-three
aggressive, thirty-five withdrawn, and thirty-three well-adjusted children were
selected, similar in age, grade, social class membership, but differing in school
performance. That the two "clinical" groups should work less effectively than
the well-adjusted in school is not surprising, but an intelligence comparison
would have been desirable. Results did not confirm hypotheses deduced from
clinical theory, and the author concludes that they "are consistent with the
general contention that behavior is mediated by central, cognitive processes"
(p. 385).

While verifying the Alschuler and Hattwick observation that there is a
relationship between age and form (use of verticals), Thomas (1951) did not
find that an experimental frustration experience induced a "regression" in the
use of either form or color. Likewise working with easel painting, Aimen
(1954) introduced nursery school children experimentally to experiences of
success and failure, but failed to discover any differences in their paintings
following the experiences. Windsor (1949) was able to verify a limited number of the hypotheses affirmed by Alschuler and Hattwick as to the relations
of certain easel painting procedures and techniques with rated personality
characteristics, by dropping to the statistical probability level of 25 per cent.
This probability level means that 25 times in 100 the relationships observed
could arise by chance alone. This level is considerably more generous than
the 5 per cent level which is often held as the minimum to establish a significant result. Windsor's observation that the validity of the method can be
increased by more information concerning the child's background, interests,
abilities and qualities, obviously raises the question of who is doing the projecting—child or teacher!

Oftentimes one must resort to "experiments of nature" in psychological
work, and there are many more papers reporting differences in drawing performance between groups selected by social or by arbitrary psychological
criteria than papers that are truly experimental. Most of these studies, unfortunately, lack careful control in the comparisons made. Alper and Blane
(1951), for example, reported a study of the finger paint and crayon work of
middle and lower class children, on the hypothesis that toilet training in the
middle class group had been started earlier, was conducted more rigorously,
and presumably was more frustrating to instinctual urges to "mess." Despite
the unfortunate finding that the groups did not differ sharply in mothers'

report of toilet training ages and regimens, the middle class children were somewhat more constricted, dependent, and destructive in their work with the art media. These differences were more noticable in use of finger paints than of crayons. Alper and Blane interpreted these findings as substantiating their hypotheses!

W. E. Martin (1955) failed to confirm Wolff's (1946) assertions about the crayon drawings of insecure children when he applied several criteria of security and insecurity, including a test devised by Wolff himself. Carp (1950) included crayon drawings of "your own family," "your very best wish," and "how you feel" with several other projective tests in a study of "psychological constriction" in children. Evaluations were based on measures of area, and number of colors used, as well as on a seven point holistic impression of constriction in the drawing. Although all these measures yielded relatively "reliable" results, judged by inter-rater agreement ranging from r's of .65 to .94, none of them correlated with behavior ratings by teachers of social and temperamental qualities, with sociometric measures contributed by the children themselves, or with other projective measures (free play constructions, and the Rorschach).

Working with small groups of children newly come to a residential school and home for normal children, Mildred Martin (1951) compared finger paintings of children adjusting well to cottage life with children who were showing distress. Using the Elkisch-Klages criteria, she found noticeable differences; the well-adjusted children showing greater rhythm, better integration, and more realism in their paintings than the poorly adjusted children, whose paintings were dominated by "rule" (rigidity), disorganization, and symbolism. The interpretation of these finger painting patterns accorded with the staff opinion of the children's adjustment. The well-adjusted were said to show in their paintings, as well as in their behavior, a greater sense of freedom, better integration of behavior, and a more realistic approach to life. Phillips and Stromberg (1948) obtained finger paintings from twenty-five "randomly selected" high school students and twenty-five detention home inmates. The groups differed significantly (P = .05) on fourteen of the seventeen points compared. O'Grady (1954), however, found that mentally retarded children used finger paints in a manner more like normal children at a comparable mental age level than like normals comparable in chronological age. The work of the delinquents in the Phillips and Stromberg study resembles, in a number of respects, that of O'Grady's mentally retarded children, calling into question a possible selection of the former's sample on intellectual factors.

It is of the greatest importance, in studies of this type, to match groups carefully on other factors that might correlate with artistic performance, to protect judges carefully from contaminating knowledge of factors, and to use appropriate statistical tests of significance. When comparing art products of two groups contrasted on some psychological criterion, it is wise to introduce a third group, selected from the middle range of the criterion continuum.

Until rigorous conditions are observed in such "experiments of nature" we must accept with the greatest caution conclusions drawn from them.

Finally, it is well to remember that projection is a mechanism that cuts two ways. All too frequently, adult associations and concepts have been projected into the interpretation of children's "projections." This fact may be construed as evidence for the general soundness of projective theory, but it does not induce confidence in the accuracy of interpretations! And altogether too often investigations have committed the methodological error of using the same group of cases for validating a hypothesis as was originally used for formulating it.

Validity of Personality Assessments Through Human Figure Drawings

In a previous section (see pp. 23–30) evidence has been presented on the use of Goodenough's scale for assessing drawings obtained from disturbed, behavior problem, and other groups of atypical children. Much of this evidence is essentially negative, when the cognitive or intellective element is allowed for. This fact may be taken as additional evidence that the principal variance in the Goodenough score measures an intellectual rather than an affective component.

It has also been shown that the more global, "intuitive" approaches, such as the Draw-a-Person technique, or the House-Tree-Person test, less circumscribed by objective scaling methods, have been widely used in personality appraisals. Machover's chapter (Frank, et al., 1953) in a collaborative study of personality is one of the most fully documented studies of the human figure drawing as a clinical tool to date. Unfortunately, the conclusions go well beyond the statistical tables. For example, it is stated that drawings by a group of adolescent girls show a "considerably greater degree of sexual wavering of identifications" (p. 97) than is found in a more mature population, data for which are *not* given. It is stated: "Consistent with her relative level of immaturity, the prepuberal girl stands out in these areas" (p. 100) (outgoing and dependency qualities); only two of seven drawing items show the prepuberal group to differ at all from the puberal group, and these differences are 11 per cent (concave mouth) and 18 per cent (arms out). The value of the paper is further marred by many assertions that are not supported by the data presented. For example, the statement is made: "Forced restraint of body impulses may be indicated by a tight waistline, a common feature in drawings of our group" (p. 90). The percentages cited for this feature in fourteen groups vary from 4 to 29, with a median at 14. Of course, the criticism may turn on the semantics of the word "common"; but it is the frequency of such general, unprecise references that weakens the scientific quality of the study.

From a very thorough review of the literature covering chiefly work with adult patients (eighty-seven references), Swensen (1957) concludes, conservatively, that "Machover's hypotheses concerning the D.A.P. have seldom been supported in the literature . . ." (p. 463). Blum's cynical observation of a few years earlier goes further: "The Draw-a-Person technique has highly questionable validity but proves to be no worse than any of the other common clinical personality assessment procedures" (Blum, 1954, p. 125). Blum's observation may explain Swensen's comment, made despite his massive array of negative evidence, that ". . . Machover's system of interpretation is probably going to continue to be used in figure drawing analysis until a more valid system is proposed . . ." (Swensen, 1957, p. 462). Possibly the augurs of ancient Sparta fulfilled a contemporary cultural purpose and utility, even though they contributed nothing to Sparta's chances on the international scene of the day; but with clinical services so costly, one just ventures to hope that less use will be made of such nonvalid systems in the future.

Furthermore, some disquieting evidence has accumulated indicating that the untrained judge does quite as well as the figure drawing "expert" in spotting the unusual cases. Thus Fisher and Fisher (1950) found that a stenographer and a psychiatrist did quite well as psychologists in judging drawings! Plaut and Crannell (1955) obtained similar results with drawings of schizophrenics and normals. While Tolor (1955) and Tolor and Tolor (1955) interpret their data optimistically, the difference obtained between elementary school teachers and psychologists is actually rather unimpressive. The Tolors likewise found that both groups of judges, and especially the teachers, were using *quality* of the drawing to judge their experimental variable (popularity of children). Similarly, Whitmyre (1953) and Feldman and Hunt (1958) have shown that clinicians' judgments of drawings are strongly influenced by the same elements that commercial artists call "artistic excellence." In this connection we may refer again to Sherman's (1958) discovery concerning the ability of children to differentiate the sexes in drawings. Woods and Cook (1954) likewise have shown that there is a marked tendency for better-quality drawings to conceal the hands or to omit them altogether, which suggests that factors other than personality dynamics in the clinical sense may be operating in such omissions.

One validation study merits more extensive discussion, not only because it is well designed, but also because it is not generally available. Stone (1952) used both an empirical and a theoretical approach. For his theoretically based instrument, he designed a figure drawing preference scale, composed of twenty-six sets of two to five pictures each. The several drawings in each set (usually three) illustrated normal and deviant conditions for one clinically familiar and often used "sign," taken from the literature concerning human figure drawings. The subject was asked to designate which of the choices was most like the drawing he would make himself. The retest reliability of this measure for a small sample was +.72.

Stone devised an empirical instrument by obtaining sets of human figure drawings (man and woman) from 492 sixth-grade children free from obvious or serious behavior abnormalities. From this population a sample of drawings by sixty boys and sixty girls were selected randomly and scored on thirty-seven "signs" selected from the human figure drawing literature. An item was scored "typical" if a clear majority of the children included it, atypical when a minority of the children exhibited it. The corrected split-half reliability for this scale was .82 for first drawing and .76 for the second. First and second drawings intercorrelated .50 for the total group.

Selected for study were six variables. Three were personality and behavior measures—a "guess who" test descriptive of social-personal qualities, a teacher rating of personality and behavior (modified Haggerty-Olsen-Wickman Scale), and the California Test of Personality. Three were ability measures—two group tests of intelligence, and the Stanford Achievement Test. Reading performance and chronological age (within the eighteen-month span included in this sixth-grade group) were also included as variables. On each of the first six variables as measured in this population, the child's status was determined as exceeding plus or minus one standard deviation, or falling between these points. Thus he was considered a deviate on one variable if he fell in the top or bottom 16 per cent. If he fell in the deviate group on two or all three of the personality and behavior measures, he was designated as "maladjusted"; if he did not fall in the deviate portion of any personality and behavior measure, he was designated as "adjusted." Drawings of these adjusted and maladjusted groups selected from the entire population were rescored by the "typicality" scale derived in the subsample. Of the original thirty-seven "signs" studied, seventeen separated the adjustment groups significantly. On the Figure Drawing Preference Record, five cards for boys and one card for girls proved statistically significant for the same criterion groups.

On the other hand, the "typicality" scores on the figure drawings correlated as highly with each of the three criterion measures of adjustment, measured across the total population, as these three measures intercorrelated. Values varied from +.23 to +.39, all significantly greater than zero. Somewhat smaller values resulted for the Figure Drawing Preference Record. With mental age partialled out, these values fell very slightly—only about two units in the second decimal place. Correlations with mental age, chronological age, school achievement, achievement test and reading achievement were negligible—all very close to zero.

The three criterion measures of personality, combined by multiple correlation methods, yielded correlations with figure drawing "typicality" scores of from .38 to .45, depending on sex and figure drawn. For the Figure Drawing Preference Record these values were .40 for boys and .31 for girls. Speaking statistically, one would usually refer to a combination of measures predicting a dependent variable, in this case figure drawing performance. Stone comments on the high validity of drawing performance shown by such substantial correlations with a multiple criterion of adjustment. Nevertheless, these values, whether or not taken as equivalent to usual validity coefficients, while considerably below those expected in performance measures, are higher than most such values reported in other studies.

While undoubtedly drawings contain "projective features"—i.e., exhibit a number of cues relating to affect, interest, typicality of personality, and the like, they cannot as yet be used alone as predictive or even as selective instruments. Stone's correlations, standing virtually alone in the literature, suggest that figure drawings might be teamed statistically with other personality measures. However, it is reasonably safe to say that the clinical enthusiasts will continue to work deductively (and intuitively) from drawings, and that use of drawings as a controlled psychometric device is still in the future.

The H–T–P method fares no better in the hands of research workers. Like the Draw-a-Person procedure, this method has developed an extensive tradition of drawing "signs" isomorphic to psychological conditions. But tests of specific hypotheses are usually negative. For example, Levine and Galanter (1953) and Bolin and associates (1956) could find no correlation between the location of a lightning scar placed on the tree in the H–T–P test and the time of occurrence of "worst event" in the subjects' lives. Jolles (1952 a,b,c; Jolles and Beck, 1953 a,b), one of the most enthusiastic and ingenious proponents of the H–T–P, who is particularly facile in his clinical interpretations, is able to support them by lowering the significance levels and over-interpreting "trends" in data which fall short of the levels selected. Jolles' paper (1952) is an example of a quantitative study which, after essentially negative findings, reaffirms the significance of the generalization with which the study began. This is altogether too common in the so-called "projective-drawing" literature.

Gunzburg (1950) accepts a discrepancy between an individual intelligence test and the IQ estimated from a figure drawing as presumptive of maladjustment, especially when supported by anomalies in the drawings of a tree and a house on the H–T–P. His study contained no control groups, and he accepted uncritically the presumptive indicators of maladjustment he found in the drawings made by his subnormal subjects. Hammer (1953) found Negro-white differences on the H–T–P to express the hostility of frustrated Negroes generally; he made no allowance for the educational and intellectual disadvantage which the Negro group invariably suffers. Tolor (1957) found no relationship of H–T–P "rigidity" signs and similar indicators on the Rorschach. Rubin (1954) found correlation values in the .60's between Wechsler-Bellevue IQ's and H–T–P IQ's, but correlations found by Sloan and Guertin (1948), while statistically significant, are even lower. The latter see no point in displacing standard intelligence measures by H–T–P estimates.

Applying Buck's criteria to the drawing of a man made according to Goodenough's instructions, Johnson, Ellerd, and Lahey (1950) obtained psychological descriptions of 209 child subjects. They compared these descriptions with teachers' descriptions of the same children. All children were in the school program of a state institution for mental defectives; their mean Binet IQ was about 50, and they included all types of mental retardation. The teachers rated the children; the psychologists rated their drawings. Psychologists and teachers achieved a comparable base in their personality descriptions by checking within each pair of eleven paired characteristics, such as "confident— lacking self-confidence," "calm-nervous," etc. Among 2,299 ratings made on the 209 children, there was agreement between psychologists and teachers 54 per cent of the time, and of these agreements 58 per cent were on positive traits and 42 per cent on negative traits.

This is certainly not a striking record for drawings as appraisal devices, assuming that a teacher's impression of child behavior has as much validity as we are likely to find (and for description of behavior this assumption appears tenable). On the assumption, however, that drawings tap fundamental aspects of personality (an assumption which some clinicians apparently are willing to make, *a priori*), teachers simply do not know their children. Yet educational research consistently (and with good reason) uses teacher judgment as a prime validating criterion!

Finally, it may be that drawing analysis has a different utility for children than for adults. The young child's pleasure in drawing has often been noted. The clinical literature is generally silent on the ease or difficulty of obtaining drawings from older subjects or patients. But in all probability youths and adults do not as willingly submit samples of their work, and those collections of drawings assembled may be much more highly selected along uninvestigated and even unadmitted psychological dimensions than is most generally recognized.

Reitman (1951) has commented that very few psychotics draw, but that schizophrenics are more productive than other classes. Vernier (1952, p. 1) is virtually alone in stating that it is very difficult to get adults to try to draw and that most adults reject the test completely. Writers on normal children's drawings often comment on the increased reluctance of older children to draw, especially in the early adolescent period, and a few with clinical reference relate this reluctance to presumed conflicts over the body and sex. More will be said on this point in a later chapter dealing with the psychology of drawing.

Goldworth (1950) has a further suggestion from his validation study of Machover "signs" with normal, neurotic, schizophrenic, and brain-damaged adults. His conclusion is that the drawing as an index to the self-image is valid only in the case of those whom Lowenfeld would call "haptics"; highly visual persons *do not* successfully project the kinesthetic aspects of the body image, which are presumably important in the drawing approach. Goldworth's well-designed study suffers from the fact that the proportion of women was not adequately balanced throughout his four samples, and this fact undoubtedly influenced the sex differences he found. Likewise, his normal group was appreciably better educated and possibly more intelligent than his three clinical groups; therefore, it is not surprising that his normals significantly excelled his clinical samples on virtually every point or quality rated, and there were fifty-one scales used altogether. That Machover's conflict signs (erasures, size changes, redrawing, reinforcement, etc.) are significantly *more* numerous in the normals should not be surprising, either. If the normals were more critical and sought (as they apparently did) to achieve good quality drawings, they would make more corrective attempts.

Summary

Aspects of affect and temperament, of attitude and personality may be revealed in an individual's drawings and paintings. This is an expression of the "projective hypothesis," used so widely in clinical psychology since World War II. Many techniques have been suggested to evaluate the symbolic and the manifest content of drawings as well as the more formal aspects of line, form and color. The results of a vast array of studies have not been nearly so positive as those of the more analytical procedures reviewed in the previous chapter.

A comprehensive review of the literature leads to the following conclusions:

1. Children as well as adults intentionally adapt lines and color in drawings to indicate moods, states or affect. However, it is not possible from the available evidence to state that there is a language of line, form or color particularly expressive of affect.

2. There is little evidence that the human figure drawing is in fact a drawing of the self, presented directly or indirectly, overtly or covertly.

3. When children are assigned the task of drawing the "self," they approach the task representatively and realistically. Handicapped children undertake this task on the same basis and in the same manner as normals. Patients with neurological damage reveal their impairment in drawings, but through gross malformations and simplifications rather than in any special or exotic fashion. Such distortions appear in their general art work as well as in the self-image picture.

4. A number of general statements based on the research literature may be made concerning the use of drawings in the clinical study of the human personality. The more cautious and generalized of these statements are plausible common sense. The more specific claims and positive assertions do not seem to have reasonable support in the accumulated evidence.

5. A survey of the research and clinical literature is persuasive; the projective hypothesis as it applies to human figure drawings has never been adequately or consistently formulated, and systems for the evaluation of such drawings have, for the most part, been exceedingly loose. Consequently, the assessment of drawings by such methods very often shows modest reliability and low validity. The more rigorous the conditions of the experiment—control of variables, matching of control samples, and the like—the lower the validity of the human figure drawing as a measure of affect and personality.

Chapter Four

Methodology
of the Revised Scale

THE LITERATURE on children's drawings shows quite clearly that the nature and content of such drawings are dependent primarily upon intellectual development. Previous to Goodenough's introduction of the Draw-a-Man technique, however, attempts to classify children's drawings were very crude. The classifications usually included only a small number of categories, to which drawings were assigned by a simple inspection, without formal analysis. The categories were defined in very general terms, thus permitting considerable variation in the classification. Such methods revealed distinctions between groups, but were of little value for individual ratings on children.

Development of the Goodenough Scale

The derivation of the 1926 Draw-a-Man scale differed from the method of approach used by previous investigators in the following respects: (1) No arbitrary decisions were made as to what constitutes intellectual merit in a drawing. (2) A double criterion for judging mental development—chronological age and school grade—was used as a basis for determining the validity of the test, and for establishing norms. Supplementary criteria were used when available. (3) Every effort was made to eliminate the subjective elements in judgments; each characteristic was defined as objectively as possible. (4) Artistic standards were entirely disregarded. (5) Standard subject matter and directions for drawing were chosen; but to allow as much freedom as possible in the working out of the task, no further specifications were made as to how the drawing should be done.

Although Goodenough had first hoped it would be possible to allow each child to choose his own subject for drawing, it soon became evident that the plan was not feasible. Without careful and systematic study of the relative difficulty of the various subjects children might choose, it would be impossible to decide, for example, whether a greater degree of ability is shown by a good representation of an easy subject, or by a poor representation of a more difficult subject. Earlier work had shown that older and brighter children tend to be more critical of their work, and are also more likely to select the "easier" subjects to draw.

In deciding upon the subject matter of the drawing, Goodenough believed the following considerations were paramount: (1) The subject must be something with which all children are equally familiar. Either the situation presented must be an entirely new one for all children, or all children must have had nearly equal opportunity to become familiar with it. The latter circumstance is probably better for very young children, since it is less likely to confuse them; also, it has the additional advantage of measuring the learning factor as shown by present accomplishment. (2) The subject must present as little variability as possible in its essential characteristics. (3) The subject must be simple in its general outline, so that even very little children will be able to attempt it, yet sufficiently complicated in its detail to tax the abilities of a youth or adult. (4) The subject must be one of universal interest and appeal, in order that motivation be maintained among children.

The human figure, a common subject in children's spontaneous drawings, was selected as fulfilling all the above requirements. The greater uniformity of man's clothing suggested that a man was a more suitable subject for the test than a woman, or a child, and was therefore chosen for the original scale.

Goodenough developed a first scale by selecting ten drawings at random from the work of children in beginning and in advanced kindergartens, and in beginning and advanced halves of each of the first four elementary grades. These 100 drawings were picked from a collection of 4,000 obtained from many kindergartens and elementary grades in an eastern city. From inspection of these small samples, changes in children's drawings with increasing age and increasing intellectual development could be discerned. No *a priori* assumptions were made as to the probable nature of these changes, and differences based on artistic effects were entirely disregarded in favor of comparative differences in details. This first scale resulted in forty separate "points" empirically selected. A point was defined as a single unit of the scale. It could be based on the presence or absence of a specified element, on the method of representation of a given quantitative or spatial relationship, or on eye-hand coordination. The points referred chiefly to the presence or absence of various parts of the body and to the relationships of these parts.

These 100 drawings were scored according to this plan. Each point was recorded separately, and curves were plotted showing the comparative numbers of successes at each age level.

Validation of the Separate Points

A threefold criterion determined the validity of each point, or unit of the scale. The requirements were: (1) A regular and (2) a fairly rapid increase in the percentage of children succeeding with the point at successive ages, and (3) a clear differentiation between the performances of children who were of the same age but in different school grades. Although the third criterion was not used in the first trial analysis because the cases had been selected on the age-grade basis, it was used in all subsequent validation of the original Draw-a-Man scale. The requirement was also made that rules for scoring be objectively defined, and broadly enough explained to cover all situations that were likely to arise.

This preliminary scale was revised, new points added, and the 100 drawings rescored according to a new plan. This new plan appeared to be satisfactory, and was extended to a new group of drawings, some 800 in number, which gave a basis for further extension and revision of the scale.

In all, five revisions of the original scale were made, the same general procedure being followed in each instance. A different set of drawings was used for each revision to avoid the error of validating a point by means of the same drawings from which it had been derived. The Draw-a-Man scale in the 1926 edition consisted of fifty-one points, each one of which conformed fairly well to the validity requirements set forth above.

The preliminary scales need not be discussed in detail. The successive revisions saw considerable change in selection of scoring points, in definition of points, and in the addition of a few points. Point 12a of this original scale is an example of the various methods tried for scoring a point, and serves to illustrate some of the difficulties encountered in the development of this scale. The discussion is from Goodenough:

The various methods tried for scoring this point were as follows:

SCALE 1.   Head smaller than trunk.

Objection: Too crude a measure. The curve showed only a slight increase in the percentage of successes at different ages.

SCALE 2.   Head length not less than one tenth or greater than one fifth of the total body length.

Objection: In many instances there appears to be a negative correlation between the size of the head and the length of the legs. Sometimes this fact is determined by the size of the sheet of paper—the child who makes a very large head and trunk being obliged to make the legs very short in order to get them on the page. Conversely, the child who makes a small head and trunk may thriftily fill up the remaining space with a pair of abnormally drawn-out legs. To compare the several parts with the total often has the effect of penalizing the child twice for a single disproportionate element.

SCALE 3.   Size of head "not grossly disproportionate to the remainder of the drawing."

Objection: Too indefinite a ruling, leading to subjective errors in scoring. The method was tried largely to see whether the point was worth using at all, as both previous methods had resulted in very unsatisfactory curves. The results obtained in this way showed clearly that the point was one which should be retained in the scale; accordingly another method of scoring was tried.

SCALE 4.   Both vertical and horizontal measurements of head less than the corresponding measurements of the trunk.

Objection: This method applies very well to full-face drawings, but is not satisfactory with profiles.

SCALE 5.   Area of head not more than one half or less than one tenth that of the trunk.

This is the method finally adopted.

It will be seen that the general procedure employed has been of the "cut and try" sort. A point which appeared to have differentiating value was noted, and a method of scoring was then devised. If the results showed a clear separation of different age and grade groups, the point was retained; if not, other scoring methods were tried. When no satisfactory scoring method could be found, the point was rejected. Typical examples of rejected points are the following:

1. *Teeth shown.*
   Up to about the age of seven, the curve shows a regular increase in the percentage of children who draw the teeth. After this age there is an equally marked decrease, a fact which renders the point useless.

2. *Attempt to show color by shading.*
   This varies according to the hardness of the lead and the condition of the point of the pencil used.

3. *Attempt to represent movement, as walking or running.*
   This point was rejected only after several attempts to score it had been made. There is little doubt as to its being, in some degree, a valid indication of intellectual maturity. The difficulty lies in differentiating between real attempts to show movement and mere bad coordination. As a result of poor coordination the drawing may seem to show one leg being raised, as in walking, when nothing of the sort was intended by the child. With the more mature drawings it is usually possible to make the distinction, but with those of the younger children it is often difficult, if not impossible, to do so.

4. *Pupils of eyes symmetrically placed, so as to focus the glance correctly.*
   Gives too much weight to eye details, and is difficult to score consistently. A modification of the point has been retained.

5. *Entire figure in correct alignment. If the full-face position has been chosen, all parts must be in full face. If the profile has been shown, all parts must face in the same direction.*

The curve shows a very marked drop from eight to ten years, due to the confusion which arises at the time of transition from the full-face to the profile drawing.

Other points were rejected for reasons analogous to those just cited. It is probable that in some instances further trials might disclose methods of scoring which would do away with the objections mentioned, but such methods have not yet been found (1926, pp. 19–21).

Development of the Present Revision

The present revision and extension of the scale has seemed desirable for a number of reasons. There has been a renewed interest in children's drawings. Much of this interest has reflected a concern with the emotional significance of drawings and the usefulness of these drawings for measuring personality differences. The Goodenough scale has been widely used in psychological clinics to assess the intellectual maturity of children (Louttit and Browne, 1947). Many who have used human figure drawings as projective devices have calculated a mental age based on the original Goodenough scale. In some cases, the discrepancy between an IQ obtained from the drawing scale and IQ's obtained from more conventional intelligence tests has been used in differential diagnosis of mental conditions, notably brain damage. At least one important source has called for a revision and the establishment of new norms of the scale (Buros, *Fourth Mental Measurements Yearbook*, 1953, pp. 291–292). More than once the idea has been voiced that the drawing task reflects somewhat differently the intellectual maturity of adolescents as contrasted with that of younger children.

It was decided that the new scale should attempt to encompass the following: (1) An upward extension into the adolescent years, following suggestions by Hinrichs (1935); (2) the exploration of new items which might increase the reliability and validity of the scale by sampling different aspects of cognitive ability; (3) the development of extended or alternate forms of the scale; (4) the development of a basis for possible projective uses of the scale.

Because of its popularity with children, the human figure was accepted as the most meaningful basis for the scale, and a test of three drawings — a man figure, a woman figure, and the drawing of the self—was then set up, to be accomplished in that order. Preliminary work revealed that children are willing to attempt these three tasks in one sitting, even kindergarten children finding this not beyond their capacities. As was anticipated, more resistance was encountered on the self drawing than on the drawing of the man or woman. Older children increasingly were reluctant to draw at all. This observation has been frequently noted, and will be further commented on in a later section of this book.

The Subjects

For testing new points and the development of new scales, a sample of urban and rural children in Minnesota and Wisconsin was selected to represent the 1940 occupational distribution according to the categories of the Minnesota Scale for Paternal Occupations. More than 300 children were tested at each grade level from kindergarten through the ninth grade. These children were drawn from schools selected to give a fair approximation of the range of occupational status. All subjects were classified on the Minnesota scale according to the occupation of the father as recorded by the child and checked with the school record.

The Revised Draw-a-Man Scale: Validation of Items

Originally it was hoped that samples as small as fifty would give sufficiently stable results for the preliminary analysis. Consequently, twenty-five boys and twenty-five girls were selected whose chronological age at the time of testing fell between five years nine months and six years two months, and between six years nine months, and seven years two months, and so on, so that the year samples were evenly distributed about a mid-value of six years, seven years, and the like. For checking purposes an additional sample of fifty children, twenty-five boys and twenty-five girls, was selected between six years three months and six years eight months, between seven years three months and seven years eight months, and the like. These samples of fifty were thus grouped about the mid-birthday. Each of such samples was stratified as closely to the socioeconomic norm as possible.

However, analysis indicated that fifty cases were not sufficient to provide stable proportions passing the separate items. Consequently, the age samples were combined into groups of 100 including, for example, from five years nine months to six years eight months. Each age sample thus was grouped around a mid-point approximately one-fourth of the way through the year; thus, six-year-olds being centered around a value of approximately six years three months and the seven-year-olds around the value of seven years three months, and so on, for each age sample.

The samples of 100 were drawn from the larger numbers available at each age to represent the U. S. distribution of paternal occupations, according to the 1940 census. A quite close fit of each age sample to this distribution was obtained.[1] It was found that computing percentages on 100 children rather than on 50 children gave substantially more stable results, and the resulting

---

[1] Tables giving data in full on these samples, and the item analysis, are on file with the Test Department of Harcourt, Brace, & World, Inc. Table A of this series gives the actual distributions of boys and girls by parental occupation for each of the age samples.

TABLE 1	Distribution, by Parental Socioeconomic Status (Occupational Group), of Age Samples for Validation of Scale Items

			AGE GROUPS							
		1960	5–9 to 8–8		8–9 to 11–8		11–9 to 15–8		TOTAL	
CLASS	TYPE OF OCCUPATION	PER CENT	N	%	N	%	N	%	N	%
I	Professional	4.3	12	4.0	12	4.0	15	3.7	39	3.9
II	Semiprofessional and managerial	10.7	18	6.0	18	6.0	25	6.3	61	6.1
III	Clerical, skilled trades and retail business	23.1	48	16.0	46	15.3	59	14.7	153	15.3
IV	Farmers	6.0	29	9.7	39	13.0	50	12.5	118	11.8
V	Semiskilled occupations, minor clerical positions and minor business	23.5	84	28.0	77	25.7	102	25.5	263	26.3
VI	Slightly skilled trades and other occupations requiring little training or ability	22.0	46	15.3	48	16.0	64	16.0	158	15.8
VII	Day laborers of all classes	10.4	63	21.0	60	20.0	85	21.3	208	20.8
Total		100.0	300	100.0	300	100.0	400	100.0	1000	100.0

age curves were much smoother. Table 1, above, summarizes the socioeconomic distribution of these age samples.

For selection of items to be included in the scale, the following criteria were used: (1) The items should show a regular and fairly rapid increase with age, in the percentage of children passing the point. (2) The items should show a relationship to some general measure of intelligence. (3) The items should differentiate between children scoring high on the scale as a whole and those scoring low on the scale as a whole.

The criterion of brightness as measured by a group intelligence test was used in place of Goodenough's over-age- and under-age-for-grade criterion. Thirty years ago the situation in the schools was such that bright children were put ahead and dull children were retained in grades. The present widespread practice of "social promotion" makes this criterion impossible, and the general availability of group intelligence measures gives a rough criterion which, along with others, helps establish the validity of the drawing score as a measure of intellectual maturity.

The first criterion was rather easily applied by computing the percentage of children in each sample of 100 passing the item. From the percentage of children earning credit on the item at each age,[2] curves were drawn for that item. An atlas of such curves supplied a ready visual check for the selection of items according to the criterion of age progression.

The second criterion was obtained by looking up the IQ in the school records. Since a number of different tests were included in the records of the several schools participating in this original study, the IQ scores were converted into standard scores based on the distribution of IQ's reported in the standardization data of the particular test, or system-wide test data for certain tests used in large school systems. Each IQ was converted into a standard measure and distributed for each year of age. Records were not available on all children; but approximately top and bottom 25 per cent groups were separated, and the percentage of these high- and low-intelligence groups passing the item was computed. Although the degree of relative exceptionality of these deviant samples differed somewhat in the several age groups, about twenty children were included in each deviant sample so that percentages could be computed.[3] An atlas of curves for each item was prepared from these data, to provide a convenient visual check for the selection of items according to the criterion of general intelligence.

On the basis of a tentative scale including approximately 100 points, a total score was derived for each child. The twenty-seven high-scoring and twenty-seven low-scoring individuals on the drawing scale for each age group were separated for analysis. The percentages of these groups passing each item [4] provide the third criterion, that of internal consistency. An atlas of curves for this criterion was also prepared.

Some 100 scoring points were tried: all of the previous Goodenough points and modification of them, Hinrich's points, and some others devised by the writer. The following data were examined: the percentage "passing" the item at each age group, the separation in per cent passing each point between brighter and duller children in each age group, and the separation in per cent passing between high-scoring and low-scoring children in each age group. By these criteria, seventy-three items were selected. This selection was somewhat arbitrarily done, as no statistical combination of the three criteria was devised. These points included a number which are inoperative in childhood but show some incidence in early adolescence. They were included to give special opportunity for adolescents to earn increments on the scale, and to

[2] These percentages, for all items in the final scale for the male figures, appear in Table B of the material on file in the Test Department of Harcourt, Brace, & World, Inc. See footnote, p. 73.

[3] These percentages for all items in the final Man scale, together with the actual number of children in each deviant group, appear in Table C of the material on file with the Test Department of Harcourt, Brace, & World, Inc. See footnote, p. 73.

[4] The percentages for all items in the final Man scale, together with the actual number of children in the high- and low-scoring groups, appear in Table D of the material on file with the Test Department of Harcourt, Brace, & World, Inc. See footnote, p. 73.

permit more careful study of the relationships among these "adolescent" items. Detailed descriptions of the seventy-three points as scoring standards for the man drawing appear in Part II of this book, which is the Manual for this revision known as the Goodenough-Harris Drawing Test.

The Draw-a-Woman Scale

Each of the children had produced three drawings: a man, a woman, and the self. Consequently, the work of these children was available to formulate a scale for the drawing of a woman. Exactly the same procedure described for the man drawings was applied to the drawings of a woman.[5] From the inspection of a series of drawings, a tentative scale was constructed. Approximately ninety items were tried, of which seventy-one survived the test of the three criteria. Detailed descriptions of these seventy-one points appear in the Manual (Part II of this book, pp. 276–291) as the scoring standards for the woman drawing.

Some comments on certain items *not* retained in the Woman scale may be of interest. In the drawing of a woman, the attempt to designate *glance* (both eyes looking in the same direction indicated by positioning of the pupils), shows some increase with age, but does not differentiate significantly between high and low scorers or between the more and less intelligent students. In the drawing of a man, there was enough association with both criteria to warrant its inclusion in that scale. *Ornamentation on the head* by the use of a ribbon, flowers in the hair, or a feminine hat, shows very little increase with age and does not differentiate sharply between intelligence groups, though it shows some differentiation between high- and low-scoring groups. Moreover, there is some tendency for older children to include this feature less often than do seven- and eight-year-olds. Therefore, the item was discarded. Originally, *necklace and earrings* were scored separately. It was found that they showed better differentiation when they were scored as necklace and/or earrings. The items were therefore combined and retained in this changed form.

Another interesting item was the *inclusion of a pattern or design on the garment*. This feature is much more frequent at ages seven and eight than at any other age and shows a steady decline with age. While at seven and eight it differentiates between the more and less intelligent pupils, it ceases to do so very quickly thereafter. The item was therefore dropped. An attempt was

[5] In the material on file with the Test Department of Harcourt, Brace, & World, Inc. (see footnote, p. 73), Table E presents the frequencies of boys and girls at each age who passed each item in this provisional scale. Because the N is 100 in each age group, the frequency totals may be read as per cents, thus offering evidence for the first criterion, that each item progress in difficulty with age. Table F presents the evidence on validity by an external criterion for the provisional Woman scale; Table G the evidence by the criterion of internal consistency.

made to score on the use of *accessories* in the garb or *action* of the figure, but this item showed no age increase or clear discrimination among certain groups. In an early analysis a peculiar characteristic, *the squaring of the lower portion of the face*, appeared to be valuable, but more complete tabulation through the age groups showed that this feature appears at eight or nine and disappears by age thirteen and is never included by more than 10 per cent of the cases. Moreover, it makes no consistent differentiation between intelligence groups.

The resulting scale of seventy-one points roughly parallels the Man scale, but differs in a number of specific aspects. It was not possible, for example, to use the ear as a scoring point in the female figure; too often the long hair conceals this organ. Earrings, when combined with necklace, became a useful substitute. *Arm movement and leg movement*, both useful items in the Man scale, did not qualify for the Woman scale. Leg movement was disqualified, possibly because of the long skirt with which many children provide their drawing in the age range where leg movement is an effective item. The point, *modeling or shading*, has been included in the treatment of the skirt rather than appearing as a separate item.

Developmental Aspects of Drawing the Female Figure

The American child drawing the female figure goes through some clear and distinctive "stages." Reference to Figures 9a through 33 on pages 79 to 86 will illustrate the following statements. (Figures 9a through 21 were drawn by boys, ranging from ages five to fifteen; Figures 22a through 33 were drawn by girls of similar ages.)

At the earliest ages the feminine figure is not perceptibly differentiated from the masculine figure. Questioning the child often reveals that whereas he distinguishes sex differences in his thinking, his symbolization of them in a drawing is insufficient to be apparent even after his explanation. One of the earliest signs of femininity is the attempt to show hair in somewhat different fashion than it is shown on the male figure. The scribbled indication of hair on the male figure is likely to be placed more on top of or on the upper portion of the head. On the female figure this representation most commonly takes the form of scribbled masses around the head, hanging down at the side of the face (Figs. 9a,b; 22a,b). Where short pencil strokes are used to indicate hair, the man's hair may stand up; in the woman figure there is a tendency for these strokes to point downward to the sides (Figs. 9b, 14, 22b, 23). While this tendency appears most commonly at age six or seven, it may appear as early as four or five in some cases. In the illustrations provided, Figures 22a and b, by a girl, are superior to Figures 9a and b, by a boy, but note that both the boy and the girl differentiate the sexes mainly by the hair. Note also that this five-year-old girl has already adopted eyebrows and eyelashes, more commonly drawn by girls than by boys, as Goodenough pointed out long ago.

In the earliest attempts at a profile drawing of the woman figure, the "pendant" mass of hair curving around the contour of the head and then hanging down the back in a rounded mass is a striking characteristic used by both boys and girls about seven or eight years of age (Figs. 13, 15). This representation gives the hair the appearance of being shaped or molded. It is carried into the full-face figure also, apparently as a more mature representation of the scribbled hanging masses noted at ages six and seven (Figs. 16, 24, 27). Still later, there may be an attempt to show styling (Figs. 18, 27, 28, 29); girls attempt this more commonly than boys. This styling may be achieved with some degree of skill in better drawings (Figs. 20, 30, 32).

By age six and more commonly by seven, there is some attempt to differentiate the dress or garb. This depiction takes the form of a triangular-shaped trunk, sometimes with a belt line across (Figs. 10, 23). This basic form may be retained even after the upper part of the trunk is differentiated from the skirt (Fig. 12). While this crude triangularity persists, the placement of the legs far apart and continuous with the line of the skirt is very common (Figs. 12, 23).

In the next advancement, the legs are brought closer together and are no longer continuous with the corners of the triangular skirt (Figs. 13, 15, 25). By this time also, the upper portion of the trunk is commonly differentiated from the skirt, usually by lines that take a different angle from the belt or waist (Figs. 13, 15, 24). Occasionally, in the transition to this representation an "hour glass" arrangement indicates the skirt (not illustrated in the examples). Still later the sharp corners of the skirt are rounded (Fig. 24) and some attempt made to drape or model it (Figs. 18, 29). Around age seven or eight, also, some children of both sexes elaborate the dress with flowers or other attempts to show a figure or pattern on the fabric (Figs. 10, 12, 16, 24, 25, 27).

The "cupid's bow" mouth or "cosmetic lips" is clearly apparent in at least one-fourth of the cases by age nine, and is increasingly used thereafter, especially by girls (Figs. 18, 27, 28, 30, 32, 33). The use of accessories, such as jewelry, purse, feminine hat, and the like, appears in some cases by age ten or eleven. Although such accessory items are seldom included in more than 10 per cent of the figures, the use of at least one accessory is present in 20 to 25 per cent of the drawings done after age eight, but shows no tendency to increase further with age.

Secondary sex characteristics, such as the indication of the breast, the modeling of the dress or skirt across the hips, or the depiction of the calf of the leg, appear frequently after age nine or ten (Figs. 18, 30). By age twelve, 50 per cent of the children include the breast and the shaped calf of the leg, and 30 per cent the hips (Figs. 20, 30). By this age, also, specific stylistic designations of sex are likely to be included in the drawings, such as a styled coiffure (Figs. 19, 20, 27, 28, 29), "cosmetic lips" (Figs. 18, 30, 32), and an indication of cheeks (Figs. 18, 20, 32). By this age, also, many children draw a long gown or "formal" dress.

It is instructive to compare the drawings of mentally retarded children with those of normals. On the woman drawing, the differences are much the same as those that have been noted on the drawing of a man.[6] On almost every point in the scale, mentally retarded children are slower than normals to achieve success. However, mentally retarded children are relatively *more* deficient on items of proportion and dimension, the treatment of shoulders, elbow joints and fingers, the elimination of transparencies, and motor coordination items (especially the treatment of lines and body contours). Mentally retarded children are relatively *less* handicapped on the inclusion of specific body parts.

[6] See Goodenough (1926, pp. 71ff., and scored examples, pp. 112–153).

Fɪɢ. 9a. Man, by boy, 5-1   Fɪɢ. 9b. Woman, by same boy

FIG. 10.   Woman, by boy, 5-3

FIG. 11.   Woman, by boy, 5-4

FIG. 12.   Woman, by boy, 6-5

FIG. 13.   Woman, by boy, 6-8

FIG. 14.　Woman, by boy, 6-10

FIG. 15.　Woman, by boy, 9-5

FIG. 16.　Woman, by boy, 10-2

FIG. 17.　Woman, by boy, 10-9

Fɪɢ. 18.   Woman, by boy, 11-5

Fɪɢ. 19.   Woman, by boy, 13-0

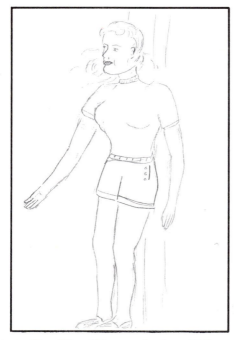

Fɪɢ. 20.   Woman, by boy, 13-2

Fɪɢ. 21.   Woman, by boy, 15-3

Fig. 22a. Man, by girl, 5-0

Fig. 22b. Woman, by same girl

Fig. 23. Woman, by girl, 5-0

Fig. 24. Woman, by girl, 7-0

Fig. 25.   Woman, by girl, 7-2

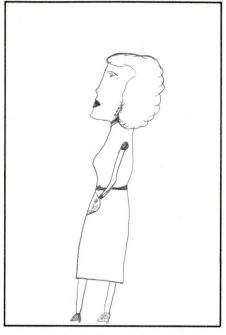

Fig. 26.   Woman, by girl, 9-8

Fig. 27.   Woman, by girl, 9-9

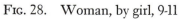

Fig. 28.   Woman, by girl, 9-11

FIG. 29. Woman, by girl, 10-10

FIG. 30. Woman, by girl, 11-3

FIG. 31. Woman, by girl, 13-3

FIG. 32. Woman, by girl, 13-3

FIG. 33.   Woman, by girl, 15-2

Some Special Scoring Problems

For some time researchers in children's drawings have noticed that older and brighter children tend to evade the difficult task of portraying the human hand. Often they do this by drawing the figure in such a position that the hand does not show; such as by placing the hands in pockets or behind the back. How should such drawings be scored? Presumably, strict adherence to scoring standards might penalize ingenious children! Table 2 (p. 87) indicates the mean total score achieved by children concealing the hand and those portraying one or both hands in three successive age groups. It is clear that the present method of scoring, which requires the presence of one or both hands, does not unduly penalize the children who draw both hands concealed. Hence, it has seemed inadvisable to introduce a correction in score when both hands are concealed.

Similarly, in preparing the scoring scale for the drawing of a woman, it appeared that enough children portray a long gown or "formal" to make the scoring of feet and legs a problem. By rule of thumb, several points were credited automatically in such instances. The age progression of scores on these items was watched carefully. When a tendency appeared for the item to increase in percentage passing with age when such allowances were made, this lenient credit was retained. Where such credit did not seem to make a difference to age progression, it was not retained. Examples of points on

TABLE 2	Mean Scores of Drawings Showing One Hand or Both Hands Compared with Drawings Concealing Both Hands

AGE	N	TYPE OF DRAWING	MEAN SCORE	S.D.
13	13	Both hands concealed	48.1	10.71
	87	One or both hands depicted	50.2	11.32
14	12	Both hands concealed	52.5	10.27
	88	One or both hands depicted	50.3	11.12
15	23	Both hands concealed	48.7	10.16
	77	One or both hands depicted	49.7	10.84

Note: The *t* for the largest observed difference, that at age 14, is 1.09, which is not significant at the .05 level.

which credit was allowed are the following: legs present, attachment of arms and legs, and arms and legs in two dimensions. Points which were *not* allowed on this basis pertain chiefly to feet and include the elaboration of the foot and any credit for shoe.

The question of whether the full-face or the profile figure in the drawing received a particular advantage is partially answered by the data in Table 3, which refers only to data for the man drawing. Although the difference is not statistically significant at any age reviewed in the table, it is consistently in favor of the profile drawings, and suggests that allowing bonus points for com-

TABLE 3	Mean Scores of Full or Partial Profile Drawings Compared with Full-Face Drawings

AGE	N	TYPE OF DRAWING	MEAN SCORE	S.D.
10	22	Profile	43.8	11.98
	78	Full-face	40.2	11.82
11	29	Profile	43.3	11.42
	71	Full-face	42.3	9.26
12	41	Profile	49.2	10.78
	59	Full-face	47.6	11.31
13	38	Profile	51.7	10.49
	62	Full-face	49.3	11.60
14	39	Profile	51.3	11.09
	61	Full-face	51.0	10.16

Note: The *t* for the largest observed difference, that at age 10, is 1.25, which is not significant at the .05 level.

pleteness in the profile presentation is too generous. The profile seems to be the more mature type of drawing, is more adequately executed, and therefore needs no additional credit. Such a correction should be made in any further revisions and restandardizations of the Man scale; it was not included in the Woman scale.

Scaling Problems

Goodenough established her scale on a point score basis and adjusted the point scores to mental age equivalents, using her age norm data. She calculated the IQ by the customary method of dividing mental age by chronological age. Her published distribution of calculated IQ's for samples of boys and girls at each age, six to twelve inclusive, permitted the calculation of standard deviations of IQ, and coefficients of relative variation at each age.

It has been shown repeatedly that because mental abilities do not develop as a strictly rectilinear function, this method of depicting mental level presents certain statistical problems. Unless the construction and standardization of the measure are very carefully conducted, there will be a variation in the standard deviation of scores from age to age, which will make a given IQ value of different significance, so far as indicating exceptionality is concerned. Theoretically and statistically, the standard deviation should increase by an amount proportionate to the increase in the mean score. This condition makes the relative variability, or the Coefficient of Variation as it is sometimes called, reasonably constant. In the 1926 Goodenough scale this requirement was roughly achieved. Moreover, the 1926 scale, as shown in the normative data, falls below the theoretical IQ average of 100 by age ten, and progressively so thereafter. Particularly is this underestimate true for boys. The review of the literature in earlier chapters includes considerable evidence that older subjects are seriously underestimated by this method of presenting the individual score.

In the literature of measurement generally, the intelligence quotient has increasingly come under criticism, for the above reasons. When Wechsler developed his Adult Intelligence Scale (1939), he abandoned the IQ in favor of a deviation or "standard score" method, though in it he attempted to retain the appearance of the IQ. He set his average at 100 for each age, and adjusted the standard deviation of scores at each age to a standard value of fifteen points. This standard deviation is somewhat more than the standard deviation of IQ's characteristically found by the 1916 Stanford-Binet and a little less than that obtained by the 1937 Binet. This procedure represents a compromise between the standard score method of representing exceptionality and the general concept of how "intelligence," as measured by the conventional IQ, distributes itself in the population. This general concept has been formed through the repeated use of these other widely used measuring devices, and through widespread familiarity with their results.

Wechsler's scales departed from the monolithic concept of intelligence and attempted to represent the measurement theory that intelligence is a mosaic of abilities. Wechsler gives standard score equivalents for raw scores on each of his ten sub-tests. Because five of these tests conform to the general principle of "verbal" materials and five to "performance" and "manipulative" items, Wechsler devised a system for combining each of five scores into the standard form described above, which would approximate an IQ distribution. He also devised a method for combining his verbal and performance "IQ's" into a full scale estimate of intelligence, also having the appearance of an "IQ."

The standard score method of measuring the child's performance has been adopted in the revision of the Draw-a-Man Test and in the Draw-a-Woman Test. Because of the dominance of the IQ concept in the literature and in professional thinking, and because of the precedent set by Wechsler, the present scales likewise have used a mean standard measure of 100, with a standard size for the standard deviation of fifteen points. In terms of the theoretical distribution of values, roughly 68 per cent of children at each age should score between the values of 85 and 115, and 99.8 per cent should score between the values of 55 and 145. Provision is also made for combining estimates of the child's ability measured separately in the Man and Woman scales. The tables for these conversions appear in Part II of this book, pages 294–301.

Chapter Five

Reliability and Validity of the Scales

THE USEFULNESS of a psychological measuring scale hinges on the consistency with which it measures whatever it measures (its reliability), and on the demonstration that it does in fact assess the abilities for which its claims are made (its validity). In the present revision reliability is evaluated in two ways: (1) the consistency with which scorers evaluate a particular set of drawings, and (2) the consistency of children's performance in the drawing task as evaluated by the scale. Validity is evaluated by: (1) considering from several angles the effects of special experience and training on drawing-test performance, and (2) relating the scale statistically to other measures of "intelligence," and to other abilities presumably related to the traits assessed by the drawing scales.

Evidence for Reliability

A number of studies (see Chap. II, pp. 21–22) have already established the consistency with which scorers can, with a minimum of training, score the Goodenough Draw-a-Man Test. Intercorrelations between different scorings range from the low .80's to as high as .96. Values commonly exceed .90.

In an unpublished study conducted by the present author, two scorers independently scored several samples of drawings by eight-year-olds and ten-year-olds. Table 4 (p. 91) gives the results, and indicates that a high level of agreement can be obtained between the scoring of briefly trained undergraduate students.

Another approach to evaluating reliability is through the study of scorers' agreement item by item. A group of thirty-six drawings, representing the work of children from seven through twelve years and including boys and girls, were given independently to three scorers after a short training period with the scales. Judge A disagreed with the normative scoring provided by the writer on 5.03 per cent of the items, Judge B on 5.05 per cent of the items and Judge C on 5.02 per cent of the items. After a conference concerning the

		MAN	WOMAN
AGE	N	SCALE	SCALE
8	75 boys	.92	.94
	75 girls	.97	.91
10	75 boys	.98	.98
	75 girls	.97	.97

TABLE 4 — *Reliability of the Drawing Scales; Intercorrelations Between Two Independent Scorers*

discrepancies, and scoring a new sample of drawings, the disagreement scores dropped to less than 2 per cent on the average for the three judges.

A number of studies have indicated correlations in the .60's and .70's between the scores of children's drawings separated by a time interval of as much as three months. McCurdy (1947) compared the variability of Goodenough IQ's derived from a long series of drawings by one boy with that of a group of children comparable to the boy in age. He concluded that the variability within the individual was about of the same magnitude as that for the group, and inferred that the individual variability of this one child's scores was more than "error of measurement," and rested on true fluctuations of ability. Unfortunately, this boy was extremely intelligent, and his mean score was quite different from the mean of the group of children his age. Hence, the direct comparison made by McCurdy is somewhat unwarranted.

In preparing the present revision of the Goodenough scale, the author administered the Draw-a-Man Test on each of ten consecutive school days to four classes of kindergarten children. The scores were translated into Goodenough IQ's, and treated by analysis of variance procedure. Results appear in Table 5 (p. 92). These results indicate that although there were significant differences between the performances of boys and girls, and between the individual children, the portion of the total variance accounted for by variation within the sequence of ten drawings was quite insignificant.

Validity: Indirect Evidence

A question frequently raised in testing is whether the examiner has an effect on the performance of the subject. The writer conducted a study in six first and second grades of two schools to assess this influence. In two examinations scheduled one week apart, the writer and the classroom teacher administered the Draw-a-Man Test according to the same instructions. In two classes the examiner tested the children first; in two classes the teacher examined the children first; and in the remaining two classes the teacher administered the test on both occasions. Table 6 (p. 92) shows that the

TABLE 5 | *Analysis of Variance of Goodenough Scores Made by Children in Four Kindergarten Groups on Each of Ten Successive School Days*

SOURCE OF VARIANCE	SUM OF SQUARES	d.f.	MEAN SQUARE	F	SIGNIF.
Between Sexes	1,056.9	1	1056.9	26.4	.01
Between Groups	16,049.0	3	5349.7	133.8	.01
Between Days (Intra-child Variation)	517.0	9	57.4	1.4	n.s.
Between Children (Individual Differences)	167,130.0	103	1622.6	40.6	.01
Remainder	36,482.0	923	39.5		
Total	221,234.9	1039			

person of the administrator had very little influence on either the mean score achieved by the class or on the rank order of children's scores within the class. In none of the classes was the difference between the two administrations statistically significant. The correlations reveal no trend or pattern indicating a systematic effect attributable to the outside examiner or the familiar classroom teacher.

Another question frequently raised concerning the validity of the Draw-a-Man Test is the effect of school art training on the test performance. In the study just cited, two of the classes were selected because their teachers were said by the art supervisor of the city to be conducting outstanding programs of art education with their children. (These teachers are marked with an asterisk in Table 6.) The results obtained in this small experiment substan-

TABLE 6 | *Effect of Examiner vs. Classroom Teacher as Administrator of the Draw-a-Man Test (Time Interval One Week)*

GRADE	N	EXAMINER		MEAN SCORE ON TEST		CORRELATION
		FIRST	SECOND	FIRST	SECOND	
1	24	Examiner	Teacher *	16.9	15.9	.60
1	21	Teacher	Teacher	18.7	18.3	.73
1	44	Teacher	Examiner	17.2	17.3	.80
2	25	Teacher	Teacher	18.6	18.6	.81
2	27	Examiner	Teacher *	21.9	21.3	.86
2	53	Teacher	Examiner	21.1	20.7	.85

* Teachers designated as conducting an outstanding program in art education.

tiate Goodenough's conclusion that: "Repeated comparisons of the work of children who have had this type of training [elementary school art], with that of children from schools in which no drawing at all is taught in the primary grades, have failed to show any consistent differences between the performance of the two groups in drawing the human figure" (1926, pp. 53–54).

Phatak (1959) made an interesting study of the relationship between the artistic merit of children's drawings and their scores obtained by the Goodenough method. From approximately 2,500 drawings made by children between the ages of five and fifteen she selected ninety-nine groups of two or three, matched for age, sex, and score on the Draw-a-Man scale. In each set, one of the drawings appeared to her to have particular outstanding artistic merit. Following the criterion that a drawing may be considered artistic if it is "pleasing, appealing, interesting," sixty raters were asked to pick the most artistic drawing from each of the ninety-nine groups, and to express their degree of confidence in their selections. These raters were divided equally among Psychology students, Fine Arts students, and Art Education majors. The judges' academic background made little difference in the drawings he selected as having "artistic merit," though Art Education majors differed from the other two groups in the number of *confident* judgments they made. Twenty-six sets of drawings were selected for further study—all those in which at least forty of the sixty judges agreed on the most artistic drawing of a set.

On only six items of the seventy-three in the revised Man scale were significant differences found between the more artistic and less artistic drawings of matched pairs. These items in general pertain to two aspects of the drawing: The artistic drawings exceeded the nonartistic on the representation of arms, the development of the hip joint or crotch and the use of a sketching technique; whereas the nonartistic drawings exceeded on three points pertaining to finger and hand detail. When the seventy-three items were grouped by such categories as (1) body parts, (2) dimensional representation, proportion and perspective, (3) clothing and activity represented, (4) precision of motor control in the execution of the drawing, and (5) location of specific body parts, a significant difference appeared between two categories: the artistic drawings showed higher clustering of points on the clothing and action items, while the nonartistic drawings exceeded on the proper location of different body parts. This study adds substantially to the evidence that the method of scoring the drawing is independent of its artistic qualities.

Goodenough's experiment to show that certain types of formal training do affect scores on this test has been reported (Chap. II, pp. 30–31). Likewise, Mott's study (Chap. II, p. 23) confirmed that drawings made after children had engaged in rhythmic games emphasizing certain body parts verbally and in body motion increased scores on the parts thus emphasized. Harris (1950), however, investigated the effect of rhythmic exercises, *not* emphasized verbally, on children's drawings. Four groups of first-grade children in two schools of a lower-middle class district were subjects for this study; a total of forty-eight boys and fifty-six girls. All drawings were made immediately after the morning routine of assembly and attendance-taking had been observed. One class served as a control group, producing a drawing of a man according to Goodenough's instructions on each of ten successive school mornings. A second class, the experimental group, expérienced a fifteen-minute exercise period in which games were led by a college student trained in choreography and dramatic exercises for children. Various musical group games and exercises emphasizing arm and leg movements were used. The room teacher then took charge and conducted the drawing test. No connection between the "visiting teacher" and the drawing period was mentioned, nor did the children at any time appear to perceive such a relationship. The remaining two classes served both as additional experimental groups and controls. One of these groups had exercises preceding the drawing during the first week and no exercises the second week. The other group reversed this procedure. All drawings were made with soft pencils on standard 8½ × 11 buff manilla paper. The children cooperated enthusiastically in every instance. For all it was the first experience of drawing with a pencil in school; only crayons had been used before.

Measurements derived from the drawings included the Goodenough IQ, measurements of leg length, arm length, head length and trunk length in millimeters, an estimate by protractor of average angle of arms and legs in relation to the vertical dimension of the picture, and a simple rating of the amount of movement portrayed in the figure. The person making the measurements knew the general purpose of the study but did not know the allocation of groups in the experimental plan. Ratings by teachers on the Haggerty-Olson-Wickman Schedule were supplied.

Several null hypotheses were tested. The chief statistical analysis used was the analysis of variance, as the most convenient technique to test the null hypothesis, using several groups. Although several classifications appear in a number of the analyses, no effort was made to test the significance of *interactions* of these sources of variance. Where more than three drawings were missing, the case was omitted from computations. In each case retained, the mean of the child's measurements was substituted for any missing estimations to secure symmetry in the analyses. It is recognized that this introduces a certain element of spurious intra-child consistency. Hypotheses and results have been reported (Harris, 1950) and are here summarized in general terms.

Hypothesis 1: That drawings made following exercise periods do not differ significantly from drawings made after no exercise with respect to: mean length of leg, mean length of arm, mean angle at which arm or leg is depicted in relation to the major vertical axis of the figure, and mean rating of motion indicated in the drawing.

This hypothesis was accepted with respect to each of the criteria noted above. The evidence suggests that motor and kinesthetic experiences are not projected into drawings; or, that a *fifteen-minute period* is insufficiently long to produce carry-over effect. This finding differs from that of Mott (1945).

Hypothesis 2: That the intra-child variance in certain dimensions of drawings does not differ significantly from the inter-child variance.

This hypothesis was rejected at the .01 level, for over-all length of figure, length of each leg taken separately, and length of each arm. This study thus gives evidence that children adopt a characteristic size for their drawing of the human figure and maintain this with relatively little variation over a period of days. There was no statistically significant sex differences in the above measurements; however, even though statistically unreliable, there was a consistent tendency for boys to draw longer arms. Goodenough (1926, p. 61) comments on boys' tendency to draw longer arms and legs than girls.

Hypothesis 3: That intra-child variance in proportions between certain dimensions of the child's drawings does not differ significantly from the inter-child variance.

This hypothesis was rejected at the .001 level for trunk to leg length, head to trunk length and arm to leg length. This finding would, of course, tend to follow from the finding of Hypothesis 2, and supports Wolff (1946) in demonstrating that certain children adopt characteristic proportions for major dimensions in their drawings.

An attempt was made to score drawings by the Wolff method, which is based on the *number* of certain types of ratios observed in major dimensions of the drawing. It was not possible for independent scorers to obtain consistent results, so this method was abandoned. A rating of introversion-extroversion based on the Haggerty-Olson-Wickman Schedule, as suggested by Olson (personal communication), was derived for each child. These ratings were correlated with gross size of drawing, with placement of the drawing on the page, with head-trunk ratio, and with trunk-leg ratio. Correlations were statistically not significantly greater than zero, and were, in fact, very close to zero.

While the studies reported here did not attempt to assess the significance of drawing style for personality, they lend support to the contention that children adopt particular styles of drawing, and that these styles tend to be consistent over a period of time.

Validity: Relationship to Other Measures

The Goodenough Draw-a-Man Test has been correlated with a number of other measures. Most of these correlations have been reviewed in Chapter II, and the pertinent data are presented in Table 7 (pp. 96–97). In addition, Ellis (1953), working with 123 emotionally disturbed children between the ages of four and nine, compared Mental Age and IQ values on the WISC and the Goodenough. For 116 children she had values on the Binet and the Goodenough. These children were for the most part below average in intelligence, ranging from the low 80's to about 110. The mean IQ's for the various age groups (although the numbers are small, from sixteen to thirty-four cases), range from the low 80's to the mid 90's. Table 7 summarizes the relevant correlation data for these groups.

TABLE 7	*Summary of Correlations Between Goodenough Scores and Scores on Other Psychological Tests*

PRIMARY MENTAL ABILITIES

CORRELATIONS

Ansbacher (1952)   100 ten-year-olds

(PMA quotients)
.40 Reasoning
.38 Space
.37 Perception
.26 Verbal Meaning
.24 Number
.41 Total test

Harris (unpublished)   164 kindergarten children

(Raw scores)
.29 Verbal Meaning
.17 Perceptual Speed
.43 Quantitative
.43 Motor
.46 Space
.46 Total score

STANFORD–BINET

CORRELATIONS

Yepson (1929)   37 institutionalized mentally retarded boys, aged nine to eighteen years   .60 (IQ values)

McElwee (1932)   45 fourteen- and fifteen-year-olds, ungraded class   .72 (MA values)

Williams (1935)   100 children, aged three to fifteen, subnormal to gifted   .80 (MA values) .65 (IQ values)

Havighurst and Janke (1944)   70 ten-year-olds   .50 (IQ values)

McHugh (1945)   90 kindergarten children   .45 (MA values) .41 (IQ values)

Pechoux, *et al.* (1947)   100 abnormal and delinquent children aged five to eighteen   .38 boys (MA values) .26 girls (MA values)

Rottersman (1950)   50 six-year-olds   .36 (IQ values)

Johnson, *et al.* (1950)   all mentally subnormal, epileptic, and brain-damaged children in a state hospital   .48 (IQ values)

Ellis (1953)   116 children in outpatient psychiatric clinic, aged four to nine years

	AGE	N	
.75	4	17	(MA values)
.78	5	19	
.69	6	20	
.79	7	26	
.92	8	20	
.60	9	14	

TABLE 7 (*continued*)

WECHSLER INTELLIGENCE SCALE FOR CHILDREN

CORRELATIONS

Rottersman (1950) 50 six-year-olds V .38 (IQ values)
P .43
FS .47

Hanvik (1953) 25 psychiatric patients, aged FS .18 (rho, IQ values)
five to twelve years

Ellis (1953) psychiatric outpatients, aged (IQ values)
eight to thirteen

V	P	FS	AGE	N
.77	.67	.70	8	16
.63	.59	.67	9	34
.17	.26	.24	10	20
.45	.46	.50	11	17
.50	.68	.62	12	19
.05	.15	.13	13	17

WECHSLER ADULT INTELLIGENCE SCALE

CORRELATIONS

Berdie (1945) 56 older, retarded adolescents .62 (Raw scores)

Gunzburg (1955) adult mental defectives V .43 (IQ values)
P .73
FS .63

MISCELLANEOUS TESTS

CORRELATIONS

Havighurst and 70 ten-year-olds (IQ values)
Janke (1944) .63 Cornell-Coxe
.48 Minnesota Paper Form-
board

Pechoux, *et al.* (1947) 100 abnormal and delin- (MA values)
quent children, aged five to .25 boys Porteus Mazes
eighteen years .27 girls Porteus Mazes

Ansbacher (1952) 100 ten-year-olds (Raw scores)
.34 Tracing McQuarrie Test
.23 Tapping of Mechanical
.16 Dotting Ability

Harris (1959) 98 kindergarten children .22 (Raw scores) Raven Progressive Mat-
rices (1947)

Spoerl (1940) 30 mentally retarded chil- Examination, presumably indi-
dren, tested during three vidual, not named (IQ values)
successive years .56 first year
.67 second year
.78 third year

The present investigator correlated the Goodenough Draw-a-Man score with results of the SRA Primary Mental Abilities test (Primary Form) for 164 children, representing seven different kindergartens. The children came predominantly from middle- and lower-class occupational groups. The results are also listed in Table 7, and suggest that the Goodenough score is more strongly associated with Quantitative and Space than with Verbal-Meaning or Perceptual-Speed abilities. While the Motor factor is not considered to be a reliably established dimension in the Primary Mental Abilities battery, it is perhaps not surprising that it shows as strong a relationship to the Goodenough score as do the Quantitative and Space components.

These data differ from Ansbacher's (1952) findings, using the Elementary Form of the PMA, which showed the Number factor scores in ten-year-olds to be very modestly related to their Goodenough scores. In his data, the Perception factor scores correlated higher with Goodenough scores than had been observed among five-year-olds. Whether these two studies reflect the changing significance of the drawing test in the hierarchy of mental abilities cannot be confirmed from these few data; certainly there is cause, from the standardization data presented in this revision, for hypothesizing that the significance of the drawing test as a measure of intellectual maturity does change with age; especially between middle childhood and adolescence. Ansbacher's total score at ten years, however, correlated only slightly less ($r = .41$), than that observed for the Primary Mental Abilities Test at age five ($r = .46$). Even though Ansbacher notes that his correlation values are attenuated because of smaller standard deviations than those reported in the standardization of the tests, they are comparable in order if not in pattern to those obtained by the present investigator. The latter's results in part confirm Goodenough's idea (1926, p. 73) and the conclusion of Havighurst, *et al.* (1946), and of Ansbacher (1952), that one thing measured by the Draw-a-Man Test is children's ability to form abstract concepts; they suggest, also, that at age five and in relation to ability to draw the figure of a man, children's handling of quantitative and spatial concepts may be relatively more important than the emerging components of verbal meaning and perceptual speed as measured by the Primary Mental Abilities Test. Possibly the verbal abstractions and concepts in which these latter factors will come to play an important role have not yet taken sufficient form, developmentally. The fact that perceptual motor skills are also involved in drawing a man is suggested by Ansbacher's correlation of .34 with the McQuarrie tracing test as well as by the present data.

The Raven Progressive Matrices test purports to assess form perception and analogical thinking abilities. However, its value is somewhat controversial (Burke, 1958) because of consistently low validity and reliability coefficients. Harris (1959) used the Raven with 100 kindergarten children selected to be representative of the U. S. urban occupational distribution. The Goodenough (revised) score showed the same correlation with this performance measure (r = .22 between raw scores) as with the Primary Mental Abilities factors reported above.

With young children, the Goodenough test score is considerably associated with intellectual maturity as assessed by the Stanford-Binet or the WISC. As would be expected, MA scores correlate more highly than IQ scores. It is probable that the drawing test also measures other aspects of psychological development. The attempt to determine what particular components of mental maturity are measured has not been entirely successful, possibly because such components are not clearly differentiated in young children (Garrett, 1946). Goodenough's original assumption that the drawing task in part reflects the ability to form concepts is probably correct. From the evidence summarized in Table 7, and in the additional studies reported here, the Draw-a-Man Test is not more allied with performance than with verbal abilities.

Relation of the Original and Revised Draw-a-Man Scales

Despite the extensive and intensive effort to develop new items that would extend the scale upward in age, it has been noted that few additional items could be found.[1] Some items added are actually elaborations or subdivisions of existing points. None has managed to extend the usefulness of the scale into the adolescent years. It is a tribute to Goodenough's insight and scholarship in her original work with children's drawings that few additional items have been found. Table 8 gives the results of comparing the old and new scales on a sample of Canadian Indian children. The correlations are undoubtedly spuriously high, because the old scale is largely contained in the new scale. Although these children tend to score higher than whites, there is no reason to believe that the relationship of their performance on old and new scales would be affected for this reason.

| TABLE 8 | *Comparison Between 1926 and Revised Draw-a-Man Scales* |

AGE	N	1926 SCALE		REVISED SCALE		CORRELATION BETWEEN 1926 AND REVISED SCALES
		MEAN	S.D.	MEAN	S.D.	
6	84	18.9	5.52	22.9	8.93	.97
8	73	25.0	6.15	30.6	8.57	.96
10	73	32.3	7.60	42.3	12.45	.98
12	79	34.3	7.06	45.7	10.91	.97
14	55	37.5	6.22	52.7	11.27	.91

[1] A comparison of percentages passing items on Goodenough's scale with percentages passing the same items in the present study appear in Chapter VIII, Plate VII, pp. 141ff.

Chapter Six

Standardization
of the Revised Man Scale
and the Woman Scale

FOR THE SELECTION and validation of items, all scoring of drawings selected for the validation samples was completed by the present author. Several psychologists tested the comprehensibility of the instructions used. Successive rephrasings of scoring descriptions were tried until reasonably clear, concise and understandable test instructions resulted.

For the standardization of the test, new samples of drawings were obtained. Through the courtesy of the Research Division of Harcourt, Brace & World, Inc., drawing tests were administered to several thousand children in four geographic areas of the country: the middle Atlantic and New England area, the South, the West Coast, and the upper Midwest.[1] For final standardization of the scale, seventy-five children were selected from this test pool at each age level from each of these geographic areas so as to represent the occupational distribution of the United States as a whole. At each age level children were selected and distributed throughout so that the sample centered at the mid-year, with an approximately equal number of children selected from each month in that age interval. An equal number of boys and girls were selected in each occupational stratum when possible. The standardization and norms, then, are based on 2,975 children, representative of the occupational distribution of the U. S. in 1950, and are distributed among four geographic areas. A summary of the socioeconomic distribution of these groups appears in Table 9.[2]

The drawings thus selected were scored by a team of assistants; undergraduate or graduate students in Psychology who had been trained in the rationale and methodology of the scales. Scorers worked independently on practice papers, until a better than 95 per cent agreement was achieved for

[1] Specifically, these schools were located in rural and urban areas of New York, Connecticut, Minnesota, Wisconsin, Louisiana, Texas, and California.

[2] The paternal occupations of this sample, for each age group, are distributed in Table H of material filed with the Test Department of Harcourt, Brace, & World, Inc.

		1960	AGE GROUPS							
				5–8		9–12		13–15		TOTAL
CLASS	TYPE OF OCCUPATION	PER CENT	N	%	N	%	N	%	N	%
I	Professional	4.3	31	2.8	32	2.8	22	3.1	85	2.9
II	Semiprofessional and managerial	10.7	116	10.3	120	10.4	66	9.4	302	10.2
III	Clerical, skilled trades and retail business	23.1	237	21.1	234	20.3	143	20.4	614	20.6
IV	Farmers	6.0	99	8.8	120	10.4	76	10.9	295	9.9
V	Semiskilled occupations, minor clerical positions and minor business	23.5	252	22.4	253	22.0	165	23.6	670	22.5
VI	Slightly skilled trades and other occupations requiring little training or ability	22.0	251	22.3	250	21.7	138	19.7	637	21.4
VII	Day laborers of all classes	10.4	139	12.4	143	12.4	90	12.9	372	12.5
Total		100.0	1125	100.1	1150	100.0	700	100.0	2975	100.0

TABLE 9 | *Distribution of Standardization Samples by Parental Socioeconomic Status (Occupational Group)*

all items in three successive test samples of ten representative papers each. The age samples were later rescored by a second team, and any differences in scoring were resolved by this team in relation to the scoring principles.

Normative Data

Table 10 reports means and standard deviations calculated for raw scores on the Man scale furnished by age samples of boys and girls. Table 11 presents these values smoothed by the three point moving average method. The smoothed data were used to calculate the standard score "IQ's" discussed in Chapter IV and presented in Part II of this book, which contains the Manual for the Goodenough-Harris Drawing Test. These standard score IQ's constitute the test norms. Tables 12 and 13 offer comparable data for raw scores of the Woman scale. The conversion tables for this scale also appear in the Manual, pages 298–301. Plates I and II (pp. 104–105) present the smoothed raw score means graphically for the Man and Woman scales, respectively.

TABLE 10 | *Means and Standard Deviations of Point Scores for the Standardization Group, Man Scale*

AGE	BOYS		GIRLS		COMBINED	
	MEAN	S.D.	MEAN	S.D.	MEAN	S.D.
5	13.8	4.67	16.6	4.92	15.2	5.01
6	19.7	5.68	19.0	5.96	19.3	5.86
7	21.6	6.78	24.3	6.95	23.0	6.98
8	26.3	7.99	27.2	7.82	26.8	7.91
9	30.0	8.53	31.2	8.95	30.6	8.76
10	36.0	10.32	37.1	9.27	36.5	9.81
11	37.6	10.67	40.6	9.84	39.1	10.38
12	39.2	11.55	42.8	10.22	41.0	11.06
13	44.1	10.81	45.4	10.91	44.8	10.86
14	44.4	9.65	44.6	8.54	44.5	9.11
15	45.5	11.07	45.5	9.25	45.5	10.19

TABLE 11 | *Smoothed Means and Standard Deviations for the Standardization Group, Man Scale*

AGE	BOYS		GIRLS		COMBINED	
	MEAN	S.D.	MEAN	S.D.	MEAN	S.D.
5	15.8	5.01	17.4	5.27	16.6	5.29
6	18.4	5.71	20.0	5.94	19.2	5.95
7	22.5	6.82	23.5	6.91	23.0	6.92
8	25.9	7.77	27.6	7.91	26.8	7.88
9	30.7	8.95	31.8	8.68	31.3	8.83
10	34.5	9.84	36.3	9.35	35.4	9.65
11	37.6	10.85	40.2	9.78	38.9	10.42
12	40.3	11.01	43.0	10.32	41.6	10.77
13	42.6	10.67	44.2	9.89	43.4	10.34
14	44.7	10.51	45.1	9.57	44.9	10.05
15	45.1	10.60	45.2	9.01	45.2	9.83

In Tables 10 through 13 levelling of the means and shrinkage of the variances are noticeable in the thirteen- to fifteen-year age groups. This finding is quite consistent with Goodenough's original observation that the test is most appropriate with young children, and with the conclusions of Eggers (1931), Levy (1931), and Cohen (1933) that no gain in score can be expected after age twelve or thirteen. Using a scale similar to Goodenough's, The Fay Test, Rey (1946) and Wintsch (1935) arrived at a similar conclusion for European children. Apparently, the expectation of Hinrichs (1935) and of Oakley (1940), that the test could be extended upwards, is not fulfilled.

TABLE 12	Means and Standard Deviations of Point Scores for the Standardization Group, Woman Scale

	BOYS		GIRLS		COMBINED	
AGE	MEAN	S.D.	MEAN	S.D.	MEAN	.SD.
5	14.5	4.97	18.3	5.73	16.4	5.70
6	18.8	6.34	21.4	6.66	20.2	6.63
7	22.9	7.93	28.7	8.84	25.8	8.89
8	28.0	7.23	30.8	8.14	29.4	7.81
9	32.0	8.64	34.4	9.22	33.2	9.01
10	36.4	9.25	40.6	9.03	38.5	9.36
11	36.6	9.57	44.0	9.93	40.3	10.44
12	38.8	9.78	45.4	9.27	42.2	10.09
13	43.9	9.49	48.0	9.53	46.0	9.72
14	43.2	9.56	48.7	9.32	46.0	9.82
15	45.0	9.19	47.9	8.06	46.4	8.74

TABLE 13	Smoothed Means and Standard Deviations for the Standardization Group, Woman Scale

	BOYS		GIRLS		COMBINED	
AGE	MEAN	S.D.	MEAN	S.D.	MEAN	S.D.
5	16.0	5.43	19.3	6.04	17.6	6.01
6	18.8	6.41	22.8	7.08	20.8	7.07
7	23.3	7.17	27.0	7.88	25.2	7.78
8	27.6	7.93	31.3	8.73	29.5	8.57
9	32.1	8.37	35.3	8.80	33.7	8.71
10	35.0	9.15	39.7	9.39	37.3	9.60
11	37.3	9.53	43.3	9.41	40.3	9.96
12	39.8	9.61	45.8	9.58	42.8	10.08
13	42.0	9.61	47.4	9.37	44.7	9.88
14	44.1	9.41	48.2	8.97	46.1	9.43
15	44.4	9.31	48.2	8.48	46.3	9.10

Sex Differences

There is a slight but quite consistent tendency for girls to score higher than boys on the Man scale (Plate I and Table 11). This tendency disappears as both groups reach the "ceiling" of the test, which clearly occurs by age thirteen. Goodenough (1926, pp. 56ff.) noted this tendency, but reasoned that it was probably due to the fact that girls tend to make more rapid progress through the grades. She attached more significance to the qualitative than to the quantitative differences between the drawings of boys and of girls, and discussed the former at some length.

PLATE
I | *Smoothed Raw Score Means, Man Drawing*

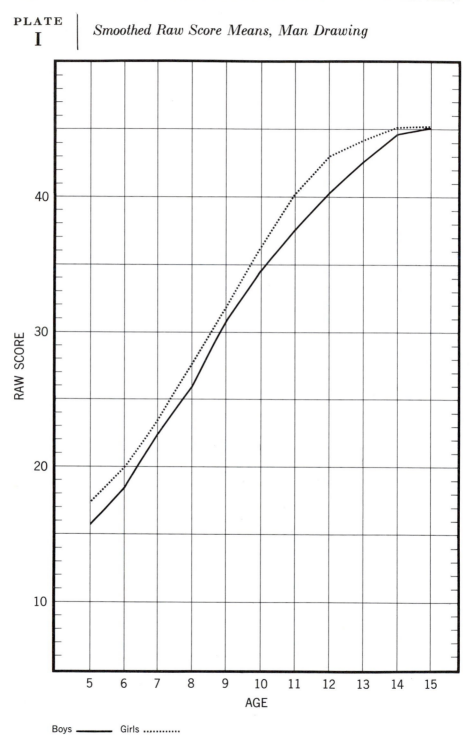

Boys ——— Girls ··········

PLATE II | *Smoothed Raw Score Means, Woman Drawing*

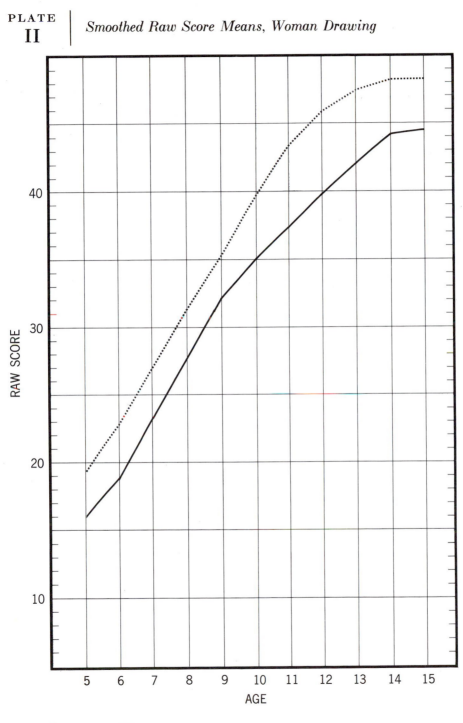

RAW SCORE

AGE

Boys ———— Girls ·············

Plate II and Table 13 compared with Plate I and Table 11 show that in the present standardization the advantage held by the girls increases appreciably in drawing their own sex. Because of marked changes in school practices with respect to grade acceleration (less than one per cent of the Midwest standardization samples had been accelerated), one can no longer accept Goodenough's hypothesis described above. The alternative hypothesis which she suggested (1926, p. 58), that perseverance, care with details, and docility (on all of which girls are generally rated higher than boys), lead to this difference, may well be the more plausible. The sex differences noted could also be due to "cultural" factors which give girls greater practice with drawing (or other finely coordinated work), or engender greater interest in and attention to people and clothing. To these suggestions should be added the fact that girls exceed boys developmentally in social interests and skills and very possibly in certain intellectual abilities. The widening discrepancy between mean scores of boys and girls, both on the drawing of the man and of the woman, as the children approach puberty may result from the relatively greater maturity of the girls.

Relationship Between the Man and Woman Scales

Table 14 contains correlations between the point scales for the even-numbered age groups. There is no discernible trend among the correlation values, by sex or by age. Using the z' transformation of Fisher (McNemar, 1949), the mean value for boys for the age groups in Table 14 is 1.006 (r = .76); for girls the value is 1.023 (r = .77). For the sexes combined the z' transformation yields a mean value of .9693, which corresponds to an r of .75. This value may be presumed to be the best estimate of the true correlation obtaining between the point scales. Although an r of .75 is not as high as the test-retest values often reported for the Draw-a-Man scale, it compares favorably with the split-half reliability of .77 (Spearman-Brown formula) reported by Goodenough (1926, p. 48). In a sense, an alternate form reliability can be logically compared with a split-half reliability.

A correlation of .75 between two reliable forms of the same test seems

TABLE 14	Correlations Between Man and Woman Scales at Selected Ages					
AGE	N	BOYS	N	GIRLS	N	COMBINED
6	150	.74	150	.73	300	.71
8	149	.75	151	.81	300	.77
10	151	.80	149	.72	300	.74
12	124	.80	126	.79	250	.79
14	127	.72	123	.80	250	.73

rather low, and suggests that perhaps different abilities are measured by the Man and Woman scales. However, each scale may measure several abilities, represented by different kinds of items, which are in fact only modestly inter-correlated. In such case the items in both scales reflect two or more rather different test components. These components, being less than perfectly measured, and combined in unknown proportions in the scales, result in modest split-half and alternate-form reliabilities. A detailed study, including factor analyses, of both scales' items might be instructive.

It is this possibility—that different "kinds" of items are combined in tests—that modern theories of intellectual development point out. Contemporary theories are beginning to suggest that the criteria of item progression and validity, plus internal consistency (in this case, total score on the drawing scale) may *force* a unity that actually blurs the measurement of several rather distinct abilities. The fact that several such abilities are all significantly age related subordinates their distinctiveness to the mere fact of age re-latedness.

Thus the Man and Woman scales may be mixtures of several only modestly related developmental abilities. Each scale may in truth be an index to the formation of concepts which are theoretically of a similar order and should show a much higher correlation. That these scales include other, uncorrelated abilities would attenuate the relationship which theoretically should obtain.

In use, the values obtained from scoring the Man and Woman drawings should probably be combined, to give a more reliable estimate of test achieve-ment. This is done quite simply by taking half of the sum of the two stand-ard score IQ equivalents, for the Man and Woman drawings respectively, which can be read from the appropriate tables in Part II, pages 294–301. The average thus obtained is a statistically more accurate estimate of the ability measured by the drawing test than that obtained from either drawing alone.

Chapter Seven

Construction
and Standardization
of the Quality Scales

A CHILD'S DRAWING of the human figure, being organized and unitary, invites an immediate appraisal as crude or excellent, as simple or detailed. Very early in the history of psychological measurement, techniques were devised for rendering such immediate judgments of *quality*, when complex products could be arranged along some general but defined continuum. Indeed, various so-called "quality scales" were applied early to children's drawings, as well as to handwriting samples, examples of creative writing, and the like.

Evaluation of Drawings by Quality Scales

The more globalistic or qualitative approach was initiated by Thorndike (1913), who applied the statistical method of judgment by equal-appearing intervals to samples of children's drawings selected from Kerschensteiner's published material (1905). While in many respects the Thorndike scale is a model of methodology, it has the limitation of beginning at age eight, when the development of drawing is already well along. It has the further flaw of containing examples of different subject matter, requiring a broader generalization and greater judgment by the examiner than a scale limited to one subject, for example, the human figure.

The Kline-Carey scale (1922 a,b), following a statistical methodology, remedied this latter defect by developing scales on four assigned topics: a house, a rabbit, a boy running, and a tree. This scale reaches from the kindergarten level to the level of high school seniors. McCarty (1924), interested particularly in the work of younger children (ages four to eight), developed scales for three subjects popular with children of that age: a person, a house, and a tree. McCarty's study was more adequate in number and representativeness of children sampled than other work available at that time. Her results showed clear-cut age progression in all drawings, and established correlations with intelligence from +.08 to +.63 in the age groups between four and eight, centering on a correlation value of +.35.

Cyril Burt in *Mental and Scholastic Tests* (1921), and in later editions, provided an age scale, from three to fourteen, of drawings of the male figure. This representative collection of drawings was obtained by taking the median example from a collection at each age level. Burt built detailed quality scales within each age level, but urged every teacher and psychologist who wishes to study drawings to construct his own scales for subjects commonly drawn by children. From such qualitative scales, Burt urged that one proceed to enumerate the technical details, and thus to develop analytical schedules for instructional and remedial purposes in the teaching of drawing.

The next phase in the wholistic approach to children's drawings appeared when Lark-Horowitz and her associates (1939) at the Cleveland Museum of Art developed a series of samples illustrating degrees of quality in children's drawings. While these samples do not constitute statistically graded scales, they do represent an arrangement in order of merit, and are designed as an aid to art teachers who must grade children's work. Kerr (1937) used a simple scaling in her study of children's drawings of a house; Tiebout (1936) developed a nine-point scale of "artistic merit" for grading children's paintings.

Of those quality scales constructed in the 1950's, Dunn's (1954) is the most elaborate and carefully devised, using a developmental point of view. He asked four judges to sort a large collection of drawings into ten piles, according to a criterion of maturity of representation. The judges then ranked the drawings within each of the ten piles. After separating by sex of subject, and determining a composite rank order for the drawings, Dunn converted the results to percentage positions from .002 to .998. He then selected twenty drawings from each set, one drawing at each five per cent interval. These drawings constitute his quality scales for the male and female figures. Dunn has used his scales principally in studies of drawings made by aging persons.

Using a considerably less elaborate scaling method, Wagner and Schubert (1955) developed seven-step quality scales for drawings of the male and female figure. Unlike other scales, theirs provides separate scoring for the full-face and the profile figure, for both the male and female figures. Their samples were obtained from the work of older adolescents and young adults, and thus do not cover the developmental period. However, their samples covered a range of quality and could be correlated with age scales. Methodologically, they used the model of the normal curve of distributed judgments. Judges divided a large pile of drawings into seven groups, graded from lowest to highest in quality. The piles were to include the following percentages: 2.5, 8.0, 23.0, 31.0, 23.0, 8.0, and 2.5. They stated, however, that "no effort was made to be exact about this distribution or to hold the rater to it" (1955, p. 3). From each stack agreed upon by three judges, model representative front and profile views were selected to be included within the final scales. Only drawings upon which there was unanimous agreement were used.

Beatrice Lantz (1955) published a scale for easel paintings made by children in kindergarten and primary grades, as well as by older retarded children. While this device is primarily a point scale, it requires that the examiner make a difficult qualitative distinction between pictures that primarily express the emotions and those that reflect mental and physical maturity. This discrimination is accomplished with the aid of verbal criteria and twelve color plates. The points of the developmental scale are based not so much on the presence or absence of specific details, as on four seven-point rating scales, using detailed descriptions at each of the seven points. These scales relate to the dimensions of Form, Detail, Meaning, and Relatedness and can be applied regardless of the "subject" of the painting. Scores on these dimensions intercorrelate from +.52 to +.87. The scale as a whole correlates substantially (+.90) with Draw-a-Man scores and appreciably (+.64 to +.86) with verbal tests of intelligence. The scale predicts subsequent reading test performance somewhat less successfully (r = +.48 to +.74). The scale is thus a modified quality scale.

The Quality Scale Method Applied to the Draw-a-Man Test

The quality scale appears to provide a convenient and economical, as well as a valid and reliable index to children's drawings of the human figure. It has the added advantage of providing a visual impression of the growth in drawing ability which no collection of points or array of scores can supply.

The present investigator and a graduate student [1] experimented with a quality scale for children's drawings of the male figure. A considerable range in quality of drawing is represented in the distance from kindergarten to high school. How many steps are needed to give a workable, yet valid, discrimination in such scales? What is the correlation with the Point scales over both limited and wide age spans? Such questions as these prompted the building of two new quality scales. The method of equal-appearing intervals (Guilford, 1954), referred to earlier in this chapter, was adopted.

Using drawings selected from those collected for the present restandardization of the Draw-a-Man Test, Frankiel (1957) experimented with a quality scale of twenty-three drawings of the male figure. The scale was constructed according to the Thurstone method using the validation sample of the present study—100 children, 50 boys and 50 girls, at each age level from five to fifteen years, stratified to represent the socioeconomic distribution in the United States, according to the Minnesota Scale for Paternal Occupations, 1950 revision. Twenty drawings, ten by boys and ten by girls, were selected from each age group according to a table of random numbers. Thus, 240 drawings were selected: 20 at age five, 20 at age five and one-half, and 20 for

---

[1] Miss Rita Frankiel.

each year of chronological age from six to fifteen. These 240 drawings were arranged in a randomized order and presented to each of twelve judges in this same predetermined random order. The judges were given the following instructions:

> You are asked to judge a number of drawings made by children of different ages. We are concerned with the ideas portrayed in the drawings rather than with the technical skill of the drawings. Thus, we are NOT interested in evaluating artistic skill as such.
>
> Inclusion and accuracy of detail, and proportion are important, as they reveal the level of MATURITY of the drawings. It is this maturity which we wish to evaluate. Please try to rate all the drawings at one sitting, since ratings done in several periods may have an error introduced.
>
> Enclosed you will find 13 manila folders numbered from 0 to 12 and a number of drawings in a predetermined random order.
>
> Group the enclosed drawings in folders 1 through 11 according to the criteria described above. Make eleven groups of drawings such that each group is EQUALLY SEPARATED from the next. Group 1 would be of least excellence, group 6 of median excellence, group 11 of greatest excellence. Thus, in going from groups 1 through 11, each succeeding group exceeds the next lower group by about the same "amount" of excellence. Categories 0 and 12 have been included so that drawings of OUTSTANDINGLY poor quality and drawings of OUTSTANDINGLY good quality may be set apart, where the judge feels that they deviate enough to place them one unit above or below all the rest.

After each judge completed his ratings, he returned the drawings to the experimenter who tabulated the ratings and put the drawings back into the prearranged order for presentation to the next judge. Thus, no judge had knowledge of how his ratings compared with those of other judges.

Because the distributions of the drawings near the ends of the scale were markedly skewed, non-parametric measures of central tendency and dispersion were adopted. All examples that had Q values of 1.00 or less were taken into consideration for inclusion in the final Quality scale; thus, restriction of range of judges' ratings became a primary consideration for the selection of drawings for the final scale. Drawings having the smallest Q values, which were closest in median placement to intervals equally spaced along the scale continuum, were chosen.

Thus, the Quality scale as finally devised consists of twenty-three drawings which range in median placement from 0.5 to 11.5, at 0.5 intervals. The score of a particular drawing to be evaluated by this scale is the median value of the scaled drawing it is judged to resemble most closely. Using all twenty-three drawings, one has a twenty-three-step, finely graded Quality scale; using alternate values from the twenty-three-step scale, one has a short, twelve-step scale. Thus, the design of Frankiel's study permitted investigation of the relative precision of a twenty-three-step and a twelve-step Quality scale.

To establish the reliability and validity of this qualitative scale, three groups of drawings, two by children homogeneous with respect to age, and one by children heterogeneous with respect to age, were used. The homogeneous age groups, each containing thirty-eight boys and thirty-seven girls, were selected at ages seven and twelve. These samples were selected to represent the occupational distribution in the United States.

In the heterogeneous group, age variance was maximized by including the work of 110 children, five boys and five girls for each year of chronological age from five to fifteen years. To restrict the effect of socioeconomic or environmental factors, these children were selected to represent only the middle occupational groups (III, IV, and V on the Minnesota Scale of Parental Occupations). At each age the ten drawings were selected randomly (except for the restriction on socioeconomic status), from an age sample of seventy-five drawings stratified with respect to paternal occupation. The samples from which these were selected were quite distinct from the samples from which the drawings were selected for the Quality scale itself. They were, in fact, cross-validation samples used for the normative data presented in this volume.

Five judges applied the Quality scales selected by the previous method to these new samples of drawings. One was an expert with the Goodenough method, two were psychologically sophisticated graduate students, and two were naive judges (an undergraduate student and a secretary) neither of whom had ever dealt with children's drawings evaluatively. Using the short, twelve-step scale, three judges rated the seven-year-olds and then the twelve-year-olds. The remaining two judges rated the twelve-year-olds first and then the sevens. The standard set of instructions used by these judges appears in the Appendix, pages 317–318. One week later, one of the psychologically sophisticated judges regraded the drawings. Two weeks after the original judgments were made, the other sophisticated judge and one of the naive judges rated the heterogeneous age group. At the same time, these judges rerated the seven-year-old and the heterogeneous groups, using the twenty-three-step scale.

The ratings assigned by each judge were correlated with the ratings given by every other judge for that group of drawings. In the instance where one judge repeated his ratings, the ratings assigned in the two sessions were correlated. Judges' ratings for each group were then correlated with the quantitative Goodenough scores for that set of drawings. Pearson product-moment correlations are given in Tables 15, 16, and 17.

Table 15 gives the pattern of correlation coefficients among the several judges. Correlations between the successive ratings of the same judge were +.85 and +.89. Correlations between judges run from +.71 to +.91. Table 16 shows that although the intercorrelations on the twelve-step scale may tend to be slightly higher, they are not significantly higher than on the twenty-three-step scale.

Table 17 gives the correlations between the ratings of the qualitative method (i.e., using the Quality scale) and the scores obtained by the quanti-

TABLE 15	Correlations Between Judges Using the Quality Scale to Rate Drawings of a Man by Seven-Year-Olds (N = 75), Twelve-Year-Olds (N = 75) and a Heterogeneous Age Group, Ages Five to Fifteen (N = 110)

| | AGE GROUP | | | | | | | | | |
| | B_1 | | B_2 | | | C_1 | | C_2 | | |
JUDGE	7	12	7	12	5–15	7	12	7	12	5–15
A	.71	.85	.79	.81	—	.74	.83	.74	.86	—
B_1			.82	.81	.91	.81	.82	.84	.83	.88
B_2						.76	.84	.77	.84	.90
C_1						.85 *	.89 *	.79	.83	—

* Repeat ratings after one week
A — Experienced judge
B_1 — Inexperienced judge
B_2 — Inexperienced judge
C_1 — Graduate student, some training
C_2 — Graduate student, some training

TABLE 16	Correlations Between Two Judges Using 12-Step and 23-Step Quality Scales to Evaluate Drawings of a Man by Seven-Year-Olds (N = 75) and a Heterogeneous Age Group (N = 110)

| | | AGE GROUP | |
JUDGE *	SCALE	7	5–15
B_1, C_2	12-step	.84	.88
B_1, C_2	23-step	.80	.87

* See explanatory statement in Table 15.

TABLE 17	Judges' Ratings of Three Groups of Children's Drawings of a Man Using 12- and 23-Step Quality Scales, Correlated with Point Scores of the Same Drawings

| | | AGE GROUP | | |
JUDGE *	SCALE	7 (N = 75)	12 (N = 75)	5–15 (N = 110)
A	12	.79	.84	—
B_2	12	.84	.80	.91
C_1	12	.82	.85	—
C_2	12	.76	.83	.89
C_2	23	.79	—	.87
B_1	12	.80	.84	.89
B_1	23	.82	—	.85

* See explanatory statement in Table 15.

tative method (i.e., using the Point scale). These values run from +.76 to +.91, depending on the group rated. The twenty-three-step Quality scale yields correlations with the Point scale no higher than does the twelve-step scale. Thus, the data of Frankiel's study (Tables 15–17) suggest that the twelve-step scale orders the drawings about as successfully as the twenty-three-step scale, either within an age group or across the range of several ages.

The judges reported that the nature of the judgmental task changed as they moved up the Quality scale. The earlier steps of the scale seemed to be distinguished from each other largely in terms of the details included in the general configuration of the body drawing. Thus, the "better" figure seems to be more representative, more detailed. Beyond the middle of the scale, from about 5.5 to the upper end, the distinction seems to involve more the increasing fluidity of the figure, rather than an increase in detail. Apparently this quality of the drawing, which here is termed fluidity, is harder to appraise than accuracy of detail, and may be the factor that makes the Quality scale less accurate than a simple quantitative approach. The greater ease and speed of scoring by the qualitative method must be weighed against the greater accuracy of the more time-consuming point-scale method.

Although the Quality scales are much simpler to use, and although they give results that correlate substantially with the Point scales, they are useful principally *because* the Point scales had been previously constructed, and their validity painstakingly spelled out, item by item. The analytical procedures of the Point scales have greatly illumined the growth of the abilities measured by the drawing test. However, the Quality scales provide a total or wholistic impression of the growth of drawing behavior portrayed in the human figure which the tables of percentages for the items of the Point scales do not give. Thus, each method has its particular advantage and affords its own useful results. In the following section the relative precision of the two types of scales as measuring devices will be considered.

Statistical Evaluation of Quality Scales for Man and Woman Drawings

By the methods described earlier in this chapter, but on independently selected samples of drawings, twelve-step Quality scales for the drawing of a man and of a woman were constructed.[2] As in the Man scale, twelve scoring values were determined by twelve carefully selected drawings, for each of which the dispersion of ratings was small, the medians being about equally spaced on a linear scale of values.

The plates for both these scales, together with instructions, scoring values, and norms appear in Part II of this volume. The statistical data pertinent to the selection of these plates appear in the Appendix.

[2] Instructions for judges as used in the final scaling procedure are included in the Appendix, pages 317–318.

The relationship of Point and Quality scales was restudied, using the newly selected plates, at ages six and ten. Drawings of a man by one of the regional samples, consisting of seventy-five children at each age, were scored by the Quality scale independently by three judges. Because using the drawings in one age sample tends to concentrate scores in a portion of the Quality scale, the following procedure was adopted: Judge X scored six-year-olds, then ten-year-olds; Judge Y scored ten-year-olds, then six-year-olds; Judge Z scored sixes and tens mixed randomly. Tables 18 and 19 report pertinent comparisons. No differences, either between variances or between means, reach the five per cent level of confidence. Nor is there evidence that the more hetero-geneous sample (Judge Z) introduces any systematic effect on the judges' scores. The success of this procedure at ages six and ten led to the scoring of the eight-, twelve-, and fourteen-year-old samples on both Man and Woman Quality scales by a single judge. This judge spread his work over a number of sittings, working first with one and then a diverse age group.

Means and standard deviations for all these age groups were computed and

TABLE 18		*Means and Standard Deviations of Quality Scale Scores Assigned by Three Raters*			
		MAN SCALE		WOMAN SCALE	
AGE GROUP	JUDGE	MEAN	S.D.	MEAN	S.D.
6 Years (N = 75)	X	2.47	1.01	2.79	.92
	Y	2.57	.91	2.85	.87
	Z	2.40	.84	2.84	.81
10 Years (N = 75)	X	4.93	1.72	5.69	1.44
	Y	4.98	1.58	5.64	1.48
	Z	4.96	1.86	5.31	1.69

TABLE 19		*Intercorrelations Between Quality Scale Scores Assigned by Three Judges*	
AGE GROUP	JUDGES CORRELATED	MAN SCALE	WOMAN SCALE
6 Years (N = 75)	X, Y	.87	.88
	X, Z	.91	.74
	Y, Z	.84	.74
10 Years (N = 75)	X, Y	.92	.88
	X, Z	.89	.88
	Y, Z	.86	.88

appear in Tables 20 and 21. The data pertaining to the Quality scales in these tables were smoothed by the three point moving average method and then plotted graphically, separately by scale and by sex. Best fitting curves were drawn through the points by inspection. From these graphs were read the estimated values of mean and standard deviations for intermediate years where actual values had not been obtained. The curves were also extrapolated to give values for ages five and fifteen. These values, as read from the graphs, are recorded in Tables 22 and 23.

In connection with Tables 20, 21, 22, and 23, reference to Tables 10 through 13 (pp. 102–103) demonstrates that the Quality scale is less sensitive to increments of performance in the upper age ranges, as would be expected from the less exact character of the measure. On the Point scale the increments between the means at ages ten and eleven and between eleven and twelve are significant at the .001 level or better. For the mean Quality scale ratings obtained at these same ages, the increments fall between the .03 and .02 levels.

Table 24 (p. 118) records the observed correlations between scores on the

TABLE 20	Means and Standard Deviations for Quality Scale on Standardization Samples, Man Drawing

| | BOYS | | GIRLS | | COMBINED | |
AGE	MEAN	S.D.	MEAN	S.D.	MEAN	S.D.
6	3.19	1.07	3.48	1.15	3.34	1.10
8	4.78	1.34	4.89	1.34	4.83	1.36
10	6.49	2.08	6.50	1.87	6.49	2.29
12	6.15	1.71	6.72	1.77	6.44	1.76
14	6.63	1.80	7.03	1.75	6.83	1.80

TABLE 21	Means and Standard Deviations for Quality Scale on Standardization Samples, Woman Drawing

| | BOYS | | GIRLS | | COMBINED | |
AGE	MEAN	S.D.	MEAN	S.D.	MEAN	S.D.
6	3.03	1.04	3.59	1.09	3.31	1.10
8	4.77	1.14	5.32	1.34	5.04	1.30
10	6.26	1.91	7.22	2.01	6.74	2.45
12	6.00	1.55	7.07	1.60	6.54	1.67
14	6.26	1.65	7.65	1.59	6.96	1.79

| TABLE 22 | | *Smoothed and Interpolated Means and Standard Deviations for Quality Scale Scores, Man Drawing* | | | | | |

	BOYS		GIRLS		COMBINED	
AGE	MEAN	S.D.	MEAN	S.D.	MEAN	S.D.
5	2.50	.95	2.90	1.10	2.85	1.00
6	3.25	1.15	3.60	1.20	3.65	1.20
7	4.00	1.25	4.25	1.25	4.15	1.30
8	4.80	1.45	5.00	1.45	4.90	1.55
9	5.40	1.60	5.60	1.55	5.60	1.70
10	5.80	1.70	6.00	1.70	5.90	1.80
11	6.20	1.80	6.50	1.75	6.30	1.90
12	6.40	1.85	6.75	1.90	6.55	1.95
13	6.45	1.85	6.80	1.80	6.65	1.90
14	6.50	1.75	6.95	1.75	6.70	1.80
15	6.45	1.65	6.90	1.70	6.70	1.70

| TABLE 23 | | *Smoothed and Interpolated Means and Standard Deviations for Quality Scale Scores, Woman Drawing* | | | | | |

	BOYS		GIRLS		COMBINED	
AGE	MEAN	S.D.	MEAN	S.D.	MEAN	S.D.
5	2.50	.90	3.00	1.00	2.75	.95
6	3.10	1.05	3.80	1.20	3.50	1.15
7	4.00	1.35	4.60	1.35	4.30	1.40
8	4.70	1.35	5.35	1.50	5.00	1.60
9	5.20	1.50	6.00	1.60	5.55	1.75
10	5.70	1.60	6.50	1.65	6.10	1.90
11	5.95	1.65	7.00	1.75	6.50	1.95
12	6.10	1.70	7.30	1.70	6.75	1.90
13	6.15	1.65	7.40	1.65	6.85	1.75
14	6.20	1.50	7.50	1.60	6.85	1.70
15	6.20	1.40	7.50	1.50	6.85	1.60

Point scales and Quality scales in the age groups for which data were available for calculation. The correlations were converted to z' [3] values and averaged across all five age groups, separately by scale and by sex. Reconverted to correlation equivalents, these means are +.84 and +.80 for boys and girls, respectively, on the Man scale. For the Woman scale, the corresponding values were +.84 and +.79.

When one examines the separate z' values, he notes that in the younger

[3] Fisher's z'.

TABLE 24 | *Correlations Between Scores on Point and Quality Scales*

| | MAN SCALE | | |
AGE	BOYS	GIRLS	COMBINED
6	.82	.87	.88
8	.88	.94	.94
10	.88	.83	.75
12	.86	.81	.84
14	.75	.69	.72

| | WOMAN SCALE | | |
AGE	BOYS	GIRLS	COMBINED
6	.81	.88	.82
8	.85	.88	.89
10	.91	.86	.73
12	.84	.79	.83
14	.77	.74	.78

ages there may be a tendency for Point and Quality scales to correlate more highly among girls than among boys. There is no discernible difference between Man and Woman scales, however. There is also a tendency for the correlation to drop somewhat in the older age groups, for both sexes and both Man and Woman scales. Therefore the differences between mean z' values for various age combinations were tested. Between boys and girls, the observed difference in each scale is significant at the .01 probability level for the mean z', taken across the five values. For each scale and sex the difference between the eight- and fourteen-year correlations is significant at the .01 probability level. It was decided, therefore, to calculate several estimates of the true relationship obtaining between the Point and Quality scales. The obtained correlation values at the six- and eight-year levels were averaged to provide an estimate for years five, six, and seven. The obtained values at the eight-, ten- and twelve-year levels were averaged to give a value for those and the intervening years. The obtained values at ages twelve and fourteen were taken to give the best estimate for the thirteen-, fourteen-, and fifteen-year levels. These operations yielded the estimates of correlation recorded in Table 25.

Plates III and IV (pp. 120–121) compare the means and standard deviations of both Point and Quality scale scores, reduced to a common base. Using the obtained means and standard deviations (boys and girls combined) at age five as a base, all other year means (i.e., age norms) were calculated as deviation scores from the five-year performance level. Reference to Plate III thus

TABLE | *Estimates of Probable Correlations Between Scores on Point*
25 | *and Quality Scales*

MAN SCALE		
AGE	BOYS	GIRLS
5 to 7	.85	.91
8 to 12	.87	.88
13 to 15	.81	.76

WOMAN SCALE		
AGE	BOYS	GIRLS
5 to 7	.83	.88
8 to 12	.87	.85
13 to 15	.81	.76

shows that, on the Man Point scale, thirteen-year-old boys score, on the average, almost five standard deviations above the five-year-old average; the standard deviation unit being the dispersion of point scores for all children at the five-year level. On the Quality scale, however, the comparable thirteen-year-old performance is only about three five-year-standard-deviations above the five-year mean or norm. Clearly, the Quality scale is not as discriminative, not as differentiating of age increments in ability, as is the Point scale, especially among older children. Up to the age of eight there is no difference between the scaling methods, in either man or woman figure, in the sensitivity of the test. By nine, the advantage of the Point scale method begins to appear, and is appreciable by age ten.

It is of considerable interest that the advantage of the Point scale method is notably greater for the man figure. Possibly the Point scale method of scoring the woman figure is not quite as revealing of changes in psychological maturity as is the man figure, and the shift to a qualitative method of evaluation does not reduce the sensitivity of the measure quite as much as it does in the man figure.

These graphs (Plates III and IV) also bring out strikingly certain other features of the drawing performance of children as measured by these scales. As we have already noted in Chapter VI, on the Point scale for the man figure girls tend to excel boys, especially up to the age of thirteen or fourteen. This difference is noticeably greater on the drawing of the woman, in which the sex difference does not disappear at ages fourteen and fifteen. It is most interesting that the Quality scale appears to increase this relative difference, and even for the man figure, accords clear superiority to the work of girls in the oldest age groups. In addition to blurring out age increments in

PLATE
III

Mean Point and Quality Scale Scores, Man Drawing

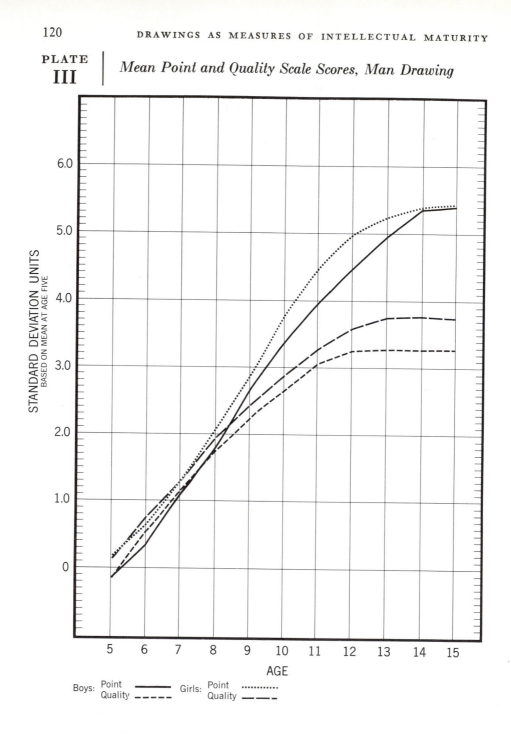

Boys: Point ——— Girls: Point ············
    Quality – – – – –   Quality – – – –

PLATE
IV

Mean Point and Quality Scale Scores, Woman Drawing

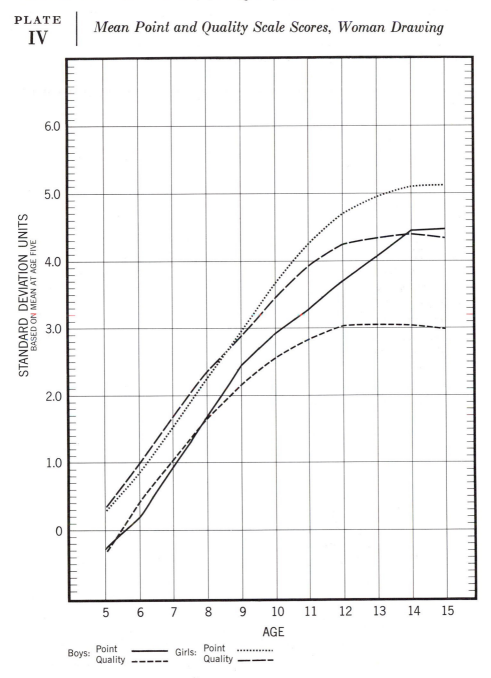

the work of older children, the Quality scale method seems to increase the relative advantage of girls over boys, and especially in drawing a figure of their own sex. Attention to detail in drawing seems to be a feminine characteristic, and the Point scale method reveals this on drawings of male as well as female figures. A qualitative or impressionistic method of evaluating drawings, while less sensitive to increments in presumed intellectual maturity measured by the scales, may be more sensitive to features of the drawings only in part captured by the Point scale method. In turn, the qualitative method captures elements more clearly related to sex than to intellectual maturity, which appears to account for a large portion of the variance in the drawing test.

When one uses the Quality scale as a quick approximation, he may wish to know the equivalent Point scale score. As we have seen, the saving in scoring effort is considerable. What loss in precision will occur by this estimation? The data necessary to this statistical relationship are provided in Tables 11, 13, 22, and 23 and in the correlation coefficients of Table 25. It is necessary to set up the regression equations for estimating Point scale scores from Quality scale scores. Because of the sex differences observed between average scores on both Point and Quality scales, the constants for predicting Point scale scores, given the Quality scale scores, are presented separately for the sexes. These constants, together with the standard errors of the estimated or predicted Point scale scores, are given in Tables 26 and 27.

A visual comparison of the reliability of Point scores estimated from Quality scale scores compared to Point scores achieved by the Point scale appears in Plates V and VI (pp. 124–125). In these plates the standard errors of estimate for the boys' data from Tables 26 and 27 are plotted, together with means and standard deviations of Point scale scores. These graphs also show the standard errors of measurement for the Point scale scores, assuming a scoring reliability of +.90, which from various studies seems a reasonable figure. Clearly, the saving in time by using the Quality scale is accompanied by an appreciable reduction in accuracy of measurement, when the Point scale equivalent is estimated according to the constants of Tables 26 and 27. Such estimates must be used cautiously, as indeed must estimates of intellectual level obtained by the drawing method generally.

Scores estimated from correlations of less than 1.00 are *regressed*; that is, they are estimated closer to the mean than they would be from actual computation. The effect of regression is progressively greater, the farther away from the mean the particular score lies. Therefore, from the data of Tables 22 and 23, standard deviation equivalents were calculated similar to those established by methods described in Chapter IV for the Point scale. These standard deviation scores for the Quality scale, possessing a mean of 100 and a standard deviation of 15 at each age, appear in the Manual in Tables 36 through 39. Although these values are based on smoothed curves of means and standard deviations for Quality scale scores, and in part on interpolated values, they are probably to be preferred to values derived from regression equations, even though they are based on more exactly computed normative statistics.

TABLE 26	*Regression Equations for Estimating Point Score (X′) from an Obtained Value on the Quality Scale (Y), and Standard Errors of Estimate, Man Drawing*

	BOYS		GIRLS	
AGE	REGRESSION EQUATION	S.E.est.	REGRESSION EQUATION	S.E.est.
5	$X' = 4.72(Y) + 4.00$	1.58	$X' = 4.36(Y) + 4.76$	2.16
6	$X' = 4.22(Y) + 4.68$	1.80	$X' = 4.50(Y) + 3.80$	2.44
7	$X' = 4.64(Y) + 3.94$	2.16	$X' = 5.03(Y) + 2.13$	2.83
8	$X' = 4.66(Y) + 3.53$	2.45	$X' = 4.80(Y) + 3.60$	3.80
9	$X' = 4.86(Y) + 4.46$	2.83	$X' = 4.93(Y) + 4.19$	4.17
10	$X' = 5.04(Y) + 5.27$	3.11	$X' = 4.84(Y) + 7.26$	4.49
11	$X' = 5.25(Y) + 5.05$	3.43	$X' = 4.92(Y) + 8.22$	4.69
12	$X' = 5.18(Y) + 7.15$	3.48	$X' = 4.78(Y) + 12.41$	4.95
13	$X' = 4.67(Y) + 12.48$	3.37	$X' = 4.17(Y) + 15.84$	6.43
14	$X' = 4.87(Y) + 13.04$	3.32	$X' = 4.16(Y) + 16.19$	6.22
15	$X' = 5.20(Y) + 11.56$	3.35	$X' = 4.03(Y) + 17.40$	5.86

TABLE 27	*Regression Equations for Estimating Point Score (X′) from an Obtained Value on the Quality Scale (Y), and Standard Errors of Estimate, Woman Drawing*

	BOYS		GIRLS	
AGE	REGRESSION EQUATION	S.E.est.	REGRESSION EQUATION	S.E.est.
5	$X' = 5.00(Y) + 3.50$	1.72	$X' = 5.32(Y) + 3.34$	2.90
6	$X' = 5.06(Y) + 3.11$	2.03	$X' = 5.19(Y) + 3.08$	3.40
7	$X' = 4.41(Y) + 5.66$	2.27	$X' = 5.14(Y) + 3.36$	3.78
8	$X' = 5.11(Y) + 3.58$	2.51	$X' = 4.95(Y) + 4.82$	4.63
9	$X' = 4.85(Y) + 6.88$	2.64	$X' = 4.68(Y) + 7.22$	4.66
10	$X' = 4.98(Y) + 6.61$	2.89	$X' = 4.84(Y) + 8.24$	4.98
11	$X' = 5.03(Y) + 7.37$	3.01	$X' = 4.57(Y) + 11.31$	4.99
12	$X' = 4.92(Y) + 9.79$	3.04	$X' = 4.79(Y) + 10.83$	5.08
13	$X' = 4.71(Y) + 13.03$	3.04	$X' = 4.32(Y) + 15.43$	6.09
14	$X' = 5.08(Y) + 12.60$	2.97	$X' = 4.26(Y) + 16.25$	5.83
15	$X' = 5.39(Y) + 10.98$	2.94	$X' = 4.29(Y) + 16.02$	5.51

PLATE | Boys' Drawing of a Man: Accuracy of the Point Scale
V | and of Point Scores Estimated from the Quality Scale

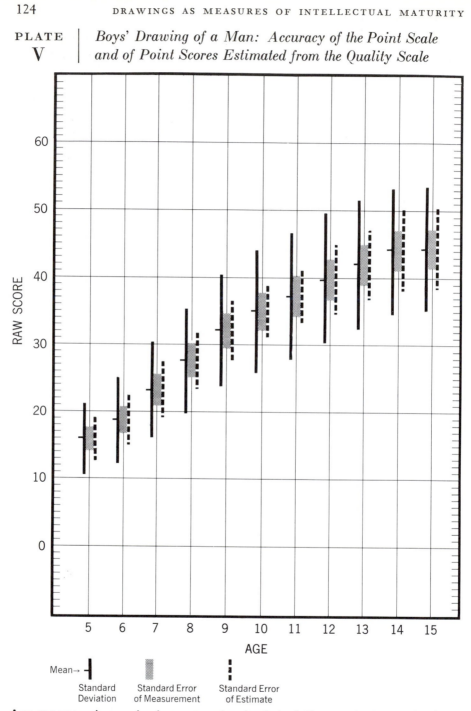

Age means; plus and minus one standard deviation, and plus and minus one standard error of measurement for the Point scale; plus and minus one standard error of estimate on predictions from the Quality scale.

PLATE
VI *Boys' Drawing of a Woman: Accuracy of the Point Scale and of Point Scores Estimated from the Quality Scale*

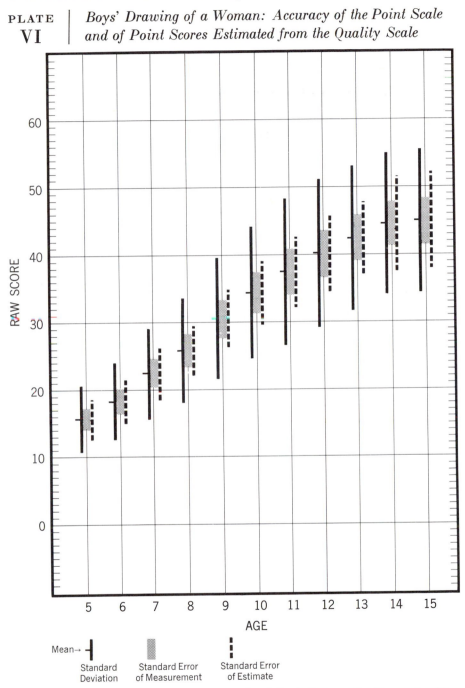

Age means; plus and minus one standard deviation, and plus and minus one standard error of measurement for the Point scale; plus and minus one standard error of estimate on predictions from the Quality scale.

Chapter Eight

Nonintellectual and Cultural Influences on Drawings

SINCE GOODENOUGH stated that ". . . the present experiment, which has dealt chiefly with the intellectual side, has by no means exhausted the possibilities which these drawings possess for the study of child development" (1926, p. 80), there has been an assiduous search for such possibilities. Chapters II and III of this book have reviewed this literature. Drawings are unmistakable indices to certain aspects of intellectual or conceptual development. They measure aspects of development that cut across cultural divisions of mankind, since children of all cultures show age progression in scores. The Goodenough scale, however, is clearly related to educational influences, as is demonstrated by the fact that many groups tend to score below American or European children, particularly in later childhood. Notable sex differences are evident. The search for idiopathic signs in drawings, whether by children or adults, has not been particularly successful; yet children are clearly idiosyncratic in their drawings—in style, in subject and in details recorded. Whether the uniqueness recorded in a child's graphic products reflects his temperament, his personality, his interests, or something else entirely has not been proved.

Sex Differences in Children's Drawings

In her 1926 monograph, Goodenough reported two trends in the data from the drawing of a man: (1) slight but consistent sex differences in mean score, favoring girls; (2) marked sex differences in the treatment of certain qualitative features of the drawing. Goodenough attributed the difference in total score between boys and girls to the method of standardizing the scoring items. Goodenough's conclusion, minimizing her observed sex differences in score, may have been encouraged also by her observation (1926, p. 13) that several European investigators had noted marked sex differences favoring boys.

Sex Differences Not Due to Standardization Procedure

The present studies have suggested that sex differences cannot be attributed to differential selection of boys and girls according to intellect, and reflect more than the effect of a few items. The sex difference in total score appears at an early age and considerably exceeds that noted by Goodenough. For the drawing of a man, the sex difference between mean scores favors girls at each year of age by about one-half year of growth. For the drawing of a woman, this difference is roughly equal to one year of growth.

Goodenough also reported a marked trend for girls to treat certain features in rather different ways from boys. These differences certainly could not be attributed to the standardization procedure. For example, girls emphasized eye detail, cheeks, "cupid's bow" mouth, curly hair, and arms no longer than head length. Boys were more likely to draw profiles, to put in the heel, to represent the figure in motion, and to draw long arms reaching below the knee. Goodenough suggested these points as the basis for a masculinity-femininity scale. Since that time a few investigators have examined these differences, reaffirming them and suggesting further that excessive "femininity" in boys' drawings may be associated with maladjustment (see, for example, Chapter II, p. 28).

An item analysis of the provisional forms of the present scales showed considerably more fluctuation than did the total scores. This is to be expected. Based on an analysis of drawings in the original standardization samples (fifty girls and fifty boys at each year of age, selected to represent the U. S. occupational distribution in terms of paternal employment), many items show differences between boys and girls in the per cent passing at each age. Some of these differences satisfy criteria of statistical significance.

Based on the simple criterion of the number of items on which one sex exceeds the other, regardless of amount, Dixon and Mood's sign test (1946) results in the information in Table 28 (p. 128). Clearly, the girls exceed the boys in the number of developmental points included in their drawings, especially in the drawing of a woman.

The following discussion is based on sex differences in performance on individual items in this revision. To be relevant to this discussion, a difference between boys and girls satisfying the five per cent level of significance had to occur in more than half the age groups from five through fifteen. All such differences, furthermore, had to favor the same sex.

On the drawing of a man, girls do consistently better on eye detail and proportion items. Boys are considerably more likely to get the nose in two dimensions. Girls definitely excel on indicating the lips and giving the line of the jaw. Girls do better on hair items and on proportion of the ears. Boys excel consistently on the proportion of the foot and indication of the heel. Girls do better on arm proportion. Girls solve the problem of clothing or figure transparencies sooner than boys, but do not otherwise tend to do better on clothing items. While girls definitely do better on motor coordination items,

TABLE | *Sex Differences in Performance on Drawing Test Items,*
28 | *Significance Evaluated by the Dixon-Mood Test*

	AGE GROUP										
	5	6	7	8	9	10	11	12	13	14	15
					MAN SCALE						
Total number of items *	86	86	86	86	86	86	86	86	86	86	86
No difference	39	32	25	20	21	8	17	11	10	15	16
Girls exceed boys	21	43	35	39	37	75	45	26	56	42	45
Boys exceed girls	26	11	26	27	28	3	24	49	20	25	25
Confidence level	n.s.	.01	n.s.	n.s.	n.s.	.01	.05	.05	.01	n.s.	.05
					WOMAN SCALE						
Total number of items *	84	84	84	84	86	86	86	86	86	86	86
No difference	25	22	20	16	10	6	9	10	9	7	5
Girls exceed boys	48	44	45	49	58	75	63	52	61	71	65
Boys exceed girls	11	18	19	19	18	5	14	24	16	8	16
Confidence level	.01	.01	.01	.01	.01	.01	.01	.01	.01	.01	.01

* Based on provisional scoring key, including items later discarded.

boys are more likely to portray action in the arms. Most of these observations confirm Goodenough's earlier work.

In the drawing of a woman, more girls than boys score successfully on the great majority of items. Again, girls do better on most facial features, but again boys exceed girls in depicting the nose in two dimensions. On the drawing of a woman, girls score more often than boys on points based on hair and hair styling. Girls also are more likely to depict jewelry. At most ages girls more frequently depict neckline and waistline of the female figure, and give a "flare" to the skirt. Boys are more likely to draw the female legs in such fashion that a distinct angle is indicated; this effect is often produced by separating the feet. Girls are more likely to draw the legs parallel.

Earlier we noted no particular sex differences in depicting garb of the male figure. In portraying the female figure, girls are much more likely than are boys to score clothing and costume points, especially at the older ages, above eight or nine. Girls also excel boys on the motor coordination items on this figure, as well as on the male figure. Motor coordination items evaluate body contours, including in the female figure such secondary sex characteristics as breast, hip, and calf of leg.

These data fit quite well into what is already known concerning sex differences in drawing performances. McCarty (1924, p. 74) noted that girls drew the human figure better than boys. Boys, however, excelled in drawing composition. In her study, girls more frequently used mass, and boys more frequently worked with outline. Zazzo (1948), in a study involving more than 5,000 children, found indisputable sex differences in handwriting and drawing. Girls excelled in the motoric aspects of drawing (coordination items discussed above may be considered as similar to Zazzo's motoric aspects), while boys excelled in the "intellectual organization of space" in drawing.

These data may further be related to information on other psychological sex differences. A common observation in the literature of sex differences is that boys appear to excel on certain general motor and performance items, notably space orientation, comprehension, and use. This observation has been repeatedly confirmed by studies of the so-called "primary mental abilities," in which boys excel on the S (Space) factor. McCarty, in the study of drawing already referred to, found that boys were superior in the use of perspective.

Interpretation of Sex Differences in Drawing

The interpretation of the sex differences noted offers something of a problem. Depending on his theoretical predilections, one can interpret the observed sex differences in different ways. In psychometric instruments sex differences are usually minimized by excluding items favoring one sex. In the long history of mental testing, the few items in intelligence measures that consistently favored one sex have either been discarded or balanced by items that favored the other sex. In constructing scales, this procedure has worked quite well, and it has been customary to speak of "no real sex differences in intelligence."

The analytical approach to abilities, however, has consistently turned up small differences in a number of dimensions, which appear at early ages and persist through childhood and into adolescence. Girls show a slight but consistent acceleration in general development and perhaps in verbal performance. Boys seem to excel in arithmetic performance, particularly reasoning. Girls do slightly better on fine motor coordinations and on tests of number and name checking. As early as age five, girls show more esthetic interests, and more interest in painting and modeling activities. Girls are often found to show greater awareness of people and personal relationships. Regardless of whether these differences arise from psychobiological or culturally derived origins, they are consistently noted from early ages in our culture and probably should be taken into account in test building. A base research question is: How does the drawing scale relate to tests of perceptual and fine motor skills as well as to cognitive and verbal factors?

Some may prefer to explain sex differences in terms of personality dynamics. Many of the differences here summarized could be related to dynamic theories of personality organization. Culturally reinforced sex differences in libidinal investment of body parts, differences between the sexes in the significance of the body image, and differences in sexual symbolism, all could be drawn upon in discussing the restandardization data. The greater relative sex differences in drawing the female figure are interesting. It may be that girls have a greater identification with sex role than do boys. Certainly there is no indication that girls reject the feminine sex role in their drawings; they do not "masculinize" the feminine figure. Moreover, it has often been observed that social values in Western cultures emphasize the male role. The fact that boys and girls are less likely to exhibit characteristic sex differences in drawing the male figure than in drawing the female figure is not surprising. That a majority of both boys and girls of all ages characteristically draw the *male* figure when only the drawing of a *person* is called for has already been noted in Chapter III. Another possibility is that girls excel in drawing the human figure because of a greater awareness of and concern with people and personal relationships. More than one of such factors is undoubtedly involved in girls' superior drawing performance.

Cultural Differences in Children's Drawings

That sex differences in drawings cannot be separated from cultural influences was suggested in the literature review of Chapter II. In various American Indian groups boys do as well as or better than girls in drawing. Among American Negro and New York Puerto Rican children, however, girls tend to excel boys, as is true also in native Japanese and Argentinian groups. Such a finding is also common in European samples. Data available to the author from a number of Eskimo schools under the jurisdiction of the U. S. Department of the Interior have confirmed the observation that sex and cultural differences in drawings are complexly related. Unfortunately, the number of cases available did not warrant an item analysis for boys and girls separately. It was possible, however, to make certain interesting comparisons with test norms. The results are reported here and suggest that more detailed studies of children who have had limited experiences with print and pictures might be fruitful.[1]

Drawings of Eskimo Children

Through the courtesy of their teachers, a total of 318 Eskimo children were tested in several remote Alaskan schools. Figures 34a–45b (pp. 135–138) are examples of these children's drawings. Table 29 presents the mean scores by age groups and compares these values with means based on the normative samples. Relative to the norm group, a consistent superiority of the Eskimo children is apparent, and the drawings showed many evidences of superior quality in performance.

---

[1] The author has in preparation a monograph which will survey anthropological, cross-cultural and other studies of the Draw-a-Man Test with so-called primitive and culturally underprivileged groups. This volume will incorporate original studies of several thousand drawings from a dozen areas of the world.

TABLE 29		*Smoothed Means for Eskimo Group Compared with Standardization Group, Man Scale*			

	ESKIMO GROUP				STANDARDIZA-TION GROUP
	BOYS		GIRLS		TOTAL	
AGE	N	MEAN	N	MEAN	MEAN	MEAN
5	3	12.3	5	17.5	15.4	16.6
6	21	17.7	19	20.8	19.4	19.2
7	11	23.8	9	26.2	24.6	23.0
8	7	30.0	5	33.4	31.7	26.8
9	7	35.3	10	37.2	36.4	31.3
10	27	41.5	10	41.1	41.2	35.4
11	16	44.5	13	43.5	44.1	38.9
12	15	47.1	19	47.7	47.4	41.6
13	23	51.3	14	49.3	49.7	43.4
14	13	52.3	12	51.5	51.2	44.9
15	18	53.8	15	52.1	52.4	45.2
16+	11	52.9	15	53.5	52.6	——

The consistent difference between boys and girls in norms, favoring girls, is not as clearly reflected in the Eskimo children's results. It should be noted, however, that the smaller number of cases in the Eskimo group introduces a considerable sampling error into the statistics. The standardization studies have indicated that small numbers produce considerably less stable average performances than N's of 100 or more in any one age group.

To increase the number of cases for computational purposes, the adjacent age groups in the Eskimo sample at the prepubertal ages were combined. The cases at ages ten and eleven were made into one group, and the cases at twelve and thirteen were made into another group. The percentages of children in these combined samples passing each item were compared with the percentages in the corresponding age groups of the norm group sample. A deviation of 15 per cent points or greater was selected arbitrarily as "significant." [2] A list of items was compiled for each age group on which Eskimo children exceeded or fell short of children in the norm samples. The two Eskimo age groups were then examined. Where a notable difference, as defined above, appeared in *both* age groups, the item was tentatively considered to be one handled differently by the Eskimo children.

Using this criterion, a number of items show cultural differences. Eskimo children are less likely to depict the neck, the ears, and to correctly place the ears. These facts seem to reflect the greater prevalence of parkas in the Eskimo

[2] Actually, this percentage difference in the middle range of the distribution corresponds roughly to a five per cent level of statistical significance.

group's drawings and is thus an artifact of the drawing situation. Due to the voluminous parka garments, elbow joints, knee joints and modeling of the hip are less likely shown, resulting in greater stiffness of figures portrayed.

Since the Eskimo boot does not have a heel, Eskimo children are less likely to indicate heels in their drawings. Figures 37, 38, and 42, however, show that when the garb is appropriate, the heel is shown. The children do have the concept of heels; their drawings are quite appropriate to the type of figure they are representing at the time. Eskimo children are also less likely to portray the arm and shoulder performing some type of movement, probably due to the loose parka (Figs. 45 a,b), though this is not invariably the case (for example, Figs. 39 and 44).

On the other hand, Eskimo children are more likely to portray with exactness the nostrils, the bridge of the nose, and, when portrayed at all, the thumb or fingers. The characteristic tendency of the Eskimo children to show a mittened hand earns for them a greater credit on the thumb opposition point and on the hand as distinct from fingers or arm in the age groups ten to thirteen inclusive. In this age group also the Eskimo is more likely to draw the arms down at the side than held out stiffly from the body. The Eskimo child is more likely to show the feet with a wide stance, that is, with toes pointing apart, or in perspective in either full-face or profile drawings. The Eskimo drawings include fewer transparencies in these age groups, and a larger percentage of them earn credit for showing a distinct costume, which of course follows from the tendency to draw the parka—the everyday costume in this part of Alaska.

Aspects of the Eskimo drawings that are distinctive and that are not apparent in the detailed scoring technique of the Goodenough method include: a greater emphasis on the eyebrow, on the nostrils and nose (as indicated above), and on general detail of facial features. There is some evidence of a general decrease in quality of the drawing in adolescence. This is not sufficiently great, however, to reveal itself as markedly in the trend of median scores as in the normative group. It is most noticeable in the increased tendency to draw the facial features and hands "sketchily." Particularly among younger Eskimo children there is a very distinct tendency to draw shorter arms and legs than in the norm group. Here again there is the possibility that the proportions of the body are distorted somewhat by so many children depicting the figures in parkas.

Another notable feature of Eskimo drawings is the great detail in which the boot, or mukluk, is drawn (see Figs. 39, 40, 41, 43 a,b, 45 a,b). It often includes a corrugated toe and heel, decorations on the upper part of the mukluk, tassels, and the like. In relation to the rest of the picture this feature is the one most likely to appear in great detail. Another feature shown on most of the drawings is the device on the breast of the parka for warming the hands (Fig. 39). This, too, is noted by most children, even the six-year-olds, and is usually presented in careful detail. The sewn and embroidered patterns around the skirt of the parka are usually portrayed elaborately (see Figs. 34 b, 39, 40, 41, 44, 45 a,b).

A breakdown by type of drawing made by children eight years and older appears in Table 30 (p. 134). The preponderance of the native costume and the relative absence of business suits is apparent. The few cowboy figures are interesting, however (e.g., Fig. 38). One of these cowboys was drawn with a cactus plant in the background! The presence of military personnel is reflected in the drawings that show individuals in uniform or in military fatigue clothing. Only three drawings included evidence of traditional Eskimo tools or weapons (Fig. 39), while several times this number included the tools or weapons of an industrial age (Fig. 40). One drawing was labelled "hunter in the old time." The airplane featured in several drawings, and the sled in only two.

Table 31 (p. 134) gives a breakdown of Table 30 by individual school. While the number of cases is quite small, particularly in some schools, the variation in "type" clearly represents proximity to military posts. While the distinction between military fatigue uniform and nondescript jacket and trousers is probably not completely reliable (e.g., Fig. 45 a), the work uniform of the military services was unmistakable in quite a proportion of those so classified (e.g., Fig. 37). The military uniform itself and the native parka were unmistakable when drawn.

Although culture influences drawings in rather obvious ways, such as type of garb, vehicles, implements, actions portrayed, these elements do not influence a Goodenough-type score. For this reason the Draw-a-Man Test has been rather widely used as a "culture free" intelligence test. Yet the data above suggest that the child's drawing of certain body features or parts is influenced by garb, and possibly by other conditions of living that call attention to particular parts or their functions. Allowance would have to be made, both in scoring and in the norms, for parts omitted in one of these cultures included in the present scoring system. Such allowance would have to be worked out empirically within each culture group. It has been affirmed (Goodenough and Harris, 1950, p. 399) that although the test may be unsuited to comparing children *across* cultures, it still may rank children *within* a culture according to relative intellectual maturity.

The present writer would further amend this position to state that, for the most valid results, the points of the scale should be restandardized for every group having a distinctly different pattern of dress, mode of living, and quality or level of academic education. This conclusion virtually rules out the scale for cross-cultural comparisons; indeed, psychologists increasingly believe that mean differences among large, representative samples drawn from varying cultures, express the gross differences in conceptual experience and training these groups have had. Further work, to determine exactly which aspects of intellectual or conceptual maturity the drawing task expresses, will be necessary to explain scientifically these observed cultural differences.

TABLE 30 | *Per Cent of Eskimo Drawings Illustrating Different Types of Garb*

	BOYS (N = 136)	GIRLS (N = 112)
Parka	43	46
Jacket and Trousers	28	24
Military Uniform	4	8
Military Fatigues	13	13
Cowboys	4	1
Indians	1	0
Business Suits	7	8
	100	100

TABLE 31 | *Per Cent of Eskimo Drawings Illustrating Different Types of Garb, by Local School*

SCHOOL	N	PARKA	JACKET AND TROUSERS	MILITARY UNIFORM	MILITARY FATIGUES	BUSINESS SUIT	COWBOY, INDIAN
Barrow	115	49	16	8	15	10	2
Kivalina	25	76	20	0	0	4	0
Meade River	9	100	0	0	0	0	0
Point Hope	39	33	27	5	20	13	2
Point Lay	18	44	34	0	22	0	0
Wainwright	42	31	35	7	12	5	10

Secular Changes Within a Culture

Children's drawings from the same culture may be compared at different points in history. If any changes have directionality with reference to some norm or standard, such changes are said to express a secular trend. If there is reason for supposing a change over time in the culture patterns of a group, or in its social values and mores, and such a secular trend in drawings can plausibly be related to this culture change, then the change demonstrates the impact of culture on drawings. Sufficient items in the scale remain unchanged from Goodenough's original formulation to permit such a study. On most points in the scale, more present-day children score successfully than did the children in Goodenough's original normative group. The discussion of these results follows on page 139.

FIG. 34a. Man, by girl, 5-10   FIG. 34b. Woman, by same girl

FIG. 35. Woman, by girl, 9-5   FIG. 36. Woman, by boy, 10-2

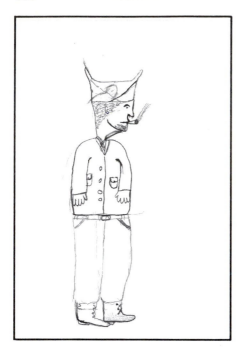

FIG. 37. Man, by boy, 10-3

FIG. 38. Man, by boy, 10-5

FIG. 39. Man, by boy, 10-9

FIG. 40. Man, by boy, 10-11

FIG. 41. Man, by girl, 12-1

FIG. 42. Woman, by boy, 13-0

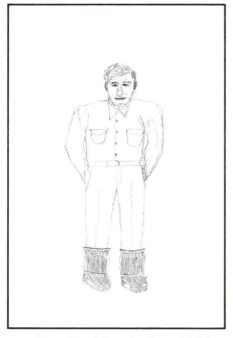

FIG. 43a. Man, by boy, 13-10

FIG. 43b. Woman, by same boy

Fig. 44. Man, by boy, 15-10

Fig. 45a. Man, by girl, 15-11

Fig. 45b. Woman, by same girl

In the present standardization children draw features of the face more poorly. Their drawings less frequently indicate the projection of the chin, or portray both nose and mouth in two dimensions. The legs are less successfully portrayed in suitable proportions. There is virtually no difference between the groups on the presence of general features of the man, such as head, legs, fingers, neck, items of clothing, costume, and the more general proportion and motor coordination items.

The drawings in the present standardization tend consistently to excel on the presence of arms and trunk, attachment of limbs, correct number of fingers, depiction of hand, head and two dimensional arms and legs, ears, eye details, chin, and forehead. Children in the present group achieve notably higher performance on hair, finger detail and thumb opposition, absence of transparencies, proportion of trunk, and coordination in drawing arms and legs. The list (p. 140) and Plate VII (pp. 141–147) present these differences.

Because this text has consistently warned against overinterpretation of drawings, it may seem presumptuous to interpret observed trends. The reader is certainly free to draw his own conclusions, but he may wish to know the author's speculations. It appears that the depiction of the most general features of the human figure shows no differences over time. However, children of the mid-1950's appear to be more successful in handling a number of body and limb details; they have particularly "improved" with respect to hair, absences of transparencies, and hand items. Since the 1920's there has been a full generation of excellent health education in the schools. The emphasis on the body, its development and its comfort, has often been singled out as a feature of mid-century American culture. These differences may reflect a greater emphasis in recent years on the body, possibly a greater "body acceptability" now than a generation ago.

Children of the 1950's, in contrast to those of the '20's, give less attention to the mouth, nose, and chin. One might be tempted to speak of a "faceless generation" characteristic of a period of conformity! The author, however, prefers somewhat less dramatic hypotheses.

Since the 1920's there has developed a new philosophy of art education. In contrast to the old emphasis on copying, on stylized patterns and design, and on the stereotyped reproduction of models, the new philosophy has emphasized freedom of expression, encouraging children to express their own ideas through art media—and, at an early age.

Also, during the second quarter of the present century, there was a virtual revolution in the attitudes of adults toward children, and in the general management and guidance of children, especially in the schools. It is often hypothesized in current child development literature that children are, as a consequence, freer, more spontaneous and expressive, and also more observant. Changes in general art education theory and in the general attitude toward handling children appeal to the author as more plausible hypotheses than the notion that greater materialism and hedonism have led to more "body emphasis" in modern drawings.

*Summary of Changes in Performance on 41 Items
Common to the Original and Revised Draw-a-Man Scales*

MARKED DIFFERENCES, FAVORING PRESENT STANDARDIZATION GROUP

Trunk in proportion
Hair shown
Hair on more than the circumference of the head
No transparencies
Finger detail
Thumb opposition
Motor coordination: arms and legs

SOME DIFFERENCES, FAVORING PRESENT STANDARDIZATION GROUP

Arms portrayed
Trunk present
Attachment of limbs
Correct attachment of limbs
Two items of clothing
Correct number of fingers shown
Hand distinct from fingers or arm
Head in proportion
Proportion: both arms and legs in two dimensions
Ears present
Pupil of eye
Eye detail: proportion
Both chin and forehead shown

VIRTUALLY NO DIFFERENCE BETWEEN STANDARDIZATION GROUPS

Head present
Legs present
Neck present
Eyes present
Mouth present
Clothing indicated
Four items of clothing
Costume complete
Fingers present
Proportion: arms
Proportion: feet
Head outline
Trunk outline
Motor coordination: features
Profile A
Profile B

SOME DIFFERENCES, FAVORING ORIGINAL STANDARDIZATION GROUP

Nose present
Nose and mouth in two dimensions
Proportion: legs
Brow or lashes
Projection of chin

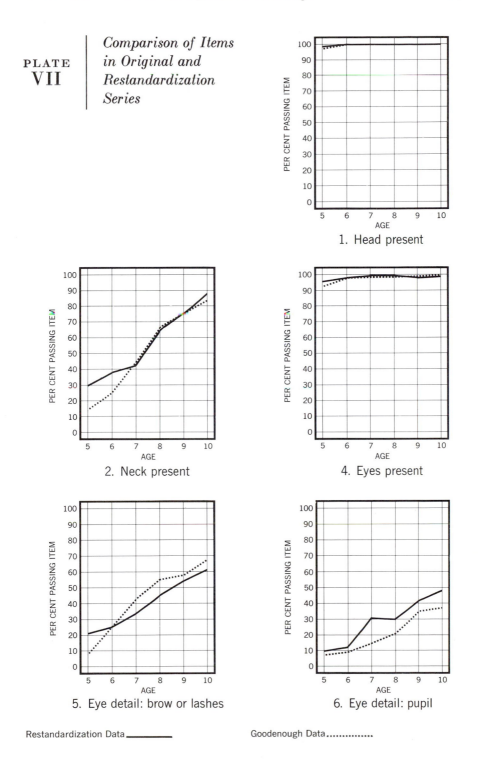

PLATE
VII

Comparison of Items in Original and Restandardization Series

1. Head present

2. Neck present

4. Eyes present

5. Eye detail: brow or lashes

6. Eye detail: pupil

Restandardization Data ————

Goodenough Data ·············

PLATE **VII** (*continued*)

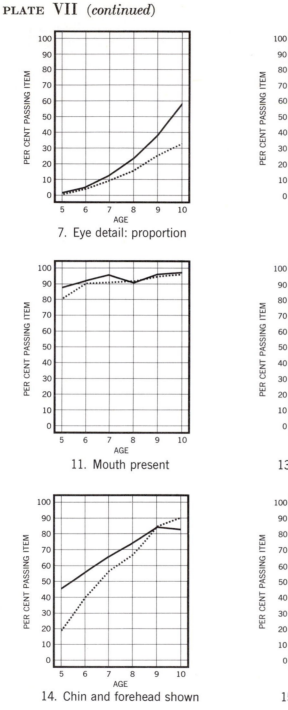

7. Eye detail: proportion

11. Mouth present

14. Chin and forehead shown

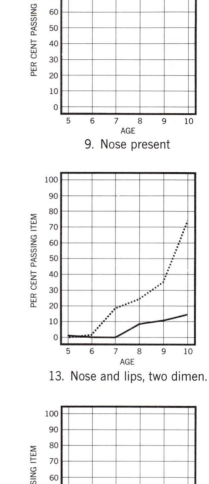

9. Nose present

13. Nose and lips, two dimen.

15. Projection of chin shown

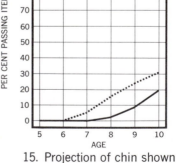

Restandardization Data _____   Goodenough Data ....

PLATE **VII** (*continued*)

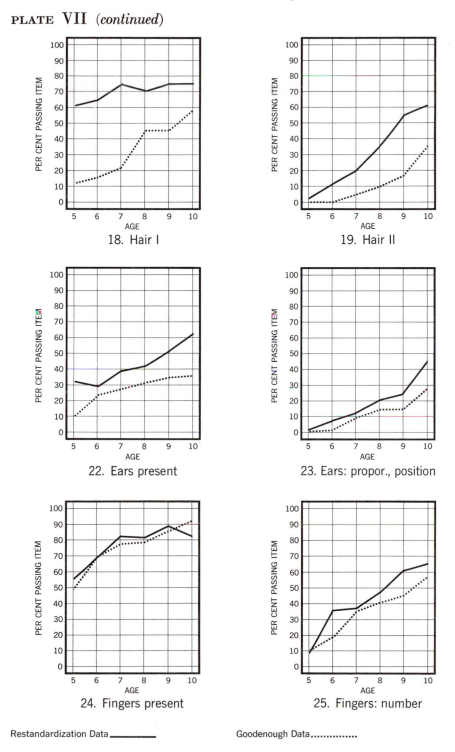

18. Hair I

19. Hair II

22. Ears present

23. Ears: propor., position

24. Fingers present

25. Fingers: number

Restandardization Data_____   Goodenough Data...............

PLATE **VII** (*continued*)

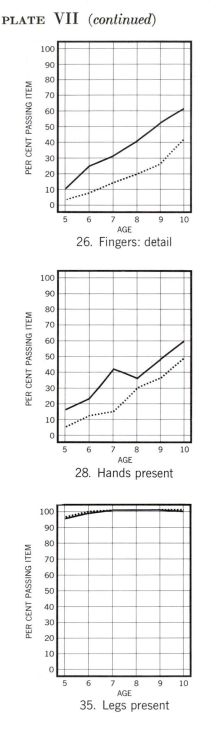

26. Fingers: detail

28. Hands present

35. Legs present

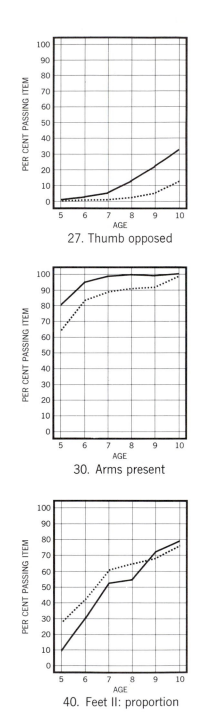

27. Thumb opposed

30. Arms present

40. Feet II: proportion

Restandardization Data ━━━━━━   Goodenough Data ....

PLATE VII (*continued*)

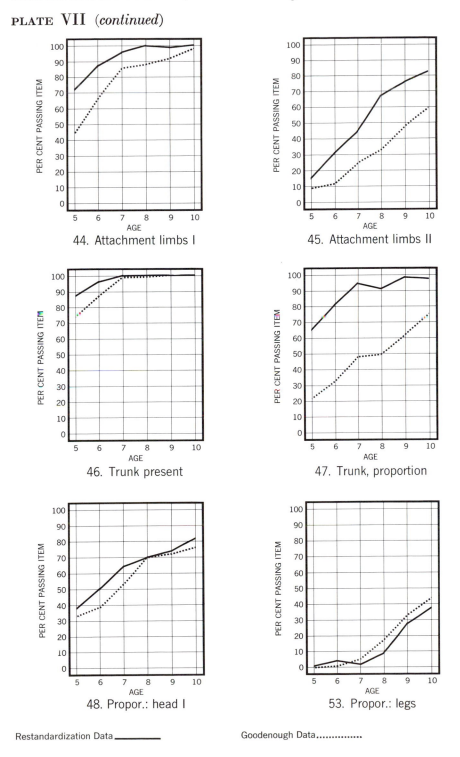

44. Attachment limbs I

45. Attachment limbs II

46. Trunk present

47. Trunk, proportion

48. Propor.: head I

53. Propor.: legs

Restandardization Data ————　　　Goodenough Data ....

PLATE VII (*continued*)

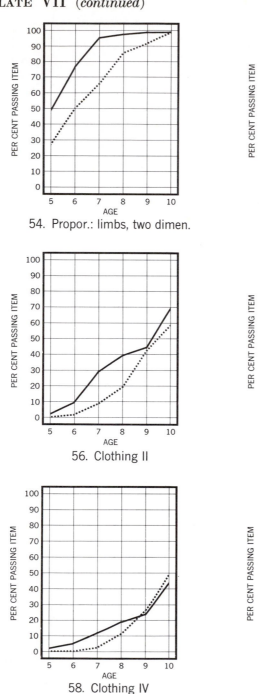

54. Propor.: limbs, two dimen.

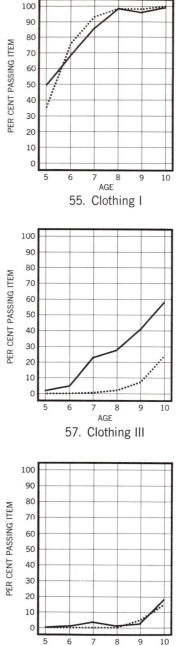

55. Clothing I

56. Clothing II

57. Clothing III

58. Clothing IV

59. Clothing V

 Restandardization Data _____    Goodenough Data ···············

PLATE VII (*continued*)

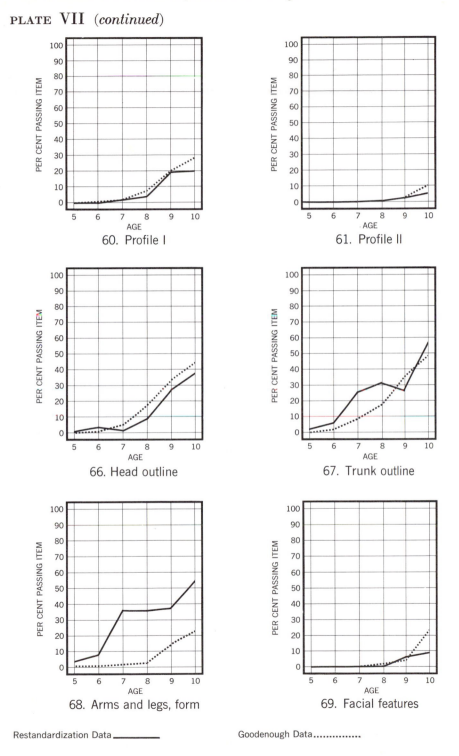

60. Profile I

61. Profile II

66. Head outline

67. Trunk outline

68. Arms and legs, form

69. Facial features

Restandardization Data ———————   Goodenough Data ....

The Use of Drawings to Diagnose Personal Qualities

A comprehensive survey of literature (Chapter III) has already indicated that drawings are not generally useful as diagnostic devices for personality study. Although seriously disturbed subjects sometimes use bizarre or distorted forms, such drawings are seldom needed to detect the condition, which is usually first noted on other grounds. The "blind" analysis of children's drawings is particularly hazardous; children use many and ingenious devices to portray their ideas, limited only by the medium or by their lack of technique or skill. What appears to the naive adult analyst as a "bizarre" feature may have a straightforward and perfectly sensible explanation in light of the child's thought and intention. Some examples from the restandardization work may serve to illustrate this point.

Figure 46 was selected by a psychologist as the work of a disturbed child, described by her teacher as "different." However, when the child described the picture as "a clown carrying balloons in a parade," the spots on the cheeks, the peculiar appendages suspended from the arms, and a number of "bizarre" features of the garb became quite meaningful. The drawing was made by a bright and very imaginative six-year-old girl. Figure 47 was drawn in a group setting by a very intelligent eleven-year-old boy. Questioning quickly revealed that he, suspecting the psychological purpose of the task, had resolved to trick the investigator! Figure 48, on the other hand, was drawn by an eight-year-old boy, of "average" mental capacity and average social background. He was described as excessively tense, rigid, unsure of himself and very compliant. He offered no explanation for the odd markings.

Thus, despite Goodenough's ingenious study of psychopathic traits in children and the modest association she demonstrated between descriptive adjectives applied to children by their teachers and certain odd features in their drawings, the usefulness of drawings for personality diagnosis remains questionable. At best, because of the many possible determinants of both detail and thematic content, the child's drawing must be understood against the backdrop of a great deal of other information about him. With sufficient information available to throw light on the drawing, the drawing itself loses significance as a diagnostic tool.

A number of studies were conducted to examine the drawings of children selected as possessing certain personality qualities to a marked degree. To select criterion groups, classroom teachers were asked to respond to "guess-who" descriptions for the following qualities or attributes: anxious, carefree, rigid, hostile, neat, extratensive, self-confident, sex-appropriate interests and attitudes, sex-inappropriate interests and attitudes, "odd," aggressive, and compliant. Elementary school teachers nominated the two or three boys and/or girls in their classrooms who best fitted the verbal descriptions supplied for each of the above-named qualities. By taking one boy and/or girl so named from each of a large number of classrooms, a "sample" of children

FIG. 46. Man, by girl, 6-1

FIG. 47. Self, by boy, 11-3   FIG. 48. Man, by boy, 7-11

was formed, having in common a notable degree of the trait named. Drawings by these children were compared with samples of drawings selected randomly from children in the same classrooms, not named for any trait. Using various analytical as well as global or judgmental approaches, the author was unable to identify any features of drawings, or kinds of drawings, that differentiated the groups.

Two other major attempts (unpublished) were made by the author to utilize descriptive aspects of the drawings. A list of "signs" or features commonly reported in the literature as significant in personality study was prepared. This list contained some eighty or ninety items including: (1) a number of linear measurements, e.g., length of nose; (2) ratios or proportions formed by combinations of these measurements, e.g., trunk width to height; (3) relationships of specific body parts, e.g., shoulder width to hips; (4) qualitative treatment of hands and hair; (5) presence of accessory objects, e.g., cigarette, necktie, baseline, background object; (6) type of costume, e.g., "fashion plate"; (7) amount of erasure; (8) quality of lines, etc.

Several major problems at once appeared. While many items could be judged on a "present-absent" basis, such as garment accessories, others had to be rated subjectively, such as amount of erasure or treatment of lines. Agreement of judges on the rated items was low. The tabulation of these items through several age samples showed no particular relationship to age, and many features occurred in an exceptionally small proportion of cases in any age group. In the latter instance it was not possible to relate the items to other features of the drawings, or to any known data about the child. It was the fruitlessness of these attempts, plus the endless variety of combinations in which drawing qualities appear, that have led the author to the conclusion that consistent and reliable patterns having diagnostic significance for personality probably cannot be found in children's drawings.

The Self Drawing as a Possible Indicator of Nonintellectual Aspects

A drawing of the self had been obtained from all children in the restandardization and normative studies. Extensive perusal of these drawings suggested that most children took the self-portrait assignment seriously, although many apparently found it quite difficult, and the older children often resisted the task.

If any of the three drawings was carelessly or incompletely done, it was most likely to be this one. But whether this fact represents a conflict within the self, a greater reluctance to tackle a specific portrait as contrasted with a generalized "man" or "woman," or a condition of simple fatigue or boredom from having completed two preceding drawings, cannot be said. It is the author's impression that all three factors play a part, but that the latter two are more common than the first. Occasionally one can detect the "flip" attitude of the wiseacre older child from a written caption or remark included in the drawing. One encounters a caricature or cartoon infrequently, a somewhat remarkable finding in view of the quite common cartoon element in the doodlings and notebook scribbles of many older school children.

From this survey a detailed guide to analysis has been developed but remains untested empirically. This analysis involves the examination of the self drawing for apparently idiosyncratic features, "juvenile" features and specific comparisons with the like-sex and opposite-sex adult figures. The Guide for Analysis of Self Drawing appears in the Appendix, pages 320–321.

The theory that has prompted the questions included in the guide to drawing analysis is relatively simple. The self drawing, *so labelled*, is the child's attempt to portray his own image as he is acquainted with it via direct inspection, mirror image, and the comments of others. This drawing will contain both realistic features as well as concepts suggested or symbolized more indirectly.

Realistically portrayed features take the form of general indications of child or youth status, such as a baseball cap, or a hair ribbon or barrette; or they include features unique to a particular child, such as glasses or freckles. The general juvenile features may reveal something of the child's developing idea of age or sex role; the unique or idiosyncratic features may reveal something of the child's self-concept.

The child may represent activities of considerable interest or significance. These activities may be portrayed directly, as reading or diving in a pool. More often they are suggested through accessory items or equipment, such as a baseball bat or a doll. He may reflect something of his sense of self-worth in his drawings, by caricature or ridicule. For example, he may: (1) draw an enormous nose on the self drawing when that feature was more realistically shown in the adult figures, (2) attach a derisive nickname as a label, or (3) use a cartooning technique. Attempting a self-portrait puts excessive demands on the child's ability to portray realistically. He may be willing to try a generalized man or woman, but his own picture challenges him and he may use the cartoon technique, popular with children, which is representational only in a general sense.

Concepts or ideas suggested indirectly may possibly show up in size or treatment relative to the adult figures. It is possible that comparisons with like- and cross-sex adult figures may relate both to identification and to the self-image. Most research heretofore has assumed this meaning of the self drawing, but the assumption needs empirical verification.

All these suggestions must be understood as tentative until tested further. But it is likely that meaningful interpretations will be fairly obvious and "close to the surface" and not require an elaborate theory of symbolism. Furthermore, the meanings will probably be readily apparent, and the child will be able to explain them in his own words.

The present investigator offers the following suggestions concerning the drawing of the self test and its further development. To yield a developmental measure, the self drawing test may be scored with either the Man or

Woman scale, as is appropriate. The qualitative analysis of the self drawing, or some modification, should be validated systematically, against personality variables in both normal and clinical populations of children. It may be that the more general, comparative approach suggested by the Guide in the Appendix, pages 320–321, will be no more useful than analytical scoring by the measurement of parts or the counting of "signs." However, preliminary work suggests that there may be some value in this more comparative approach.

In any event, further studies of drawings should be made on children tested individually rather than in groups. This requirement will add much to the cost and the time involved in the research; but with so little evidence of universal symbols, it will be necessary to observe the child's procedures and behavior sequences, and especially his verbal behavior as it relates to the drawing. A systematic post-drawing inquiry would be very helpful. If, as seems to be the case, much of the drawing act reflects cognitive processes, the investigator should bring out as many verbal correlates of these processes as possible, along with the graphic correlates.

In discussing drawings with young children the author has always been impressed by the seriousness with which they approach the task. He has found, as undoubtedly teachers have discovered, that it is unwise to ask a child, "What can it be?" or "What is it a drawing of?" Rather, the courteous request, "Tell me about it" elicits a great deal of discussion, without affronting the child. Most young children regard their drawings, which usually are the product of intense effort however brief the time required, as important pieces of work. The author has found it advantageous to describe his interest in advance, and to request the drawings as gifts "for his collection." This courtesy to children invariably wins their cooperation and willingness to part with their work.

The Relative Significance of Affect and Cognition in Drawings

The results of the analyses reported in this and previous chapters seem to reinforce the author's position that drawings primarily express cognitive processes. Children's drawings are much more likely to reveal concepts than affective processes, except insofar as the latter become caught up in expressions of knowledge, recognition, and awareness.

It has long been an axiom in psychology that temporary or mild states are continuous with more permanent or intense states of the same kind. Thus, if drawings reflect diagnostically the emotions of chronically upset children, the same signs should, in lesser degree perhaps, occur in drawings made when a child is temporarily upset.

Researchers are reluctant to manipulate children's feelings experimentally, and for good reason. In a few studies, however, children have produced drawings under conditions of frustration or gratification. These studies have shown general deterioration or improvement in the drawing as a whole; the appearance of specific features or affect symbols has not been noted. The literature on the art of psychotics suggests that deterioration of meaning is the usual effect of mental disease, and that it is knowledge about or the cognitive meanings of the subject matter drawn that suffers, not the drawing skill itself.

A child is seldom asked to draw while known to be emotionally upset, unless the drawing situation itself is stressful for him. In this case, if stress is experimentally increased, it is more common to get outright refusal, or a deteriorated product, than a drawing that contains specific symbols of affect.

Art educators have long held that the activity of drawing may be quite as valuable educationally as the product. Considering drawing or painting as psychological therapy, the *process* may be much more important to the patient than the *product*. If this is true, it is all the more important when conducting research to capture the *sequences* by which this product is achieved, many of which will not show in the end result. More descriptive research should be done on the process of drawing, and on the verbalization of the ideas and thoughts that accompany the act of drawing.

If the act of drawing is looked upon as expressive of ideas and of problem-solving attempts, where the problems are those of both conceptual and graphic organization and arrangement, the study of the drawing act in the early teens may take on a special significance. The dramatic "leveling off" after age twelve or thirteen to which these studies attest may indicate that a shift in "center of gravity" of thought processes is in fact occurring. A number of studies of mental processes and abilities have suggested that in early adolescence the child shifts over from habits of relatively concrete thought to much more abstract thinking and reasoning. No studies have shown that this occurs in saltatory fashion; yet as one views the properties of thought processes of ten- and eleven-year-olds in contrast with thirteen- or fourteen-year-olds, he is struck by the noticeable difference in ability to formulate and apply general principles.

Attractive though this hypothesis may be, certain alternative hypotheses must be recognized. One view, often associated with Garrett (1946), though others have held it also, would have it that the composition of "intelligence" changes during childhood and adolescence, becoming more differentiated, complex, and highly organized. This issue has been controversial, such persons as Swineford (1947) and Doppelt (1950) holding that there is relatively little change in the principal components in intellectual growth during childhood and adolescence. That the change in the drawing task involves something other than a simple progressive change in the intellective components of intellectual maturity is attested by the relatively abrupt termination of growth increments in early adolescence, and by the fact that intercorrelations of the test with other measures hold up quite well through later childhood.

Another hypothesis is simply that the test itself has been quantitatively "exhausted"; that is, since the number of scorable points on the drawing of a human figure is finite, the "ceiling" of the test is reached by early adolescence. This hypothesis has some plausibility, in view of the extent to which it was necessary to canvass small details to find possible additional points. Indeed, a number of the points that appeared to be useful in later childhood were "technique" points such as shading, foreshortening, and perspective. These points, from the evidence, measure something other than cognitive content and add little to the measure as a whole. This hypothesis, that the task of drawing the human figure ceases to measure conceptual growth largely because there is a finite limit to the details which can be recognized and used, is also consonant with the evidence.

A child's drawing of an object may convey much of his thoughts and generalizations about the concrete aspects of that object. As he is impelled more and more to consider properties arising not out of appearances but out of functions and relationships, the representativeness of graphic portrayal no longer suffices. Unless he masters the techniques developed by the artist to suggest properties and relationships, he must abandon his attempts to portray his concepts and understandings graphically. Verbal techniques, much more highly practiced, and considerably more suited to portraying abstract properties and relationships, take over. Indeed, the child is encouraged to abandon artistic attempts by the very increase of his verbal powers of comparison, evaluation, and criticism. By these powers he detects and condemns the deficiencies of his graphic portrayals.

Hence, as Lowenfeld maintained (e.g., 1947, and again in 1957), the period of early adolescence *is* a critical one for the creative graphic process. If the youth can be encouraged to explore and learn through this period of increasing discouragement and rejection, he may find that he can continue his graphic productions both as cognitive and as truly esthetic communications. The fact that drawing changes from a primarily cognitive process to include other, possibly esthetic and affective elements, may make the drawing act for adults more truly "projective," in the clinician's sense.

Chapter Nine

The Psychology of Drawing: Empirical Conclusions Concerning Drawing Behavior

AS WAS POINTED OUT early in this volume, research on children's drawings may be divided into several phases of interest. Following the early general and descriptive studies, there appeared a succession of empirical studies focussing on many relatively limited aspects of the drawing process. To establish a foundation for a theoretical approach to drawing behavior, the present chapter organizes this diverse, scattered and particulate literature under a series of empirical generalizations. Chapter X will discuss more fully the several investigators who have made an approach to a theory of children's drawing behavior. From these two discussions, and from a review of recent developments in the study of perception and cognition, it may be possible to point toward a reconciliation of apparently divergent psychological viewpoints and to formulate a "psychology" of children's drawing activity.

1. *The earliest scribbles are more than random markings. They are patterned by the mechanical arrangement of the hand, wrist and arm as a multiple jointed lever; they are probably modified by the scribbler's visual observation and to a very limited degree by relations within the drawing field.*

a. *Early scribbles show a circular character.* Since the 1920's, the prerepresentative stages of drawing or scribbling have received considerable attention. That the young child's crayon or pencil scribbles are not fortuitous, but represent the expression of movements for which the arm as a complex lever is well constructed, has been noted by Bender (1932, 1938), Bender and Schilder (1936), and others. Side-to-side sweeping movements of the entire arm, and then of the wrist and forearm produce slightly curved lines. Perceiving the mark produced by the crayon probably reinforces the tendency to produce those marks; thus, scribbles become patterned. With the added motor control coming from maturation or experience, or both, the slightly curved lines become more and more circular, forming loops and then whorls. In the motor movements basic to the production of lines can be seen the operation of the laws of developmental direction.

Seeman (1934) found the whorl to be characteristic of the drawings of all infants and young children, regardless of race or culture. The whorl gradually evolves into the "stick-man," in which the circle still predominates but to which various appendages are added in accordance with cultural influences. The apparently universal occurrence of the "whorl" led Read (1945) to a rather curious theory of the development of child art. This theory combines some observations from early descriptive accounts on the subject with ideas drawn from psychoanalytic theories and typology, apparently influenced by Jung. Read advanced the theory of "primordial images," exemplified by the circle, whorl, and radiating lines that appear in the drawings of young children. He believes that these forms represent "electrostatic patterns produced in the cortex by normal phenomenal experience" (p. 189), a concept apparently borrowed from Gestalt psychology. To the present writer, this does not appear to add much to the generally accepted belief that all behavior with cognitive components is mediated through cortical action.

Special mention should be made of Rhoda Kellogg's monumental collection of young children's scribbles, described by her in a privately published booklet (1955). From observations of many children aged two to five, while crayoning or painting, and from the study of many thousands of scribbles, she has constructed a classification for the myriad forms produced. Her ingenious vocabulary and classification attest to the complexity of the problem.

Kellogg identified twenty Basic Scribbles, starting from the simple dot and straight vertical, horizontal, diagonal, and arc lines, through "roving" lines, to various modifications of the imperfect circle. These simple, basic line forms may appear in the work of all children, and the twenty Basic Scribbles encompass all the forms she has observed. These basic forms are variously combined into six Diagrams: the Greek Cross, Square or Rectangle, Circle or Oval, Triangle, Odd Shaped Area, and Diagonal Cross. In turn, these Diagrams are combined into at least thirty-six Combines, and then into innumerable Aggregates (in which three or more Diagrams combine, with or without additional Scribbles).

Kellogg has stressed the fundamental pleasure children obtain from scribbling; how the process is self-reinforcing and "self-teaching"; and how, gradually, the forms produced combine with the child's perceptions and intent to yield simple representations of human figures, houses, and animals. She is convinced that an orderly sequence appears in drawing development, but is chary of describing it precisely, due to its complexity and varied mode of expression. Her work appears to have been influenced by Jung's (e.g., 1950) theories, through Read (1945), whose contributions will be reviewed later. As is true of many other art educators, Kellogg believes that the child's expression should be natural—unhampered by adult guidance or naming. Furthermore, she believes that the child's drawings may reveal facts about his perceptions and understandings.

b. *Innate aspects of motor action may control the origins of drawing behavior.* Extensive and analytical studies of infants putting crayon or pencil to blank paper have yet to be made, though some interesting work on chimpanzees has been reported. Schiller (1949) believes that innate aspects of motor action (such as grasping, pointing, shaking, carrying, placing, pulling) form the basis for learning manipulative patterns, including problem solving, subject, of course, to physical limitations imposed by the media. These innate propensities, plus the limiting conditions just described, are elaborated into "characteristic," "preferred," or "habitual" manipulative movements by a process of serialization rather than selection. The unifying mechanism appears to be the reinforcing effects of such basic manipulative activities. It has long been noted that there is an "exploratory" or manipulative tendency in animals, becoming especially noteworthy in primates. Apparently, the effects produced by action become important reinforcements in all types of learning, perceptual and cognitive as well as motor, giving manipulative behavior an additional "drive" quality. The generalization of such responses to non-associated stimulus conditions must be considered to be independent of "expectation" and "purpose" and remains one of the most difficult aspects of learning to explain. "Expectation," or set, may itself be a learned response (Harlow, 1949).

c. *Primate scribbles show orientation in space.* Schiller (1951) has reported observations of a chimpanzee with a propensity for "scribbling" with crayons. Short dashes or zig-zag lines were characteristic; curved lines seldom appeared. The subject, Alpha, reacted according to perceptual features of figure and ground. She first oriented to the corners of the blank sheet, and then to the center. An outlined square in the center of the sheet focussed her efforts on the square, which was "colored" over by many heavy marks; attention to the corners of the page was completely inhibited. If the square was presented off center, the scribbling was placed in the largest open area to "balance" the figure, in about half the cases. Triangles, more frequently than circles or squares, seemed to serve as "figures" evoking symmetrical scribbling.

A solid geometric form with a part cut out concentrated the animal's marking efforts on the "cut out" area. Continuous but incomplete outlines were not completed. Scattered spots did not define a field and were ignored. Symmetrical arrangements of spots with one or more spots missing concentrated marking activity in the missing locations. This reaction did not occur if the number of spots was less than about six. Attention to a "figure" diminished after two or three minutes and the whole sheet filled up with scribbles. Schiller noted that Alpha was much more interested in the activity than in its effects or in the finished product, yet she would not "draw" with a pointed stick and rejected a pencil when the point broke, or when a broken pencil was offered her.

Desmond Morris, an English biologist, obtained drawings and paintings from thirty-two primates of four species. By far his best "artists" were chimpanzees, often considered psychologically closest to man among the primates. One chimp in particular proved a most apt pupil, and a preliminary report (1961) dealt mostly with this animal's work. Morris noted a basic "fan-shaped" pattern of strokes made by push-pull movements of the arm; only after long experience (two or three years) did these develop into side-to-side or circular movements noted early in the human child's development. Morris' observation that the young human child appears to favor horizontal rather than vertical strokes suggests that he has done some work with human infants, but it has not yet been reported.

As did Schiller's subject, Morris' chimpanzee clearly "drew"; he kept his work under visual-perceptual control. Given a plain sheet, he distributed his marks over the entire area. Given a sheet with a large imprinted rectangle, the chimp treated the rectangle as a frame, confining his marks within the delineated area. A much smaller rectangle was treated as an object, with marks around and converging on the rectangle. A small grey square on a large white sheet was similarly treated when centrally located. If the square were placed off center, the chimp's markings converged on the largest open space, thus "balancing" the design offered by the figure on the white field. Similarly, a vertical line dividing a sheet into halves was ignored, marks being scattered across the entire field. A vertical line placed off center was counterbalanced by "scribbles."

It is Morris' (1962) belief that the human infant goes through the same stages as the chimpanzee initially, but is capable of going much farther, developing the early scribbles into definite forms. Apparently some fundamental figure-ground relationships operate in perception, coincidentally with the earliest patterning of motor activities. The coordination of visual regard and motor expression in higher primates, including man, becomes the basis of drawing and perhaps of art.

Busemann's work (1950) with children two to four years old found that some children ignored stimulus figures (angle, rectangle, circle) on the drawing sheet, while others oriented their scribbles and crude drawings to such figures. He, too, utilized field-theory language in discussing his results.

Stotijn-Egge's account of drawings by severely mentally retarded children in the Netherlands (1952) gives a comprehensive account of the genesis of drawing in terms of motor behavior, concept formation and cognitive elements. She did not, however, examine the children's perceptual orientation to the page in the act of drawing.

d. *Drawing and writing show analogous patterns of early development and may have similar origins.* To the very young child "writing" and "drawing" are much the same. Legrün (1938) described a series of developmental stages by which the two forms of graphic expression become differentiated. The progress is from completely unorganized scribbles with no apparent design, to forms of a more definite shape, with occasional attempts at letters of the alphabet. Hildreth (1936) also reported on the early stages of handwriting shown by 170 children between the ages of three and six years. She was able to differentiate seven levels of progress in writing, beyond which further improvement seemed to involve mainly a higher degree of accuracy, neatness, and speed. Both Legrün and Hildreth noted that letter-like forms usually appear earlier than true letters, and that irregular scribblings tend to give way to arrangement in forms of lines or rows as the concept of writing evolves. To a certain extent both activities are imitative in that the incentive to create forms with pencil or crayon probably comes from observing others draw and write. Prudhommeau (1948) has remarked that self-criticism in drawing appears earlier than it does in writing.

2. *The majority of young children show a common directionality in drawing simple forms. This directionality in the drawing act is probably influenced by components of motor development. The way the object drawn is oriented on the page is also predictable for most children, and likewise may be related to motor development.*

a. *Directionality in drawing shows developmental trends.* The development of directionality in drawing was the subject of an extensive investigation by Gesell and Ames (1946). Approximately 1,500 drawings were secured from children between the ages of eighteen months and seven years, most of whom were tested semiannually, and from twelve adults. The tasks included drawing a vertical and a horizontal stroke in imitation of the examiner, copying a cross, a circle, a square, and a rectangle with a diagonal, and copying a diamond from a printed form. Of the reported findings, the following seem to be reliably established: (1) For both the vertical and horizontal strokes the average length of line increases as age increases. This probably reflects more purposeful action as well as improved control in use of the hand. (2) Symmetry in the form of the cross improves with age, as does the tendency to make the cross by means of two intersecting lines (rather than half-lines to the point of intersection, then completed by a separate line). (3) Younger children commonly draw both the square and the diamond using four separate lines. Older children and adults usually draw the square using a single continuous line, but are likely to use four downward strokes for the diamond. Gesell and Ames also note the usual errors in copying the square and the diamond, but these are too well known to require description here.

Gesell and Ames (1946) found no consistent relationship between directionality and handedness. Rice (1930a), however, had 293 subjects ranging in age from two-and-one-half to fourteen copy the diamond presented in both the horizontal and the vertical position. She found that right-handed subjects commonly follow a clockwise system in making the strokes. Although her number of left-handed subjects was too small to yield highly dependable results, the indicated trend is that left-handed subjects follow a counter-clockwise system. Other findings are similar to those obtained by Gesell and Ames.

b. *Orientation of the figure on the page appears to be related to handed-*

ness, but, with age, comes under the influence of cultural conventions of reading and writing. Orientation in the direction depicted in railway trains drawn by kindergarten and primary grade children in Japan and Formosa was studied by Iinuma and Watanabe (1937). They have presented the following figures: of 1,648 drawings collected, 26 were front views, and the direction of 105 could not be determined. Of the remainder, more than 80 per cent of the trains were shown traveling toward the left.

Stimulated by this report, Ballinger (1951) asked Indian children of the Southwest to illustrate this subject: "A boy is riding across the desert on a horse. Suddenly it starts to rain and he must hurry to his home." Three hundred and ninety-three paintings and drawings were analyzed according to a series of criteria. Fifty-seven per cent oriented the human figure toward the left; 21 per cent to the right; 1 per cent gave a frontal interpretation, and 21 per cent gave mixed or indeterminate interpretations. (In addition, some subjects introduced a dog or other figure, facing in an opposite direction to the main figure.) It should be noted that Ballinger interpreted the drawing as a whole, using clues to show direction of rain, wind, etc., not merely the direction of the horse and rider. Thus, of the drawings showing direction, 73 per cent were oriented, as a whole, to the left, and 27 per cent to the right. Ballinger made the interesting observation that when a group of older adolescents (ages fourteen to twenty-one) were separated from the total, the percentages differed. Of the younger children, 82 per cent oriented to the left; while of the older group, only 52 per cent oriented in that direction.

Hildreth (1941) reported a similar left-orientation tendency in the drawings of the boy whom she studied; however, no exact figures were given. Among right-handed children, unwillingness to cover their work with the hand that holds the pencil seems the best explanation for this tendency. This point has been particularly stressed by Østlyngen (1948) and by Zazzo (1950). A similar trend has been noted in drawings of animals and in profile drawings of human figures; both usually face toward the left. Zesbaugh (1934) noted this in her analysis of more than 10,000 drawings of a mailman.

Jensen (1952a) asked children in Egypt and Norway, and from various social and educational backgrounds in America to draw a human profile. In each group the majority of profiles faced left. Egyptian children in almost the same proportion as American rural children (66 per cent) faced profiles to the left. Urban and high socioeconomic status American children significantly exceeded this proportion, while Norwegians gave the highest percentage of left-oriented drawings. Jensen concluded:

> Although the majority of our S's faced their profile drawings toward the left, the left-to-right reading habit is not regarded as the chief determiner of profile orientation. There is a possibility that the left-to-right reading habit may strengthen a tendency for left orientation and that the right-to-left reading habit may weaken such a tendency. Probably there are other cultural factors affecting profile orientation but they are not identified. Profile orientation may be slightly affected by handedness (1952a, p. 83).

This conclusion is further supported by Jensen's study (1952b) of almost 9,000 Japanese children, the majority of whom also faced their drawings to the left. However, there is a steady and significant decline in such orientation with age, and with experience in right-to-left reading practice. At age fifteen, the per cent facing the profile to the left approaches 50, or the theoretical "chance" figure. It should be recalled, however, that Ballinger noted a similar trend in Navajo children, whose reading experience was from left to right.

Dennis (1958) also observed children's drawings in culture groups contrasted in orientation of handwriting: Americans who write English and Lebanese who write Armenian—from left to right; Lebanese and Egyptians who write Arabic—from right to left. Approximately half the children in each sample oriented the drawing to the top and to the side of the page on which writing is normally begun. In each sample, the remaining half began their drawing in various other positions on the page. His data on drawing behavior are consonant with a habit-transfer hypothesis but do not explain the variation within the group.

Cases of inversions in the up-down orientation of children's drawings are reported by Belart (1943), Billing (1935), and Gerald (1928). For the most part, interpretations are the same as those generally given for inversions found in the writing of young children. Although Pearson (1928) regards his cases of inverted drawings as very unusual at the ages specified (five to six years), they are actually more common than he supposed, as any kindergarten teacher will testify. It has been observed that primitive peoples entirely unacquainted with the conventions of printing and of pictures have considerable difficulty at first in relating the idea of "up" with the top of the paper. Graewe (1935) observed that one of the first distinctions to appear between the human and animal figures as drawn by young children is the vertical orientation of the human figure and the horizontal orientation of the animal figure.

c. *Features of motor development other than handedness also influence developmental trends in drawing.* Naville (1950b), working with children's paintings, concluded that the young child's tendency to daub before he produces lines is actually an exteriorization of gross, diffuse smooth muscle and autonomic activity. Once highly controlled striped muscle activity becomes possible, lines appear, and drawings become increasingly socially conditioned as to form, material and instrument preferred. Belves (1950) noted that as they grow, children normally move from graphism, to filling in pre-drawn sketches, to direct painting.

d. *The motor behavior in the drawing act serves to guide the production, especially in work by preschool children.* As long ago as 1913 Rouma observed that young children name their first drawings according to fancied resemblances after completion. Later, while engaged in drawing, they will name the work in terms of some feature produced quite fortuitously. It is only later still that children announce in advance what their drawings will be. Rey (1950) affirmed that older children also do not draw solely from a mental picture of their subjects but are influenced by the drawing process itself. After a stroke has been made, the child artist sees and uses cues in the changed sketch and thus is progressively guided in making further strokes. The drawing act is thus governed by factors intrinsic to the process, and some of these may reflect Gestalt principles. Bender (1932) has made much of this point. From evidence on perceptual processes in children, to be discussed later, it appears that young children are relatively more influenced by motor aspects of drawing; secondary schemata arising out of experience, and visual imagery play a more important role in later years.

Child psychology has long recognized the significance of motor activity in the child's exploration of his world, his language growth, his concept formation and his social development. It is, thus, not surprising to discover that the motor components of a complex, expressive act may be significant, especially in the early phases of its organization.

e. *Although his motor behavior may guide a child's execution and interpretation of his drawings, his work after the acquisition of speech primarily reflects comprehension and cognition.* In a study to be discussed more fully later, Meili-Dworetzki (1957) concluded that the preschool child commonly interprets drawings much as he performs them; that is, the same limitations of idea that appear in drawings appear also in children's discussions of the drawings. An unpublished study by Campbell (1958), conducted experimentally with carefully chosen samples of children, amply confirmed Meili-Dworetzki's finding that children interpret drawings in much the same manner as they produce them. Campbell showed a simple "face" with two lines projecting below to twenty children in each of seven age groups. Over half the three- and four-year-olds, and one-sixth of the five-year-olds called these "legs"; all the children six and over saw this feature as a "neck." When asked to copy a simple profile face, no three-year-olds, only a sprinkling of four-year-olds, about half of the five-year-olds, but a large majority of the six-year-olds and seven-year-olds, and all of the eight-year-olds and nine-year-olds complied. Thus, the relationship between comprehension and execution in young children is close, and one probably cannot logically or empirically separate the motor from the cognitive in interpreting children's drawings.

That the child interprets drawings in the manner of his execution, and that he moves from simple to complex forms, extends also to his preferences in art. French (1952) conceived the idea of relating the features displayed by children's drawings and paintings to the elements of pictures they preferred and rejected. Selecting the ages of seven and eleven as representing two rather different stages, he hypothesized that children will respond favorably to those pictures whose organizational pattern is comprehensible to them. He further hypothesized that these aspects of organization which are comprehensible are the same as those characteristic of the productions of children at particular developmental stages. Where younger children use clear-cut unbroken unaccented lines, older children often experiment with sketchy and incomplete lines; where younger children use unvaried color locally within drawn outlines, older children often use variegated, blended colors to suggest effects of texture and atmosphere; where younger children represent objects in flat, two-dimensional outlines, older children attempt linear and aerial perspective, use overlapping, and reduce size with distance; where younger children isolate forms, older children experiment with composition and attempt to represent the entire figure from a consistent point of view.

French, an artist, prepared thirteen pairs of simple representational pictures equated as to content but varying according to the above-listed principles. A group of elementary school teachers consistently preferred the more complex member of each pair, whereas 83 per cent of first-grader's choices went to the simpler members of each pair. No sex differences appeared at any point in his study. Interestingly, the tendency to prefer the simple forms *increased* from kindergarten to the second grade and then decreased thereafter, and sharply so after the third grade. Had the investigator prepared his simple compositions to reflect the elements used by kindergarteners, would his results have shown a straight line rather than a curvilinear trend? Possibly the representational work of preschool children is so very simple and rudimentary that satisfactory experimental stimulus pictures, matched as to content, could not be prepared. French, however, has demonstrated his point—that children's preferences differ from adults' due to differences in comprehension.

3. *Children's drawings represent objects as they perceive them. Even the simplest, most "primitive" drawings are wholes, yet contain discernible parts. With increased age this whole or Gestalt quality of drawings shows a progression; it is more detailed, and at the same time more complexly organized.*

a. *Children's drawings are at first influenced more by concrete features than by abstract properties of objects.* The Goodenough method of scoring drawings has shown conclusively that the representation of features of the human figure increases with mental growth. Evidence from many other sources suggests that a similar process occurs in the representation of other familiar objects. Age norms in Goodenough's and the present study show that the appreciation of abstract properties of the human figure, such as relative size or proportional and spatial relations between parts, develops much more slowly than the awareness of the existence of parts. Goodenough, as well as others, long ago observed that children seem to depict first the parts which have a particular significance for them at the time. It may be that this increase in detail is related to the visual process itself; children may perceive the whole or the largest masses earliest, and then supply the detail as visual experience increases. (In Chapter X evidence on children's perception is explored in greater detail.)

Meili-Dworetzki (1957) has reported on long-term detailed observations of children in family and neighborhood settings and on drawings collected from over 100 other children two to seven years of age, in both free and controlled settings. She concluded that the concept of the human body and its parts is derived more from seeing others than from experiencing the self physically. The infant's and young child's awareness of his own body seems to follow a definite sequence: hands, feet, face, trunk. From age two to four, the feature most prominent in the child's awareness of his own body is his abdomen, or belly. The abdomen is prominent in his conversation and in his attention to his own body. This portion of the anatomy, however, plays virtually no role in the perception and image of others, as evidenced by oral sentence completion tasks, definitions tests, and general interviews and discussions. Rather, the child's awareness, or image, of other persons' bodies is concentrated on the head (especially the eyes), followed by a global awareness of the total figure, within which the various parts slowly become differentiated.

In his drawing of the human figure, as we have seen, the child manifests much the same order of awareness. Head (and face) and the vertical dimension dominate, the latter indicated either by a line or (more commonly) by an undifferentiated, elongated form. Often the global, "rest of the body," comes after the appearance of the face. Meili-Dworetzki reports a most interesting phenomenon; the child at the scribbling stage can often tell more about the human body orally than children who have already begun to depict the human figure. When asked to describe parts of the body, there is very little progress in the number of parts enumerated between the ages of two and five!

Meili-Dworetzki also asked a number of children to tell her how to draw a man, what to draw first, and so on. Most children described or listed only those parts which they themselves included in drawings. Their oral descriptions and their drawings were almost identical, with the exception of the very youngest subjects who could not draw at all. Older children, five-, six-, and seven-year-olds, drew more parts than they mentioned orally. Meili-Dworetzki hypothesized that children develop an underlying graphic pattern (head and legs; later, head—trunk—legs) for the human figure. Through a certain compression the child becomes preoccupied with achieving a synthesis of parts which previously seemed unconnected. This synthesis, or structure, is all he can keep in mind. As he becomes aware of a coordinating principle, he states in words less of the figure's complexity than he did before he recognized any order. Thus it is possible that there is an interaction or "feedback" between perception and reproduction in drawing, such that the child's perceptions and drawing representations reinforce or modify one another in the construction of concepts.

b. *In comprehending the concrete features of objects, young children may depend on tactual and kinesthetic cues relatively more than do older children, who seem to depend primarily on visual cues.* The importance of the tactile sense in perception has only recently been recognized (Frank, 1957; Philip Solomon, *et al.,* 1961) although Revesz (1950) and Lowenfeld (1939) both gave it a considerable place in their discussions of the art of the blind. Lowenfeld particularly considered the tactile sense to be a more primitive, fundamental mode of apprehending reality; one closely linked to affect. Volkelt (1926) observed that in their drawings children frequently emphasize the pointedness and angularity of objects, and exaggerate dimensions to portray movement. He believes these qualities express children's perceptions rather than their immaturity or lack of skill with a pencil.

Mira (1940) has presented an elaborate theory of the kinesthetic-motor expression of temperament in drawings, but apparently has conducted no research to test his hypotheses. Young children seem to live closer to their sensory and motor experience than do adults; they possess fewer abstractions and less complex structures of meaning for classifying their perceptions. Hence, young children use more emotional referents, identify aspects of objects with immediate sensory experience, and the like, as many investigators have pointed out. In a later discussion of the organismic theory of children's drawings, this point will be more fully discussed.

Research on tactual stimulus localization appears to show a developmental shift from tactual to visual localization in sighted subjects (Renshaw, *et al.,* 1930). In form discrimination studies, young children quite commonly trace with their fingers, apparently finding kinesthetic and tactual cues helpful to visual perception.[1]

The influence of motor components on cognition has long been affirmed by child psychology. Mott (1945) with children, and Geck (1947) with college students have shown that adding kinesthetic experience to visual and auditory impressions improves the quality of drawings. Mott had children exercise parts of the body as a group "game" before drawing the human figure. Geck emphasized specific tactual and kinesthetic experience by having students explore manually a modelled human head before sketching it. Practical manuals for the training of artists have long stressed this point.

c. *As children grow in maturity they draw objects as increasingly differentiated, yet organized, wholes.* As they grow older children depict more features in the objects represented. The parts always fit the representation; the object is always a unity. Indeed, incongruities are taken to suggest abnormalities in mental growth.

Variations in style resulting from differences in manner of perceiving part-whole relationships at different ages were studied by Kobayashi (1937) and by H. Martin (1932). These investigators, however, regarded the child's product as evidence of the child's perception. Both found that with age there is an increasing tendency to perceive an object or figure as a differentiated whole, rather than as a conglomeration of parts. Much the same results are reported by Kato (1936) for Japanese kindergarten children who were asked to draw from a doll model of a man. At first only the main parts were drawn, then details were added, until finally the concept of the figure as a whole with differentiated parts was indicated. The careful, detailed observations of Meili-Dworetzki (1957), already mentioned, support this view. Probably both theories are correct: (1) Children's drawings present a progressively differentiated *conception,* regardless of the children's immediate perceptual experiences. (2) Increasing skill in technique enhances the represented conception. Ignat'ev (1950) applied a technique similar to Barnhart's (see below), but concluded

[1] This view, as will be shown later, assumes considerable importance in Bell's (1952) analysis of the psychology of drawing.

that children's drawings reflect more their understanding of the task, and the techniques required, than their perception of the world. He urged drawing instruction to sharpen perception and give an understanding of the drawing task itself.

d. *The organization of a drawing containing many objects, as the organization of the details of an object, proceeds according to a describable sequence of stages.* The hypothesis that, in drawing, children proceed from the whole to the parts is not entirely confirmed by Barnhart (1942), who constructed an ingenious device for studying the problem. It consisted of a frame in which the drawing surface covered a sheet of carbon paper which, in turn, covered a long sheet of paper wound on a roller. At intervals of one minute, while drawing, the subject was asked to pause while the lower paper was pulled out to the length of one panel. This made it possible to determine the order of drawing. Fifty-two children between the ages of five and sixteen years were asked to make a picture of children playing in the snow in a park. Some children, chiefly the older ones, began with a broad outline of the entire picture and later filled in the details; but the younger children more frequently completed each detail separately before passing on to the next. The complexity of the subject is likely to have been a contributing factor in this case, but it would be interesting to know what characteristics other than age differentiated the two groups.

Barnhart further examined the manner in which space was depicted by children of different ages. His findings are very similar to those obtained by Stern (1909) and others many years ago. At first there is no apparent concept of graphic portrayal of space; objects are scattered at random over the paper.[2] This is followed by a linear form of representation in which objects are arranged in a row, usually upon a ground line. Next comes a period of ranked space in which there are two or more rows. The ground lines in the background are either straight or curved to indicate relative distance. This technique shows only a rudimentary idea of perspective. A transitional period follows leading to the final idea of "true space," with recognition of such factors as perspective, partial concealment of objects in the background by those in the foreground, foreshortening, and the like. Lack of skill may still lead to very crude ways of depicting these factors. These are essentially the stages described by Lowenfeld (1957).

4. *Central or cognitive factors appear to be crucial in determining developmental features of children's drawings.*

a. *In drawings of a model, changes appear which are associated with age and, presumably, with mental level.* As a test of mental development, Rey (1947) experimented with children's drawings of small wooden cubes piled in different arrangements and viewed from different angles. He assumed that a

---

[2] Even at age five or six, association between persons or objects is shown by placing them near each other or even in juxtaposition; but the concept involved seems to be that of a functional relationship, rather than that of position in space.

concrete model would reassure the timid child who lacked imagination. Age changes were evident, but the test was scored by a rating procedure that allowed a total variance of only six points; such a "test" is necessarily limited in power. Rey's data show that reassured or not, children are decidedly limited in the ability to draw from three-dimensional models.

Osterreith (1944) studied the child's ability to copy, both from inspection and from memory, a line drawing of complex geometric design. Scoring this drawing on a point basis, he found negatively accelerated age curves, which levelled off at about nine years. On the other hand, Neubauer (1931) reported that adolescents, when asked to decorate and complete an outline drawing of a teapot, showed a distinct age progression in use of color, geometric patterns, composition, and the emergence of idealistic and realistic types. These findings differ markedly from those generally reported for adolescents unselected as to aptitude for graphic art. To copy a complex geometric design, for which the child has no memory image or schematic referents, may actually be a somewhat different perceptual-conceptual task than to draw a figure for which considerable associations exist. "Decorating and completing" a basic outline may differ as a psychological task from constructing the figure, just as drawing a familiar object may differ from copying a complex geometric figure.

Townsend (1951) conducted a study designed to identify certain correlates of the ability to copy. He used geometric figures—a total of fifteen items including the Bender-Gestalt designs—with a large group of children six to nine years of age. He rated the children's work on: (1) the inclusion of components, (2) general form, (3) correct orientation, and (4) a "preciseness" element not adequately defined in the report, but seemingly a rating of size relationship to the model. The battery also included tests of form perception, motor skill, and intelligence. His results showed that copying ability of children may be much more highly correlated with form perception than with motor skill. When mental age was controlled, for example, form perception correlated $+.18$. This finding led the author to suggest that in both form perception and copying, higher mental age permits more adequate form comprehension. In general, copying skill correlated more highly with mental age than with chronological age; this ability increased to about C.A. seven and slowed down thereafter, whereas it increased to M.A. eight before slowing. Gollin (1960) has published some simple designs useful for studying the ability of young children to copy.

Campbell's study (1958), already referred to, contained the suggestion that alterations in copying a model result from perceptual errors. While Campbell used a wholistic approach to discuss his findings, he denied that Gestalt laws could entirely explain his observations. For example, given an incomplete schematic drawing of the human body (arms missing, and legs not joined to the trunk), many of the three-year-olds, most of the fives and sixes, and all the sevens and older added arms. Only a few children at each age filled in lines to attach the legs without adding the arms. Campbell concluded that evidence for a "strength of Gestalt" feature of children's drawing was thus not entirely confirmed.

Campbell also presented an angle of 41 degrees, first as an open angle, and then as part of a parallelogram, with instructions to copy it. Not all children, especially among the younger groups, could do this; but of those who attempted it, the four-year-olds overestimated the angle by 18 degrees, on the average, whereas all the older children came, on the average, within 4 degrees or less of the model. In copying the parallelogram, the tendency to produce a rectangle, and thus to overestimate the angle, was much stronger, especially among the fours, fives, and sixes, where the overestimation was close to 40 degrees. The overestimation was less for children aged seven and older.

Campbell's hypotheses, which he believed were confirmed by these data, stated that children's drawings exhibit simplification tendencies because systematic biases affect human cognition, and these biases are stronger in less experienced individuals. The origin of these biases was discussed in a paper by Campbell and Gruen (1958), which treated the progression from simple to complex drawings as a molar law of learning. Some of the bias is perceptual and apparently inherent. One effect of experience (i.e., learning) is to overcome this initial bias; another is to produce more complex cognitive structures.

Campbell believed his findings also demonstrated that children's perceptions differ from those of adults *not* just as randomly imperfect versions of adult performances, but as systematic (hence, developmental) deviations. To check this hypothesis further, he included an optical illusion test (length of lines), ingeniously presented so as to eliminate failure due to misunderstanding and incompetence. He found that while all age groups were influenced by the illusion, the younger children were much more susceptible to it.

b. *When a time interval occurs between viewing the model and making the drawing, systematic rather than aimless modifications take place in drawings.* Graewe's intensive study (1932) of over six thousand drawings, by subjects from the preschool to the adult level, included both free drawings and drawings from a model, with later reproduction from memory. His treatment of the data is descriptive only; there are no tables and few quantitative statements of any kind. However, his long and intensive study of the problem enabled him to make many keen observations with respect to developmental changes relating to: (1) the tendency to perseveration, (2) the trend toward concreteness, and (3) the manner of representing space or perspective, foreshortening, and the like.

It has been recognized that adults' perceptions tend to incorporate the new into the known or familiar. Goodenough (1926) cited two early studies, by Paulsson (1923) and by Albien (1907) to show that a subject's perception of *meaning* in a stimulus influenced what he selected to draw and the manner of his depiction. Albien reached the fairly modern conclusion that the primary factors in the ability to reproduce a recalled figure are: (1) directed observation and analysis followed by (2) the organization of many partial elements into a unified whole. He also concluded that observation *per se* is less important than the relationships observed.

Both of the above-mentioned researchers anticipated the now better-known studies of Gibson (1929) and of Carmichael, Hogan, and Walter (1932), that showed the effects of idiosyncratic aspects of perception upon drawing reproduction. Gibson intended to study how observers learn to reproduce correctly a number of geometrical figures, and the decay of this learning over time after stimulus presentation has ceased. He discovered that he could not complete his study as designed because the exact reproduction of a figure never occurred, even after numerous presentations! He noted that modifications occurred systematically and suggested that at least five "modes of apprehension," based on five ways in which reproductions were modified from stimulus figures, could be consistently discerned among his subjects. The most frequent mode reflected the influence of figures previously exposed in the series. The next most frequent mode reflected a perceived similarity between the figure presented and a familiar object; the reproduction was modified to resemble more closely the object the figure was seen to resemble. Another mode of apprehension was more common on broken or interrupted figures; these figures were often "completed" in reproduction, but sometimes more decisively broken or separated into components. Less commonly, reproductions were influenced by verbal tags or descriptions attached in the perception of the stimulus figures. A final mode consisted of straightening curved lines.

Gibson took his experiments to indicate that conceptual materials, in the absence of visual models, influence reproduction of visually perceived forms, and this process follows systematic lines of occurrence, reflecting the manner in which the figure is apprehended. He concluded that his data argued against a single law of perception and for the existence of a variety of perceptual habits which arise in individual experience.

The famous sequel study, by Carmichael, *et al.*, showed that descriptive words associated with ambiguous figures "slanted" reproductions in the direction of the object suggested by the words, overriding idiosyncratic associations of observers. Both of these studies emphasize that form perception and reproduction are greatly influenced by experience, both past and present.

c. *A tendency to simplify or to concretize the model when it is reproduced from memory has frequently been reported.* An experiment by Kröber (1938) incorporated explicit kinesthetic and motor elements into perception and examined the effect on drawing from memory. More than four thousand children between the ages of thirteen and sixteen years drew from memory a picture of a formboard into which they had previously fitted eighteen simple geometrical figures—a circle, a square, a star, etc. Half of the subjects made the drawing immediately after fitting the forms in place; the remainder, after a lapse of two hours. No age differences were noted within the range covered, but boys reproduced more figures than girls, though the sex differences were not large. The more complex the figure, the more likely it was to be modified in accordance with its "meaning" for the subject.

Lark-Horowitz (1936), who compared children and adults with respect to their ability to draw a series of figures from memory, found that although on the average the adults did better than the children, there were many adults who drew considerably simplified representations, as do children. She commented particularly on the interrelationship, or "interlinkage," of different sensory modalities in producing the memory image. Due to this interlinkage, drawings by different persons vary in accordance with the type of sense impression dominant in that person when the image was formed.

Rostohar (1928) had elementary school children reproduce from memory a number of designs, some of which were in black and white, others in color. After each unsuccessful attempt the original was again exposed and a new trial given. This was continued until an approximately correct copy was made, or until it became apparent that no further improvement was likely. Examination of the successive trials showed that two different methods were employed in building up the memory image. Some children proceeded from the general contour to the details, while others worked from the parts to the whole. Retests at weekly intervals indicated that the process of forgetting followed in reverse order the same general plan as the process of learning. Children belonging to the first group forgot the details before the general form was forgotten; those of the second group retained details after the main figure could no longer be recalled.

Two papers by Slochower (1946 a,b) described the attempts of children between the ages of five and ten years to reproduce line drawings of a geometrical figure in each of three media—pencil and paper, clay, and Tinker Toy. The younger children kept to the two-dimensional forms shown in the models with only such minor variations as were necessitated by the medium used. Children of nine and ten, however, showed a definite tendency toward the construction of three-dimensional forms when the clay and Tinker Toys were used. Slochower also found, as have others, a definite tendency to simplify the more difficult forms and an increase, with age, in accuracy of reproduction.

d. *A tendency to amplify or "interpret" a model reproduced from memory has also been reported.* Burton and Tueller (1941) found that children may *amplify* a drawing for the purpose of giving it more meaning. These investigators asked nursery school children to make successive copies of a schematic human face until they refused to make more. Children frequently added elements to the "face"; the results were similar whether the model remained before the children or was removed after the first reproduction.

The Burton and Tueller study may be considered a "satiation" experiment, of which the work of Lewin (1935) was the prototype. Lewin compared the drawing performances of normal and feeble-minded children. Bender (1940) conducted a similar experiment with children suffering from organic brain damage. All these investigators found that when it serves to give concrete meaning to a relatively abstract symbol, the tendency to amplify is more common than the tendency to simplify. However, this is true only when the original stimulus is well within the child's ability to copy, and seems to him an imperfect or incomplete representation of the object he conceives it to depict. In spite of the complexity of studying the conditions under which children amplify in copying designs and under which they simplify, more research should be done in this area.

With the purpose of studying behavior under increasing frustration, Seashore and Bavelas (1942) obtained a drawing of a man, using Goodenough's instructions. Upon completion of the drawing, they immediately asked the subject to make another man, "this time a better one." This request was repeated until the children refused, or until a maximum of fifteen drawings had been obtained. Apart from overt verbal and motor behaviors showing frustration, ten of the fifteen subjects progressively produced lower scores, though many were quite erratic in this trend. Some appeared to show "escape efforts" by adding extraneous elaborations—designs, flowers, etc.—to their drawings.

e. *The tendencies to simplify and to amplify, or "interpret," are also present in the drawings of children who copy directly from models.* Hildreth (1944) commented on the tendency among children to simplify that which is too difficult, or to give meaning to that which is meaningless. Both Sorge's (1940) work with rural and urban European children and Homma's (1937) work with Japanese children lead to a similar conclusion and suggest that the tendency is geographically widespread. Portocarrero de Linares (1948) studied 1,375 girls from the public schools of Lima, Peru, ranging from kindergarten to sixth grade. Each subject copied a series of eight designs printed on the test blank. Most of the designs were highly conventionalized representations of common objects, such as a table or a fish. The following eight categories appeared: (1) entirely correct reproduction, (2) correct except for minor errors in proportion or symmetry, (3) amplification, i.e., the addition of elements not present in the model, (4) simplification, (5) deformation, (6) broken structures in which changes were made in the conventionalized figure in order to bring about a closer resemblance to the real object, (7) concretization, in which realistic changes were introduced into the conventionalized example, and (8) confabulation, in which the subject apparently drew pictures at will, with no attempt to copy the model.

There was general improvement with school grade for all the models, but a comparison of changes in the various categories is interesting. In all grades and for all models, simplification was much more common than amplification. In sixth grade, for example, the relative proportions were 12.9 per cent to 0.6 per cent. Concretization and confabulation were largely confined to the kindergarten and preparatory classes except in the case of the much-conventionalized fish, for which the percentages in the former category continued to make up an important percentage of the total throughout the first four grades.

Burkhardt (1933) attempted experimentally to control the complexity of familiar forms and meaningless figures by equating them in terms of the number of lines and angles. Alterations of form, which in Burkhardt's opinion represent "improvements" from the child's point of view, were much more common in copying familiar forms than in copying meaningless figures. Apparently, unless a child is able to see some meaning in a figure at the start, he is not likely to improve upon it. Although Portocarrero de Linares did not classify her figures with respect to their meaningfulness, it may be noted that her Models II and VIII, which appear to be the least abstract in her series, do tend to show more alterations in the direction of concreteness than the others.

Prudhommeau (1947) devised a "test" of eighteen line drawings, to be reproduced from direct inspection rather than from recall. His published results are limited to case studies and general statements of trends and do not include statistical data. Unlike virtually all other investigators, he concluded that the young child's simplified or "schematic" drawing results not from conceptual limitations but from limitations of time, attention and energy. To the present writer, the few cases presented in detail appear to represent only very advanced or intellectually gifted children.

Apparently, no universal statement can yet be made with respect to the tendency to add or omit elements in drawings made from memory or from examples; this varies with the difficulty and meaningfulness of the material. Moreover, difficulty and meaningfulness are not absolute factors, but depend on the maturity and knowledge of the subjects. Complex figures, especially those that are not familiar, tend to be simplified by children as well as by adults. Under some conditions, amplification, by the addition of details necessary to give a more obvious meaning, may occur.

It is hard to escape the conclusion that the person's cognitive content is fundamental; both simplifications and amplifications usually lead to "meaningfulness"—the incorporation of the object into a familiar body of concepts.

f. *In children's drawings, language development and use are related to drawing performance.* In an earlier discussion, Mott's study (1945) was cited as showing the influence of motor involvement on children's drawings. It should be remembered that children not only went through a motor drill with respect to body parts, but named the parts in chorus as they proceeded with the drill. As may be recalled, these children showed gains in Goodenough scores, based largely on the body parts involved. That Harris (1950) failed to find any effect of rhythmic body exercise on Goodenough scores may have resulted from the fact that children's attention was not drawn *verbally* to the motions and postures of arms and legs; the exercise was a dance, demonstrated in pantomime.

In a comprehensive study of mentally retarded children up to age fourteen in the Netherlands, Stotijn-Egge (1952) found the same drawing sequence observed in normal children of about three to eight years of age. However, none of her "non-performing" children (those who made no drawings at all) possessed words; "scribblers" in every case had a few words, and nearly half of them had speech; all children who achieved recognizable drawings of objects had more or less acquired language. The "drawers" preferred to draw the human figure, but all except one could copy a circle, square and vertical cross. Fewer were able to copy a triangle or rhomboid. Only a small proportion could copy a tree, table, or house. About half of those with language drew one or more of the following objects on request: animal, house, car, boat. Very few of these could draw a bottle or a cube placed before them as a model.

While these results are extremely suggestive, they cannot be taken as proof that language is necessary to successful drawing. Children with serious language defects, due to deafness for example, do produce drawings, although the performance is somewhat retarded (Shirley and Goodenough, 1932). Research on children's concepts uniformly concludes that concepts are greatly enhanced by language. Bühler (1930) considered that the development of language first aids drawing and ultimately defeats it as a mode of expression.

Summary

From his earliest years, the child's pencil or crayon marks have *form*. This form is due partly to the mechanical arrangements of the human hand and wrist, and partly to developmental trends in the achievement of complex motor control. The way in which form is achieved, through the directionality of marking movements and the orientation of the object on the page, likewise seems to be a matter of handedness and factors of motor development; cultural conventions of directionality are overlaid on these primary preferences. Motor aspects of the drawing act, however, at all stages of development have some influence on the *form* of drawings and on the manner in which drawings are developed.

From the very outset, also, the child's drawings have *meaning*. This meaning is of much greater significance than explained by motor factors controlling the substance and arrangement of drawings. The child's progress from simple to more complex form, his preoccupation with concrete features of objects and, as he grows, his increasing ability to represent more such features in his drawings, may well depend upon his perceptual experience with objects. In deriving meaning, young children seem to depend more on motor and kinesthetic experience than on visual experience. Older children become increasingly "visual." These "improvements" with age and experience are such that with maturity children's drawings become increasingly more differentiated, yet remain organized wholes.

Children never portray objects exactly as they appear. In their drawings, they select, modify, and even add to what may be perceived in the object. These tendencies occur whether objects are copied from models or drawn from memory. The "meaningfulness" of the object to the child, even more than its difficulty (complexity and amount of detail), influences the drawing that is made. This effect can be noted regardless of the maturity of the child. Language seems to be closely related to the child's ability to draw; this fact adds strength to the conclusion that drawing for the child is primarily a cognitive process.

Chapter Ten

The Psychology
of Drawing: Theories

MODERN SCIENCE considers theory the *sine qua non* for experimentation and the discovery of laws. While, as has been shown, there are many descriptive and empirical studies of drawing, there are relatively few experimental investigations. This lack may occur because so few investigators have taken comprehensive theoretical positions concerning children's drawing behavior. Points of view exist more as philosophies than as empirically based theories. This chapter presents the more articulate theoretical positions that have appeared. It is hoped that this discussion will stimulate more truly experimental studies of drawing behavior.

In psychology, two implicit (and sometimes quite explicit) opposing viewpoints have long existed concerning the nature of the organism's development and function; that between nativists and empiricists. Although this distinction is no longer valid, it still appears in the literature of children's drawings. The fundamental question is how drawing, basically a succession of pencil or brush marks, becomes organized into form. Two or three writers have taken a *nativistic* position, holding that organization is given either by properties intrinsic to the stimulus field or intrinsic to the nervous system of the stimulated organism. These writers have tended to use the concepts of Gestalt psychology to express the intrinsic or "given" nature of organization in drawing behavior and its products. Two principal writers, likewise borrowing Gestalt concepts and language, state their positions in terms of an interaction between organism and its environing stimulus *field*. These writers have referred to their position as "organismic," but are more clearly wholistic than behavioristic in their thinking. Another general theoretical position uses the conditioning effects of experience to show how complex representations result from very simple beginnings. Several major contributors have taken such *empiricistic* positions and have used terms and concepts that in one form or another have come down from associationistic psychology. As will be shown, however, their interpretations are not based on simple mechanistic viewpoints. Rather, they are based on the interaction of a perceiving, learning organism and a succession of environmental stimuli, some of which are created by the organism's responses. The emerging viewpoint is, thus, empirical, organismic, and transactional.

With the possible exception of the most explicitly Gestalt-based theories, all discussants have noted the phenomena catalogued by the empirical studies reviewed earlier in this book. Although the theorists have generalized from these phenomena in rather different terms, all in one way or another found *concepts* and *cognitive processes* at the core of the drawing process. Except for a passing interest in line and geometric form, often noted in children age six or seven, spontaneous drawings uniformly depict *objects known in experience*.

Theories Implying an Inherent Organization

That the structure of children's drawings evolves, at least in part, through inherent features of children's physical and mental development is implicit in many discussions. To a greater or lesser degree such a theory is implicit in all so-called "developmental" approaches to creativity or to the expression of aptitudes. The notion, expressed most simply, is that the urge to express oneself is bound up with the potential, or capability, of the individual; all that capacity needs is an opportunity and some encouragement. Such a view has, in one form or another, been implicit in virtually all theories of art education and in many views of general education, especially in the elementary school.

That drawings are governed by laws of structure and form in the stimulus field is held in one way or another by many who are not formally identified as Gestalt theorists. Obviously, drawings require at least two psychological processes—perceptual (visual sensory) and expressive (motor). A third process, cognition, presumably mediating between perception and behavior, is sometimes posited also. The Gestaltists hold that perceptual processes, controlled by hypothesized neural actions in the brain, cause all stimulus situations to be experienced as "patterned" into figure-ground relationships. The responding organism is thus selectively oriented to the stimulus field. His motor responses are likewise patterned by neural activity, and may also be subject to Gestalt principles.

The literature on visual perception demonstrating the Gestalt principles is well known and will not be discussed here. The qualitative, subjective phenomena of art have appeared to be conveniently expressed by Gestalt theory, with its emphasis on wholes, organization, and phenomenalism generally. It is not surprising, therefore, that psychological theorists who approach art, or art theorists who seek a rapprochement with psychology, have generally turned to Gestalt psychology.

Gestalt Theories of Drawing

Britsch (1926) was one of the most clearly avowed Gestalt theorists in the field of art. His influence in the United States has been largely mediated by the writing and lectures of Henry Schaefer-Simmern (e.g., 1950), who has both crystallized and extended Britsch's original viewpoint. According to Schaefer-Simmern, drawing, as well as all artistic activity, has an intrinsic or inherent character whereby it evolves from simple to more complex forms. This feature is as much a part of drawing as growth is of the embryo, or the organism. However, graphic art follows a natural sequence only when untrammelled by artificial instruction. Though the end result is representative drawing, the child's early efforts (when untutored) are not to portray what he sees, what he remembers, or what he conceives abstractly.[1] Rather, his drawings follow strictly developmental laws, based on Gestalt principles of the contrast of figure and ground, the contrast of horizontal and vertical ("greatest contrast of directionality"), the "variability of direction," and the achievement of "unity" (organization) in this variability.

The child uses a form of conceptualization different from abstract conceiving, which results from knowledge. "Their [children's drawings] existence can be explained only as the result of a definite mental activity of conceiving relationships of form in the realm of pure vision" (1950, pp. 12–13)—an activity that may be called "visual conceiving" and its pictorial realization, which is "visual conception." What the child draws is, thus, not an idea resulting from a visual model. He draws much more than he knows; he draws a visual structure not based on knowing but on this inner process of visual conceiving. Schaefer-Simmern states:

> The term visual conception is used in a literal sense, to designate that which is conceived or begotten in the mind and which causes the birth of a visual configuration of form, that is, the *artistic form*. Mental activity that transforms the multiplicity of visual impressions into self-created visual unities leads to visual cognition. Visual cognition is the result of an immediate mental digestion of visual experience into a visual synthesis of form; it is not the result of an accumulation, registration, or reproduction of mere facts by means of conceptual activity (1950, p. 13).

This distinction between visual conceiving and abstraction is not commonly made in the usual psychological treatment of cognition. Indeed, the distinction as phrased by Schaefer-Simmern does not appear in Gestalt psychology, though he seemingly believes that the laws of Gestalt psychology govern his process of "visual conceiving."

While much of Schaefer-Simmern's writing is, to the psychologist, conceptually unclear and couched in confusing terms, his results with children are undeniably remarkable. Under his guidance, children and adults of limited social and intellectual backgrounds have produced complex and pleasing graphic compositions. It is quite possible, however, that the intrinsic patterns he finds are the result of his own teaching, much as he abjures such influence. One notes in his book a striking similarity from example to example and from child to child; such standardization is suspect, in view of the variation found in virtually all psychological characteristics and behavior. Reitman (1951,

---

[1] The term "abstract" is used here and elsewhere in this chapter in its psychological sense, as the consideration of a quality of an object apart from the object itself.

p. 138) has observed that the art products of mental patients clearly reflect their therapists' viewpoints; it is entirely possible that drawing "style" is learned in the very process of eliciting that "natural achievement" which is confidently expected by the teacher. Certainly the history of art amply illustrates the influence of a master on his pupils.

A much more psychologically sophisticated treatment of graphic art from the Gestalt viewpoint has resulted from the extensive work by Rudolph Arnheim (1954), who also owes an intellectual debt to Britsch. Arnheim's theory is systematic, and uses the laws and principles of Gestalt psychology, including the hypothetical cortical forces that pattern perception and behavior, to explain the observed facts of children's drawings.

For Arnheim, every act of seeing is a visual judgment, which is not affected by the intellect, but is spontaneous. In his theory, visual perception is central, and features inherent in the stimulus properties of objects as they are organized in the act of perception are of primary importance. Arnheim considers balance to be fundamental. Balance is a dynamic property inherent in cerebral processes that tend toward equilibrium in a complex, interactive, "field" relationship. Physical and perceptual equilibria are not to be conceived as identical; perceptual equilibrium has its own laws, though they may operate in an analogous fashion to those which establish physical equilibrium. Indeed, the operation of these laws in the stimulus field has effects in the psychological field. For example, balance eliminates ambiguity and disunity in the psychological field of forces. Conversely, the operation of these laws in the psychological field tends to achieve balance in the production of graphic art, where balance is known as "composition." Gestalt psychology seeks to formulate these laws.

Arnheim believes his position has cosmic significance. Just as all living processes are to be conceived of in dynamic terms, as active, striving and becoming (showing a continual effort to organize competing forces into some kind of equilibrium), so compositional balance in art "reflects a tendency that is probably the mainspring of all activity in the universe" (Arnheim, 1954, p. 21).

Such a theory related to graphic art inevitably places considerable emphasis on formal elements. These elements are conceived dynamically, however, because the basic psychological forces are continually organizing and reorganizing perceptions. Arnheim states: "A work of art is a statement about the nature of reality. From an infinite number of possible configurations of forces, it picks and presents one. . . . The work of art is the necessary and final solution of the problem of how to organize a reality pattern of given characteristics" (1954, pp. 21–22).

While the study of art may be approached from the analysis of finished products, it is instructive to consider the psychological processes involved in the behavior creating the works of art. The child's product is quite different from the adult's; simpler, less differentiated and complex. This situation comes about chiefly because the child reacts *visually* rather than *conceptually* (i.e., abstractly). The five-year-old's concept of a hand is that of radially spreading fingers—a visual impression; "fiveness" does not exist because such a concept is verbally (i.e., abstractly), not visually, presented. Children's drawings start with simple over-all features. While they draw what they see, they draw *less* than they see. They are limited by the medium they use, and achieve a *similarity in essential structural features*, but not isomorphic identity. The schooled artist does better because he has learned more possibilities (and techniques) in the medium. Arnheim believes that the development of children's art is a true prototype of the development of artistic form in general (1954, p. 134) and thus may properly be likened to "primitive" art. Because art is basically part of human motor activity, it reflects physiognomic (kinesthetic and affective) as well as descriptive elements. Because of this property, graphic art may be said to have "projective" significance.

Arnheim notes a developmental progression in perceptual processes and hence in the child's graphic work. He believes, however, that stages exist only in a general and theoretical sense. He describes these stages using Gestalt principles. The emergence of parts from wholes by a process of differentiation is central to these principles. The so-called incongruities of the child's drawings ("errors" of depth, dimension, and transparencies, etc.) are all the natural outcomes of childish logic, operating within the limitations of his medium. Such "errors" are his natural and ingenious solutions to problems posed by attempting three-dimensional visual representations in a two-dimensional medium. Some of the artist's solutions to these problems such as the "painterly style" and "aerial perspective" are beyond the child's reach and will not usually be spontaneously discovered by him. The young child's pictures are meager in content not because he fails to observe, but because his skill in representation does not permit him to incorporate much of what he has seen. Moreover, "the development of pictorial form rests on basic properties of the nervous system, whose functioning is not greatly modified by cultural and individual differences—hence child art is 'universal' " (p. 167).

Like Schaefer-Simmern, Arnheim believes that the broad brushes, fluid paints, and finger paints, so dear to the "expressive" school of thought in art education, actually constrict the child and compel in his work a narrow, one-sided picture of his potentiality. Significantly, Arnheim asks whether this constriction may in turn influence the child's understanding. In reacting to the dangers of copying models exactly, perhaps, as he says, art education has prevented the child from clarifying his observation of reality and hindered him from learning to create order!

An English art educator, Read (1945), has drawn heavily on Gestalt theory but, as has been pointed out, owes considerable to Jung's psychoanalytic theories as well. In the Gestalt notion that phenomenal experience produces cortical "electrostatic patterns," he finds the basis both for thought processes and for Jung's "primordial images," which in turn reveal unconscious processes of psychological integration. Although his theory is eclectic and unsystematic, Read has influenced art education.

"Organismic" Theories of Children's Drawings

The viewpoints represented under this broad term have stressed the continuing interaction of organism and environment as a developmental, adjustive process. These theories have been phenomenological, describing behavior from the viewpoint of the experiencing self or agent. They have drawn an analogy between the concepts of physical growth and concepts of behavior organization. Thus, they have used concepts of behavioral maturation and learning, stressing successive stages. These viewpoints, more readily than behaviorism, admit "cognitive processes," even "mental contents," as constructs or concepts. Consequently, it is not surprising to find that concepts or ideas are central to the organismic approach to children's drawing.

All studies of concept formation (e.g., Vinacke, 1951, 1954) and the language systems that embody them, especially those of children, seem to reveal a sequence of differentiable operations that can be called perception, abstraction, then generalization. Moreover, with development there is a definite change in these operations toward increased elaboration and differentiation. Objects at first noted as generally similar, later are seen to differ in certain respects. Such separation is accomplished as smaller details are discriminated by closer attention, by repeated comparisons with other objects in the same class, and often by sheer increase in total perceptual and cognitive experience. The fundamental aspect of this process seems to be the "eduction of relations," discerned in the earliest perceptions of children (Line, 1931).

Children's cognition, involving processes of perception, abstraction, and generalization, has been described in detail by Werner (1948), who has contributed a number of terms to what he has specifically called an organismic view of children's thinking. Basically, the young child's cognitive structure is less *differentiated* than it will become. With differentiation will also come superordination and subordination—the organization of simple concepts into patterns and meanings. Thus, the adult is cognitively more *organized*, and hence more *complex*, than the child.

Werner also considers the young child's cognitive processes as *concrete*, even though limited processes of abstraction and generalization manifest themselves very early. The child reacts to objects primarily in terms of their tangible properties, rather than in terms of their complex relations to other objects or to other experiences; he reacts to things perceived *directly* rather than to ideas about them. He grasps relationships between objects as given directly in his experience before he grasps relationships as understood or anticipated. He requests his doll or ball when he sees it in the room before he asks for the object to be brought to him out of its storage place in the cupboard. He can pile blocks into a "tower" long before he can understand piling as forming a particular construction, as a wall. He can copy a block building directly from a model before he can construct it from a picture.

Similarly, the child draws objects, or persons as objects, long before he portrays persons in relationship to each other or to objects in his environment. In these early drawings of a person a few salient features stand for the whole—

first the head; then head and appendages; then head, trunk, and appendages, and so on. Throughout development, processes of differentiation, organization and hierarchization can clearly be discerned.

Not only are young children's concepts more concrete and less differentiated than they will later become, they are also more *diffuse* in organization. This feature is particularly well illustrated by having children copy geometrical forms. Werner reproduced the drawing of an eight-year-old girl instructed to copy a six-sided pyramid atop a cylinder (see Fig. 49) combining two general features, roundness and angularity. How a child combines two qualities, wholeness and pointedness, in copying a diamond is shown in Figure 50. Volkelt (1926) showed that the diffuseness in organization of the child's percepts and concepts is not simply a matter of immaturity of motor coordination. In an experiment requiring choices, young children consistently preferred "primitive" reproductions of geometric forms to more highly articulated copies. The studies of French (1952), Meili-Dworetzki (1957), and Campbell (1958) have been noted; all of them agree with Volkelt that the child's "understanding" or conceptualization is limited, as is his ability.

FIG. 49. Six-sided pyramid on a cylinder, drawn by an eight-year-old girl

FIG. 50. Copies of a diamond-shaped figure drawn by four- and five-year-old children

The above figures are from Heinz Werner, *Comparative Psychology of Mental Development*, 1948, p. 120. Reprinted by permission of Follett Publishing Co., Chicago.

The young child's diffuseness of cognitive organization likewise contributes to his lability in interpreting his own work. As his work on a drawing proceeds, the young child's "purpose" or declaration of subject may change.

Werner (1948, p. 154) uses the expression *syncretism* to designate the condensation of complex meanings into simple forms. Such syncretism is a common feature of children's drawings as well as of their speech. Syncretism has two aspects: One simple form may stand for a complex object, and one form may combine aspects of different objects. A simple mark, or somewhat later a knob, represents foot and shoe alike, and only later is the shoe specified, first by heel, then by laces, or perhaps by sole edge and ornamentation. So "penny" or "nickel" designates all coins, and only later do differential names and values appear.

Also, various characteristics derived from different objects or experiences may be *condensed* into a composite. Such syncretism occurs in drawings that combine (somewhat in the fashion of dreams or fantasy) specific features of several different objects that have impressed the child; for example, one six-year-old's "man" for some time showed the painted cheeks of the clown in the circus, and the balloon which the child himself had purchased there. The modification of copied objects toward familiar objects, noted in the previous chapter, is an illustration of syncretism, and is achieved both by adding to and subtracting from the perceived stimulus.

Physiognomic Perception in Language and Drawing

In studying perception Gestalt psychologists have long emphasized the prepotency of the global over the particularized, the closed or completed over the open or incomplete. Werner notes that these tendencies also appear in children's drawings, even the earliest ones. The crudest "man" is a completed figure, however "bloblike" or nonrepresentative it may appear to the adult. The circularity or "wholeness," whether of head, or head-and-trunk in combination, always appears in children's drawing.

When the dominant total qualities have a particular emotional significance for the child, Werner speaks of *emotional perspective* (1948, pp. 148 ff.). This term refers to the exaggeration of those features of an object or of an experience having *affective* rather than *cognitive* significance for the child. Students of children's language have long observed that the early vocabulary is heavily weighted with words having affective rather than cognitive meaning (Lewis, 1951, p. 148; Markey, 1928, pp. 127 ff.). Werner explains this observation as resulting from the *physiognomic* quality of children's perceptions and concepts (1948, pp. 67 ff.). The physiognomic mode of perception, presumably used extensively by animals, children and primitives, arises from the fact that objects are understood first and most fundamentally through the motor-affective attitudes of the observer, who projects his own kinesthetic and visual cues onto the objects. Objects known thus by their actual or imputed dynamic qualities contrast with objects known through their "geometrical-technical," or matter-of-fact qualities.

Because the young child often uses language expressive of his own feelings and motor states to describe things-in-action, his thinking is said to be anthropomorphic, or *animistic*. Werner attributes the child's tendency to personify animals and inanimate objects to his physiognomic mode of perception and cognition, and considers animism to be a more elaborate and developed form of the same tendency (Werner, 1948, p. 75). As in language, drawings express affective, kinesthetic-motor and "concrete" meanings before they express cognitive, abstract ideas. Werner has described certain experiments on the expressive quality of lines, noted earlier in this book, as illustrative of physiognomic perception.

Professor van der Horst (1950), in his work in the Netherlands, was also impressed by this physiognomic quality of children's graphic art. For young children the *act* of drawing, not the *product*, is important. This, we have seen, is strikingly characteristic of the chimpanzee artist (Morris, 1962). Motor, kinesthetic and affective elements, says van der Horst, are more significant than visual-perceptual and cognitive aspects. The more drawing becomes a collection of parts (i.e., the more differentiated it becomes in the work of more mature, complex, differentiated personalities) the more its function resembles language. Because at the same time language skills are increasing (and, because the culture finds language so much more adequate for communication) the child leans more and more on language. Adolescence is, thus, a crucial period in the child's development of language and of drawings for communication.

Van der Horst also makes explicit the interesting point, implied by some others, that as the child's inner life becomes richer, more complicated and more abstract, drawing becomes a *less* adequate means of expression. Being a concrete activity, drawing is less adequate than is language for the expression of abstract ideas. Drawing activity declines in late childhood and early adolescence, not so much because it is inadequate for expressing new ideas and feelings appearing at this time, as because more adequate modes of expression have become available.

It is well to note van der Horst's emphasis on *cognitive* expression, for many writers who emphasize the expressive value of drawing and painting (particularly when viewed as a projective technique) refer to *affective* content. This point is important, because the evidence of many researches is that the cognitive aspects of drawing persistently obtrude themselves. Perhaps it is the affective aspect of expression in drawing that must be cultivated. The "natural" function of drawing as a symbolic system, whether to convey affect or cognition may be immaterial. In our society, as in most societies with a complicated material culture and a highly visual mode of education, children's drawings seem inevitably to gain the *carrier function* for cognition.

The impact of the visual world on a more fundamental method of comprehending has been particularly stressed by Lowenfeld's important experimental demonstrations of *haptic perception* (1939, 1945). The haptic mode of apprehending reality presumably draws heavily on tactual and kinesthetic modalities, and tends to be displaced by the visual mode as the person matures. Lowenfeld's haptic perception, thus, is closely akin to if not identical with Werner's physiognomic perception. Lowenfeld, however, developed his position more as educator than as scientist. His later writings (e.g., 1957) seek to evangelize a viewpoint in art education. More than others in art education, Lowenfeld has recognized that there are various avenues and styles for the expression of concepts, and seeks to represent the validity of all methods. His approach is consistently through the *experience* of the child, not through techniques for visual presentation. He asks children to draw their experiences, every attempt culminating in a discussion of the "how." Somewhat earlier than van der Horst, and in much the same terms, Lowenfeld (1947) also drew attention to the crisis in the development of graphic expression occurring at about the time of adolescence.

Lowenfeld's discussion of drawing development is not formally "organismic." It is "Gestaltish," but without reference to Gestalt laws. Lowenfeld's theory becomes organismic when he emphasizes the growth of the child through his continuing experience (i.e., interaction with environment) and when he emphasizes a progression through stages of development. While Lowenfeld rejects the classification of children's work according to "objective" criteria, his own more subjective criteria of artistic development (which for him is largely healthy emotional development) necessarily reflect a visually oriented, concept-valuing culture. He recognized this problem more explicitly in his earlier experimental work (Lowenfeld, 1939, 1945). Although Lowenfeld agrees with Werner that drawings express concepts or meanings, Werner is more concerned with how perception modifies concept formation; Lowenfeld with how concept formation modifies the drawing product.

The position Lowenfeld has taken is related primarily to personality development but is broadly educational rather than narrowly clinical. He views art experiences as stimulating growth in all conceivable dimensions. In particular, and unlike Read (1945), the function of art education is not so much to bring to awareness the content of the unconscious, as to activate passive knowledge. The mechanism is the development and enhancement of the self, or ego, through creating pleasing results with color, line, and form, and through expressing highly individual ways of viewing the world.

Lowenfeld believes that the haptic and visual types, discussed earlier, require different guidance and instruction to develop optimally. Psychological and educational harm results from imposing instruction inappropriate to the child's disposition; hence, Lowenfeld's emphasis on the teacher's need to observe and encourage the child's individual drawing procedures until the child's mode is determined. In a highly visual world, it is inevitable that the development and expression in many naturally haptic children will be distorted. The result may be mixed types and a predominance of the visual type.

From a psychologist's viewpoint, Lowenfeld's dual personality types may be overly simple, and his analysis of perception technically inadequate. However, more than others in art education, Lowenfeld has discerned the developmental character of children's concepts, the great variety of ways in which children meet and solve problems, the desirability of encouraging individual patterns of growth in assuring strong ego development, and the essentially unique character of personality. Psychologically, Lowenfeld's emphasis on observation of the child at work, as a key to understanding individual patterns of growth, is sound. Motor and kinesthetic, as well as visual and cognitive, aspects of experience have educational significance. Lowenfeld's discussions contain a wealth of ideas for the child psychologist and the student of experimental esthetics to work into research problems.

An Experimental Evaluation of Werner's Theory

The only experimental study based on Werner's "organismic" theory of drawing is that by Graham, Berman, and Ernhart (1960). These investigators started with Werner's concepts that young children's drawings show such "primitive" characteristics as tendencies to close open figures, to simplify complicated figures, and to increase symmetry. Using a drawing task in which three-, four-, and five-year-olds were asked to copy each of eighteen simple geometrical forms, all children were scored on each of the above tendencies. These evaluations showed that children's tendencies to simplify or to close incompleted, "open" figures decreased somewhat with age, but so did the logically opposite tendencies—toward complication and openness of reproduction. The percentage of drawings *less* symmetrical than the stimulus figures increased with age to four years and then decreased. The percentage of drawings *more* symmetrical than the stimuli decreased after age three-and-a-half, but less dramatically. Measures of eight indications of accuracy of reproduction (such as closure of gaps, tendency to curve or to straighten lines, number of parts, orientation of the drawing, intersections, and the like) *increased* uniformly from age three. Rejecting Werner's concepts of hierarchic organization and of discontinuity as explanatory principles in the development of drawing, the authors concluded "that the reproductions increasingly approach the original in all dimensions and that, in the course of so doing, errors both of under- and over-estimation occur" (1960, p. 358). Unlike Campbell (1958), they would possibly argue that children's errors *are* randomly distributed over- and under-estimates, though they admit this feature shows only when analyzing a sample of drawings. "Errors" may tend to be systematic in a particular drawing, because some aspects of drawing improvement may be learned before others; for example, the detection and reproduction of a gap in a line may be handled adequately before the reproduction of angles is learned.

The work of Graham, Berman, and Ernhart, however, seems not to invalidate the conclusion of Gibson and others that older children and adults tend to distort figures in the direction of apparent similarities to "meaningful" objects. Nor does this study controvert the well-established fact that children show "syncretism," i.e., allow simplified schemata to stand as adequate representations of complex perceptions, either in representative drawing or in copying. The figures used were the simplest forms, and the details examined were the most molecular features of these forms—tendencies in the handling of junctures of lines, direction of lines, and the like. Seldom did more than one opportunity for "simplification" appear in a single form. It may be that such elements, taken one by one in the simplest forms, appear to be treated randomly; in more complex forms, however, simplifications or "styles" consistently appear. The authors, indeed, allow for such happenings as "indirect consequences" of gradual improvement in accuracy.

It may also be that one set of descriptive terms and concepts applies adequately at the level of analysis, and another set may work successfully at a more molar level, or with more complex figures. Indeed, this problem is a difficult one to handle experimentally, since the experimental conditions for younger and older children cannot be equated. Young children are not capable of responding to complex test stimuli due to lack of learning; when a year or more of learning and growth has been accomplished, so that they can handle more complex stimuli, the experimental problem is different. It is possible that both the extremely analytical approach and one which works with larger, more complex units can be useful, depending on the phenomenological level at which one approaches the material.

Theories Assuming that Organization in Drawings Is Given by Experience

In contrast with theories which assert or imply that drawings represent an expression of implicit neurological patterns "given" in the mind, are those which seek to be rigorously empirical. These theories account for organized behavior in terms of the organism's repeated contacts with its environment, mediated by sensory processes. Florence Goodenough was perhaps the first to give a comprehensive account of children's drawings wholly in empiricistic terms. Her theoretical statement began with a consideration of sensation and perception, and assuredly no theory of drawing can be formulated apart from consideration of perceptual processes. A great many studies of perception in children have appeared since her discussion. The findings of these studies will be reviewed to establish a basis for a theory of children's drawings in contemporary language.

The Organization of Visual Perception

Perception has long been considered central in psychology (Boring, 1950, p. 304). In recent years much attention has been given to the role cognitive contents and affective functions play in limiting or qualifying perception. It is now rather generally accepted that many species, including man, orient to patterned rather than to nonpatterned stimuli (Fantz, 1958). Modern discussions, however, make no more extensive assumptions than this concerning intrinsic or native processes in perception. Cognitive contents, when hypothesized, are understood as built up empirically. Since early visual perception occurs in a three-dimensional world, perception in space, "in the round," is the modal experience, and some cues to depth perception are probably acquired preverbally. Studies in transposition learning indicate that *form* as such is discriminated by very young children, and that with increasing age the response to form generalizes. Apparently, too, this process of visual discrimination and generalization is greatly helped by language (e.g., Jeffrey, 1953; Spiker and Terrell, 1955; Norcross and Spiker, 1957).

Skeels (1933) found that the visual discrimination of formboard pieces occurs before the ability to perform adequately with the board, presumably before all the motor components necessary to handling and fitting are mastered. Stevenson and McBee (1958) noted that young children discriminate three-dimensional shapes more readily than two-dimensional shapes. Rice (1930b) showed that plane figures can be recognized despite their changing orientation, and suggested that although the ability to discern orientation or disorientation is learned, it appears rather suddenly at about age five. Hunton (1955), however, has affirmed that even two-year-old children may recognize disorientation in complex pictures. It is generally believed, however, that visual perception continues to improve throughout childhood, as the child learns to discriminate and organize more and more aspects of the visual field.

Engel (1935) observed that very young children (under three-and-a-half) are more responsive to form than to color; this focus of interest shifts to color between three-and-a-half and six years, and thereafter shifts slowly back to form. This finding confirmed the work of Brian and Goodenough (1929), who observed that in sorting geometrical shapes, the majority of children shifted from a preference for form, to color, and back to form at different age periods. This returning interest in form may well be reflected in children's drawings, which increasingly depend upon differentiated form from five or six to about twelve years of age. Brian and Goodenough noted that brighter children tended to be somewhat advanced in this form-color transition; Engel that intelligent children were "form-reactors." Livson and Krech (1956) noted that intelligent adults are better able to handle asymmetrical patterns, both visually and conceptually. These observations should be more fully investigated.

Whether children perceive globally or analytically is an old controversy, with evidence for each point of view. One of the most detailed attempts to validate Gestalt theory in perception (Rush, 1937) found evidence for principles of proximity, similarity, and continuity in making visual groupings of dots. Rush found it necessary to add the aspect of direction, also, and reported that preference for the horizontal direction in patterns decreases with age. No one principle of perception, however, was absolutely compelling, and there were marked interactions among them. Apparently, perception is a complex process, and any attempt to analyze it into components results in arbitrary distinctions and definitions, which must be qualified under particular circumstances of application.

Children generally have more difficulty than do adults in perceiving embedded figures, although Street (1931) demonstrated no marked age change in recognition of incomplete pictures after age six. Gollin (1960), however, showed that kindergarten children performed more poorly than adults in recognizing incomplete pictures of familiar objects, though not markedly inferior in terms of possible score. Adults also benefitted relatively more from practice in recognition. Ghent (1956) found that children have a great deal of difficulty perceiving separate figures (whether familiar objects or geometrical forms), when they are not clearly set apart from each other. Piaget and Albertini's (1954) important study of intersecting and incomplete forms is of interest here. They found that young children had the greatest difficulty seeing gaps in lines as necessary elements in a total figure. Such gaps were seen invariably as interruptions or breaks. Only later in development could children perceive the gap as part of the whole figure. The most readily perceived incomplete forms involved short gaps in straight lines, followed by gaps in curved lines or arcs. Forms involving missing oblique lines and/or corners were most difficult to perceive; apparently angles or corners are important orientational cues.

Incomplete forms were much less successfully perceived than intersecting forms. Dotted line figures were difficult for children under six or seven, and intersecting dotted line figures almost impossible to perceive. That children ultimately can perceive incomplete forms may occur because secondary "good Gestalten" (in addition to primary Gestalten due to field effects) arise from perceptual activity and become a "perceptive schema" to facilitate recognition of the figure. In essential agreement with Gibson (1929) and many others (see pp. 168 ff. this volume), Piaget and Albertini noted that young children tried to make familiar objects out of incomplete forms.

In a world where certain forms are endlessly repeated, perceptual learning seems to give a compelling quality to regular forms early in life. Leuba (1940) arranged pill boxes in simple configurations (circle, square, triangle) and "baited" one with candy in the subject's presence. After a brief delay, during which the arrangement was screened from view, children had difficulty locating the box in which they had seen the candy placed. When the critical stimulus was placed adjacent to the configuration, there was no difficulty whatsoever. Moreover, there was relatively greater success when the critical object was located at or next to the end of a line, as in a corner, suggesting again the importance of ends and corners in perception of wholes. One recalls the finding of Schiller (1951) that the chimpanzee oriented first to the corners of a sheet of paper, and the just-mentioned Piaget and Albertini finding concerning the importance of angles and corners.

Attneave (1957) believed that the number of turns or changes in direction in the profile of a figure is the chief component in the perception of complexity. Graham and others (1960), in an experiment already described, found that discontinuity or acuteness of change in direction, as for example an angle, seems to be the principal factor in determining the difficulty of a form to be copied. It is not possible to say whether this difficulty occurs in the perception of the form, in the motor execution, or in both. Helson (1953) pointed out that in visual perception there are "anchoring stimuli" or elements which are preponderant; corners, ends, or isolated objects may constitute such elements early in perceptual learning. It may well be that when children draw the human figure they depict those aspects which serve as "anchor points," in the order in which they appear in perception—the head, facial features and limbs being the earliest emergents.

It has long been known that young children, responding to pictures, seem to concentrate primarily on separate objects or details; attention to relations among objects comes much later. A study of Rorschach responses (Hemmendinger, 1953) showed the youngest children responding globally, with increasing attention to detail at ages six to eight, and these details being integrated into larger wholes around nine or ten. Ames and others (1953) reported similar results at slightly different ages and also reported that color and form responses show a marked increase with age. Rorschach blots, however, are irregular, and the relationships among them repeat few of the usually experienced relationships observed in the world of familiar objects. On the hypothesis that less frequently experienced stimuli are more "strange" or "difficult," it is not surprising that the general sequence—perception of the undifferentiated whole, to perception of details, to perception of relationships among parts—comes somewhat later with respect to the Rorschach than to more "meaningful" forms.

It is difficult to say whether we are dealing with a definite sequential process or whether this impression of succeeding phases arises out of the features of perception to which *we* choose to attend. Analysis and organization may proceed simultaneously, both processes advancing to include more, and more complex, aspects. A pioneer study of children's perception (Line, 1931) affirmed that the eduction of relations is one of the *earliest* features of children's perceptions, albeit at a rudimentary level. Line, moreover, discerned two types of perception of relations. One of these seems to occur more commonly and perhaps is more primitive; the other is more critical, discriminative, and occurs as there is a special need for clearness. The first is the cognizing of items "as" related; the second is the thought-like judgment "that" the items are related. Moreover, the "as" relationship, being less specific or explicit, can be applied more generally and has almost the character of a configuration or Gestalt. It is this less specific feature of perception, according to Line, that particularly characterizes the young child's work.

More than one investigator, puzzling over the problem of organization in perception, has concluded that *both* synthesizing and analytic processes occur, and that *both* show progressive features. The attempt to establish correlations between stimulus changes and the perceiving organism's discrimination of these changes has not affirmed one viewpoint to the exclusion of the other in this old controversy.

From these studies of perception and from the generalizations of empirical studies of drawing discussed in the previous chapter, one may conclude the following: Children perceive form very early; comprehend simple (i.e., with few corners and angles) more readily than complex forms, and familiar (i.e., frequently experienced) more readily than unusual or unfamiliar forms. More-over, there is great variation among children in perceptual performance. The overwhelming dominance of form in all visual experiences assures that mark-ings-on-paper will likewise show form, building on the patterns given to the first scribbles by the mechanics of hand and arm. The great variation among children, both in perception and in drawing, seems to belie the notion of in-nately patterned visual-motor Gestalts, except possibly in the most general sense; even these "Gestalts" may be determined by the mechanical arrange-ments of the hand and arm, and by a tendency to orient perception to corners, or to angles formed by joining lines. Very quickly, however, drawings depict familiar, "meaningful" forms. Copies of less familiar outline drawings tend to modify in the direction of the "meaning" originally suggested to the child artist. Thus, once again we come to the idea of concept formation and cogni-tion as central to children's drawings.

In drawing complex objects, or making compositions involving a number of objects, the organization process seems to proceed by two modes: by building up from part structures, or by delineating details within the more general out-line. Any given child may use both procedures. Rostohar's (1928) interesting implication, that these two "styles" of procedure represent different thought patterns, or personality organizations, may well be an oversimplification, but the problem needs more thorough investigation.

Perception and Object Recognition

Both Darwin (1877) and Perez (1888) considered that when the child recog-nizes objects seen in a mirror as images and not as the objects themselves (as shown by his turning away from the mirror to find the object therein re-flected), one of the earliest stages in the ability to recognize objects in pictures has been reached. In the world of primitive man the natural "mirror" furnished by pools of water undoubtedly brought about a similar recognition of the self-image. However, as observers of extremely primitive groups have often com-mented, the recognition of the photographic or pictorial image does take prac-tice or experience (Nissen, Machover and Kinder, 1935), though apparently the adaptation is rather quickly made by adults. In the case of very young children, this adaptation seems to require added maturity and an accumulation of experiences with discriminations and perceptions. Goodenough (1926) spoke of recognition as "association by similarity," and drew on the theory of identical elements.

However, as has been often pointed out, in perception certain elements be-come more essential than others; also, the arrangement and pattern of ele-ments become significant in facilitating recognition. Thus, it is tempting to use general or even vague Gestalt and phenomenological terms, especially in dis-cussing perception, recognition, and concept formation in older children. One cannot, however, describe the infant's experience in phenomenalistic terms, even though one may take this position with respect to adult psychology. Goodenough (1926), in laying a foundation for her analysis of drawing behavior, stayed with a more objective framework. Her ideas, though expressed in the associationistic terms of her day, still adequately embrace the more modern data and concepts concerning perception.

In her explanation of object recognition, Goodenough made certain assumptions about the "experience" of the newborn child. His mental life was considered as an unorganized flow ". . . of sensations which force themselves upon the developing consciousness with greater or less insistence, according to the intensity of the physical stimulus and the immediate condition of the receiving organism" (1926, p. 67). It is central to associationistic views that in the continuing flow of such experience, the repeated associations of certain sensations bring about the discrimination of the separate sensations and also the grouping of sensations into patterns. Possibly one of the earliest discriminations made is between recurring groups of sensations (hence, "familiar") and novel sensations (hence, "unfamiliar"). In such patternings of sensations come the first crude perceptions of objects. Goodenough considered such early association and recognition processes to be closely related to the conditioned reflex. However, she also found in these processes the beginnings of the analysis, discrimination and comparison central to the conscious cognitive processes of later life.

Goodenough hypothesized that the infant of a few weeks probably recognizes his mother through the combined action of a great number of impressions, using all sensory modalities. Little by little, the infant becomes able to substitute a more limited number of such impressions for the total, so that the visual sight of mother or the sound of her voice alone is sufficient for recognition. Since Goodenough's description, the literature on perception and on learning has more and more emphasized discrimination. Discrimination is perhaps not so much a substitution of a few clear impressions for a vague "totality" as it is the learning, through repeated stimulation, of salient features and the relations among these features. This use of a limited number of cues has been referred to as a "coding process" (e.g., Attneave, 1957; E. Gibson, 1961).

The process of discrimination, involving analysis, comparison, and abstraction, permits the child increasingly to substitute central equivalents of peripheral experience for concrete sensory experiences. Eventually a small snapshot of his mother is recognized in spite of changes in size, color, and dimensionality. This is known as the "constancy phenomenon" in perception, and has long fascinated psychologists. Thus, perceptual constancies can be considered in part as based on firmly established *concepts.*

The most complete theoretical analysis of object perception and recognition has been supplied by Piaget (1953), according to whom the object concept is constructed empirically, little by little. The child first distinguishes and recognizes stable groups of impressions. These groups of impressions are subjective dispositions or attitudes rather than images in the child's mind. Object recognition thus at the outset involves the infant's recognition of his own reaction rather than the object itself. In this process simple reflexes are basic; for example, Piaget finds the prototype of all object recognition in the nursling's discrimination of the nipple from other surfaces.

Piaget links the concept of object with the concept of space, and the concept of causality with the concept of time. These four primary concepts are essentially preverbal and are fundamental to the capacity for object recognition. They grow out of primitive assimilative and accommodative relationships between the infant and his environment. With these four concepts, and the consequent capacity for object recognition, and with the assistance of the language system, the child constructs the elaborate structure of verbalized concepts involved in cognition. In relation to Piaget's description, it will be noted that the very first experiences of the child with pencil or crayon come *after* the development of object recognition, but early in the process of concept formation aided by language. The development of the child's drawing thus is coordinate with, and probably closely linked with, the development of the system of verbalized concepts we commonly understand as cognition.

Concept Formation and Cognition

From the discrimination and recognition of particular objects the child moves on to grouping objects into classes according to recognized similarities. This is the basis of concept formation (Vinacke, 1951, 1954). Studies of children's language processes have shown that very simple concepts exist almost as soon as symbols (sounds used as signs) or words exist. Thus, the ability to form concepts depends on the increasing ability to analyze, to abstract certain elements from the total impression created by an object, and to reconstruct the object psychologically in terms of those elements that repeated experience has shown to be essential or invariant. This process of concept formation is the core of *cognition*, or the knowing, thinking, and reasoning we generally subsume under mental or intellectual processes.

Brian and Goodenough (1929) speculated that the sequential shift in preference from form to color and back to form really illustrates concept formation. They hypothesized that attention is first given to discriminating among the members (species) within the more general class (genus) and later to making differentiations within separate species. Still later, as the separate aspects at the species level are mastered and the child can readily shift his attention from one aspect to another, a new process of organization and evaluation of these partial elements occurs. According to this hypothesis, mastery moves from a general concept of the whole, to a more differentiated examination and mastery of the components, back to a new, more highly organized concept of the whole. Intensive studies of the process of concept formation (e.g., Vinacke, 1951, 1954) suggest that some such sequence probably does occur. However, these studies also indicate that a given child is simultaneously at different levels with respect to different concepts, and that a clear-cut progression in concepts occurs only as a construct, not in actual fact.

Concepts may also be viewed as *expectancies* to which new perceptions are referred, somewhat as hypotheses to be tested. Moreover, concepts are formed, changed, enlarged, or subdivided by a feedback process wherein the idea is continually tested in new contexts and modified accordingly (Brown, 1958).

Concept formation is, thus, thoroughly empirical. In this context the tendency of adults as well as children to draw unfamiliar or incompletely perceived objects as familiar objects becomes understandable. The unfamiliar or ambiguous stimulus is assigned to a known class (familiar concept) in terms of certain salient elements or properties. In this context, also, the biassing effect of strongly formed concepts on new perceptions also becomes understandable. The concept establishes a kind of "response set" in terms of which incoming percepts are received. The perceiving organism plays, in a sense, a more active, *cognizing* role in this theoretical framework than in the framework of the Gestalt psychologist.

How unfamiliar or vague referents become assimilated into the child's ideational structure is illustrated by two interesting studies. Nagy (1953a) asked children to draw various human visceral organs, locating them in an outline of the body. The 400 subjects were from age four to eleven. Presumably these children, to the extent that they had studied anatomy and physiology at all, had talked about body organs but had never seen them. Possibly they had some assistance from medical charts or diagrams; the report does not comment. Although the author reported from the viewpoint of body-image theory, the study is even more interesting as an investigation of concept formation where minimum reference to visual objects is possible. When asked to identify and portray the organs responsible for "thinking," "breathing," and "digestion," very few children at any age attempted representative drawings; the great majority used vague, undifferentiated open or closed forms. For example, the brain was often confused with the bony skull; the lungs shown by a roundish form, or by a cluster of veins in a globular mass; the stomach as a roundish figure, in no cases showing the digestive tract. Lungs were located within the torso by over half the children, but in the approximate correct location by only one-third. The stomach was placed in the abdomen only 8 per cent of the time, being in the chest or shoulders in two-thirds of the drawings. Actually, children identified parts and tissues of the organs by name more successfully than they diagrammed them. The study assuredly indicates that the anatomical concepts of elementary school children at best are very vague.

In another study Nagy (1953b) found that children have a clearer image of germs. The majority of young elementary school children tended to draw germs as abstract figures—circles, dots, triangles, ovals, etc. Most older elementary children moved toward an animal-like, wormlike, or insectlike representation. Germs are understood as producing disease and sickness, and as entering and leaving the body through the mouth. The Nagy studies illustrate the power of visual perception and of symbolic processes in forming concepts. The studies also show the necessity for some kind of conceptual structure into which new information can be fitted.

Cognition and Drawing

Goodenough discerned cognitive elements in the genesis of children's drawings. For little children, drawing is a language—a form of cognitive expression

—and its purpose is not primarily esthetic. Nor is it, she affirmed, simply a matter of reproducing the visual image; rather, "the child draws what he knows, not what he sees," to use Luquet's (1913) phrase. In defense of this position, Goodenough cited the researches of Clark (1902), who asked children to draw an apple with a skewer running through it. The skewer entered the apple on the side turned toward the viewer and emerged from the side turned away from him. The model was so placed that none of the children could see the apple as a plane figure with the skewer entering or leaving exactly at the edge. Invariably the younger children drew the skewer as extending straight through the apple from side to side and visible throughout its length. Somewhat older children realized that a portion of the skewer could not be seen and depicted it so; but they, too, depicted a plane figure. Only in the work of older children was there an occasional attempt to reproduce the apple in perspective. Before this stage the model served only as a cue for an idea; "given the idea, the nature of the drawing was no longer dependent upon the image immediately present" (Goodenough, 1926, p. 73).

Goodenough concluded that an analysis of drawings requires hypothesizing certain higher thought processes, involving discriminations, associations and generalizations of details and of relations. These processes furnish the person with concepts and enable him to manipulate these concepts. She discerned individual differences among persons in the ease and success with which they perform such operations. In keeping with the ideas of her time she conceived these differences as constituting a psychological dimension, the extremes of which could be named as "bright" and "dull." Her own statements are appropriate here:

> It seems evident, then, that an explanation of the psychological functions which underlie spontaneous drawing of little children must go beyond the fields of simple visual imagery and eye-hand coördination and take account of the higher thought processes. It has been said that the ability to recognize objects in pictures, an ability which must obviously precede any real attempt to represent objects by means of pictures, is dependent upon the ability to form associations by the similarity of certain elements which are common both to the picture and to the object, in spite of the dissimilarity of other elements. Analysis and abstraction are clearly involved, but only the final result is present in consciousness. The three-year-old child who recognizes the photograph of his mother cannot tell you by what means he is able to do so, and even the adult finds such a task difficult. In order to represent objects by means of pictures there must be, however, a conscious analysis of the process, of the intermediate steps by means of which the desired result is to be obtained. It is necessary to select from out the total impression those elements or features which appear to be characteristic or essential. This analysis must be followed or accompanied by observation of relationships. The relationships to be observed are of two kinds, quantitative and spatial. The former determine the proportion, the latter the position, of the various parts of the drawing with reference to each other. Very great individual differences are found among children with respect to the extent to which these

functions keep pace with each other. In general it may be said that the brighter the child, the more closely is his analysis of a figure followed by an appreciation of the relationships prevailing between the elements which are brought out by his analysis. Backward children, on the other hand, are likely to be particularly slow in grasping abstract ideas of this or any other kind. They analyze a figure to some extent, and by this means are able to set down some of its elements in a graphic fashion, but the ability to combine these elements into an organized whole is likely to be defective and in some instances seems to be almost entirely lacking. It is this inability to analyze, to form abstract ideas, to relate facts, that is largely responsible for the bizarre effects so frequently found among the drawings of backward children—the "*Zusammenhangenlosigkeit*" to which Kerschensteiner has called attention (1926, pp. 73–74).

If the child's drawings depend primarily on his concept of an object rather than upon the immediate visual image, it becomes possible to understand two phenomena of children's drawing: (1) As children mature, drawings increase in complexity, yet always retain a quality of wholeness. (2) Developmental adaptations or changes in children's drawings do not remain fixed from the time of their first appearance.

Concepts become more differentiated as the child increases his contacts with objects under different circumstances, and as he discriminates more and more aspects of them. His drawings likewise show more and more parts. With added experience, the child's concepts become increasingly abstract; they encompass *relationships* among aspects of an object, and they include relationships among objects. Children's drawings of the human figure likewise include more abstract elements, such as appropriate proportions of limbs, head, trunk, assignment of the figure to a class through the use of clothing or accessories, the depiction of activity, and the like. After about age five, any drawing of a man is recognizable as a man, containing the major features; modifications are toward increasing elaborations of the basic concept, toward the inclusion of more abstract elements.

As in most new performances or skills, only gradually do elements of the new attainment become a consistent feature of the total performance. While the progress in drawing, from the simple concepts governing the drawing of the four-year-old to the complex and highly developed ideas of the ten-year-old, shows a series of quite marked changes, this development is brought about by specific features which at first appear sporadically and only later become fixed. When the very young child who draws head, trunk, and legs begins to add the arms he does not do so invariably; as his concept develops the arms tend more and more to become an essential part and are more consistently shown, until the child no longer considers his drawings complete without them. Goodenough's words cogently summarize:

It may thus be said that at any given time a child's drawing will consist of two parts—the first part embracing those characteristics which have already become an integral part of his concept of the object drawn, and consequently appear invariably; the second part including the elements which are in process of becoming integrated and are therefore shown with more or less irregularity. The frequency with which any given characteristic tends to appear is a function of the extent to which it has become integrated into the developing concept, and a measure of the weight which should be given to it as an index of concept development (1926, p. 75).

Such a theory can account for the marked instability of performance from drawing to drawing noted in the work of retarded children, who seem to develop more slowly than normals. It can also account for peculiar features of drawings by children with particular types of defects (Burt, 1921, 1947; Bender, 1938, 1940).

No data have ever appeared to controvert the general import of Goodenough's observations and conclusions. Rather, the increased body of data serves to fill in the process she outlined. Drawings of objects are based on concepts; concepts are based on experience with objects. Experience increases the aspects of objects that are reacted to, understood and incorporated in drawing. Not only are the *number* of these aspects increased by experience; the *relationships* among them are grasped more completely. Thus, with experience, a larger number of concrete aspects and, what is more important, more abstract aspects are understood and used in drawings.

Another significant theoretical discussion of children's drawing has been supplied by Bell (1952), who has also attempted a basis for the so-called "projective significance" of drawings. Basically, his theoretical approach is empirical and associationistic, as is Goodenough's, but it also falls back on the neurological assumptions of Gestalt theory. Where Goodenough emphasized the associational mechanism basic to percepts and concepts, Bell has given more recognition to the various sensory processes, in keeping with more recent attention to these components of perception. Bell's view recognizes that the very young child's perception of his world depends relatively more on tactual, kinesthetic, and organic receptor mechanisms—the epicritic and protopathic sensibilities. With development, as his world becomes more complex and his store of experiences and meanings increases, he comes to depend more and more on his distance receptors—vision and audition. Thus, Bell's discussion is related to the "organismic" theories covered earlier.

As the child develops, the hand replaces the mouth as the significant contact organ, and the tactile modalities tend to replace taste, although the kinesthetic sense continues to be an important avenue of perception. The hand can, with appropriate equipment, produce scribblings, which are then noted visually and serve to stimulate further movements. Gradually, control of the hand is achieved, as simple push-pull or sweeping movements are supplanted by circular movements. This progression has been observed by many investigators, as we have seen. In turn, these simple visual-perceptual experiences are organized with reference to the continuing kinesthetic-tactual experience, and gradually the element of differentiation in visual imagery is brought in as a control-ling device. As this occurs, roughly between five and eight years, the child begins the representation of many objects in his drawing. Still later comes the initial use of abstract, verbal-symbolic imagery, both in verbal and pictorial representation. Bell considered that it is the difficulty of giving concrete repre-sentation to abstract, symbolic images that causes many children to give up drawing at this period and to lean more on handwriting as a graphic form of communication.

Bell has schematized his view as a progressive spiral, circling from an undif-ferentiated to a differentiated state and returning to a state of integration at a different level. At this new level earlier processes are still used but so skillfully and automatically that they are carried forward without conscious effort or, indeed, awareness. The prime mover in this process is assumed to be field activity of neural processes in the brain.

The several levels of integration Bell discerned, from simple to more com-plex, are: oral kinesthesis, direct manual kinesthesis, indirect or referred contact kinesthesis, visual-perceptual, visual figure imagery, visual figure-ground imagery, and verbal-symbolic imagery. The first three or four of these levels are included in the preschool period, and the child normally enters stage five by the kindergarten age. The correlation of these stages with successive dominant modes of children's drawings are fairly obvious. Bell believes that the successively longer periods of time occupied by each stage attest both to the slowing down of the rate of brain development and to the greater com-plexity of succeeding integrations.

From Bell's assumptions come several important hypotheses concerning drawing behavior. While growth factors set the nature of successive levels and the pace with which they are traversed, various environmental influences determine the particular way in which each stage is realized, thus accounting in part for individual differences among children at the same stage. Moreover, in the process, as in most developmental phenomena, features most recently acquired are most readily disrupted by dramatic upset in the environmental or field forces. Such upset leads to distortion of drawing phenomena in a given stage, or to regression to an earlier stage. Gross disruption at any level would have a pervasive influence on all following stages; the earlier the stress occurs, the more devastating its effect on total functioning. Bell seems to believe that these hypotheses have virtually the character of axioms and, consequently, have significance for the use of drawings as diagnostic clues in clinical analy-sis. His hypotheses should be more fully investigated.

Complex Experience, Perception, and Cognition

In recent years research on perception has not only investigated how sen-sory processes give rise to elementary perceptions; it has also investigated molar aspects of individual and social experience. The fact that, in perception, cer-tain elements in a composite may suggest a likeness to another object was held by Alberti several hundred years ago to be the origin of art (Janitschek,

1877). Irregularities on a rock or tree stump suggested the bear, or other totem object, and with slight modification became the image or statue of the venerated creature. In the cave art of Spain and France it has been noted that the primitive artists used irregularities on the rock walls to give an appearance of the third dimension to figures.

Such a process may be related to what modern clinical psychology conceives of as projection in drawings.[2] The perception of selected elements in an essentially unorganized context of stimuli causes the viewer, by association, to "see" the likeness to some other object. What he sees is thus in part conditional upon his associations; he "projects" onto the materials before him the meanings aroused by the association of the elements common to this experience and to previous, more highly organized experiences. A recent writer in art history and theory (Gombrich, 1960) has made much of this activity on the part of the observer. The human mind is not simply a repository of learned associations but is active; this activity is a constant striving for meaning, assessing, comparing, reassessing the materials of immediate perception in terms of previous associations. This emphasis on the dynamic, complex character of perception is a striking feature of recent research and writing on perception. The previous chapter and numerous references in the present chapter furnish a convergence of many investigations on the generalization that drawings of unfamiliar or ambiguous designs are modified, both by addition and subtraction of elements and often in the direction of familiar objects, by the individual experience of the viewer.

It has been noted that children may name their earliest random scribblings in terms of some chance resemblance they perceive, and that in the attempt to complete or perfect the chance resemblance is found the first real attempt at graphic expression. Goodenough (1926, p. 69) pointed out that it is not necessary to suppose that these associations are entirely spontaneous. In many cases associations are probably stimulated by questions or comments of older persons, and in the modern world the child's previous visual experience with pictures is of great importance. Meili-Dworetski's careful investigation (1957) of the circumstances surrounding children's drawing suggests that imitation is significant; not the imitation of a particular model, but the imitation that grows out of the many comparisons, comments, and discussions occurring when children draw freely, in unsupervised settings.

Sherif extended perceptual research to include the influence of social factors in perception (1935, 1936), demonstrating that perceptual processes are influenced by "social norms." The individual's perceptual experience is modified by experiencing stimuli in the presence of other experiencing subjects. Physiological, social, or psychological conditions of need have also been experimentally controlled in recent years, with the discovery that all such variations in conditions of the organism influence perception. Gombrich's lectures

---

[2] An extensive literature has already been reviewed (Chapter III) showing an association between emotional concepts and certain properties of line and form.

(1960), already mentioned, are among the latest to stress what the artist as producer and the viewer as consumer each contributes to the "experience" of a drawing or painting.

Witkin's monograph (1954), investigating the relationship of "styles" of perceptual habits to personality structure, offers some data on the relationship of human figure drawing elements (scored according to Machover's signs) to modes of visual perception. His discussion utilizes concepts from both Gestalt and dynamic clinical psychology. Those adults who perceptually are more influenced by the field tend to include Machover figure drawing signs indicating that they: (1) place a low evaluation on their bodies, (2) exhibit infantile defenses against anxiety, (3) lack self-assurance, and (4) exhibit passivity, together with signs of uncontrolled hostility. It is scarcely possible, from the brief scoring scale presented, to check these figure drawing scoring signs against the Goodenough-Harris scoring system advanced by the present work. However, close scrutiny of the items strongly suggests that "immature" drawings would likely contain a good many such Machover signs. The suggestion is that adults, who for whatever reason, make poor quality drawings containing features more likely to be used by children, are those who tend to be "field dependent" and "nonanalytical" in perception.

Witkin's material on children is incomplete (the number of cases at three different age levels is very small and no measures of intelligence or of maturity other than age were used), yet the results are extremely suggestive. It appears that the relationships between personality and both "orientation to the field" and "independence of the field" in perception were moderately high for adults. Both measures of perception showed marked age changes between ten and thirteen years with less of an age trend both prior to and after thirteen years. Thus children, contrasted with adolescents and adults, are much more influenced by the field in perception, hence are less perceptually analytical. Boys are more analytical (field independent) than girls. The relationship between personality and perception noted in adult data is not so clearly evident in children below age thirteen, although what relationships exist tend to parallel those in the adult data. Although characteristic sex differences appear in the perceptual habits of adults (females are more field dependent), the data on children are too meager to admit of statistically stable trends, and none appear in the tables. The hypotheses are intriguing, however, though the results are less clear-cut than those of Stewart (1955).

Stewart studied "personality style" in the self-portrait drawings of adolescents. He rated thirty-one formal and stylistic elements, such as realism, symmetry, rhythm, firmness of line, etc. and factor analyzed the intercorrelations among these ratings. It would be instructive to investigate the relationship between the figure drawing elements in adult drawings and their cognitive, perceptual and personality factors. It may be that "quality" of drawing carries sufficient correlation in the internal consistency sense to account for much of the relationship that Witkin observed.

McFee (1961) placed a different evaluation on the Witkin data. She extended and corrected Lowenfeld's visual and haptic modes of perception to incorporate Witkin's findings concerning "posturally oriented" (field independent) and "visually oriented" (field dependent) modes of space perception. Most people use some compromise between these modes, but individual differences and sex differences may be found, depending on the receptors (kinesthetic-tactual versus visual) preferred. McFee's account places greater confidence in Witkin's meager (and statistically unreliable) data for children than does the present writer. McFee concluded that child-rearing practices make girls more "field dependent" and "visual" in their perceptual habits, and more emotionally dependent in their social and psychological relationships.

In addition to noting Witkin's visual and postural orientation to space, McFee drew a distinction between visual concepts and cognitive concepts, between visual learning and cognitive learning. The distinction is based on perceptual processes. *Visual concepts* are "derived from form and surface elements of objects as seen in space and light, as opposed to *cognitive concepts* of objects derived from past learning" (p. 54). McFee concluded:

> We have suggested that people need all four kinds of ability in handling information to deal adequately with experience—cognitive understanding, awareness of visual details, use of both postural and visual receptors for getting information from the environment (p. 54).

Her use of "visual concepts" suggests the ideas of Britsch and of Schaeffer-Simmern, discussed earlier, which have not been defined adequately in psychological terms. To the present writer, cognition cannot be so easily separated into "visual" and "cognitive" elements.

Perception is assuredly a complex process; growing up in a complex world seems to involve a transactive process of stimulation, learning and development such that cognitive concepts dominate most children's drawings. It is possible that special training could alter this state of affairs. McFee asserts: "Children who are aware of the existence of the constancies—color, size, and shape—can reduce their limiting effects by learning to observe visually as well as cognitively" (1961, p. 60). The necessity of overcoming habituated expectancies and sets (i.e., cognitive concepts) in "seeing" has long been known to artists. It may well be that McFee is correct when she affirms:

> Visual training increases the wealth of material the children have to work with. If visual training becomes rigid and authoritarian it may inhibit creative activity, but if it is used to motivate visual curiosity and exploration it should widen the range of creativity of students. Much more effect of light and color, of form and line will become available for children to use. *They* will go beyond *cognitive* categorizing and see many more details and significant relationships as they respond to their environment, both visually and cognitively (pp. 63–64).

These hypotheses may be fruitful for future research.

To the present writer, the available literature on perception and drawing, and the materials of the present study suggest that the overriding significance of intellectual and conceptual factors in the early years obscure the perceptual-personality relationships, and dominate the production of children's drawings. It is possible that perceptual styles which result in discernible personality relationships emerge more clearly after the drawing task has ceased to be a test of conceptual maturity in the cognitive sense. "Cognitive styles" in personality may be a complex resultant of a long-continued process of learning and development, requiring many prior learnings.

Use of Reduced or Simplified Structures

It has repeatedly been shown that in drawing figures that are unfamiliar or ambiguous, a child tends to modify the form of the stimulus; often this modification takes the form of simplifying the originally perceived model. Luquet (1913) took this to be an essential feature of the child's drawing, reflecting inadequate concepts. He noted that the child draws first according to the principle of "intellectual realism" and later according to the principle of "visual realism." That the child "draws what he knows, not what he sees" may be used to account for the "transparencies" in children's drawings, or the "unfolding" of complex objects when the child has not mastered the techniques of perspective.

Numerous investigators, however, have noted that the child does not draw *all* that he knows. Goodenough remarked that the child selects those items "which to him are so essential or characteristic that they occur to him spontaneously without suggestion from outside sources" (1926, p. 76). That such meanings may be either cognitive or affective or both was early observed by Sully (1903). Organismic theories of children's drawings have given a central place to this tendency to condense or simplify, holding that a child cannot perceive the complex form in its more abstract aspects until he no longer cognizes concretely, as noted earlier. In this connection it is interesting to recall Mott's (1939) observation that to require children four to seven-and-a-half to draw a particular *type* of man, as a policeman, farmer or cowboy, serves to involve them relatively unsuccessfully with special details. Their drawings of "a man" in Mott's study were invariably superior to their drawings of a specified type of man.

Goodenough (1926) stressed cognitive factors in accounting for this attenuation in drawings:

> A three-year-old child will point to his hair when asked to do so, but 50 per cent of nine-year-old children are entirely content to draw the human figure without a vestige of hair, although these same children include in their drawings such non-essential features as flashing scarfpins, elaborate hat bands, pipes, canes, etc. The problem which the child has to meet is primarily one of selection, of determining which ones of a vast number of items really furnish the key to the situation. Knowledge of a fact does not in itself guarantee that this fact shall be shown in a drawing; its importance must also have been

evaluated. Terman has shown [3] that the majority of seven-year-old children *know* the number of their fingers when the question is put to them; yet only 31 per cent of unselected seven-year-olds show the correct number in their drawings when no suggestion is made. The difference can hardly be due to technical difficulty; at least it is hard to see why it should be any more difficult to draw five fingers than to draw four or six, or, as occurred in the case of one kindergarten child, twenty-nine on one hand the thirty-six on the other! Carelessness, in the sense of lack of appreciation of the importance of details, is undoubtedly one of the factors involved; yet when one notices the care with which some of these drawings have been finished, and the effort which has apparently been expended upon them, it appears evident that carelessness, in the ordinary sense of the term, is not an adequate explanation for the discrepancy in the findings by the two methods. The determining factor appears to be the presence or absence of the definite stimulus, "How many?" In the one instance, that which is measured is the memory of a particular percept; in the other, the integration of that percept into the concept of which it is a part (pp. 76–77).

In this connection Goodenough also pointed out how children, in arriving at the ability to define verbally a concept in terms of significant and essential features, often are entirely satisfied with a definition which includes only one or perhaps none of the essential characteristics of an adequate conceptual definition. She concluded: "There is a distinct difference between knowledge of facts and appreciation of their relative significance" (1926, p. 78).

Nor can "appreciation of their relative significance" be built by calling attention to already-known, affectively appreciated, and verbalized features. One advanced four-year-old made a typical schematic drawing, including head, trunk, arms and legs. He was then asked to clothe his figure. When he appeared to ignore the request, it was given in more specific terms by the designation of particular items such as supplying buttons and trousers. Again he shrugged aside the suggestion. When further pressed on the point, he verbalized his behavior with some astonishment, saying: "But he's dressed like I am," and with sweeping motions of his hands he designated his new shirt and trousers, in which he had been attired shortly before making the drawing. Although the items of clothing were undoubtedly very important to him, he was satisfied to indicate an attired figure by a schematic drawing. The reluctance to include some definite representation of clothing persisted even when the examiner showed the boy how to designate buttons and trousers. The simple schema was quite sufficient, even though his awareness (both cognitively and affectively) included many more elements. The author has noted this reaction among many preschool children; [4] although some children will designate by

---

[3] In studies concerned with the 1916 Stanford-Binet tests.

[4] An experimental investigation by the present author, incomplete at this writing, suggests that children who fail initially to draw an item differ widely in this reaction, even at age four. The observation stresses the point made earlier by Meili-Dworetzki (1957) and others, that a child's drawing reflects what he chooses to put down on paper, not the full range of his understanding.

very simple marks in the appropriate location the parts called to their attention. For these children the *location* of the part seems to be sufficient. Lack of
skill in handling the medium may be involved.

Possibly in depicting a concept by drawing, the progression is the same as
that observed for perception—from undifferentiated whole, to partial differentiation, to more complete differentiation. Simultaneously with this process,
however, there occurs a kind of organization or integration, the two proceeding hand-in-hand. That the child locates the part suggested to him, using a
simple pencil mark or a symbol of the crudest form, may indicate a partial
differentiation of the concept, and at the same time its integration into the
whole figure. Whatever the solution to this problem, the fact remains that,
progressively with age, all children include more aspects in their drawing of the
human figures, and these aspects are at all times organized into a patterned,
"whole" representation.

"Schemata" or "Symbolization" in Drawings

The child's abbreviation or simplification in drawing may be a part of the
problem facing any artist—that of selecting what is to be drawn. No one can
draw the complete detail he sees, or depict the full concept he knows. He must
represent *schematically* that which would be beyond either the time allotted or
his ability. Virtually all investigators have observed that children's drawings
abbreviate or simplify the image in ways characteristic both of the age level
and of the particular child. The notion of an underlying graphic pattern, or
schema, in children's drawings has, however, been interpreted in different
ways. Sully (1903) saw such schemata as convenient simplifications. These
simplifications are successfully enlarged and elaborated as the child's ability to
handle both the medium and his own ideas expands. Goodenough (1926),
like Luquet, accepted schemata as embodying the features of reality holding
particular significance for the child. Gombrich (1960) used the term "schema"
to designate the particular concepts and techniques that control the artist's
choice of subject matter and his ways of handling it. The "schema" depends
in part on the medium adopted as well as the concepts expressed, a point made
much of by Gombrich in the history of graphic art, but also acknowledged by
Arnheim (1954) and by Lowenfeld (1957). Lowenfeld further sees the
schema as the form concept a child holds at a particular time and which he
characteristically uses in drawing, when no directed experiences influence him
to change his concept (1957, p. 133).

Read (1945) saw the schema as the individual child's escape from his ever-
present vivid images. Because his images are inadequate to express feelings,
the child invents "a visual symbol, a cipher in this language of line, which will
express his feelings, communicate its quality to others, fix it in the shifting
world of appearances" (1945, p. 131). As the child acquires the machinery of
conceptual thought, the vividness of his emotional imagery decreases, the
realism of his drawings increases, and the schema declines. In Read's thinking, the schema is as much a matter of the individual child as of an age level.

Eng (1931, 1957) in contrast with Read, and in agreement with the present writer's position, held that children's drawings are schematic not because of the greater significance of affect for children, but because their concepts are more concrete, less differentiated and abstract, and their drawing techniques limited. Early drawing is *ideomotive*; the child repeats lines and forms many times until he has a *formula*, which becomes virtually mechanical. It is this formula that he draws, even when he is given a model. The idea is present; the learned response is executed. Children produce more realistic drawings as their concepts become clearer and more differentiated, and as their skill with the medium increases.

Drawing reflects visual perception, which occurs primarily in a three-dimensional world. The child who draws either what he sees or what he knows must conform to the limitations of a two-dimensional surface. This necessity creates quite a few problems. The schema a child adopts represents his crude solution to these problems. The more adequate (but never complete) solutions achieved by artists do not occur to young children. Older children may discover some of them (such as overlapping, foreshortening and use of lines to suggest perspective, etc.) empirically by trial and error, or by noting photographs and pictures. Indeed, more than once it has been suggested that these elements of "reality" are of no consequence in the conceptual world of the child, becoming significant only as the primacy and conventions of the visually presented world are thrust upon him (e.g., Lowenfeld, 1939).

Karl Bühler, in effect, subscribed to this general view, but emphasized the verbal rather than the visual presentation of reality (1930). Bühler used *schema* to designate the distortions of drawing peculiar to the child; he saw these stylizations as a consequence of language, which "models the mind of man according to its requirements" (1930, p. 114).[5] By the time the child can draw more than a scribble (by age three or four), an already well-formed body of conceptual knowledge, formulated in language, dominates his memory and controls his graphic work. The highly schematic drawings of childhood result from this fact. Drawings are graphic accounts of essentially verbal processes. The sometimes chaotic appearance of children's drawings merely mirrors the fact that their verbal accounts are as yet unordered by the space and time sequences controlling the verbal productions of mature persons. As an essentially verbal education gains control, the child abandons his graphic efforts and relies almost entirely on words. "Language has first spoilt drawing and then swallowed it up complete" (Bühler, 1930, p. 120).

Bühler summarized his view: "It is in the main language which is responsible for the formation of concepts and therefore for the reorganization of mental life and the dominance of conceptual knowledge over concrete images" (1930, p. 124). The eminent art educator, Herbert Read (1945, pp. 130–31), already mentioned, offered a similar point of view, but emphasized the decline, with age, of vivid imagery as the verbal equipment for conceptual

---

[5] This is a point of view associated with Benjamin Whorf's work on language.

thought takes over. For Read, the schema was essentially the reflection of an image, a position which modern psychology has pretty much abandoned.

In art, the more mature and sophisticated expression of the schema is known as "style." The problem of style, i.e., the use of characteristic forms or techniques by individuals or during periods in the history of art, is very complex. Gombrich (1960) considered it to be the core of the psychology of art, and addressed his entire series of fascinating essays to the topic. One of the best brief discussions of the problem is by Schapiro (1953).

Considering style from the standpoint of history and criticism of art, Schapiro notes that style has a reality, though it appears to defy precise definition. Artifacts and works of art can correctly be assigned to periods on the basis of appearance and configuration of elements. Yet, attempts to analyze style into basic components often fail, as do mathematical approaches. It has been necessary to retain the vague and unsatisfactory language of qualities. Of the several theorists whose work he reviews, Schapiro proposes the system of Löwy (1907) as particularly adapted to children's drawings. Löwy bases his analysis of representative art on a progression from its beginning in schematic or stylistic "conceptual representation" according to the memory image to its conclusion in perspective representation according to the direct perception of objects. Löwy lists seven stages; starting from the designation of parts of figures and their shape and movement by few typical forms, to the representation of three-dimensional space in which action takes place. The student of children's drawings cannot escape considering these issues; he is continually impressed by the fact that the work of individual children is often recognizable, as well as by the fact that there are styles or schemas that characterize stages in a child's development of representative drawing.

In adult art, stylization or symbolism may arise from accentuation of certain features in realistic representation, permitting a few characteristic elements to convey the idea of the object as a whole. Thus, conventionalization may arise quite as much out of visual representation as from the more undifferentiated presentation of certain key ideas, noted in the work of the young child. Adam's warning (1954, p. 42), that we not read too much into the art work of primitive peoples, has its parallel in children's drawings. Adam specifically noted that so-called "cubism" in certain Gold Coast art was really due to conditions of the deep shadow in which people in that hot country work; they must use simple shapes if they are to see anything at all! Sometimes enthusiastic adults read similar "styles" into the work of young children, forgetting that they may merely be struggling with problems of media and technique.

A Possible Reconciliation of Theories

Theories of learning based on association concepts have long been dominant in psychology, and in Goodenough's work have been used to explain children's drawings. Yet, when the fact of patterns in perception and in graphic execution becomes evident, writer after writer either adopts Gestalt principles and theory outright (as Schaefer-Simmern and Arnheim), or adopts some modifications, utilizing the concepts of field, figure, ground, and pattern. The organismic interpretation usually includes the idea of patterned growth determined by field forces rather than by point-to-point influences, as in associationistic theory. Numerous writers have found it desirable to adopt such wholistic or dynamic concepts. Werner, perhaps, gives the most comprehensive and theoretically organized account of drawing from this viewpoint, yet his work remains largely descriptive. Such writers as Bell, Bühler, Campbell, Gombrich, and Witkin, while holding to associationistic learning theories in the main, find they must at some points call on the more global concepts of Gestalt or organismic theory. Only Graham and colleagues (1960) avoid these terms; they do so, however, by examining children's behavior in a very limited task.

Two views on perception have been advanced which may aid in reconciling these apparently divergent conceptions. Hebb (1949) posited hypothetical cell assemblies in the central nervous system to explain perceptual learning. Eleanor Gibson (1961), following Attneave (1954), drew upon the constructs of information theory to explain "meaning" in perception. Both accounts provide a theoretical basis for concept formation and thus both are potentially useful in a psychology of drawing, though neither have made much reference to drawing behavior.

McFee (1961) alone has attempted to assemble material from the psychology of perception as a basis for procedures in art education. Her view stresses the interaction of developing child and environing culture, and the complex relationship of personality and perception. More than the present writer, she accepts and incorporates the somewhat ambiguous and incomplete evidence from "social perception" research into her strongly social and educational viewpoint. She does not attempt to examine psychologically how percepts are organized into concepts, but divides concepts into the visual and cognitive—a distinction not generally made in the psychological literature. Her discussion, however, is lucid and informative and her applications to education logical and challenging.

A Neuro-Psychologic Theory of Perception Applied to Drawing

To apply Hebb's (1949) constructs and concepts to children's drawings it must be assumed that the child's behavior is socially reinforced by attention of others (comment, praise), or that the child exhibits a primitive exploratory or manipulative tendency. Confronted with paper and pencil, the child manipulates the materials in such fashion that his behaviors are subject to fairly rapid reinforcement and thus to modification. With age and learning the behavior becomes more complex, and the situation in drawing becomes essentially an adjustive one, with numerous problem-solving aspects.

Hebb notes from studies of perception (1949, p. 31) that the observer commonly perceives much more than he requires to make a discrimination; thus, he commonly responds to only part of the perceived figure. As we have seen, studies of drawing recognition and production reveal that there is reconstruction of figures from a few parts which have been perceived. The slopes of a few lines, their direction and distance from one another suffice to establish the entire figure when that figure has been learned. But in this process there is often reconstruction by the perceiver—he fills in gaps in the perception, or modifies the new or less well learned from his earlier experiences, calling on the well learned. Hebb believes that what the child learns essentially from visual training is to note the direction of lines and the distance between points, separately for each grossly separate part of the visual field (Hebb, p. 47). All early perceptions involve the elements of straight lines and points (lines and points in turn subsuming angles), and regularly curving lines. It is Hebb's theory that learning these perceptual elements as elements, and as combinations in complex patterns, involves a prolonged learning period (Hebb, p. 81) and much manipulative contact with objects.

Hebb describes a neuropsychological basis for the visual fixation of successive points on the contour of an object, leading to "inspectional sweeps," and to noting the intersections of lines. Intersections become the focus of greatest perceptual activity, and in the perceptual field correspond to corners of objects. The eye, then, tends to seek out the contours of a figure and follow them, irregularly, and with reversals. Numerous investigators have seen angles and corners as significant in perception, though difficult to manage in reproductive drawing. Thus it is Hebb's contention that straight lines and angles are fundamental in perception, not fully innate but partly so, and necessary to be learned before it is possible to perceive more complex patterns. He states:

> If line and angle are the bricks from which form perception are built, the primitive unity of the figure might be regarded as mortar, and eye movement as the hand of the builder (p. 83).

Thus, for Hebb the figure-ground relationship of Gestalt psychology is fundamental, yet not sufficient to explain the phenomena of perception. Likewise, motor activity alone cannot explain the organization of perception, yet it plays an essential role, leading to manipulation of objects, to tactual and kinesthetic reinforcement of visual perception, and to further definition of the visual correlates of form.

Hebb hypothesizes "cell assemblies" in the nervous system, functional linkages of neurones through electrochemical action, which account for the phenomena of association in learning. When an irregular object is seen from different points of view, each grossly different pattern of stimulation requires the establishment of a separate set of cell assemblies. If sight of the object from one direction is followed by sight from another, these separate assemblies develop interfacilitating connections, and ultimately the object arouses the same total neural activity, regardless of the vantage point of the observer. Thus, patterned perception acquires "constancy," and each perception involves *conceptual* activity, an activity not *directly* controlled by sensory processes, except as parts of the pattern were originally stimulated by sensory stimulation. Because of this conceptual activity, children's drawings, considered as visual reproductions, often contain "errors"—the child draws as he knows, not as he sees. By the same token the experienced artist, by deliberately introducing distortions in his painting, utilizes and incorporates the conceptual activities of the viewer. As has been shown, children often cannot tell wherein their drawing differs from what is actually presented to the eye. Whereas organismic theory says the object is still incompletely differentiated, Hebb says perception, refined by many experiences, has constructed a conceptual activity, triggering more cell assemblies than would the simple perception of the moment. The child has not yet built up the interfacilitations among separate cell assemblies to establish the constancies necessary to complex perceptions.

Hebb's position is that human learning "early" in development is rather different from "later" learning. For one thing, it occurs much more slowly, is graded in amount, and is built up steadily by small increments. Later learning occurs much more rapidly, sometimes on a single trial basis, may show the "all-or-none, quantum-like character of insight," and masters much more complex material. This "later" learning can occur only because of the cell assemblies built up by the slower, more detailed processes of "early" learning. Indeed, there is, as Harlow has pointed out (1949), a "learning how to learn," and this phenomenon occurs particularly in intelligent or problem-solving behavior as contrasted with rote learning; with meaningful material as contrasted with "nonsense" material. The child's many perceptual experiences with lines and points prepare him, when motor coordinations allow him to manage the pencil, to record the simplest elements of a complex figure. His motor learning along with his perceptual learning give him an increasingly complex schema with which to represent the human figure. This complex schema is essentially conceptual.

Administering formboard tests to West African native children, Nissen, Machover, and Kinder (1935) attributed the children's poor scores to slowness in identifying shapes rather than slowness in movement. They were inexperienced with the components of the required perceptions, the regular geometric forms omnipresent in more complex, "civilized" cultures. This observation is most instructive when the drawings of children in nonliterate or underdeveloped cultures are considered. Children inexperienced in recognition and production of conceptual schemata appropriate to pencil and paper are at a distinct disadvantage in the drawing task. Moreover, this disadvantage increases with age, as progressively older groups of children commonly fall farther and farther below Western white norms.

Hebb argues (1949, pp. 89–95), from experimental evidence as well as from the logic of his theory, that to perceive an object from many aspects requires a more complex learning process than to perceive it from one aspect. Such learning takes longer and is gained more readily the higher the animal is in the phylogenetic scale. The theory accounts for the observed fact that perception of an object's location is more readily achieved than perception of the object itself, especially if the object is near and is seen from different aspects. The theory thus accounts also for constancies in perception, which men attain but with which lower animals have difficulty. This theory, too, is relevant to drawing the human figure, inasmuch as the child acquires the capacity to draw this figure only as a result of about ten years of perceptual experience; and not all children manage to achieve the feat even then. Hebb's theory would account for the perception and reproduction of certain features, or "anchor points," in the human figure before others, thus in turn accounting for the schematic figures drawn by the young child. It would likewise account for the facts that: (1) the preschool child makes little distinction between the male and female form, (2) the young primary school child uses stylistic symbols to designate sex, and (3) the older child achieves naturalistic reproductions of male and female figures. It would also account for the fact that the preschool and early primary child draws a generalized man, and the older child a specific kind of man (e.g., with an occupation, or social role).

Hebb points out (1949, p. 133) that a concept is not unitary. There is a central core or meaning, often carried by a symbol, word, or words, and a fringe of contents varying from time to time, depending on circumstances of arousal. Elements from this fringe translated into symbols become, in time, incorporated into the core. Recombinations of such "core" meanings is what is meant psychologically by "restructuring."

A similar process occurs in children's drawings of the human figure. There is a schema, a certain minimal "core" of lines and shapes, which is rather constant from time to time for one child, and indeed from subject to subject of approximately the same degree of experience. This "core" or symbol is the organized Gestalt of organismic theorists. From time to time new elements are added to this core, selected from more peripheral awareness and from more recently differentiated and discriminated aspects of the human figure.

These elements vary from time to time, as perceptual experiences and specific learning become incorporated into the "core." The process from peripheral awareness to incorporation in the core has been well described by Goodenough and quoted earlier in this text. The child knows of the existence of a feature, such as a foot, shoe, or pocket, long before he draws it. At first its location on the figure is noted by a mark and later by a simple form. Only later still does the recognizable feature appear occasionally in the child's drawing. Its invariable inclusion in the drawing comes even later. Thus, the drawing of the human figure, a common and much-experienced object, as a concept subject to improvement through learning, becomes a useful index to intellectual maturity.

"Coding" of Perception, Concept Formation, and Drawing

Eleanor Gibson (1961) has reconciled processes of differentiation and association identified in perception, borrowing from information theory the important distinction between "coded" and "uncoded" stimuli. When "meanings" are given directly, or are contained in the stimulus, as light reflected from a tree, one speaks of uncoded stimuli; the referent is unequivocal. When meanings exist because of convention, usage, arbitrary definition, as in words, diagrams, coins, and the like, one speaks of coded stimuli; the referents are man-made and arranged. Gibson writes: "The identification of coded stimuli is learned, and the learning probably involves an associative process. But the association with the code symbol or referent must be *preceded* by *differentiation* of the stimuli to be coded" (1961, unpublished paper). Before the response (the referent in the code) can be associated to the stimulus, the stimulus must be successfully and consistently discriminated from other stimuli in its general class. In other terms, the observer must learn to discriminate the *invariant* aspect or property of the stimulus, or its particular class.

According to Gibson, children first identify a dimension (e.g., size, or weight) in experience and then increase precision of perception within the dimension by progressive differentiation (discrimination). Children very early learn invariants in the properties of objects about them (e.g., size) as a basis for their concepts. To this learning of progressive differentiation several sense modalities and countless experiences (i.e., trials) contribute. Because the process becomes very complex, even in such basic and commonly acquired properties as size and weight, it continues well into late childhood and early adolescence. Gibson fails to see how associative processes have much to do with the early phases of this learning—awareness of the pertinent dimension and increasingly precise discrimination of it. In learning coded stimuli—those to which words or other symbols are attached—associative processes are unmistakably involved. In learning language, phonemes must first be discriminated, then meaning begins to be attached to phonemic combinations through repeated association.

Both Hebb and Gibson thus make a distinction between early and later aspects of the learning process, though both admit that these "phases" may proceed simultaneously. Undoubtedly this is true in part because the organism is always involved in so many different learnings. Both investigators are in effect describing concept formation. The evidence repeatedly affirms that the drawing of a man is the graphic portrayal of a complicated concept, and that it improves as the child matures partly by increase in skill but chiefly by the more adequate discrimination (i.e., differentiation) of the concept, with the attendant attachment of meaning. As a process develops, increases in complexity and in the organization of subprocesses change the "nature" of the process. Eleanor Gibson and particularly Hebb employ this idea.

Summary and Conclusions

The material on children's drawing demonstrates clearly that the drawing function changes as the child matures. Drawing is first a means of expression wherein perceptual and motor aspects are inextricably bound with rudimentary concept formation. In time, the motor expression aspect of drawing becomes less and less important; the conceptual and communicative aspects more and more significant. As concepts become more sharply defined and controlled by visual percepts, the child's drawing of the human figure becomes more definitive, more indicative of a class, type, or particular individual, until his ideas outrun his technical skill and self-criticism increasingly intervenes to discourage drawing. In this process the child's increasing dependence on visual reality and on words to express that reality undoubtedly plays a part. He struggles with technique to achieve the effects he wants partly by sheer trial-and-success discovery, and partly by imitation from photographs and sketches observed. Unless he develops a measure of facility spontaneously or through instruction, the child abandons drawing.

Drawing becomes an esthetic expression for those older children, adolescents, and adults who have developed a measure of skill and can use it to communicate their concepts of design, arrangement, balance, and composition. This is not to deny that younger children form such abstract esthetic concepts; they do, but undoubtedly at a much more rudimentary level. Nor is this to deny that drawing expresses affect or feeling; it does, particularly for young children, but at the motor expression level. For those older children and adolescents who can master technique and manage to conceive the activity in terms of values in addition to visual realism, drawing may express affect at a more abstract, conceptual level. It is the writer's belief that research on the drawings of adolescents and adults could profitably attend to these abstractions, including the so-called "formal elements" of line, form, mass, balance, and proportion. Stewart (1955) and Lark-Horowitz and Norton (1960) have also made this suggestion. But such research will require that subjects be given fairly extensive training. It should be remembered that further progression in drawing performances is not found beyond ages twelve or fourteen. This is because most children have stopped spontaneous drawing by that time, thereby reducing or eliminating their opportunities for further learning in the medium.

Chapter Eleven

Children's Art

T H E   S T U D Y of children's drawings from a psychological viewpoint, even those drawings made in response to specific instructions, cannot be divorced from the study of art. When Goodenough came to her conclusions concerning the psychology of children's drawing, there had been very few studies on art production or on the psychology of esthetics. Many more such studies now exist in the literature.

Psychology and Art

Any theory of art must ultimately be a theory of perception and cognition and must also include affect or feeling. The cognition may not be verbal-abstract; it may be "imagistic," form-representative or even form-abstract. However, it will most probably involve those psychologically ill-defined concepts and constructs comprising the area known as esthetics.

Art has been approached as (1) *representative* of reality, (2) interpretative or *expressive*, and (3) *abstract*, in which the focus is on color, line, form, surface, space, and their interrelations. *Representation* is essentially illustration; the delight of the artist and of the viewer is in the life-like re-creation of some image or impression. *Expression* is often illustration plus purposeful distortion or selection to create an effect for both artist and viewer. The *abstract* is, in a sense, decorative; the satisfaction for both artist and viewer is in the use and interrelations of color, line, shape, and space. This last usage of art is highly abstract, as that term has been used in this volume, in that relationships among properties represent a step removed from the properties themselves, which in turn are the invariants in the perception of diverse objects or experiences, discussed in the previous chapter.

Representative, expressive, and abstract art are not mutually exclusive. The pleasing illustration selects and interprets familiar visual forms; the expressive drawing transmits emotion by form and design, often by distorting familiar objects or placing them in unusual settings; the abstract design is often expressive, and may also relate symbolically to familiar cognitive contents. Representative and expressive art that continues to please over long periods of time usually satisfies the principles of abstract art.

Thus, from a psychological viewpoint, art is exceedingly complex. To the psychologist, art consists of equivalences, or at least of relationships, between objects and ideas. The attempt to reduce these equivalences to formulae, whether in principles of physics or in pure mathematics, has not been widely accepted. Up to the present, there remains a nebulous area in experience, both in the production of a sketch and in the viewing of it, wherein something "creative" occurs (perhaps a recombination of elements). This essentially "psychological" experience has persistently defied conversion into the systematic symbols of mathematics or logic.

Is psychology properly concerned with things of the "mind," with experience as opposed to observable behaviors? Such was its usage in the early days of psychology, though modern scientific psychology has largely settled this question by concentrating on observable behavior. To the extent that art, whether seen as an interpretation of experience or as the result of behavior, is viewed as embracing some indefinable element, it remains *psychological* in the older sense of the term rather than *behavioral*, as this term is used today.

There is still another exceedingly troublesome problem in formulating a psychology of art. Science is analytical; analysis seems to destroy the completeness of the esthetic experience, and to lose the essential quality of the artistic product. But psychology has both humanistic and scientific aspects. A psychology of art and drawing in the rational or in the intuitive, effective sense of the discipline would yield one form of truth. A psychology of art and drawing in the research tradition of behavioral science would yield quite a different form of truth. The two would be supplementary, but they would probably defy reduction to common terms.

Aspects of Art and Children's Drawings

Thus far this volume has dealt largely with analytical, behavioristic approaches to drawing as representation, and to a lesser extent as expression. There have been a few systematic studies of children's use of the elements of art—color, line, mass, space, surface, and their interrelations—shape, form, proportion, balance, design, symmetry. There have been studies of techniques such as perspective, shading, and the like. Schools of instruction have been built around such elements and technique. Individual "style" can often be discerned in the use of elements and techniques and, as has been pointed out, peculiar treatments of these aspects of drawings have been the basis for "projective analysis" of personality.

Formal Elements in Drawing

Education in America and England has, in recent decades, viewed the art period as an opportunity for children's free expression rather than for teaching art techniques. This may account for the relatively few studies dealing with formal elements in children's work. The McCarty study (1924), one of the best of these, was done when the theory of art education permitted the teaching of techniques. Although she studied the work of young children who had had little or no art instruction, her approach was in harmony with the art education of that day. From spontaneous drawings made by more than 30,000 children, McCarty found that while at age four more than 70 per cent of children used outline principally, and somewhat less than 30 per cent used mass, there was a steady change in the preference for these techniques. By age eight, the ratio was approximately 60–40, with the larger proportion using mass principally, though at least a third combined the two elements.

McCarty also evaluated the appearance of proportion, balance (symmetry), and perspective, all of which were virtually nonexistent in drawings of four-year-olds. Proportion, as shown by reasonably effective use of relative size among objects in a picture, appears first and in the largest proportion of cases (approximately one-fourth of children achieving some success by age eight). Balance or symmetry in the arrangement of forms or objects remains quite foreign to eight-year-olds, less than four per cent showing this element. As in other studies of children's use of linear perspective, notably those of Clark (1897) and of Kerschensteiner (1905), the McCarty study noted its virtual absence in children under age eight.

Leroy's (1951) study of perspective in the drawings of French children was limited to reproductions of three objects—an auto, a house, and a boat. The study also included children's recognition of absurdities in pictured perspective. Although Leroy found that the use of perspective appears as early as age four and is reasonably common by age eight, American experience based on the free drawings and requested human figure drawings of children suggests that attempts at perspective are quite infrequent before ages eleven or twelve. Malrieu (1950) found that perspective appeared at about age ten. The present author found very small but increasing percentages of children using perspective at ages ten to fifteen.

The absence of these formal elements or features in execution does not mean that children are not aware of them. The Binet-type intelligence tests consistently place the beginnings of esthetic appreciation at five years, and the delight of young children in natural beauty and in color and design has long been noted and used in kindergarten practice. As in so many aspects of development, understanding or appreciation precedes spontaneous use.

Ellsworth (1939) analyzed the free easel paintings of twenty nursery school children as a means of studying the early stages of compositional design, particularly with respect to the relative use of line and mass. She found that if design was apparent, it most frequently took the form of a simple figural element placed in rows, columns, or concentric circles. Lines were more often used for the figures; mass more often when filling in backgrounds.

A more extensive study in this area was made by Cockrell (1930), who collected 1,550 paintings from three nursery schools, with a total enrollment of sixty children between the ages of twenty months and six years. Cockrell reported that the devices most frequently employed in composition were contrast and opposition, and these occurred in almost every painting. Balance of line, mass, or color was observed in 637 paintings; repetition in 262 instances; rhythm of movement in 180 paintings; and symmetry in 93 instances. All paintings showing symmetry were made by the same thirteen children. Unfortunately, little information is given concerning the abilities and personality traits possibly differentiating these thirteen children from their classmates. Cockrell concluded that training in design is unnecessary for young children.

Toward a Systematic Psychology of Children's Art

To the studies of proportion, balance, design, symmetry, and the like, in children's drawings must be added the series of systematic studies carried out by Norman Meier and his students at the University of Iowa. It is to be regretted that these promising early studies were not followed by others. Of the three monographs published by Meier only the first (1933) deals specifically with the art of children. Its several papers, written by Meier's students, will be considered here.

Daniels (Meier, 1933, pp. 1–11) described an ingenious method for studying the recognition of compositional balance. Pairs of block designs, one of which was balanced in composition and the other unbalanced, were constructed within recesses in a wooden frame and presented visually to children. The balanced model was sometimes on the right, sometimes on the left. The task of the child was to duplicate with a set of blocks either of the two models he wished. After he had finished he was asked to look at the models again and to choose the "nicer" one. Thirty-eight children were subjected to 185 experimental situations. Among all the children's models, there were only eighteen clear attempts to copy the unbalanced design, and the unbalanced compositions were preferred in only thirty-one choice situations. The author stated conservatively, that because neither of these proportions is reliably greater than chance, the results indicate that "no child evinced a definite *preference* for the unbalanced design" (Meier, 1933, p. 9).

Jasper (Meier, 1933, pp. 12–25) made use of four devices for studying rhythm in graphic forms. In all four tests regular progress with age was observed, but other findings were of little significance. Whorley's careful analysis of the literature on the subject of rhythm (Meier, 1933, pp. 26–45) suggested that three elements of compositional unity be studied—emphasis, balance, and fitness. A test was designed for each. Emphasis was studied by requiring the child to arrange four toy trees around a birdbath. Balance or symmetry was studied by the child's arrangement of the trees around a central archway. Fitness was evaluated by the child's arrangement of furniture within a doll house. Scale values were obtained by utilizing the median value given by art experts to each of a series of photographed arrangements chosen to represent a roughly graded series. Scores were assigned by comparing the children's arrangements with photographs as standards. Children under four obtained low scores on these scales. With age improvement occurred, but even among the adults success was far from universal. The test yielded very high reliability coefficients for the method, but inspection of the scatter diagrams suggests that the figures reported are in error by a considerable amount.

Children's sensitivity to color harmony was evaluated by Williams (Meier, 1933, pp. 46–50) in a brief methodological report. A doll-dressing procedure was used that included two identical sets of small dolls. Each doll in the set was dressed in a different color. The dolls were handed to the subject one at a time, together with four scarves of different colors. The child was asked to choose the scarf that he thought "would look nice with the doll's pretty dress." One of the scarves was a harmonizing color; the other three were chosen to give as poor an effect as possible. Walton (Meier, 1933, pp. 51–62) applied Williams' method to discover that ideas of color harmony prevalent among young children differ materially from those of older persons in the culture. Both means and medians show a steady *decrease* up to the age of seven, after which improvement occurs until the adult level is reached. The small sex difference observed consistently favored the girls. There was no relationship of the score on this test to intelligence, and a small group of children considered to be gifted in art performed only slightly better than a group judged to lack artistic ability.

These studies demonstrate that some of the subjective aspects of art, such as balance, symmetry, and harmony can be defined and studied experimentally. They show that young children demonstrate the formal elements of art in a rudimentary fashion and utilize these elements increasingly as they grow older. These principles are probably learned from incidental visual stimulation of the environment. It should be possible to investigate this learning systematically. The variables of age, intelligence, and experience could be controlled and the application of acquired knowledge and skill could be studied.

The "golden section"[1] and its more complex formulation as "dynamic symmetry" has long been a favorite subject for experimentation in the psychological laboratory. Using 100 subjects at each of four levels—preschool, third and sixth grades, and college, Thompson (1946) investigated preference for a series of 12 rectangles that were of uniform length but varied in width from a width-length ratio of 0.25 to 0.75. The preschool group favored no particular rectangle or group of rectangles. Adult (college student) preferences stabilized in the 0.50 to 0.65 range. There was steadily increasing similarity to adult preferences in the third- and sixth-grade groups. The culture seems to orient preference toward certain width-length proportions, with adults noticeably rejecting the 0.70 and 0.75 proportions. Cordeau (1953), however, claims that about half of the children who make spontaneous drawings of rectangles approach the dimensions of the golden section; whereas less than ten per cent of the same children *choose* preferentially a rectangle of this dimension.

---

[1] "The golden section is the division of a line into two parts, so that the square on the one part is equal to the area of the rectangle formed by the whole line and the other part" (Drever, J. *Dictionary of Psychology.* Baltimore: Penguin, 1952).

Whether a particular complex quality of the person known as *talent* exists, and to what extent its components can be identified, still evades rigorous analysis. Meier concluded that talent is composed of a number of qualities in the possession of which people differ markedly at birth. Ordinarily these qualities develop in all persons, in proportion to the potential with which a person starts. Great talent consists in the possession of high potential in all necessary elements. Meier's studies suggested such a theory to him, although they did not demonstrate it; nor did his several papers dealing with differences between children presumed to be gifted in art and those presumed to lack talent, help his argument. Even though these studies are almost unique in the psychological literature, they can be said to have only begun to approach the subject.

The Factor Analysis of Drawing

Factor analysis is widely used to organize the fragmentation brought about by analytic procedures. Differing measures of the same complex of phenomena can be intercorrelated; and the components which parsimoniously account for the observed interrelationships among measures can be defined mathematically. From these definitions psychological inferences may be drawn, depending on the investigator's knowledge of and insight into the components he has defined and measured. It is important to remember, however, that such a technique can only organize the measures put into it. Because factor analysis requires correlations, it is natural for the investigator to study easily measured aspects of drawings. Few such factor analytic studies have been made of art products, and it is not surprising that these studies have dealt largely with ratings of formal qualities of drawings.

Martin and Damrin (1951) rated drawings produced by thirty-one children on eleven five-point scales, including such variables as symmetry, firmness of line, expansiveness of the drawings as a whole, expansiveness of individual parts, pressure, continuity of strokes, and distinctness of features of individual figures. A factor analysis applied to these ratings, while based on too few cases for firm determination of factors, was interpreted as yielding three factors designated as Maturity, Balance, and Quality of Strokes. The first of these probably represents the psychological component assessed by Goodenough's method; the latter two clearly refer to more formal elements. The relation of these factors to psychological measures was not investigated.

Lark-Horowitz and Norton (1960) reported a factor analysis of ten characteristics rated on several hundreds of crayon drawings contributed by as many children, six to fifteen years old. The characteristics included such items as use of blended color, balance in grouping, intentional asymmetry, and line treatment. Each drawing was rated dichotomously as to whether the characteristic contributed to its artistic quality. It is perhaps significant that the percentage of drawings achieving an artistic or esthetic rating on each of the ten characteristics ranged from 4.0 to 21.2, with a median value at 7.9 per cent. Thus, the correlations (tetrachoric) were based on extremely asymmetrical distributions of ratings, in which only a small number of drawings achieved the positive rating. Entirely apart from the statistical problems this situation creates, it is evident that this study did not deal with abilities or qualities shown by most children.

Seven of the ten characteristics correlated +.37 or higher with chronological age. A Developmental, or Age, component thus became a logical first factor to extract, and a principal factor solution of the intercorrelations was designed for this purpose. The following variables contributed substantially to the Developmental factor: realism; attempt to use shape in an artistic rather than clearly outlined manner; suggestion of a specific style in painting; diversity of means of indicating motion; consistent and effective use of the crayon medium; bold, blended, or graded (textured) treatment of area; bold, subtle, or delicate use of line; chronological age.

A Style factor accounted for almost as much of the variance as the first factor. To this factor were related the use of color; use of shape in artistic manner; suggestion of a particular style; effective use of the medium; and treatment of areas. The third factor, less clearly defined, seemed to be a Motion factor. To it were related balance in grouping; purposeful asymmetry of arrangement in contrast with symmetry or haphazard placement; and the number of ways in which motion was suggested.

The Developmental factor probably includes some aspects of drawing revealed more explicitly by the Goodenough method. It is possible that the realistic or representational quality, diversity of ways of indicating motion, and use of line characteristics are based on the same elements that Goodenough (and the present studies) have found to relate so substantially to age. The use of shape, the suggestion of a particular style, the consistent use of the medium, and the treatment of area characteristics less obviously incorporate Goodenough-type scoring elements; they are more global and qualitative in nature, yet they appear to correlate positively with age.

The Lark-Horowitz studies are unique in using concepts of art other than conventional formal elements. The studies show that quantitative methods can be successfully and meaningfully applied to concepts defined and judged by artists. From the descriptions supplied by the authors, it appears that a psychologist probably could not make reliable discriminations without training in the application of the concepts; they are not self-evident from the verbal descriptions supplied. From the percentage of the drawings contributing to the various characteristics hypothesized by Lark-Horowitz and her colleagues, it is evident that a set of concepts other than those defined by either Goodenough or Martin and Damrin were evaluated.

A different approach was made by Stewart (1955), who evaluated self-portraits obtained under standard conditions from adolescents in the classic Berkeley longitudinal study. The experimental design required independent ratings by three judges on each of thirty-one variables, using seven-point rating scales. These variables included such stylistic and formal qualities as realism, symmetry, rhythm, naturalism, firmness of line, etc. The judges studied definitions of the variables and discussed them before making their ratings. The reliability (inter-judge correlation) of ratings varied from +.10 to +.83; most of the variables having "an adequate degree of reliability for research purposes" (Stewart, 1955, p. 97). These variables resemble those of Martin and Damrin more than those of Lark-Horowitz and colleagues.

Stewart's data were treated separately for boys and girls. While similar clusters appeared in both analyses, the patterns suggest that perhaps there should be differences in the psychological interpretation of the clusters found. Among boys, the following factors (or clusters of components) appear to exist: (A) technical skill and esthetic quality; (B) naturalistic representation; (C) static symmetry; (D) width and variability of line; and (E) angularity (i.e., tendency to use angular forms). For the girls, the first factor appeared to break into two separate clusters—technical skill, and esthetic quality and rhythm. Clusters B, C, D, and E appear with much the same components as in the boys' data but less clearly delineated or differentiated. Girls' drawings, however, yielded a seventh cluster, designated as emphasis on movement, which did not emerge in the boys' drawings as a separate factor. Certain of these factors, notably B and possibly A, may overlap the aspects of drawings evaluated by the Goodenough method. That a developmental or age factor did not appear in this study is probably due to the fact that the artists were adolescents, homogeneous in age.

Scores for the several factors were estimated for the children, unfortunately from the same drawings used to derive the factors. These factor scores were correlated with adjustment measures ("Guess Who" tests, personality and interest inventories) and behavior ratings (self-ratings and teacher ratings). The resulting coefficients were low but in some cases were significantly greater than zero. For example, among boys, skill quality (cluster A) seemed to be associated with self-dissatisfaction and neurotic introversion; among girls, this cluster related to creativeness and adjustive-introversion tendencies. Cluster D in boys was related to dominant extraversion; to sociability and adjustment in girls. All statistically significant correlations fell considerably below a value useful for prediction in the individual case.

The factor peculiar to girls, which included "emphasis on mouth" as well as "movement," was associated with personality ratings of self-assertion and striving for recognition. It will be recalled that movement in drawings is a "masculine" characteristic. Stewart's finding may reflect only that girls who draw similarly to boys tend to resemble boys in aggression. This would be an interesting hypothesis to investigate, especially since girls characteristically draw a small dainty mouth.

Stewart recorded the fact that adolescent boys with some artistic talent tend to be rated as self-dissatisfied and neurotic. By adolescence, art interests and activities are rather generally accepted as relating to the feminine role in our culture. Boys with strong propensities toward art may experience considerable role conflict, especially in adolescence when status and sex-appropriate roles are so very important.

A finding of this revision and extension of the Goodenough scale may also throw light on Stewart's observation that girls draw more "stereotyped" or standardized self-portraits than do boys. It has been shown that girls are relatively more superior to boys in drawing the female figure than in drawing the male figure. Moreover, girls tend consistently to excel on facial features, hair, and presence of accessories (such as beads, etc.). Attention to facial details in drawings is a feminine characteristic, possibly greatly encouraged by the massive advertising campaigns of the cosmetics industry. Facial details do not group themselves with other clusters of attributes. It may be that girls, with their greater skills in drawing and attention to detail, achieve a superior schema for portraying the female figure, and it is this schema that comes through in the self-portraits. The fact that girls' clusters do not differentiate as well as do boys' may also result from the general superiority of girls in human figure drawings; a consistently higher pattern of intercorrelations among aspects of drawing would tend to blur the separate factors.

By plotting the factor scores for all the boys, Stewart discovered several fairly distinct types of factor profiles. When representative work for each of these "types" was studied, Stewart found it feasible to attach names of well-known "schools" of art to examples. The Realistic or Naturalistic self-portrait was executed with average skill, contained much shading, had smooth lines, and was curved and regular. The Decorative or Expressive self-portrait lacked shading, was flat, schematic, and very symmetrical. The Primitive type was rigidly symmetrical and non-naturalistic, crude and unskilled, with wide and variable lines. A fourth type was high on skill and esthetic quality and tended toward the Decorative. The fifth type resembled the Naturalistic type but showed a higher degree of skill. The sixth type was clearly Expressive, being asymmetrical, high on movement, vivid in style, with wide and variable lines. Adjective check lists applied to the "artist" subjects revealed clusters of adjectives characteristically applied to each of the six types of artist.

Thus, depending upon the variables defined and the ratings made, the results of factor analyses fit or rationalize certain more general or intuitive impressions of drawings. Moreover, the Stewart study suggests a low but positive correlation between features of adolescents' drawings and personality qualities, a finding not well established by the investigations of clinical psychologists reported in Chapter III. The Stewart study of drawing styles is one of the few studies with positive findings in the personality area.

Child Art and Personality Development

This review has noted several art theorists who have attempted to utilize well-established psychological concepts and principles in formulating their approach to teaching art. Notable among these have been Arnheim, Lowenfeld, Gombrich, Schaefer-Simmern, and to a lesser extent, perhaps, Read. Their opinions are often unique and always strongly expressed. Even among contesting viewpoints, however, there is close agreement on the idea that artistic activity can have an impact on the person usually described as enriching, freeing, or enhancing to personality development. This effect on the development of normal children is one of the bases for justifying art in the modern school curriculum. It is also one of the reasons for using art in the treatment of psychologically disturbed children and adults.

Three projects, rather differently oriented philosophically, illustrate the developmental effects of graphic art. One was the quite unsophisticated, almost accidental, experience of an artistically untrained teacher with a group of neglected aboriginal waifs on a government reservation in Australia. Another occurred at the hands of an art teacher in an evacuation camp and school for boys in war-torn England. The third was a demonstration and experiment with mentally retarded children and adults and with juvenile delinquents by an art theorist and educator in New York City.

The experience at Carrolup, Australia (Miller and Rutter, 1952) is instructive. Mr. White, a teacher, apparently had a genuine liking for the neglected outcasts in his school, mostly older children and young adolescents. He also had an interest in music and the dance and quickly sensed the capacities of his children for these activities. These activities seemed to awaken a responsiveness in the previously apathetic children. Through practical attention to personal sanitation and appearance, Mr. White built up their sense of worth. Then he tried graphic art. Although Mr. White knew literally nothing about sketching and painting, he encouraged "scribble patterns," using crayons to fill in spaces and interstices. He quickly discovered that the children enjoyed this activity and were able to create surprisingly varied and pleasing effects. The school inspector, himself an amateur artist, was struck by this fact, supplied materials, and encouraged Mr. White to permit the children to experiment freely. Says Mary Miller, who reported the experience:

> Any actual instruction they received in the use of the media was from Mr. Crabbe (the inspector) during his brief, very occasional visits. In the second year of their art development, he showed them how to apply a graded wash and how it was possible to draw with a brush, though he was sensitive lest he should hamper them with directions or in any way interfere with the characteristic style they were developing. Those who seek a clue to the origin of this style will not find it in Mr. Crabbe's own delicate, academically finished paintings (Miller and Rutter, 1952, p. 43).

Following Mr. Crabbe's suggestion to encourage children to observe, Mr. and Mrs. White took the youngsters on walks, helping the children to notice more and more detail in nature about them—a crouching rabbit, the peculiar shapes and patterns of bark on the trees, of hollows and bumps on tree trunks, and the tracery patterns of tree limbs against the sky. Through this technique and through Mr. White's suggestion that they illustrate their written work in school, the children developed a habit of writing out descriptions of what they saw, using small sketches to illustrate the details. Notable to the teacher, the school inspector, and the visitors who came to see the work was the marked contrast in appearance, alertness, poise, interest, and school performance of these children to others. Part of the children's personality development was undoubtedly enhanced by Mr. White's interest in native history and tradition, and by his telling the youngsters about native guides famous in the early days of the country.

Clearly, the effect of this experience was to develop conceptual as well as visual images in the children and to encourage them to draw the world as they saw it. Observation was reinforced by the assignment to translate their visual impressions into words. Yet their work did not fall into photographic realism. In their use of form and color the children achieved surprisingly original effects and interpretations, as the plates in Miss Miller's book show. Whereas much untrained aboriginal art is schematically realistic, portraying what is *known to be* rather than what is *seen*, these children moved ahead to draw what they *saw*, not what they *knew*. They re-created rich and varied mental images. In writing of the effect of the experience on the children's work, Miss Miller says:

> No doubt suggestions that these children may have developed more interestingly if left alone are surely made in ignorance of their story, as are also the regrets expressed that this is not "aboriginal art." The work is that of children of aboriginal blood who know as little of the art forms of their forefathers as they do of the moderns, or, for that matter, of any artists of our own society. They were no more or less influenced than any of their kind with eyes to see and ears to hear in a white man's world. But what they produced was something spontaneous and unique in itself (1952, p. 65).

And she adds further,

> It can only be said that Australia has not seen the like of this work before, and, despite the fact that so many people of aboriginal blood are artistically inclined, it is doubtful whether the phenomenon of Carrolup—an unusual combination of circumstances and a vital teacher-pupil relationship—will ever occur again (1952, p. 65).

The experiment in England took place at the Whiteacre Camp (Dunnett, 1948), a war-time evacuation camp and school for older children and adolescents. During the five years the camp operated, it saw a changing population of some 900 boys, 200 being present at any one time. As a part of their regular school experience all these boys were given stimulating experiences with graphic art by a teacher who obviously liked them and who regarded art as enriching, contributing to a sense of freedom, self-confidence, and self-respect.

This teacher was not concerned with art for art's sake, but with using art to contribute to personality enrichment and enhancement. She appreciated the evacuee's natural desires to make and to possess things of their own, and introduced and encouraged the use of various art forms. She convinced these boys that their work was truly art, meritorious in its own right. Using discussions of the work of great artists, she combined art appreciation with the experiences in art production. She encouraged the development of individual interest and taste by the free expression of likes and dislikes, accepting as valid all honest expressions. Gaining confidence, many of the boys did develop marked preferences in pattern and design. Once freed from the idea that visual conceptions must always be imitative, and also freed from fears of making mistakes, their artistic expressions became happy, intense, and varied.

Schaefer-Simmern's experiment in New York (1948) was based on a much more explicit and clearly developed theory of art and of art education. But like the Whiteacre experience, it was also based on the assumption that artistic capacity is a natural attribute of all human beings. Using a theory of self-expression, with due regard for encouragement of unique and individual conceptions, Schaefer-Simmern's experiment achieved surprising results in mentally defective adolescents and adults and in a group of delinquent adolescents. In this study, as in the Carrolup and Whiteacre experiences, the evidence points out the enhancing effects of long-continued, satisfying experiences with artistic media. Schaefer-Simmern emphasizes that as the individual achieves increasing self-confidence and freedom from preconceived notions, his art product improves and exhibits unfolding Gestalts or patterns of graphic expression. These patterns, he believes, are intrinsic to the psychological process whereby visual concepts are translated into drawings; their unfolding follows definite developmental trends.

In all three experiences reviewed above, certain common elements appear. These may be summarized as follows:

1. The children are generally eleven or twelve years of age and older.[2]
2. There is a teacher who believes firmly in the efficacy of art for personality enrichment and development.
3. This teacher also believes firmly, indeed passionately, in the potential of children for goodness and growth.
4. These teachers bring about in children an intense experience of the environment which is direct and concrete, but is also one stage removed from immediate sensation and perception. The concrete experiences are somehow converted into images, visual and verbal.

At the Whiteacre Camp, for example, Ruth Dunnett encouraged children to collect stones and other objects of nature, which were examined, compared and contrasted, sorted, and classified in many different ways. Fruit pits, eggs, acorns, branches, leaves, bits of bark, and similar objects were studied.

---

[2] The author considers this an important circumstance for the artistic and expressive development that resulted. Most of the children were close to the end or already past the period when drawing is principally calligraphy.

These studies were enhanced by handling, comparing, and discussing the materials. The comparison and sorting emphasized attributes of form, color, texture, and the like, but also emphasized generalizations.

In the Australian experiment, Mr. and Mrs. White took the children on many nature walks, requiring them to observe details of trees, animals, plants, and, upon returning, to attempt to draw in different poses and situations the things they had seen. Both experiments stressed discussion by the children of their experiences and of the items they had collected or seen.

5. The child comes to see his artistic expression as a means of conveying his unique experience, which is both emotional and cognitive in character.

6. The children work extensively with artistic media. Children must make many drawings, many paintings, do much clay work, to adapt the hand to the tools and to explore the possibilities of the medium itself.

7. Instruction in technique comes relatively late, only after the children have had clear perceptual and cognitive experiences and have developed a desire to communicate these experiences. Techniques then become aids in this communication.

In the Australian study, the supervisor on rare visits to the bush school would make a few specific suggestions on technique, or supply new materials with which to work with a word or two about handling them. At the Whiteacre Camp, the children themselves began to discuss the technical uses of perspective, balance, line, color, and the like, as they experimented with the materials. The teacher always followed the children's own lead, making a suggestion, directing their exploration by a question, showing one or two methods of solving a child's problem after the child had verbalized his problem and his attempts to solve it. Miss Dunnett says: "The boys were forever discovering technical details about drawing and painting, and as time went on they asked more and more direction and absorbed it avidly" (Dunnett, 1948, p. 36).

In the Whiteacre experiment interest was maintained and experimentation encouraged by having the children try one medium, then another, returning occasionally to earlier experiences to explore them further. The teacher directed, allowing only limited freedom of choice in media at any one time, but seeing to it that experience varied constantly.

8. Children learn technique from each other, as well as from the teacher.

It is interesting to note that Schaefer-Simmern elicits a striking similarity of pattern in his subjects which he interprets as a developmental mode of expression inherent in the "visual conceiving" process. It has also been pointed out that pupils of an enthusiastic art teacher often show a homogeneous and identifiable "style," even when technique is not consciously taught. Such a "style" appears in the work of the several Australian children illustrated in Miss Miller's book; apparently they learned modes of expression from each other, as their teacher did not draw. The Whiteacre children's work, like the work of Viktor Lowenfeld's pupils, shows a variety of effects. But perhaps this fact of recognizable style is less significant than that a warm, enthusiastic, and inspired teacher gets children to believe in themselves and in their abilities to communicate through drawing, disengaging them from cramping preconceptions of pictorial reproduction.

Summary

Any discussion of the psychology of children's drawings is incomplete without reference to studies of children's art more broadly considered. Graphic art has been conceived as *representation* or illustration, as *interpretation* or expression, and as *abstract* or, in a sense, decorative. Art, thus, is complex, serving different functions and motives. Psychologically, art must be discussed in experience constructs; behavior theory at present seems inadequate to treat fully the phenomena of art.

Studies of children's use of color, line, space, surface, and their interrelations—shape, form, proportion, balance, symmetry, and design—show progressive trends as children master the mechanics of the medium and the perceptive and cognitive processes necessary to conceptualization. Skill in the use of these formal elements is attained through very complex learnings. Entirely apart from specific instruction, there are discernible convergences and trends in children's work.

Studies employing factor analyses show that detailed, analytic evaluations of drawings can be accounted for in terms of a limited number of general factors. One of these is clearly an Age, or Maturity factor; others may be described as balance or arrangement, quality of line or stroke, style or artistic or esthetic quality, and movement or rhythm. There is evidence, moreover, that by adolescence, these factors have clustered sufficiently to suggest that some children recognizably follow one or another of the three major functions served by art. There is realistic or naturalistic work; there is expressive work, and there is work that is highly skilled and primarily esthetic. A fourth "primitive" type possibly represents the work of those who have not progressed beyond earlier, cruder representations.

Art education has emphasized the psychological consequences of encouragement of free, imaginative work. Three "experiments" in art education, although quite different in theoretical orientation, showed a convergence of features. All had as subjects older children or adolescents encouraged by enthusiastic teachers. These teachers stressed direct observation of and sensorial experience with the environment, urging motor and perceptual manipulations, and the verbalization of perceptions. The teacher emphasized the value of each child re-creating in his own way his perceptual experience through the artistic medium. They motivated intensive practice, and added instruction in technique late in the process, only to aid individual children solve particular problems. In this process children learned from trial and success and from each other as well as from the teacher. All three projects reported a "freeing" of affective expression and the enhancement of personality development.

Chapter Twelve

Summary and Conclusions

THIS BOOK has surveyed the directions that research on children's drawings has taken, reported a program of research on drawings as measures of intellectual maturity, and reviewed the major theoretical positions relating to a psychology of children's drawings.

The study of children's drawings has long followed the descriptive tradition. The stages of children's drawings are now rather well delineated. The drawing of the human form, particularly that of the male, reveals progress in the child's concepts such that an index can be derived from his inclusion of body detail. This index provides a measure of intellectual maturity that correlates substantially with tests of so-called general intelligence, and relates to the ability to do abstract thinking. It does not correlate more highly with esthetic, motor, perceptual, or performance-test abilities than it does with verbal or conceptual abilities. Children's drawings of the human figure do not appear to be valuable as measures of interest, temperament, affective or personality factors; the large part of the variance seems to be accounted for by cognitive, conceptual factors. Those who persistently seek clues to the child's affective life in his drawings may have underestimated the importance of cognition in personality development and integration. It has been shown that drawings do tell us about the conceptual, intellectual component of personality.

Contributions of This Research

Specific studies reported in this book have shown that:

1. The human figure continues to be a favorite drawing subject for children, who strive to represent it as it appears visually.

2. It has been possible to derive a Draw-a-Woman scale which parallels the Draw-a-Man scale.

   a. The scales are offered on a point score basis, with tables for converting them to standard scores with a mean of 100 and standard deviation of 15.

    b. The intercorrelation of the two scales falls somewhat below the reliability of either scale alone.

    c. The female figure is more "culture bound" than the male figure, and perhaps less stereotyped and more susceptible to individual interpretation. This conclusion accords with Goodenough's supposition in her earlier study.

3. It is not possible to extend the scale upward in age as an index of the same abilities measured in children between the ages of four and fourteen.

    a. There is much evidence in the literature and in this study to support the hypothesis that visual realism and self-criticism operate to discourage children's representative drawing efforts.

    b. Individual scoring points cease to show an age increment in the early teens; some even show an age decrement at age fifteen. This decrement occurs when points are lost as children attempt a "sketching" technique to suggest rather than portray a feature.

4. Contrary to the evidence of many older studies, girls in Western cultures do better on the drawing test than do boys. Whether there is a true shift in drawing in Western cultures over the past fifty or sixty years is difficult to say. This change may reflect both educational and cultural changes.

    a. This difference exists to a relatively greater degree on the Woman than on the Man scale.

    b. On both scales, there are certain items on which girls excel and certain ones on which boys excel.

    c. There are certain features that are handled differently in "style" by the sexes.

5. Compared with the standardization data of 1926, children today perform substantially at a higher level on many items in the test. The reason for this is not at once apparent.

6. Educational influences are significant in shaping and modifying the basic schemata that children adopt when they draw the human figure. The suggestion is that cultural peculiarities or patterns, as well as sex differences, do exist, and these probably reflect general visual as well as pictorial influences.

7. The Drawing of the Self may, possibly, be more useful in studying nonintellectual psychological factors. Although this drawing has been less completely evaluated, it is the author's impression that its general dimensions follow the lines established for the Man and Woman drawings. Children do attempt, however, increasingly with age, to portray

juvenile and idiosyncratic features. In other words, they try to present themselves as they characteristically appear in dress, with favorite possessions, and the like.

8. Quality scales for convenient and rapid scoring of the Man and Woman drawings have been developed and standardized. These scales are not as sensitive measures of development as the Point scales, especially after age eight or nine. Moreover, the Quality scales tend to magnify the sex differences observed on the Point scales.

The Descriptive Psychology of Drawing

From a review and synthesis of the research literature, it is possible to draw some general conclusions and propositions concerning the psychology of children's drawings. Though the great bulk of the literature is descriptive and empirical, and though very few writers have acknowledged systematic theory, major contending theoretical positions may be discerned. Throughout the extensive review it has been noted that an analytic approach contends with a wholistic or organismic viewpoint. The former appears primarily in descriptive and theoretic research papers; the latter in some theoretic papers, but primarily in art and art education theory, and in interpretative and clinical studies of personality. In general, it appears that the analytic method has yielded more fruitful results and has built up the more scientifically impressive literature. This literature has firmly established the major psychological correlates of children's drawings in the area of concepts and cognitive processes. Wholistic, interpretative approaches, however, have called attention to persisting problems which the analytically inclined have tended to brush aside. Wholistic approaches have emphasized the complexity of the drawing process and its essential relationship to the child's maturity in other respects. They have thus catalyzed, corrected, and returned research to the level of observed phenomena.

Likewise, various discussions divide on the need fulfilled by the drawing act: the communication of ideas, expression of inner feeling or affective states, or the expression of a more abstract, purely esthetic satisfaction in use of color, line, mass, space, surface. Again, depending upon one's theoretical and practical position and the details of drawing behavior to which he attends, he may find evidence for any position. If he is an academic or developmental psychologist, he is likely to view drawing as signifying cognitive content. If he is interested in personality development and deviations, is a clinician and therapist, or is an art educator, he is likely to favor the emotional expression hypothesis. If he is interested in esthetics, and the more abstract aspects of human thought, he may emphasize abstract esthetic satisfaction in his interpretation of art.

Actually, drawing seems to satisfy all of these motives. At any age, elements of all of these motives are evidenced in children's drawings, but the relative emphasis shifts with development. The very young child seems to gain an intense satisfaction, largely affective in nature, from the motoric expression involved in scribbling and drawing. Then, for a short time, around age six or seven, an interest in form and pattern as such may appear. Increasingly, however, his drawing becomes a form of language—a way of expressing concepts and ideas. It is thus a form of *calligraphy*, a kind of elaborate and stylized writing. At the same time, however, the child becomes increasingly adept at handling line, mass, and space, and interrelating these to produce shape, form, proportion, balance, and design in his drawings of familiar objects. In effect he is discovering the techniques of graphic art. But primarily his drawings at this time express the growing complexity of his concepts of concrete objects and their interrelationships.

With increasing skill in and dependence on verbal communication, the calligraphic aspect of drawings tends to be displaced. Most children become so dependent upon verbal techniques, so aware of the criterion of visual realism which is forced on them by an overwhelmingly visual, even pictorial, culture, and so critical of their inability to achieve visual effects commensurate with this criterion, that they give up drawing altogether.

This state of affairs (occurring in late childhood) is recognized quite generally and is much deplored by educators. A number of prominent art educators have demonstrated in different ways the possibility of reducing the tendency to self-criticism and reinforcing the satisfactions in motoric and emotional as well as conceptual expressions, so that graphic and other art forms can become a satisfying expression for children and adults. It is possible that only under these circumstances does drawing predominantly serve a truly esthetic function. This effect, however, requires considerable effort and requires mastery of a number of complex skills. Moreover, skill in the creative use of form, proportion, balance, symmetry, and design probably also requires the kind of highly abstract concepts which do not appear until adolescence.

All students of children's drawings recognize that there are distinct developmental features in the drawing process. Those who have described successive stages in the depiction of the human figure invariably discern the same or closely similar stages. Children *do* adopt similar devices for portraying the human figure at roughly similar ages. Some authorities think of these stages as the result of limits set by the child's nature. A child is limited by the present stage of his cognitive or conceptual development and cannot achieve results more complex than those he portrays. Others think of the stages as *necessary phases in the successive organization* of a complex response, wherein one stage must be mastered before the child can go on to the next.

It is this latter notion of successive stages that has proved more intriguing psychologically. Some have felt that there is an unfolding of inherent patterns and that this process, if we only knew how to read it, could tell us more of the evolving child mind. Such was pretty largely the earlier view. A more contemporary view believes that the child's stages of drawing depict successive steps in his attainment of complex concepts and his discovery and mastery of intricate techniques for delineating these concepts within the limitations of the medium—crayon or pencil on a plane surface.

Stages in Children's Drawings

Indeed, one can discern three very broad stages in which drawing seems to fulfill rather different functions psychologically. There is a very early phase, wherein the pleasure is primarily in making marks on paper; these marks gradually assuming form and character. The child's interest is less in what he achieves than in the act of producing effects. This is the stage that has been discerned so clearly in higher apes and in infants.

The next general phase consists of imitative and reproductive drawing. In this, the child progressively attains the concepts necessary to depicting the human figure as it appears to the eye. The successive stages of this general phase in drawing describes a progression in conceptual maturity, based on increasing differentiation and organization of detail. This general phase of drawing also sees the attainment and incorporation of increasingly complex concepts, so that drawings in this period become a simple but clearly defined index to cognitive complexity.

The third broad phase is much less often realized in individual development. This phase, it would seem, is the use of graphic elements according to learned techniques and principles of design, arrangement, balance, and the like, to produce esthetically pleasing effects as well as to communicate conceptually to others. This stage includes the development of art as "illusion" in Gombrich's sense. It is the stage at which true esthetic effects can be achieved, in which deep satisfaction may be gained in both the process of production and the product achieved. This stage may also include daring experiments in abstract use of line, form, and design.

Most authorities also recognize that the child's progression through the stages is seen in the schemata which he uses to depict the human figure. A schema is a characteristic way of depicting the human form through emphasis on particular forms and elements; it changes with development and learning. A characteristic schema is also identifiable within the individual child's work. Some authorities choose to find a universal symbolism in children's work, depicting ideas or truths not available to them cognitively but arising out of the individual or racial unconscious. The present author has found no particular evidence for this viewpoint, at least in experimental work. Others believe that such symbolism is determined by the culture. Cross-culture studies show, however, that the culture determines chiefly the peripheral or elaborative aspects of schemata, and are more influential in later than in earlier childhood. The general schema seems to be determined by psychological processes —perception and conceptualization of the human form, which processes are similar from culture to culture.

All authorities recognize that something occurs at adolescence which, for many children, puts an end to representative drawing. Some discern in this cessation evidence of increasing psychological and motivational conflicts, particularly over sex and body. Others attribute this cessation to the increasing preeminence of language in usefully delineating cognitive content, or concepts. Still others point out the child's increasing ability to judge his drawing as a conceptualization and representation of visual reality, and his increasing self-criticism of technique. For the first position, there is very little positive, and some negative, evidence. There is some psychological and social evidence for the second. For the third position, there is persuasive psychological evidence that when visual representation assumes an inordinate significance, as it does in a technological society with its emphasis on pictures and diagrams, the child becomes markedly aware of the photographic or visual image, grows self-critical and gives up his drawing, unless he is able to master techniques for achieving effects that he understands and wishes to achieve.

All authorities recognize, over and above the characteristic schemata already discussed, unique or individual features in children's work. Authorities vary in the significance they attach to this fact. Some discern in these individual variations evidence of individual children's interests and attitudes. Others see deep emotional significance in these variations. The position that seems most plausible recognizes these individual variations as embroidery on a central core of meaning, dependent upon perceptual-conceptual learnings.

A Distinction in Theoretical Approaches

As has been stated, all scientific efforts to describe the drawing process or to develop psychological theory concerning drawing behavior have stressed children's drawings as *representative*, as expressive of concepts or cognitive content. It is at the point of defining how concepts arise, and how drawings reflect concepts, that a sharp separation occurs.

Those investigators who have been influenced by Gestalt theory tend to discern in children's drawings the same principles that pattern visual perception. There is a hierarchical arrangement of figure and ground, and within figures there occurs a patterning which follows the dynamic laws of Gestalt psychology. Organization among the elements consistently appears and dominates the elements. As the child matures, this organization comes to include more and more elements and to express increasingly complex relationships among the elements, but form, quality, and organization are ineluctable.

Because early perceptions are limited to simple, potent attributes of objects and of the visual field, drawing representation in young children is simple and schematic. Because perception everywhere follows the same psychological laws, drawing schemata are similar from child to child and from culture to culture. As perceptions differentiate, concepts elaborate, and drawings become less schematic and more visually accurate from an adult viewpoint. Differences among children in depicting the human form begin to appear in these more elaborate concepts; cultural differences likewise appear, as concepts begin to include cultural characteristics, such as garb. But at any level, the drawing truly represents the child's perception and conception.

One must recognize that such wholistic ideas have long been prominent in the discussions of drawing and art. However, the preference, in accounts of children's drawing behavior, for the global language of these theories may come quite as much from the desire to encompass complex activities as briefly and as simply as possible, without an intricate description of all the contingencies in a highly variable phenomenon, as from an intellectual predilection for Gestalt principles as such. The use of such terms descriptively, moreover, possibly has stood in the way of more analytic accounts which might have uncovered other organizational principles. Analytical concepts have been powerful in science and, though perhaps less commonly used in the study of children's drawings, have nevertheless demonstrated their power in the Draw-a-Man technique and its interpretation.

Investigators schooled in the constructs of associationism, conditioning, and more recently behavior theory, have analyzed concept formation in terms of the association of perceptual elements with behavioral responses. By discriminative learning, which often requires repeated experience (i.e., "trials"), a particular stimulus becomes linked with a particular response. When the organism responds to stimuli closely resembling the initially effective stimulus, some learning theorists speak of stimulus generalization. In a sense, concept formation might be considered as a form of stimulus generalization; the continuum along which the stimulus, cognitively apprehended, generalizes and becomes the concept.

Some learning theorists, however, object to the concept of stimulus generalization, holding that "generalization" is merely the absence of discrimination. In such case the stimuli that occasion the response have not been fully discriminated or differentiated. This undiscriminated stimulus situation, cognitively apprehended, is a broad concept; once it is discriminated or differentiated, new concepts or subconcepts appear. In concept learning, verbal or other symbolic components take their place in stimulus-response chains.

Although such ideas present some logical difficulties, the learning process—the linking of behavior elements to stimuli by contiguous repetition, elicitation, and reward, or emission and reinforcement—taken over time, may be seen as progressive, yielding more complex structures. In these terms, the analysis of drawings becomes the linking of perceptual-motor units (concepts) with other perceptual-motor units (markings on paper). In this process, a kind of self-correction through the observation of effects undoubtedly occurs, and the reinforcements provided by adults and other children are also important. Concepts are enlarged by including in the conceptual class additional examples from new experiences in which similar elements are discriminated. Concepts are made more precise by subdividing the conceptual class according to some newly discriminated dimension of variable elements.

That a commonly experienced object is portrayed by children of successive ages (and therefore of greater experience) in such manner that drawings can be graded or scaled, is evidence that the concept involved modifies in a systematic way with increased experience. Concept development is not purely fortuitous, because the environment and its reinforcements are not random. Children acquire concepts socially, in a world of existing concepts. It is possible in these terms to trace a continuum of perceptual-motor experiences from the scribblings of the ape, to the work of the very young human child, to the art of the older child.

There is a temptation to observe that an investigator will favor one or the other of these two modes, the wholistic or the associationistic, depending on his assumptions, the phenomena he wishes to "explain," and the dimensions of drawing behavior or product he selects to study. This is too easy a solution; all phenomena reliably observed and reported should be susceptible of explanation parsimoniously. Recent developments in research and theory concerning perception offer a possible solution.

Drawing and Perceptual-Conceptual Development

Hebb's theory of behavior organization seems to bridge the gap between the associationistic and wholistic approaches. His point of view recognizes "early" and "later" types of learning, and provides a neurological basis for each type. The difference is not one in kind so much as in level of complexity of neural organization. The former is built up out of particulars and is more adequately described by associationist terms. The latter incorporates the perception and recognition of patterns and draws more generously upon concepts reminiscent of field theory. The child's drawings depict his understandings as well as his perceptions, and his understanding is built upon his accumulation and organization of learned response elements.

Eleanor Gibson's application of information theory concepts to perception can be used to show how concept formation proceeds as a hypothesis-testing, trial and correction process. Having attained object perception, the child discriminates likenesses and differences in the more prominent attributes of objects in his experience. At first, discrimination and recognition involve the total sensorium but, with age, depend increasingly on the distance receptors, particularly sight. Linguistic forms increasingly available to him permit him to "code" these attributes and thus assign the objects to classes. Thus, concepts are formed. A new object, the properties of which may be presumed to satisfy the elements of a class, is perceived and tested against the class. It is included, or excluded, or the class concept changed, depending on the corrective information coming in from the person's manipulations, or from other people who mediate the culture's rules. This process enlarges and changes as the child enlarges his store of tested concepts. He handles larger, more abstract classes, and he handles more subclasses, as he discriminates more attributes of objects, and as he comes to treat relationships among objects as well as attributive features of objects. The process is a continuing interplay between the *system* of concepts the person has formed, and the *system* that is his social and cultural environment.

Studies of children's reasoning (e.g., Vinacke, 1952) show that children use induction and deduction at all ages, but that induction is relatively more common in childhood, with deduction becoming characteristic of adolescents and adults. Concept formation involves the discrimination and abstraction of attributes, and generalization to classes—processes which are found in inductive reasoning. Deduction, a more "mature" process developmentally speaking, requires a store of functioning concepts and generalizations from which particular inferences may be made. It is probably significant that children's spontaneous drawings, which appear to reflect concept formation, correspond to the years when induction is the relatively more important mode of reasoning. Spontaneous drawings decline as children progressively increase their capacity for deductive thinking. It has been noted that Piaget attributed *concrete operations* to the childhood years, and *formal* (logical) to the years of adolescence, a distinction which obviously parallels the one we have been describing in reasoning.

This set of constructs seems to describe how children draw the human figure and to explain the schemata and developmental sequences as adequately as any theoretical terms and constructs yet proposed. These constructs parallel distinctions made by others in children's modes of reasoning. What is now needed are experiments based on the several theories described. To invent modes of manipulating experience in ways hypothesized from theory will tax the ingenuity of the experimenters.

Possible Experimental Approaches

In the past, experimental variation has been achieved by selection of cases wherein cumulative learning experiences can be assumed to be quite different along one or more designated dimension of experience. For example, retarded children, normals, and bright children of the same chronological age have been compared. Children of similar intelligence but having had, for a period of months, teachers quite different in artistic interests and teaching emphasis, have been compared. Boys and girls have been compared, on the grounds that in complex and subtle ways the socialization process is different for the sexes. Normal and emotionally disturbed individuals have been compared. To a lesser extent, children from markedly different cultures have been compared. Thus, essentially descriptive studies of drawings have outlined the effects on concepts (often inadequately defined) of the long-continued repetition of this or that general dimension of experience, modified by the many uncontrolled but correlated features of training and environment.

It can reasonably be assumed that some, if not many, crucial determinants of drawing organization are the consequences of long-continued stimulation. This is the logical conclusion from the orderly yet slow changes described in the various developmental studies. Other determinants may be "discoveries," both in perception and in drawing technique, which permit a new but important modification of a concept to emerge. It is at this point that theoretical and methodological ingenuity may permit the most rapid advance. If an effect depends on many trials, apart from sheer lapse of time and hypothesized central structure changes, such an effect will be difficult to demonstrate experimentally. Children will work at a task only so long. If an effect depends on noting a different relationship among aspects of the concept, such a relationship can be demonstrated to the child (i.e., he is "taught" it), and the consequent effects on his drawing performance may be observed.

For example, "meaningless" and "meaningful" visual forms may be constructed as stimuli and concepts developed experimentally, both with and without verbal "names" to define them. Children may be asked to reproduce them graphically under specified conditions. It may even be possible, with preschool children carefully selected in terms of probable parent cooperation, experimentally to control fairly pervasive dimensions of the environment, such as the amount and kind of pictorial stimulation, the kind and amount of drawing practice. In any case, research designs should attempt to provide long-continued periods of practice, as well as testing more immediate effects. Many of the phenomena described in the literature undoubtedly have resulted from the "overlearning" which is so characteristic of children's ordinary experience in contrast with the laboratory experiment.

Children's Drawings as Art Forms

As he has remarked several times, the author has repeatedly been led to the literature and concepts of art and art education in his long peregrination through children's drawings. Though he has not made the point a focus of quantitative study, he may be permitted certain final observations on the controversial issue of whether children's drawings can have artistic merit. One must first distinguish between children having truly esthetic experiences (which they assuredly do), and the esthetic merit which can be assigned to their drawing products (which has been questioned). He must also make the distinction between a criterion of merit *other* than representation and the criterion of skill or craft in "illusion," according to Gombrich the heart of representative art.

By present-day norms, graphic art may certainly embrace more than the standards of the representative tradition, which seemed to culminate about a century ago. Consequently, children's work, immature or primitive when judged by the developed canons of these representative traditions, *can* express artistic merit, judged by other, appropriate criteria. Children, in our culture at least, do not seem to develop an awareness of these criteria on their own. Strong affective attitudes of "liking" or "disliking" operate in children; and children's unguided expressions of liking seem to favor the visual realism of the representative tradition. This fact makes the art education of older children and young adolescents so crucial and often determines whether or not they continue to experience pleasure in drawing.

Finally, it seems that graphic ability, judged by whatever standard, will not develop unless the individual is in a social and educational setting which places considerable importance on drawing according to that standard, and encourages the individual to achieve according to the standard. Techniques can and must be learned if the individual is to continue to grow in his graphic effort past childhood. Experimental work is lacking to indicate how much practice and what motivation will get the older child to develop high-quality drawing performance. Some, indeed, believe that there are "innate" elements necessary to superior graphic ability. However, as Goodenough pointed out long ago, graphic ability which achieves representative drawing of esthetic or artistic merit cannot be discerned in young children; such appears only after certain psychological (cognitive) processes have run their course, and the child has mastered techniques appropriate to the medium.

Much the same can be said about graphic art traditions other than the representative. Impressionism, cubism, two-dimensionalism, and the like, also require complex concepts and techniques which must be acquired after expression of the child's growing visual and conceptual awareness has run a certain course. These techniques and concepts, whether in the representative tradition or according to more recent art theory, seem quite beyond discovery by unaided childish exploration with drawing materials. Such techniques, as the history of art seems to show, have been slowly, almost painfully, worked out by highly experienced, mature individuals.

As Mursell (1950) has pointed out in his analysis of the esthetic response, "skill in any art should be regarded as a refinement of insight" (p. 189). Insight and understanding assuredly assume an adequate body of concepts; these may require varied experience and an extended learning period. Thus, while the psychological study of children's drawings leads to the study of graphic art, the two approaches are distinct in process and aim. In most literate cultures the forces toward concept formation and toward visual criteria for the evaluation of drawing induced on the child are overwhelming. These matters must be mastered before art may become the vehicle of the more abstract and complex concepts of esthetics. Hebb's distinction of early and later learning comes to mind. We may see in children's drawings, however, the origin and development in rudimentary form of processes on which more complex esthetic concepts and performance may later be built.

Part Two

The Test Manual

Administering the Test

The Goodenough-Harris Drawing Test may be administered to children individually or in groups using essentially the same directions. Preschool children, and children being studied clinically, should be examined individually. Kindergarten and primary-grade children may be successfully examined in groups if an assistant is present to help children who have any difficulty following the instructions. Although these children can generally print their names, the examiner or the classroom teacher must complete the rest of the information on the front of the test booklet.

Individual examinations should always be followed by some informal interrogation to clarify any ambiguous aspects of the drawings. The examiner should start by saying: "Tell me about your picture." Throughout the interrogation period the examiner should try to get at the child's intentions in the drawings, and should avoid making assumptions or direct suggestions. For example, if a child does not spontaneously identify an ambiguous part of his drawings, the examiner may ask (pointing): "What might that be?" The child's responses should be recorded, and his identification of parts written directly on the drawings.

Each child should be provided with a pencil and a test booklet.[1] Crayons should *not* be used. The number two or two-and-one-half pencil is preferred. See that pictures and books are put aside, to reduce the likelihood of copying.

Have the children fill in the information requested on the cover sheet of the test booklet. With children of elementary school age it is best to ask them as a group to complete the items one at a time, the examiner directing the task, as follows:

> Where it says "Name," *print* your name. Print your first name, and then your last name.

> Now draw a circle around one of the words "Boy" or "Girl," to show whether you are a boy or a girl.

---

[1] Published by Harcourt, Brace & World, Inc., New York.

Now print the name of this school.

Where it says "Date of Drawing" put today's date. This is _____.

Where it says "Grade," put your grade in school. (In groups, say: This is the _____ grade.)

Where it says "Age," write how old you are *now*.

Now listen carefully: When were you born? Where it says "Birth Date," first write the month when your birthday comes, and then the date of the month. Is it November fourteenth, or January second? Write whatever date it is. Then put the *year* you were born. Do you know that? If you do, put it down. If not, just leave it blank. (*Note:* Birth dates should *always* be checked with official records. Ages should be taken to the nearest month.)

Now, where it says "Father's Occupation," write down what he does for a living. Tell what he does, not just where he works. For example: "He owns and runs a farm." "He's a foreman in the body shop of the Smith Motor Company," or "He runs machines at the Williams Pattern Works." Write down exactly the kind of work he does for a living.

When the children have finished supplying the face sheet data, have them fold it back so that the space for the first drawing, and *only* the first drawing, is exposed. Now say:

I am going to ask you to make three pictures for me today. We will make them one at a time. On this first page I want you to make a picture of a man. Make the very best picture that you can; take your time and work very carefully. I want to see whether the boys and girls in _____ School can do as well as those in other schools. Try very hard, and see what good pictures you can make. Be sure to make the whole man, not just his head and shoulders.

When the drawings have been completed, say a few words of praise and have the children turn over the sheets to the space for the second drawing. Then say:

This time I want you to make a picture of a *woman*. Make the very best picture that you can; take your time and work very carefully. Be sure to make the whole woman, not just her head and shoulders. (*Note:* With very young children it may be appropriate to say: . . . **picture of a woman, a mommy.**)

When this drawing has been completed, praise a bit more lavishly than before as a means of keeping up interest. Then demonstrate how to refold the sheets so that the two completed drawings are inside and the space for the third drawing is now face up. Now say:

This picture is to be someone you know very well, so it should be the best of all. I want *each of you to make a picture of yourself—your whole self—not just your face.* Perhaps you don't know it but many of the greatest artists liked to make their own portraits, and these are often among their best and most famous pictures. So take care and make this last one the very best of the three.

Children under age eight or nine should have a short rest period between drawings two and three. Ask children to put down their pencils, stretch their arms and flex their fingers, to relax from the tension imposed by concentration and effort.

While the children are drawing, stroll about the room and encourage those who are slow or who seem to have difficulty by saying: "These drawings are very fine; you boys and girls are doing very well." *Do not make adverse comments or criticisms, and do not give suggestions.* If any child wishes to write about his picture, he may do so at the bottom of the sheet.

If children ask for further instructions, such as whether the man is to be doing anything particular like working or running, say: "Do it whatever way you think is best." Avoid answering "Yes" or "No" or giving any further specific instructions to the children.

The importance of avoiding every kind of suggestion cannot be overemphasized. The examiner must refrain from remarks that might influence the nature of the drawing. He must also see to it that no suggestions come from the children. They should not hold up their drawings for admiration or comment. Young children sometimes accompany their work with a running commentary, such as: "I am giving my man a soldier hat," or "Mine is a big, big man." A firm but good-natured, "No one must tell about his picture now. Wait until everybody has finished," will usually dispose of such cases without affecting the general interest or suppressing the child's enthusiasm for his work.

There is no time limit for the test, but young children rarely take more than ten to fifteen minutes for all three drawings. If one or two children are slower than the rest, it is best to collect papers from those who have finished and allow them to go on with their regular work while the slower workers are finishing.

In older groups, above the fifth or sixth grade, it may be necessary to offer strong encouragement to some children, who will say they can't do the task. In these groups it may also be desirable to say:

You are to make three drawings, one on each of the three pages of this folder. The instructions are at the top of each page. When you have finished one drawing go right on to the next, until you have finished all three.

In this case, it is well to have two examiners who can walk about the room speaking to individuals who seem reluctant to attempt the task.

The following special circumstances should be noted: (1) A child may spoil his drawing and wish to start again. In such case he should be given a fresh test booklet and be allowed to try again. All such instances should be noted on the margin of the booklet after the child has finished his work. (2) Above the second grade (rarely below), a child may draw a bust picture only. When it is evident that this has been the intention, a fresh test booklet should be given, and the child told to, "Make a whole man." Both drawings should be preserved for comparison.

General Scoring Instructions for the Point Scales

The test can be scored by any person capable of following instructions faithfully. Learning how to score is not difficult but does require study, patience, and willingness to follow instructions painstakingly. It cannot be emphasized too strongly that very careful study of this Manual is imperative if results are to be of any value. With practice, the gain both in speed and accuracy is very considerable. The experienced person can score twenty or thirty drawings an hour, although the beginner may complete no more than five an hour.

Because subjective judgment is required to score some items, perfect agreement between two scorings cannot be expected. In practice, however, agreement will be quite high. (See Chapter V for inter-scorer studies.) On the more subjective items, a scorer will develop his own standards and reduce the "random error" in his score. He will, however, introduce a small "constant error" with respect to another scorer's judgment.

These general scoring instructions should be followed:

1. To learn to score the Man Point scale, study carefully the illustrative drawings on pages 264–269 of this Manual. Read the requirements for scoring the different items for the Man scale on pages 248–263. Note in the illustrations whether a score has been given for the item under consideration and fix clearly in mind the principles governing this scoring. After these principles are adequately understood, turn to the drawings on pages 270–272 and practice independent scoring.

The section dealing with requirements for scoring the Woman scale, pages 276–291 should be similarly studied. The drawings of the female figure on pages 79–86 of Chapter IV can then be used for practice. (The accepted scoring of these drawings appears in the Appendix, pp. 322–327.)

The scorer should refer to the sections on scoring requirements when there is any doubt. Even after considerable experience, restudying a point occasionally is necessary, since there is a tendency to reinterpret some scoring items; particularly those that allow for more subjective judgment.

2. Each item is scored as pass or fail, according to the rules set forth in this Manual. A credit of 1 is allowed for each "pass" with no half credits given.

The raw score is the sum of these credits, and is the score which is used to find the standard score in the appropriate tables.

3. It facilitates work considerably if the standard test blank or booklet is used. Spaces are provided next to each drawing for entering the scoring. Mark a "plus" or "check mark" for each item passed; a "zero" for each item failed. This record makes possible the rechecking of scores point by point—a procedure always desirable when inexperienced scorers are used. It also guarantees that items will not be omitted in the scoring.

4. A special Short Scoring Guide for each Point scale appears on pages 275 and 292 of this Manual. These Guides are for the use of experienced scorers only. After a reasonable amount of practice, the numbers and cue phrases contained in the Guides may suffice; continual reference to the detailed scoring requirements becomes unnecessary.

5. In practice, drawings will be found that the examiner is unable to score at all. According to standardization studies, these excessively bizarre drawings occur no more frequently than once or twice per thousand cases over age five. When such cases are found, it is well to question the children individually to obtain their own explanations of their drawings. Often, seemingly unusual features merely reflect a child's inability to portray his ideas clearly.

Goodenough designated as "Class A" those drawings in which the subject matter could not be recognized. Her description follows:

> In drawings of this class the subject cannot be recognized. The total possible score is either 0 or 1. If the drawing consists merely of aimless, uncontrolled scribbling . . . [see Fig. 51, p. 244] [2] the score is 0. If the lines are somewhat controlled and appear to have been guided by the child to some extent, the score is 1. Drawings of this type most frequently take the form of a rough square, triangle, or circle, very crudely done. Not infrequently several of these forms are included in a single drawing . . . [Fig. 52]. If a drawing of this kind contains much detail, it is always well to call upon the child for an explanation, since occasionally it will be found that such a drawing belongs in Class B, rather than in Class A. Figure . . . [53] is an example.
>
> In questioning a child about his drawing, great care must be taken to avoid suggesting the expected answer. Be sure that his confidence has been gained before asking any direct questions. Then, after praising his drawing, say, "Now tell me about your picture. What are all these things you have made?" If this does not elicit a response, point to one of the items and say in an encouraging tone, "What is this?" If he is still unable to respond, or if, as is frequently the case, he calls each part in turn "a man" then the drawing should be scored as Class A; but if, on the other hand, he names the various parts in a logical fashion, it should be scored according to the rules given for Class B [3] (1926, pp. 90–91).

[2] Figures in brackets refer to figures in the present volume.

[3] Goodenough's "Class B" drawings include all those that can be recognized as attempts to represent the human figure, no matter how crudely. Figure 54 is an example.

FIG. 51.

FIG. 52.

FIG. 53.

FIG. 54.

Fɪɢ. 51. Man, by boy, 4-2. Class A. Raw Score 0; Standard Score 55 or less; Percentile Rank 1

Fɪɢ. 52. Man, by girl, 4-2. Class A. Raw Score 1; Standard Score 62; Percentile Rank 1

Fɪɢ. 53. Man, by boy, 4-11. Class B. Raw Score 6; Standard Score 83; Percentile Rank 13

Items credited: 4, 5, 9, 11, 24, 55

Fɪɢ. 54. Man, by girl, 5-0. Raw Score 8; Standard Score 73; Percentile Rank 4

Items credited: 4, 9, 30, 35, 39, 46, 47, 53

6. The cover sheet of the standard test booklet provides spaces for entering the raw scores, the standard score equivalents, the percentile ranks and the averaged standard scores, which represent a combined estimate of the child's intellectual maturity. It is not permissible to combine partial scores selected from two drawings for the total score, nor is it permissible to combine scorings of the better features of two drawings. The total raw scores must first be obtained on each drawing separately.

7. Various qualitative aspects of the drawings, such as pressure of the pencil, placement on the page, size, and erasures, are not scored, but should be noted. In the absence of other evidence, it is better to interpret erasures as a sign of the child's dissatisfaction with his work than as evidence of personal insecurity or self-dissatisfaction. Virtually all children will at some time erase and redraw some feature of their drawing; particularly older children who are more critical of their work. Some children do a great deal of erasing and redrawing, and it is probable that in these cases the score obtained is an underestimate of their true intellectual maturity.

Uses of the Drawing Test

While almost any adult can learn to score drawings with reasonable accuracy, psychological training is necessary to adequately understand the results. Such training should include, at the very least, college course work in statistics and theory of tests and measurements, as well as supervised practice in administering and scoring various psychological tests. Moreover, as the examiner gains experience in using a variety of tests, his understanding of the potentialities and limitations of particular tests will grow. His own research with tests and his study of the published research will add immeasurably to his understanding.

This Drawing Test does *not* yield a score that is identical with the IQ derived from a well-administered individual intelligence test. Although the correlation between an individual intelligence test result and the Goodenough-Harris Drawing Test score is quite substantial for children between the ages of five and ten, the examiner should not be misled. When important decisions are to be made about children, such as placement in a special class, or provision of financial aid, the most complete and accurate psychological measurements should be available. One or more individual intelligence tests administered by a certified or licensed psychologist should be given. The results of the Drawing Test may be used to select those children who should receive more detailed attention. The Drawing Test may supply important additional evidence of severe intellectual and conceptual retardation.

A psychologist may use the Drawing Test to get an initial impression of a young child's general ability level. Because most children like to draw, the test may be used to gain a child's cooperation for more complex tasks to follow. The psychologist may wish to gain some idea of the potentiality of a deaf child who cannot be tested with the usual verbal tests. Anthropologists and psychologists have used this test to get a crude index of mental development of children for whom no appropriate standardized tests are available. However, as has been pointed out in Chapter VIII, such results may to an unknown extent be attenuated by the children's lack of educational experiences.

A primary teacher who wishes quickly to arrange her children in order of intellectual maturity can use the Quality scale. She will obtain a more accurate order if she uses the Point scale. By either scale she may misjudge a few children in her group; but if she is an alert observer who understands various signs of intellectual and conceptual maturity, she will quickly correct these initial misjudgments. Some test results that underestimate a child's ability are due to the child's carelessness, inadequate motivation, or his lack of interest. A somewhat larger proportion of test measurements that differ from each other are probably due to differences in patterns of abilities. In these cases the difference between two test results is not a product of momentary circumstances but a "real" difference—one that keeps correlations between tests from being very close to 1.00.

Psychologists often make judgments about children based on the discrepancies between test scores, particularly where the tests differ in their type of content. When a variety of tests are given, differences in the relative exceptionality from test to test for any one child is sometimes taken to indicate "patterns" of ability or even to suggest the operation of special personality characteristics. The Drawing Test lends itself particularly to this thinking because its content is so different from the usual intelligence test.

As has been pointed out in this book, discrepancies between test scores, considered to be test "patterns," are of doubtful value. Research often shows that many hypotheses related to such usages are not substantiated, even when the interpretations are made by well-trained clinical psychologists. For example, it is thought that severely brain-damaged children may do much more poorly on the Drawing Test than on a well-standardized measure of vocabulary. Such may indeed be the case, but not invariably. Only a person thoroughly acquainted with the peculiarities of particular tests, and aware of the vagaries of psychological measurement generally, should attempt to interpret discrepancies between the Drawing Test score and some other test of mental ability.

There has been a tendency in recent years to interpret a child's drawings in terms of his "creativity," special interests, or deep psychological problems or conflicts. The literature review in Chapter III shows that there is little confirmed basis for such use of children's drawings. Rather, as the evidence in this book amply shows, the child's drawing reflects his concepts which grow with his mental level, experience, and knowledge. Consequently, the Goodenough-Harris Drawing Test is best used as a measure of intellectual maturity and should not be used for other purposes.

Requirements for Scoring the Draw-a-Man Scale

ITEM	DESCRIPTION
1. Head present	Any clear method of representing the head. Features alone, without any outline for the head itself, are not credited for this point.
2. Neck present	Any clear indication of the neck as distinct from the head and the trunk. Mere juxtaposition of the head and the trunk is not credited.
3. Neck, two dimensions	Outline of neck continuous with that of the head, of the trunk, or of both. Line of neck must "flow" into head line or trunk line. Neck interposed as pillar between head and trunk does not get credit unless treated definitely to show continuity between neck and head or trunk or both, as by collar, or curving of lines.

Credit

No Credit

4. Eyes present	Either one or two eyes must be shown. Any method is satisfactory. A single indefinite feature, such as is occasionally found in the drawings of very young children, is credited.
5. Eye detail: brow or lashes	Brow, lashes or both shown.
6. Eye detail: pupil	Any clear indication of the pupil or iris as distinct from the outline of the eye. Both must appear if both eyes are shown.
7. Eye detail: proportion	The horizontal dimension of the eye must be greater than the vertical dimension. This requirement must be fulfilled in both eyes if both are shown; one eye is sufficient if only one is shown. Sometimes in profile drawings of a high grade the eye is shown in perspective. In such drawings any triangular form approximating the following examples is credited.

Credit

8. Eye detail: glance

Full Face: The eyes obviously glancing. There must be no convergence or divergence of the two pupils, either horizontally or vertically.

Credit

Profile: The eyes must either be shown as in the preceding point, or, if the ordinary almond form is retained, the pupil must be placed toward the front of the eye rather than in the center. The scoring should be strict.

9. Nose present

Any clear method of representation. In "mixed profiles," the score is plus even though *two* noses are shown.

10. Nose, two dimensions

Full Face: Credit all attempts to portray the nose in two dimensions, when the bridge is longer than the width of the base or tip.

Credit

No Credit

Profile: Credit all crude attempts to show the nose in profile, provided tip or base is shown in some manner. Do not credit simple "button."

Credit

No Credit

11. Mouth present

Any clear representation.

12. Lips, two dimensions

Full Face: Two lips clearly shown.

Credit

Profile:

Credit

No Credit

13. Both nose and lips in two dimensions

Bonus point given when Items 10 and 12 are passed. See preceding items for accepted forms.

14. Both chin and forehead shown

Full Face: Both the eyes and mouth must be present, and sufficient space left above the eyes to represent the forehead; below the mouth to represent the chin. The scoring should be rather lenient. Where neck is continuous with face, placement of mouth with respect to narrowing of lower portion of head is important. The sketches below illustrate mouth placement.

Credit   *No Credit*

15. Projection of chin shown; chin clearly differentiated from lower lip

Full Face: Modeling of chin must be indicated in some way, as by a curved line below the mouth or lip, or point of chin indicated by appropriate facial modeling, or dot or line placed below mouth near lower limit of face. Beard obscuring chin does *not* score. *Note:* Distinguish carefully from Item 16. There must definitely be an attempt to show a "pointed" chin to credit this item. This point is credited most frequently in profiles.

Credit

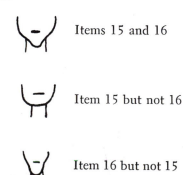

Items 15 and 16

Item 15 but not 16

Item 16 but not 15

16. **Line of jaw indicated**

Full Face: Line of jaw and chin drawn across neck but not squarely across. Neck must be sufficiently wide, and chin must be so shaped that the line of the jaw forms a well-defined acute angle with the line of the neck. Score *strictly* on the simple oval face.

Credit

ACUTE ANGLES

No Credit

Profile: Line of jaw extends toward ear.

Credit

17. **Bridge of nose**

Full Face: Nose properly placed and shaped. The base of the nose must appear as well as the indication of a straight bridge. Placement of upper portion of bridge is important; must extend up to or between the eyes. Bridge must be narrower than the base.

Credit

No Credit

Profile: Nose at angle with face, approximately 35–45 degrees. Separation of nose from forehead clearly shown at eye.

Credit

No Credit

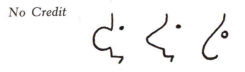

18. Hair I   Any indication of hair, however crude.

19. Hair II   Hair shown on more than circumference of head and more than a scribble. Nontransparent, unless it is clear that a bald-headed man is portrayed. A simple hairline across the skull on which no attempt has been made to shade in hair does *not* score. If any attempt has been made, even in outline or with a little shading, to portray hair as having substance or texture, the item scores.

Credit

No Credit

20. Hair III   Any clear attempt to show cut or styling by use of side burns, a forelock, or conformity of base line to a "style." When a hat is drawn, credit the point if hair is indicated in front as well as behind the ear, or if hairline at back of neck or across forehead suggests styling.

21. Hair IV   Hair shaded to show part, or to suggest having been combed, or brushed, by means of *directed* lines. Item 21 is never credited unless Item 20 is; it is thus a "high-grade" point.

Credit

No Credit

22. Ears present   Any indication of ears.

23. Ears present: proportion and position   The vertical measurement must be greater than the horizontal measurement. The ears must be placed somewhere within the middle two-thirds of the head.

Full Face: The top of the ear must be separated from the head line, and *both* ears must extend from the head.

Credit

No Credit

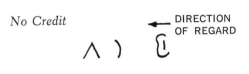

Profile: Some detail, such as a dot, to represent the aural canal must be shown. The shell-like portion of the ear must extend toward the back of the head. (Some children, especially retarded boys, tend to reverse this position, making the ear extend toward the face. In such drawings this item is never credited.)

Credit

No Credit   ← DIRECTION OF REGARD

24. Fingers present	Any suggestion of fingers, separate from hand or arm. In drawings by older children, where there is a tendency to "sketch," credit this point if any suggestion of fingers occurs.	

25. Correct number of fingers shown

Both hands necessary if both hands are shown. Credit this point in "sketchy" drawings by older children, even though five digits may not be definitely discerned.

26. Detail of fingers correct

"Grapes" or "sticks" do not score. Length of individual fingers must be distinctly greater than width. In well-executed drawings, where hand may appear in perspective, or where fingers are indicated by "sketching," credit this point. Credit also those cases in which, because the hand is obviously clenched, only the knuckles or part of the fingers appear. This last will occur only in high-quality drawings where there is considerable use of perspective.

27. Opposition of thumb shown

Fingers must be indicated, with a clear differentiation of the thumb from the fingers. Scoring should be very strict. The point is credited if one of the lateral digits is definitely shorter than any of the others (compare especially with the little finger), or if the angle between it and the index finger is not less than twice as great as that between any two of the other digits, or if its point of attachment to the hand is distinctly nearer to the wrist than that of the fingers. Conditions must be fulfilled on both hands if both are shown; one hand is sufficient if only one is shown. *Fingers must be present or indicated;* "mitt" hand does *not* score, unless figure is definitely in winter garb, wearing mittens.

Credit

No Credit

28. Hands present

Any representation of the hand, apart from the fingers. When fingers are shown, a space must be left between base of fingers and edge of sleeve or cuff. Where no cuff exists, arm must broaden in some way to suggest palm or back of hand as distinct from wrist. Characteristic must appear on both hands if both are shown.

Marginal Credit

29. Wrist or ankle shown

Either wrist or ankle clearly indicated as separate from sleeve or trouser. A line across the limb to indicate the end of sleeve or trouser, although credited in Item 55, is *not* sufficient here.

Credit

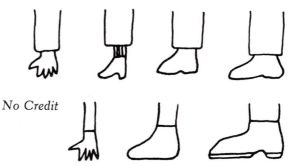

No Credit

30. Arms present

Any method of representation clearly intended to indicate arms. Fingers alone are not sufficient, but the point is credited if any space is left between the base of the fingers and that part of the body to which they are attached. The number of arms must also be correct, except in profile drawings when only one arm may score.

31. Shoulders I

Full Face: A change in the direction of the outline of the upper part of the trunk which gives an effect of concavity rather than convexity. The point is scored rather strictly. The ordinary elliptical form is never credited, and the score is always minus unless it is evident that there has been a recognition of the abrupt broadening out of the trunk below the neck which is produced by the shoulder blade and the collar bone. A perfectly square or rectangular trunk does not score, but if the corners have been rounded, the point is credited.

Credit

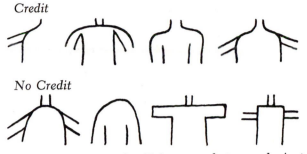

No Credit

Profile: The scoring should be somewhat more lenient than in full-face drawings, since it is more difficult to represent the shoulders adequately in the profile position. A profile drawing, in this connection, should be understood to mean one in which the trunk, as well as the head, is shown in profile. If the lines forming the outline of the upper part of the trunk diverge from each other at the base of the neck in such a way as to show the expansion of the chest, the point is credited.

32. Shoulders II

Full Face: Score more strictly than previous item. Shoulders must be continuous with neck and arms, and "square," not drooping. If arm is held from the body, the armpit must be shown.

Profile: Shoulder joint in approximately correct position. Arm must be represented by double line.

Credit

No Credit

33. Arms at side or engaged in activity

Full Face: Young children generally draw the arms stiffly out from the body. Credit this point when at least one arm is down at the side, making an angle of no more than 10 degrees with the general vertical axis of the trunk, unless the arms are engaged in some definite activity, such as carrying an object. Credit when hands are in pockets, on hips, or behind back.

Credit

10° OR LESS

Profile: Credit if hands are engaged in definite activity, or if upper arm is suspended even though forearm is extended.

34. Elbow joint shown   There must be an abrupt bend (not a curve) at approximately the middle of the arm. One arm is sufficient. Modeling or creasing of the sleeve is credited.

Full Face:

Credit

Profile:

Credit

No Credit

35. Legs present   Any method of representation clearly intended to indicate the legs. The number must be correct: two in full-face drawings; either one or two in profiles. Use common sense rather than a purely arbitrary scoring. If only one leg is present, but a rough sketch of a crotch is included, showing clearly what the child has in mind, score the item. On the other hand, three or more legs, or a single leg without logical explanation should be scored minus. A single leg to which two feet are attached is scored plus. Legs may be attached anywhere to the figure.

36. Hip I (crotch)   **Full Face:** Crotch indicated. This is most frequently shown by inner lines of the two legs meeting at point of junction with the body. (Young children usually place the legs as far apart from each other as possible, and this never scores.)

Credit

Profile: If only one leg shows, buttock must be shaped.

Credit

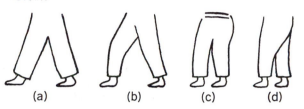

(a)   (b)   (c)   (d)

37. Hip II

Preceding item earned with credit to spare. Drawing gives a better idea of the hip than required for passing preceding item. Examples (b) and (d) on Item 36 are credited here also; (a) and (c) are not.

38. Knee joint shown

There must be, as in the case of the elbow, an abrupt bend (not curve) at about the middle of the leg, or, as is sometimes found in very high-quality drawings, a narrowing of the leg at this point. Knee-length trousers are not sufficient. Crease or shading to indicate knee is scored plus.

39. Feet I: any indication

Feet indicated by any means: two feet in full-face; one or two in primitive profile. Young children may indicate feet by attaching toes to the end of the leg. This is credited.

Credit

40. Feet II: proportion

The feet and legs must be shown in two dimensions. Feet must not be "clubbed"; that is, the length of the foot must be greater than its height from sole to instep. The length of the foot must be not more than one-third or less than one-tenth the total length of the leg. The item is also credited in full-face drawings in which the foot is shown in perspective, longer than wide, provided the foot is separated in some way from the rest of the leg, and not merely indicated by a line across the leg.

Full Face:

Credit

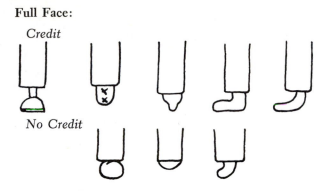

No Credit

41. Feet III: heel

Any clear method of indicating the heel. In full-face drawings, credit the item arbitrarily when the foot is shown as below, provided there is some demarcation between the foot and the leg. In the profile, the instep *must* be indicated.

Credit

42. Feet IV: perspective

Foreshortening attempted in at least one foot.

Credit

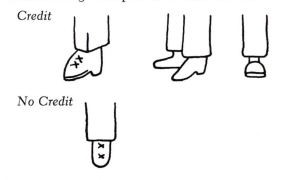

No Credit

43. Feet V: detail

Any one item of detail such as lacing, tie, strap, or shoe sole indicated by a double line.

44. Attachment of arms and legs I

Both arms and both legs attached to the trunk at any point, or arms attached to the neck, or at the juncture of the head and the trunk when the neck is omitted. If the trunk is omitted, the score is always zero. If the legs are attached elsewhere than to the trunk, regardless of the attachment of the arms, the score is zero. If only one arm or leg is shown, either in full-face or in profile drawings, credit may be given on the basis of the limb that is shown. If both arms and legs are shown, the members of each pair must be attached approximately symmetrically. Arms attached to the legs score zero.

45. Attachment of arms and legs II

Legs attached to trunk, and arms attached to the trunk at the correct point. Do not credit if arm attachment occupies one-half or more of the chest area (neck to waist). When no neck is present, the arms must *definitely* be attached to the upper part of the trunk.

Full Face: When Item 31 is plus, the point of attachment must be exactly at the shoulders. If Item 31 is zero, the attachment must be exactly at the point which should have been indicated as the shoulders. Score very strictly, especially in those cases where Item 31 is zero.

Profile: Do not credit if both the lines delineating the arm extend from the outline of the back, or if the point of attachment either reaches the base of the neck, or falls below the greatest expansion of the chest line.

46. Trunk present

Any clear indication of the trunk, either one or two dimensional. Where there is no clear differentiation between the head and the trunk, but the features appear in the upper end of a single figure, the point is scored plus if the features do not occupy more than half the length of the figure; otherwise, the score is zero, unless a cross line has been drawn to indicate the termination of the head. A single figure placed between the head and the legs is always counted as a trunk, even though its size and shape may suggest a neck rather than a trunk. (This ruling is based on the fact that, when questioned, a number of children whose drawings showed this peculiarity, called the part a trunk.) A row of buttons extending down between the legs is scored zero for trunk but plus for clothing, unless a cross line has been drawn to show the termination of the trunk.

47. Trunk in proportion, two dimensions

Length of the trunk must be greater than breadth. Measurement should be taken at the points of greatest length and of greatest breadth. If the two measurements are equal, or so nearly so that the difference is not readily determined, the score is zero. In most instances the difference will be great enough to be recognized at a glance, without actually measuring.

48. Proportion: head I

Area of the head not more than one-half or less than one-tenth that of the trunk. Score rather leniently. See below for a series of standard forms of which the first is double the area of the second in each pair.

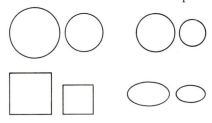

49. Proportion: head II

Head approximately one-fourth trunk area. Score strictly; over one-third or under about one-fifth fails the item. Where crotch is not shown, as in some profiles, consider belt or waist at about two-thirds down total trunk length.

Credit

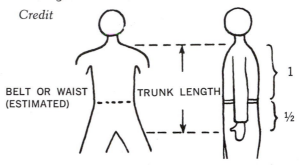

50. Proportion: face

Full Face: Length of head greater than its width. Should show a general oval shape.

Profile: Head definitely elongated. Face longer than "dome" of skull.

51. Proportion: arms I

Arms at least equal to the trunk in length. Tips of hands extend to middle of hip but not to knee. Hands need not necessarily extend to or below the crotch, especially if legs are unusually short. In full-face drawings, both hands must so extend. Score by relative *lengths*, not *position*, of arms.

52. Proportion: arms II

Arms taper; forearm narrower than upper arm. Any tendency to narrow the forearm except right at the wrist, is credited. If both arms show clearly, tapering must occur in both.

53. Proportion: legs

Length of the legs not less than the vertical measurement of the trunk nor greater than twice that measurement. Width of either leg less than that of the trunk.

54. Proportion: limbs in two dimensions

Both arms and legs shown in two dimensions. If the arms and legs are in two dimensions, the point is credited, even though the hands and feet are drawn in linear dimension.

55. Clothing I

Any clear representation of clothing. As a rule the earliest forms consist of a row of buttons running down the center of the trunk, or of a hat, or of both. Either alone scores. A single dot or small circle placed in the center of the trunk is practically always intended to represent the navel and should not be credited as clothing. A series of vertical or horizontal lines drawn across the trunk (and sometimes on the limbs as well) is a fairly common way of indicating clothing, and should be so credited. Marks to indicate pockets or sleeve-ends also get credit.

56. Clothing II

At least two articles of clothing (as hat and trousers) nontransparent; that is, concealing the part of the body which they are supposed to cover. In scoring this point it must be noted that a hat which is merely in contact with the top of the head but does not cover any part of it is *not* credited. Buttons alone, without any other indication of the coat, are *not* credited. Two of the following must be present to indicate coat: sleeves, collar or neckline, buttons, or pockets. Trousers must be clearly intended by belt, fly, pockets, cuff, or any separation of feet or leg from bottom of trouser leg. Foot as an extension of leg does not score, when a line drawn across the leg is the only way of indicating the separation of foot and leg.

57. Clothing III

Entire drawing free from transparencies of any sort. Both sleeves and trousers must be shown as distinct from wrists or hands and legs or feet.

58. Clothing IV

At least four articles of clothing definitely indicated. The articles should be among those in the following list: hat, shoes, coat, shirt, collar, necktie, belt, trousers, jacket, sport shirt, overalls, socks (pattern). *Note:* Shoes must show some detail, as laces, toe cap, or double line for the sole. Heel alone is not sufficient. Trousers must show some features, such as fly, pockets, cuffs. Coat or shirt must show either collar, sleeves, pockets, lapels, or distinctive shading, as spots or stripes. Buttons alone are not sufficient. Collar should not be confused with neck shown merely as insert. The necktie is often inconspicuous and care must be taken not to overlook it, but it is not likely to be mistaken for anything else.

59. Clothing V

Costume complete without incongruities. This may be a "type" costume (e.g., cowboy, soldier) or costume of everyday dress. If the latter, it should be clearly recognized as appropriate; e.g., sport shirt on man, cap appropriate to hunting outfit, overalls for farmer. This is a "bonus" point, and must show more than necessary for Item 58.

60. Profile I

The head, trunk, and feet must be shown in profile without error. The trunk may not be considered as drawn in profile unless the characteristic line of buttons has been moved from the center to the side of the figure, or some other indication, such as the position of the arms, pockets, or necktie shows clearly the effect of this position. The entire drawing may contain *one*, but not more than one, of the following three errors:

1. One body transparency, such as the outline of the trunk showing through the arm.
2. Legs not in profile. In a true profile at least the upper part of the leg which is in the background must be concealed by the one in the foreground.
3. Arms attached to the outline of the back and extending forward.

61. Profile II

The figure must be shown in true profile, without error or any body transparency.

62. Full face

(Include partial profile, where attempt is to show figure in perspective.) All major body parts in proper location and correctly joined unless hidden by perspective or clothing.

Essential items: Legs, arms; eyes, nose, mouth, ears; neck, trunk; hands and feet. Parts must be in two dimensions. Feet may be in perspective, but not in profile, unless they turn "out" in opposite directions.

63. Motor coordination: lines [4]

Look at the long lines in arms, legs, and trunk. Lines should be firm, well-controlled and free from accidental wavering. A few long lines may be retraced or erased. The drawing need not achieve very smoothly "flowing" lines to earn credit. Young children sometimes "color in" with their pencils; examine carefully the fundamental lines of their drawings. Older children frequently use a "sketching" technique readily distinguishable from the uncertain, wavering lines resulting from immature coordination. If the general effect is that of firm, sure lines showing that the pencil was under control, credit the item. The drawing may be quite immature and still score on this point.

64. Motor coordination: junctures

Look at the juncture points of lines. They must meet cleanly without a marked tendency to cross or overlap, or leave gaps between the ends. A drawing with few lines is scored more strictly than one with frequent changes in direction of line. A "sketchy" drawing is ordinarily credited even though the junctures of lines may seem uncertain, since this is a characteristic confined almost entirely to drawings of a mature type. Some erasures may be allowed.

65. Superior motor coordination

This is a "bonus" point for good pencil work on details as well as on major lines. Look at the small detail as well as at the character of the major lines. All lines should be firmly drawn, with correct joining. Pencil work in fine detail—facial features, small items of clothing, etc.—indicates a good control of the pencil. Scoring

[4] Items 63, 64, and 65 concern the *quality* of the child's control of the pencil. These items evaluate the firmness and sureness of line, quality of line junctions, "corners," etc.

should be quite strict. Erasures and/or redrawing invalidate this item.

66. Directed lines and form: head outline [5]

Outline of head must be drawn without obviously unintentional irregularities. The point is credited only in drawings where the shape has developed beyond the first crude circle or ellipse. In profile drawings, a simple oval to which a nose has been added does *not* score. Scoring should be rather strict; the contour of the face must be developed as a unit, *not* by adding parts.

67. Directed lines and form: trunk outline

Same as for the preceding item, but here with reference to the trunk. Note that the primitive "stick," circle, or ellipse does *not* score. The body lines must show an attempt to follow an intentional deviation from the simple ovoid form.

68. Directed lines and form: arms and legs

Arms and legs must be drawn without irregularities, as in above item, and without tendency to narrowing at the points of junction with the body. Both arms and legs must be in two dimensions.

69. Directed lines and form: facial features

Facial features must be symmetrical in all respects. Eyes, nose, and mouth must all be shown in two dimensions.

Full Face: The features must be appropriately placed, regular and symmetrical, giving a clear appearance of the human form.

Profile: The eye must be regular in outline and located in the forward one-third of the head. The nose must form an obtuse angle with the forehead. The scoring should be strict; a "cartoon" nose is not credited.

70. "Sketching" technique

Lines formed by well-controlled short strokes. Repeated tracing of long line segments is not credited. "Sketching" technique appears in the work of some older children and almost never occurs under age eleven or twelve.

71. "Modeling" technique

"Lines" or shading must indicate one or more of the following: garment creases, wrinkles or folds, other than trouser press; fabric; hair; shoes; "coloring in"; or background features.

72. Arm movement

Figure must express freedom of movement in both shoulders and elbows. One arm suffices. Credit hands on hips or in pockets, if both shoulders and elbows are apparent. A definite activity need *not* be indicated.

73. Leg movement

Freedom of movement portrayed both in hips and knees of the figure.

---

[5] Items 66–69 concern the child's deliberate direction of the pencil to produce a good form. The child's work must show that he has exercised control, firmly and surely.

Scoring Examples

Fig. 55.

Fig. 56.

Fig. 57.

Fig. 58.

Fɪɢ. 55.   Man, by girl, 3-11. Raw Score 5; Standard Score 87; Percentile Rank 19

Items credited: 1, 4, 11, 30, 35

Fɪɢ. 56.   Man, by girl, 5-0. Raw Score 19; Standard Score 105; Percentile Rank 63

Items credited: 1, 4, 6, 9, 11, 18, 22, 23, 24, 25, 27, 28, 30, 35, 39, 44, 46, 48, 55

There are clearly five digits on each hand, one of which is oriented quite differently from the others, in each case.

Fɪɢ. 57.   Man, by girl, 9-6. Raw Score 34; Standard Score 104; Percentile Rank 61

Items credited: 1, 2, 3, 4, 9, 11, 14, 18, 22, 23, 24, 28, 29, 30, 31, 32, 35, 39, 40, 44, 45, 46, 48, 50, 51, 52, 53, 54, 55, 56, 57, 58, 63, 64

Figure considered to show snowsuit.

Fɪɢ. 58.   Man, by boy, 12-6. Raw Score 53; Standard Score 117; Percentile Rank 87

Items credited: 1, 2, 3, 4, 5, 7, 9, 10, 11, 14, 15, 16, 17, 18, 19, 20, 24, 26, 27, 28, 29, 30, 31, 32, 33, 35, 36, 39, 40, 41, 42, 43, 44, 45, 46, 47, 48, 50, 51, 52, 53, 54, 55, 56, 57, 59, 62, 63, 64, 65, 67, 68, 71

Since this drawing shows the hand in profile, a compromise scoring is effected; strict on number of fingers (Item 25), but liberal on their shape (Item 26) and on the presence of a hand (Item 28).

FIG. 59.

FIG. 60.

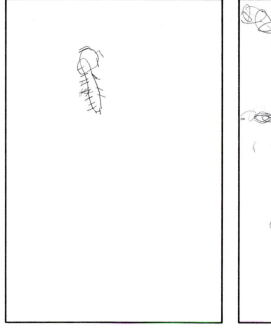

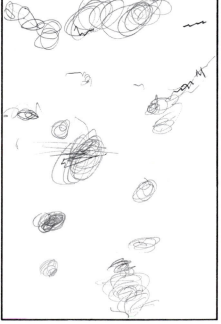

FIG. 61.

FIG. 62.

Fɪɢ. 59. Man, by girl, 6-6. Raw Score 9; Standard Score 72; Percentile Rank 3

Items credited: 1, 4, 9, 11, 14, 22, 30, 35, 39

Stanford-Binet (L) IQ 82

Fɪɢ. 60. Man, by boy, 6-9. Raw Score 4; Standard Score 62; Percentile Rank 1

Items credited: 1, 4, 9, 11

Stanford-Binet (L) IQ 65. Child in special class.

Considerable incoordination with tentative diagnosis of mild cerebral palsy. Handedness not differentiated. The examiner repeated the request to "Draw a whole man" after original figure was produced. This request led to perseverative circular drawing. The circular drawing seemed to mean "the whole man" to him.

Fɪɢ. 61. Man, by boy, 7-10. Raw Score 4; Standard Score 59; Percentile Rank 1

Items credited: 1, 24, 46, 47

Stanford-Binet (L) IQ 47. Child in special class. Speech and motor control very poor.

Could have credited Items 30 and 35; Item 24 was credited because so many marks suggest the impression of "many digits."

Fɪɢ. 62. Man, by boy, 8-6. "Class A" drawing; cannot be scored.

Stanford-Binet (L) IQ 34. Child in special class.

FIG. 63.

FIG. 64.

FIG. 65.

FIG. 66

FIG. 63.   Man, by boy, 9-11. Raw Score 15; Standard Score 74; Percentile Rank 4

Items credited: 1, 4, 9, 11, 18, 22, 24, 26, 30, 33, 35, 44, 46, 47, 55

Stanford-Binet (M) IQ 81. Child in special class; spastic paralysis.

FIG. 64.   Man, by boy, 12-5. Raw Score 31; Standard Score 87; Percentile Rank 19

Items credited: 1, 2, 4, 5, 9, 10, 11, 24, 29, 30, 31, 33, 35, 36, 39, 40, 41, 44, 45, 46, 50, 51, 53, 54, 55, 56, 57, 58, 59, 63, 64

Stanford-Binet (L) IQ 80

Note: Bridge of nose (Item 17) is questionable; cannot tell how high it extends.

FIG. 65.   Man, by girl, 15-8. Raw Score 48; Standard Score 105; Percentile Rank 63

Items credited: 1, 2, 3, 4, 5, 6, 7, 9, 10, 11, 12, 13, 14, 15, 17, 18, 19, 20, 22, 24, 25, 27, 28, 29, 30, 31, 32, 33, 35, 36, 39, 40, 44, 45, 46, 47, 48, 52, 54, 55, 56, 57, 58, 63, 64, 66, 69, 70

Stanford-Binet (L) IQ 76; WISC 72 (V, 69; P. 82). Child in special class. Note the discrepancy in test results.

FIG. 66.   Man, by boy, 16-6. Raw Score 12; Standard Score 53; Percentile Rank 1

Items credited: 1, 4, 9, 11, 30, 35, 44, 45, 46, 55, 63, 64

WISC IQ '5 (V, 46; P, 43). Child in class for "trainables."

Note segmented character of arms and legs; a perseverative characteristic not uncommon among retarded children. Coordination quite good.

Children older than the norms provided in Tables 32–35 should be considered as age 15.

Scoring Practice (*Accepted scoring on pp. 273–274*)

FIG. 67. Man, by girl, 3-9

FIG. 68. Man, by girl, 5-6

FIG. 69. Man, by boy, 10-9

FIG. 70. Man, by boy, 10-6

Fɪɢ. 71. Man, by boy, 10-9

Fɪɢ. 72. Man, by boy, 10-8

Fɪɢ. 73. Man, by girl, 12-9

Fɪɢ. 74. Man, by boy, 8-9

FIG. 75. Man, by boy, 15-8

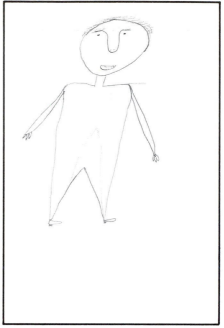

FIG. 76. Man, by boy, 17-2

FIG. 77. Man, by girl, 17-0

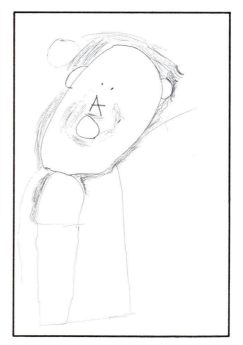

FIG. 78. Man, by boy, 19-0

Fig. 67. Man, by girl, 3-9. Raw Score 12; Standard Score 117; Percentile Rank 87

Items credited: 1, 4, 9, 11, 18, 19, 24, 28, 30, 44, 46, 63

Fig. 68. Man, by girl, 5-6. Raw Score 12; Standard Score 85; Percentile Rank 16

Items credited: 1, 4, 9, 11, 14, 18, 22, 30, 35, 39, 55, 63

Fig. 69. Man, by boy, 10-9. Raw Score 41; Standard Score 110; Percentile Rank 75

Items credited: 1, 2, 3, 4, 6, 9, 10, 11, 14, 18, 19, 24, 26, 28, 29, 30, 31, 32, 33, 34, 35, 36, 39, 40, 43, 44, 45, 46, 47, 48, 50, 52, 54, 55, 56, 57, 64, 66, 67, 68, 72

Note that the shape of fingers (Item 26) is credited even though the correct number of fingers (Item 25) is not.

Fig. 70. Man, by boy, 10-6. Raw Score 50; Standard Score 124; Percentile Rank 95

Items credited: 1, 2, 3, 4, 7, 9, 10, 11, 14, 15, 16, 18, 19, 22, 23, 24, 25, 26, 27, 28, 29, 30, 31, 32, 33, 35, 36, 39, 40, 41, 42, 44, 45, 46, 47, 48, 49, 51, 52, 53, 54, 55, 56, 57, 58, 59, 62, 63, 64, 70

Fig. 71. Man, by boy, 10-9. Raw Score 4; Standard Score 54; Percentile Rank 1

Items credited: 1, 11, 18, 35

Stanford-Binet (M) IQ 42; (L) 41. Child in class for "trainable" children.

The sole feature of the face could be scored either as mouth or nose; a mouth is more commonly intended.

Fig. 72. Man, by boy, 10-8. Raw Score 28; Standard Score 90; Percentile Rank 25

Items credited: 1, 2, 4, 9, 11, 18, 19, 22, 23, 24, 25, 27, 28, 30, 31, 35, 39, 40, 44, 45, 46, 47, 51, 53, 54, 55, 63, 64

Stanford-Binet (M) IQ 88; WISC 76 (V, 84; P, 72). Child in special class.

Fig. 73. Man, by girl, 12-9. Raw Score 7; Standard Score 45 (estimated); Percentile Rank 1

Items credited: 1, 2, 30, 35, 39, 44, 46

Stanford-Binet (L) IQ 45; (M) IQ 39. Child in class for "trainable" children.

FIG. 74. Man, by boy, 8-9. Raw Score 14; Standard Score 77; Percentile Rank 6

Items credited: 1, 4, 9, 11, 18, 24, 30, 35, 39, 44, 45, 46, 47, 54

Stanford-Binet (L) IQ 53. Child in special class.

FIG. 75. Man, by boy, 15-8. Raw Score 56; Standard Score 115; Percentile Rank 84

Items credited: 1, 2, 3, 4, 5, 6, 7, 9, 10, 11, 12, 13, 14, 15, 16, 17, 18, 19, 22, 23, 24, 26, 28, 29, 30, 31, 32, 33, 34, 35, 36, 37, 39, 40, 41, 42, 43, 44, 45, 46, 47, 48, 49, 50, 51, 52, 54, 55, 62, 63, 64, 67, 68, 69, 70, 71

WISC IQ 89 (V, 79; P, 102)

This is a superior drawing by a boy whose verbal performance on an individual intelligence test is considerably lower.

FIG. 76. Man, by boy, 17-2. Raw Score 19; Standard Score 63; Percentile Rank 1

Items credited: 1, 2, 4, 5, 9, 10, 11, 18, 24, 30, 35, 36, 39, 40, 41, 44, 45, 46, 64

WISC IQ 54 (V, 55; P, 54). Child in special class.

Eyebrow (Item 5) is faintly indicated on original, in addition to supraorbital ridge. Youth older than norms is interpreted in relation to values of fifteen-year-olds.

FIG. 77. Man, by girl, 17-10. Raw Score 15; Standard Score 50; Percentile Rank 1

Items credited: 1, 4, 5, 6, 22, 24, 30, 35, 39, 44, 46, 54, 55, 63, 64

Stanford-Binet (M) IQ 18; WISC 30 (V, 43; P, 38). Child in class for "trainable" children.

FIG. 78. Man, by boy, 19-0. Raw Score 8; Standard Score 47 (estimated); Percentile Rank 1

Items credited: 1, 4, 9, 11, 18, 22, 30, 46

Stanford-Binet (M) IQ 51

Indication of hair was perseverated around entire head and around contours of trunk. Arms are questionable but were credited, liberally.

Short Scoring Guide *

MAN POINT SCALE

1. Head present
2. Neck present
3. Neck, two dimensions
4. Eyes present
5. Eye detail: brow or lashes
6. Eye detail: pupil
7. Eye detail: proportion
8. Eye detail: glance
9. Nose present
10. Nose, two dimensions
11. Mouth present
12. Lips, two dimensions
13. Both nose and lips in two dimensions
14. Both chin and forehead shown
15. Projection of chin shown; chin clearly differentiated from lower lip
16. Line of jaw indicated
17. Bridge of nose
18. Hair I
19. Hair II
20. Hair III
21. Hair IV
22. Ears present
23. Ears present: proportion and position

24. Fingers present
25. Correct number of fingers shown
26. Detail of fingers correct
27. Opposition of thumb shown
28. Hands present
29. Wrist or ankle shown
30. Arms present
31. Shoulders I
32. Shoulders II
33. Arms at side or engaged in activity
34. Elbow joint shown
35. Legs present
36. Hip I (crotch)
37. Hip II
38. Knee joint shown
39. Feet I: any indication
40. Feet II: proportion
41. Feet III: heel
42. Feet IV: perspective
43. Feet V: detail
44. Attachment of arms and legs I
45. Attachment of arms and legs II
46. Trunk present
47. Trunk in proportion, two dimensions
48. Proportion: head I

49. Proportion: head II
50. Proportion: face
51. Proportion: arms I
52. Proportion: arms II
53. Proportion: legs
54. Proportion: limbs in two dimensions
55. Clothing I
56. Clothing II
57. Clothing III
58. Clothing IV
59. Clothing V
60. Profile I
61. Profile II
62. Full face
63. Motor coordination: lines
64. Motor coordination: junctures
65. Superior motor coordination
66. Directed lines and form: head outline
67. Directed lines and form: trunk outline
68. Directed lines and form: arms and legs
69. Directed lines and form: facial features
70. "Sketching" technique
71. "Modeling" technique
72. Arm movement
73. Leg movement

* For use only after the scoring requirements have been mastered.

Requirements for Scoring the Draw-a-Woman Scale

ITEM	DESCRIPTION

1. Head present — Any clear method of representing the head. Features alone, without any outline for the head itself, are not credited for this point.

2. Neck present — Any clear indication of the neck as distinct from the head and the trunk. Mere juxtaposition of the head and the trunk is not credited.

3. Neck, two dimensions — Outline of neck continuous with that of the head, of the trunk or of both. Line of neck must "flow" into head line or trunk line. Neck interposed as pillar between head and trunk does not get credit unless treated definitely to show continuity between neck and head or trunk or both, as by collar, or curving of lines.

Credit

No Credit

4. Eyes present — Either one or two eyes must be shown. Any method is satisfactory. A single indefinite feature, such as is occasionally found in the drawings of very young children, is credited. Credit also, in mature drawings attempting perspective, any indication of the eye by contour of the profile, as:

5. Eye detail: brow or lashes — Brow, lashes or both shown.

Full Face:

Credit

Profile:

Credit

No Credit

6. **Eye detail:**
   pupil

Pupil shown. Credit any clear indication of the pupil or iris as distinct from the outline of the eye. Both pupils must appear if both eyes are shown.

7. **Eye detail:**
   proportion

The horizontal measurement of the eye must be greater than the vertical dimension. This requirement must be fulfilled in both eyes if both are shown; one eye is sufficient if only one is shown. In profile drawings, any triangular forms which approximate the example below are credited.

Profile:

Credit

No Credit

8. **Cheeks**

Credit modeling or "shading" on cheeks or at mouth corners. Credit also "cosmetic cheeks"— circular spots on cheeks. In drawings which attempt perspective, credit any indication in *contour* of face.

Credit

9. **Nose present**

Any clear method of representation. In "mixed profiles," the score is plus even though *two* noses are shown.

10. **Nose, two**
    dimensions

Full Face: Credit all attempts to portray the nose in two dimensions, when the bridge is longer than the width of the base or tip.

Credit

|| ∧ ⌂ U L db L ப ⱳ ⩎ ∠

No Credit

△ ∪ ο ∨ ∧ • ⋈ ∠ ••

Profile: Credit all crude attempts to show the nose in profile, provided tip or base is shown in some manner. Do not credit simple "button."

No Credit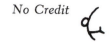

11. Bridge of nose

Full Face: Nose properly placed and shaped. The base of the nose must appear as well as the indication of a straight bridge. Placement of upper portion of bridge is important; must extend *up to or between the eyes.* *Bridge must be narrower than the base.*

Credit

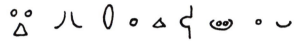

No Credit

Profile: Nose at angle with face, approximately 45 degrees. Separation of nose from forehead clearly shown at eye.

Credit

No Credit

12. Nostrils shown

Any attempt to portray nostrils as holes, dots, or to show "wings."

Credit

No Credit

13. Mouth present

Any clear representation.

14. Lips, two dimensions

Two lips clearly shown.

Full Face:

Credit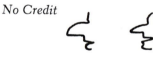

Profile:

Credit

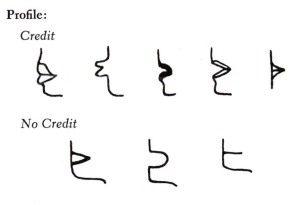

No Credit

15. **"Cosmetic lips"**

Any clear attempt to show "Cupid's bow." Score based on the outer shape. Two lips need *not* be shown.

Credit

16. **Both nose and lips in two dimensions**

Bonus point given when both Items 10 and 14 are passed.

17. **Both chin and forehead shown**

Full Face: Sufficient space must be left above the eyes to represent the forehead, and below the mouth to represent the chin. The scoring should be rather lenient. Where neck is continuous with face, placement of mouth with respect to narrowing of lower portion of head is important.

Credit

No Credit

Profile: The point may be credited when the eyes and mouth are omitted, if the outline of the face shows clearly the limits of the chin and forehead. Score leniently if forehead is covered by hat brim; more strictly if covered by hair.

18. **Line of jaw indicated**

Full Face: Line of jaw and chin drawn across neck but not squarely across. Neck must be sufficiently wide, and chin must be so shaped that the line of the jaw forms a well defined acute angle with the line of the neck. Score *strictly* on the simple oval face.

Credit

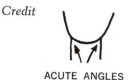

ACUTE ANGLES

Profile: Line of jaw extends toward (but not all the way to) the ear or across the neck.

Credit

No Credit

19. Hair I	Any indication of hair, however crude.
20. Hair II	Scribble closely conforming to head, *or*

Full Face: Shaped masses suggesting braids or locks each side of face.

Credit

Profile: Mass dependant in back.

Credit

21. Hair III	Style suggested by indentation at temple, or bangs, or shaped at lower ends, or both. General "style" achieved. Distinctly better design than Item 20.
22. Hair IV	Use of directed lines to indicate a part, texture, or combing. Superior style achieved.

Caution: Score strictly; superior style may be achieved with *outline* sketching, but this does not score. Directed lines to indicate hair texture must appear, and be better than "coloring in."

23. Necklace or earrings

Any clear indication. Distinguish necklace from neckline or collar of dress. Earrings without ears (which may be concealed by hair) should be credited.

24. Arms present

Any method of representation clearly intended to indicate arms. Fingers alone are not sufficient, but the point is credited if any space is left between the base of the fingers and that part of the body to which they are attached. The number of arms must be correct, except in profile drawings when only one arm may score.

25. Shoulders

Full Face: A distinct change in the direction of the upper part of the trunk, which gives the effect of a *"rounded corner."* The ordinary elliptical form is never credited. There must be an abrupt broadening of the trunk below the neck, which then turns downward into the arms or sides of the trunk. Square corners fail.

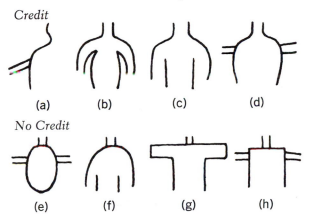

Credit

(a)   (b)   (c)   (d)

No Credit

(e)   (f)   (g)   (h)

Profile: Somewhat more lenient where the trunk as well as the head is shown in profile. If the lines that form the upper part of the trunk diverge from each other at the base of the neck so as to show the expansion of the chest, credit the point.

26. Arms at side (or engaged in activity or behind back)

Full Face: Young children generally draw the arms held stiffly out from the body. Credit this point when at least one arm is down at the side, making an angle of no more than 10 degrees with the general vertical axis of the trunk, unless the arms are engaged in some definite activity, such as carrying an object. Credit when hands are placed on hips or behind the back.

Credit

10° OR LESS

No Credit

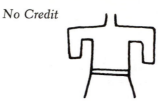

Profile: Credit if *hands are engaged in definite activity,* or if upper arm is suspended, even though forearm is extended.

Credit

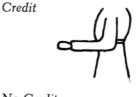

No Credit

27. Elbow joint shown   There must be an abrupt bend (not a curve) at approximately the middle of the arm. One arm is sufficient. Modeling or creasing of the sleeve is credited.

Full Face:

Credit

Profile:

Credit

No Credit

28. Fingers present   Any indication of fingers. Mitt hand does not score even if thumb is shown.

29. Correct number of fingers shown   If both hands are shown, the correct number on each is necessary, unless there is a clear attempt to portray hand activity which would conceal the correct number. Credit drawings produced by older children who try a "sketching" technique, even though five digits may not be definitely discerned.

Credit

30. Detail of fingers correct   "Grapes" or "sticks" do not score. Length of individual fingers must be distinctly greater than width. In well-executed drawings, where hand may appear in perspective, or where fingers are indicated by "sketching," credit this point. Credit also those cases in which, because the hand is obviously clenched, only the knuckles or part of the fingers appear. This last will occur only in high-quality drawings where there is considerable use of perspective.

31. Opposition of thumb shown   A clear differentiation of the thumb from the fingers. Scoring should be very strict. The point is credited if one of the lateral digits is definitely shorter than any of the others (compare especially with little finger), or if the angle between it and the index finger is not less than twice as great as that between any two of the other digits, or if its point of attachment to the hand is distinctly nearer to the wrist than that of the fingers. Conditions must be fulfilled on both hands if both are shown, unless hand is grasping something; one hand is sufficient if only one is shown. Five digits are necessary for thumb to score. *Fingers must be present or indicated;* "mitt" hand does *not* score unless subject is definitely shown in winter garb, wearing mittens.

Credit

No Credit

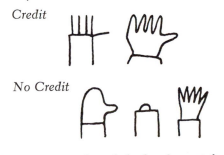

32. Hands present   Any representation of the hand, apart from the fingers. When fingers are shown a space must be left between base of fingers and edge of sleeve or cuff. Where no cuff exists, arm must broaden in some way to suggest palm or back of hand as distinct from wrist. Characteristic must appear on both hands, if both are shown. "Mitt" hand with thumb does not score unless figure obviously is wearing mittens.

Credit

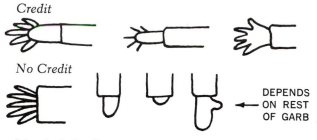

No Credit

                          DEPENDS
                                          ← ON REST
                                             OF GARB

Marginal Credit

33. Legs present

Any method of representation clearly intended to indicate the legs. There must be two legs in full-face drawings, and either one or two, in profiles. Credit where long skirt hides legs or feet.

34. Hip

Full Face: The principal axes of the legs must form a distinct angle. The distance between the ankles must be greater than the distance between the inner surfaces of the legs at the skirt line, and the difference must be more than can be accounted for by contours of the calf and ankle. Do not credit in the case of a long gown.

Credit

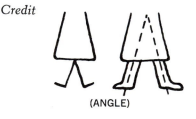

(ANGLE)

No Credit

(PARALLEL)

Profile: Credit when legs form angle, as in walking. Credit in standing figure, when one leg is shown, or when two appear in true profile.

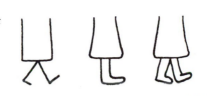

Credit

35. Feet I: any indication	Feet indicated by any means: two feet in full-face; one or two in profile. In the case of a long gown, credit this item.
36. Feet II: proportion	**Full Face:** Feet must be longer than wide, or drawn in perspective.

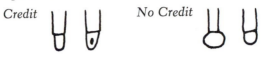

Credit   *No Credit*

Profile: Horizontal dimension of fore-part of foot must be greater than vertical dimension. In the case of a long gown, credit only when foot is indicated in some way, as by the tip appearing beneath the edge of the gown, etc.

Credit

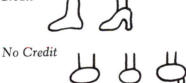

No Credit

37. Feet III: detail	Foot or shoe must show some ornamentation, such as a buckle, tie, strap, or sole. In the case of a long gown, do *not* credit unless foot is shown.
38. Shoe I: "feminine"	Credit any clear attempt to depict a feminine shoe as opposed to "brogan" or other thick, solid shoe. Note especially attempts to depict slender toe or arch, high heel, open toe, or straps. If heel is crucial point, it should be at least one-third of total height of shoe at that point. Shoe must be marked off from leg, either by a line or by profile shaping. In the case of a long gown, credit only when shoe is shown.

Credit

39. Shoe II: style	Shoe must be clearly feminine and "styled," i.e., clearly a pump, tie, open toe, wedgie, saddle-shoe, etc. In the case of a long gown, credit only when clearly shown.

40. Placement of feet appropriate to figure

Full Face: Feet turned "in" or "out," or in perspective. Do not credit primitive feet.

No Credit

Profile: Credit both feet turned in direction of head. Do not credit when feet are absent, except where long gown hides feet.

41. Attachment of arms and legs I

Both arms and legs attached to the trunk at any point, or arms attached to the neck, or at juncture of head and trunk when neck is omitted. Do not credit if either arms or legs are missing. Credit where dress hides legs and/or feet. If the trunk is omitted, the score is always zero. If the legs are attached elsewhere than to the trunk, regardless of the attachment of the arms, the score is zero. If only one arm or leg is shown, either in full-face or profile drawings, credit may be given on the basis of the limb that is shown. If both arms and legs are shown, the members of each pair must be attached approximately symmetrically. Credit where long dress hides legs and/or feet. Be careful to distinguish this item from Item 25.

Credit

42. Attachment of arms and legs II

Arms attached to the trunk at the correct position. Legs attached to the bottom of the trunk or skirt and not continuous with vertical line or drape of the skirt. Credit this point if both feet and legs are hidden by long gown.

Legs:

Credit   *No Credit*

Arms: **Full Face:** Where Item 25 is failed, attachment must be exactly at the point where the shoulders should have been indicated. Score very strictly, especially when Item 25 is zero. Do not credit if arms at their place of attachment occupy as much as one-half or more of the distance from the neck to the waist. The following sketch illustrates when Item 41 but *not* Item 42 scores:

(See also Item 25, a, e, h, for examples which credit Item 41 but *not* 42.)

Arms: **Profile:** The attachment of the arms must be indicated at a point approximately on the median line of the trunk, at a short distance below the neck, this point coinciding with the broadening of the trunk which indicates the chest and shoulders. If the arms extend from the line which outlines the back, or if the point of attachment reaches the base of the neck, or falls below the greatest expansion of the chest, the point is not credited. Credit Item 41 but *not* Item 42.

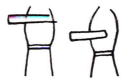

43. Clothing indicated	Clothing indicated by buttons or pockets on the simple ellipse, triangle, or trapezoid figure. Credit if there is definitely a skirt, even if no buttons or pockets are shown.
44. Sleeve I	Indicated by any means.
45. Sleeve II	Indicated by more than a simple cross line. Must show button, cuff, double line, puffed sleeve (long or short), or sleeve definitely wider than the arm which protrudes from it. Where a strap or strapless gown is clearly indicated, credit both Items 44 and 45. When hands are so placed that possible cuff is hidden, do *not* credit unless short sleeve is clearly indicated. *Note:* Be careful not to confuse bracelet or wristwatch with sleeve.
46. Neckline I	Any dress line at neck other than that produced by chin or jaw. Any crude single line, straight or semicircular. Distinguish carefully from necklace.
47. Neckline II: collar	Collar indicated. Neckline must be "V'd" or definitely shaped in some other manner.
48. Waist I	Whether or not a belt is shown, the direction of the body contour must change perceptibly at and/or below the waist. If *no belt or waist is drawn*, a gentle,

continuous curve does not score; there must be an abrupt change in body line.

Credit

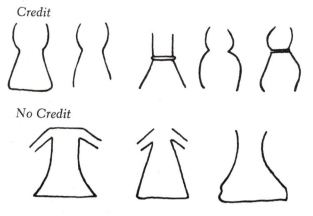

No Credit

49. Waist II

A distinct belt (two lines), sash, sweater, or blouse hem must be indicated by means *better than a single horizontal line*.

50. Skirt "modeled" to indicate pleats or draping

Irregular hemline not sufficient; lines, shading, or sketching must appear.

Credit

51. No transparencies in the figure

There must be a garment on the figure that is clear and complete. Clothing must show neckline, sleeves, skirt hem, or slacks. No body lines may show through clothes that would ordinarily conceal them.

52. Garb feminine

Young Children (under 8): Skirt must be a distinct feature, and the body must appear in *two* distinct segments.

Credit

No Credit

Older Children (8 and over): Credit any dress or skirt. Where slacks, breeches, or overalls are shown, credit only if the style of blouse or pants is distinctly feminine, apart from hair, face, or breast indication. Slacks may be judged by absence of fly and by placement of pockets.

53. **Garb complete, without incongruities**

Garb must contain all these elements: shoes, sleeves (hands must protrude), dress and neckline or sleeves, or skirt and blouse (or jacket). *Exceptions:* Slacks, blue jeans, sports garb, formal dress which may obscure shoes. These are credited.

54. **Garb a definite "type"**

Types may include: formal gown, sports garb (shorts, slacks), "school garb," "dress up," house dress (should include apron), or "suit" (jacket and skirt).

55. **Trunk present**

Any clear indication of the trunk, either one or two dimensional.

56. **Trunk in proportion, two dimensions**

Length of trunk greater than breadth. In drawings by younger children, where the trunk may not be clearly differentiated from the skirt, judge body area as including skirt.

57. **Head-trunk proportion**

Young Children (under 8): Score in relation to *body area*, excluding head when no differentiation between waist and terminus of trunk or no indication of skirt is shown.

Older Children (8 and over): Credit drawings that indicate a garment but do not suggest a waistline, if the head is no larger than one-fourth or smaller than one-eighth of the body (including garment) area.

Profile: Score more leniently. Judge more on the length of head in relation to the length of chest area. If two lengths are about equal, or if head is the shorter length but not less than one-fourth the chest length, credit the item.

58. **Head: proportion**

Full Face: Length of head greater than its width. Should show a general oval shape.

Profile: Same requirement as full-face drawing, but exclude hair in estimating width.

59. **Limbs: proportion**

Length of arms and legs greater than width. When arms score, credit the item even if feet are concealed by long dress.

60. **Arms in proportion to trunk**

Both arms *longer* than length of trunk from shoulder (or base of neck) to waist, but not more than twice this length.

Young Children (under 8): Arms must be equal to body length.

Older Children (8 and over) : Credit drawings that portray dress or skirt if arm length is at least half of dress length (shoulder to hem of skirt) but not as long as hem.

61. Location of waist   This item evaluates child's ability to *locate* the waist. Waist located below one-third of total length of figure, crown to toe, but not below one-half of total length. (Crown is considered the top of the head, including hair but not hat.) Waistline must be indicated by belt, or by some distinct change in body contour. Do not credit when trunk and dress are indicated by uninterrupted curve, with no indication of waistline.

62. Dress area   Dress area below waist must be as large or larger than trunk area above waist but not more than twice as large (three times as large in profile). Credit if formal gown is clearly represented. For slacks, include the area occupied by the legs but not the feet. Define as waist a waist *line* however indicated, or estimate location from an obvious narrowing of body, or widening of hips. Do not credit in drawings by young children showing no trunk or body contours.

63. Motor coordination: junctures   All lines meet cleanly, without overlap or intervening space. Emphasis is on the juncture of lines, regardless of the character of lines.

64. Motor coordination: lines   Lines are firm, cleanly made, continuous and "controlled." If "sketchy" judge the basic character of the body lines created by the shorter pencil strokes. Both curved and straight lines must be handled with assurance. Do not credit in a drawing with extensive redrawing and erasures.

65. Superior motor coordination   Credit this point in all cases where Item 64 is achieved without redrawing or erasures, and where the total effect of lines is neat, clean, and "sure."

66. Directed lines and form: head outline   The drawing must show the contours of the head and/or face. Simple circle or ellipse to which projecting features have been added does not score.

No Credit

67. Directed lines and form: breast   Any attempt, by modeling or by contour, to indicate the feminine breast. In full-face drawings, credit strapless gown if top is curved.

Credit

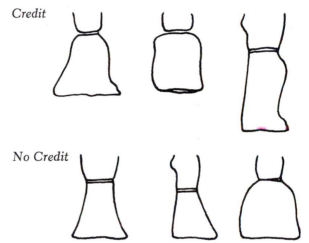

68. Directed lines and form: hip contour

Full Face: Hips indicated by distinct convexity below waistline. This must occur on both sides. Note that wide, uniformly curved bell-shaped flaring skirt does *not* score.

Profile: Convexity must be indicated over hips and buttocks.

Credit

No Credit

69. Directed lines and form: arms taper

Wrist and/or forearm distinctly narrower than upper arm. Credit the point whether achieved by narrowing of sleeve or by shaping the bare arm. Where long, full sleeves are clearly indicated, credit this item.

70. Directed lines and form: calf of leg

Leg shaped better than a taper. Definite calf must be shown. Score strictly.

71. Directed lines and form: facial features

Facial features must be symmetrical in all respects. Eyes and mouth must be shown in two dimensions; nose may be indicated by dots.

Full Face: Features must be appropriately placed, regular and symmetrical, giving a clear appearance of the human form.

Profile: The eye must be regular in outline and located in the forward one-third of the head. The bridge of the nose must form an obtuse angle with the forehead. The scoring should be strict; a "cartoon" nose does not get credit.

Short Scoring Guide *

WOMAN POINT SCALE

1. Head present
2. Neck present
3. Neck, two dimensions
4. Eyes present
5. Eye detail: brow or lashes
6. Eye detail: pupil
7. Eye detail: proportion
8. Cheeks
9. Nose present
10. Nose, two dimensions
11. Bridge of nose
12. Nostrils shown
13. Mouth present
14. Lips, two dimensions
15. "Cosmetic lips"
16. Both nose and lips in two dimensions
17. Both chin and forehead shown
18. Line of jaw indicated
19. Hair I
20. Hair II
21. Hair III
22. Hair IV
23. Necklace or earrings
24. Arms present
25. Shoulders
26. Arms at side (or engaged in activity or behind back)

27. Elbow joint shown
28. Fingers present
29. Correct number of fingers shown
30. Detail of fingers correct
31. Opposition of thumb shown
32. Hands present
33. Legs present
34. Hip
35. Feet I: any indication
36. Feet II: proportion
37. Feet III: detail
38. Shoe I: "feminine"
39. Shoe II: style
40. Placement of feet appropriate to figure
41. Attachment of arms and legs I
42. Attachment of arms and legs II
43. Clothing indicated
44. Sleeve I
45. Sleeve II
46. Neckline I
47. Neckline II: collar
48. Waist I
49. Waist II
50. Skirt "modeled" to indicate pleats or draping
51. No transparencies in the figure

52. Garb feminine
53. Garb complete, without incongruities
54. Garb a definite "type"
55. Trunk present
56. Trunk in proportion, two dimensions
57. Head-trunk proportion
58. Head: proportion
59. Limbs: proportion
60. Arms in proportion to trunk
61. Location of waist
62. Dress area
63. Motor coordination: junctures
64. Motor coordination: lines
65. Superior motor coordination
66. Directed lines and form: head outline
67. Directed lines and form: breast
68. Directed lines and form: hip contour
69. Directed lines and form: arms taper
70. Directed lines and form: calf of leg
71. Directed lines and form: facial features

* For use only after the scoring requirements have been mastered.

Instructions for Converting Raw Scores to Standard Scores

To find the standard score equivalents for a given child, certain values are needed—the child's age and his raw score on each drawing. Calculate his age in years and months. Score each drawing to find his raw score—the total number of points he has earned. On the face page of the test booklet, enter a separate raw score for each drawing. Turn to the appropriate conversion table in this section (Tables 32–35). Separate tables are provided for boys and girls, and for the Man and Woman scales. Because the standardization samples were constructed so as to center at the mid-year in each age group, a child six years and no months old, and a child six years and eleven months old is each considered to be six years old. Enter the conversion table in the appropriate age column and in the row corresponding to the calculated raw score. The value in the table at the intersection of the row and column is the child's standard score. As explained in Chapter IV, this score expresses the child's relative standing on the test in relation to his own age and sex group, in terms of a mean of 100 and a standard deviation of 15. Thus, a standard score of 120 tells us at once that a child is one and one-third standard deviations above the average of his age and sex group.

Because standard measures can be averaged directly, it is possible to obtain an average measure on the Man and Woman drawings by summing the two standard scores and dividing by two. The result is a more reliable estimate of the child's maturity as measured by drawings than his score on either test alone. However, because the correlation of the two measures is somewhat below the reliability of either scale, measured on a test-retest basis, the two scales may be considered to evaluate somewhat different functions. The psychologist may wish, therefore, to keep the two estimates distinct.

It is possible to score the Self drawing with the Point scale of the appropriate sex and use it as a third estimate of intellectual maturity as measured by the Drawing Test. There is less precedent for doing this, however, since the empirical relationships have not been worked out on the Self figure, using the Point scales. The self-portrait has not been standardized and must, therefore, be considered as only a tentative measure of maturity.

TABLE		
32		*Table for Converting Raw Scores to Standard Scores*

Drawing of a Man, by Boys

RAW SCORE	CHRONOLOGICAL AGE IN YEARS													RAW SCORE
	3*	4*	5	6	7	8	9	10	11	12	13	14	15	
0	68	55	53	52	51	50	49							0
1	73	61	56	54	53	52	50							1
2	77	66	59	57	55	54	52	50	51					2
3	82	70	62	60	57	56	54	52	52					3
4	86	74	65	62	59	58	55	54	54	51				4
5	91	78	68	65	62	60	57	55	55	52				5
6	95	83	71	68	64	62	59	57	56	53				6
7	100	87	74	70	66	63	60	58	58	55	50			7
8	104	91	77	73	68	65	62	60	59	56	51			8
9	109	96	80	75	70	67	63	61	60	57	53			9
10	113	100	83	78	72	69	65	63	62	59	54	50	50	10
11	118	104	86	81	75	71	67	64	63	60	56	52	52	11
12	122	109	89	83	77	73	69	66	65	61	57	53	53	12
13	127	113	92	86	79	75	70	67	66	63	58	55	55	13
14	131	117	95	89	81	77	72	69	68	64	60	56	56	14
15	136	122	98	91	84	79	74	70	69	66	61	58	57	15
16	140	126	101	94	86	81	75	72	70	67	63	59	59	16
17	145	130	104	96	88	83	77	73	72	68	64	60	60	17
18	149	134	107	99	90	85	79	75	73	70	65	62	62	18
19	154	139	110	102	92	87	80	76	74	71	67	63	63	19
20	158	143	113	104	94	89	82	78	76	72	68	65	64	20
21	163	147	116	107	97	90	84	79	77	73	70	66	66	21
22	168	152	119	110	99	92	85	81	78	75	71	68	67	22
23	172	156	122	112	101	94	87	82	80	76	73	69	69	23
24		160	125	115	103	96	89	84	81	78	74	70	70	24
25		164	128	117	105	98	90	86	83	80	75	72	72	25
26		169	131	120	108	100	92	87	84	81	77	73	73	26
27		173	134	123	110	102	94	89	85	82	78	75	74	27
28		177	137	125	112	104	95	90	87	83	80	76	76	28
29			140	128	114	106	97	92	88	85	81	78	77	29
30			143	131	116	108	99	93	90	86	82	79	79	30
31			146	133	119	110	100	95	91	87	84	80	80	31
32			149	136	121	112	102	96	92	89	85	82	81	32
33			152	138	123	114	104	98	94	90	87	83	83	33
34				141	125	116	105	99	95	92	88	85	84	34
35				144	127	118	107	101	97	93	89	86	86	35

* These values have been calculated from samples which are not as representative as the age samples from 5 through 15 years. They are likely to be a little high for unselected or more adequately representative samples. They are offered as tentative guides for use with pre-school groups.

TABLE 32 (*continued*)

RAW SCORE						CHRONOLOGICAL AGE IN YEARS								RAW SCORE
	3	4	5	6	7	8	9	10	11	12	13	14	15	
36				146	130	119	109	102	98	94	91	88	87	36
37				149	132	121	110	104	99	96	92	89	88	37
38					134	123	112	105	101	97	94	90	90	38
39					136	125	114	107	102	98	95	92	91	39
40					138	127	116	108	103	100	96	93	93	40
41					141	129	117	110	105	101	98	95	94	41
42					143	131	119	111	106	102	99	96	96	42
43					145	133	121	113	108	104	101	98	97	43
44					147	135	122	115	109	105	102	99	98	44
45					149	137	124	116	110	106	103	100	100	45
46						139	126	118	112	108	105	102	101	46
47						141	127	119	113	109	106	103	103	47
48						143	129	121	114	111	108	105	101	48
49						145	131	122	116	112	109	106	105	49
50						146	133	124	117	113	110	108	107	50
51						148	134	125	119	115	112	109	108	51
52						150	136	127	120	116	113	110	110	52
53							137	128	121	117	115	112	111	53
54							139	130	123	119	116	113	113	54
55							141	131	124	120	118	115	114	55
56							142	133	125	121	119	116	115	56
57							144	134	127	123	120	118	117	57
58							146	136	128	124	122	119	118	58
59							147	137	130	126	123	120	120	59
60							149	139	131	127	125	122	121	60
61								140	132	128	126	123	122	61
62								142	134	130	127	125	124	62
63								143	135	131	129	126	125	63
64								145	137	132	130	128	127	64
65								146	138	134	132	129	128	65
66								148	139	135	133	130	130	66
67								150	141	136	134	132	131	67
68									142	138	136	133	132	68
69									143	139	137	135	134	69
70									145	140	139	136	135	70
71									146	142	140	138	137	71
72									148	143	141	139	138	72
73									149	145	143	140	139	73

TABLE 33 | Table for Converting Raw Scores to Standard Scores

Drawing of a Man, by Girls

RAW SCORE	3*	4*	5	6	7	8	9	10	11	12	13	14	15	RAW SCORE
0	66	58	50	50	49									0
1	70	62	53	52	51	50								1
2	74	66	56	55	53	51								2
3	78	70	59	57	55	53	50							3
4	83	74	62	60	58	55	52							4
5	87	78	65	62	60	57	54	50						5
6	91	81	68	65	62	59	55	51						6
7	96	85	70	67	64	61	57	53	49					7
8	100	89	73	70	66	63	59	55	51	49				8
9	104	92	76	72	69	65	61	56	52	51				9
10	108	96	79	75	71	67	62	58	54	52				10
11	113	100	82	77	73	69	64	59	55	54	50			11
12	117	104	85	80	75	70	66	61	57	55	51			12
13	121	107	87	82	77	72	67	63	58	56	53	50		13
14	126	111	90	85	79	74	69	64	60	58	54	51		14
15	130	115	93	87	82	76	71	66	61	59	56	53	50	15
16	134	119	96	90	84	78	73	67	63	61	57	54	51	16
17	139	122	99	93	86	80	74	69	64	62	59	56	53	17
18	143	126	102	95	88	82	76	71	66	64	60	57	55	18
19	147	130	105	98	90	83	78	72	68	65	62	59	56	19
20	152	134	107	100	92	86	80	74	69	66	63	61	58	20
21	156	137	110	103	95	88	81	75	71	68	65	62	60	21
22	160	141	113	105	97	89	83	77	72	70	66	64	61	22
23	165	149	116	108	99	91	85	79	74	71	68	65	63	23
24	169	152	119	110	101	93	86	80	75	72	69	67	65	24
25	173	156	122	113	103	95	88	82	77	74	71	68	66	25
26	177	160	124	115	105	97	90	83	78	75	72	70	68	26
27		164	127	118	108	99	92	85	80	77	74	72	70	27
28		168	130	120	110	101	93	87	81	78	75	73	71	28
29		171	133	123	112	103	95	88	83	80	77	75	73	29
30		175	136	125	114	105	97	90	84	81	78	76	75	30
31			139	128	116	106	98	91	86	83	80	78	76	31
32			142	130	118	108	100	93	87	84	81	79	78	32
33			144	133	121	110	102	95	89	86	83	81	80	33
34			147	135	123	112	104	96	91	87	84	83	81	34
35			150	138	125	114	105	98	92	88	86	84	83	35

* These values have been calculated from samples which are not as representative as the age samples from 5 through 15 years. They are likely to be a little high for unselected or more adequately representative samples. They are offered as tentative guides for use with pre-school groups.

TABLE 33 *(continued)*

RAW SCORE	CHRONOLOGICAL AGE IN YEARS 3	4	5	6	7	8	9	10	11	12	13	14	15	RAW SCORE
36				140	127	116	107	100	94	90	87	86	85	**36**
37				143	129	118	109	101	95	91	89	87	86	**37**
38				146	131	120	111	103	97	93	91	89	88	**38**
39				148	134	122	112	104	98	94	92	90	90	**39**
40				151	136	124	114	106	100	96	94	92	91	**40**
41					138	125	116	108	101	97	95	94	93	**41**
42					140	127	118	109	103	99	97	95	95	**42**
43					142	129	119	111	104	100	98	97	96	**43**
44					144	131	121	112	106	102	100	98	98	**44**
45					147	133	123	114	107	103	101	100	100	**45**
46					149	135	124	116	109	104	103	101	101	**46**
47					151	137	126	117	110	106	104	103	103	**47**
48						139	128	119	112	107	106	104	105	**48**
49						141	130	120	114	109	107	106	106	**49**
50						142	131	122	115	110	109	108	108	**50**
51						144	133	124	117	112	110	109	110	**51**
52						146	135	125	118	113	112	111	111	**52**
53						148	137	127	120	115	113	112	113	**53**
54						150	138	128	121	116	115	114	115	**54**
55							140	130	123	118	116	115	116	**55**
56							142	132	124	119	118	117	118	**56**
57							143	133	126	120	119	119	120	**57**
58							145	135	127	122	121	120	121	**58**
59							147	136	129	123	122	122	123	**59**
60							149	138	130	125	124	123	125	**60**
61							150	140	132	126	125	125	126	**61**
62								141	133	128	127	126	128	**62**
63								143	135	129	128	128	130	**63**
64								144	137	131	130	130	131	**64**
65								146	138	132	131	131	133	**65**
66								148	140	134	133	133	135	**66**
67								149	141	135	134	134	136	**67**
68								151	143	136	136	136	138	**68**
69									144	138	138	137	140	**69**
70									146	139	139	139	141	**70**
71									147	141	141	141	143	**71**
72									149	142	142	142	145	**72**
73									150	144	144	144	146	**73**

TABLE 34 | *Table for Converting Raw Scores to Standard Scores*

Drawing of a Woman, by Boys

RAW SCORE	3*	4*	5	6	7	8	9	10	11	12	13	14	15	RAW SCORE
0	68	55	56	56	51									0
1	73	61	59	58	53	50								1
2	77	66	61	61	56	52								2
3	82	70	64	63	58	53								3
4	86	74	67	65	60	55	50	49						4
5	91	78	70	68	62	57	51	51	49					5
6	95	83	73	70	64	59	53	52	51					6
7	100	87	75	73	66	61	55	54	52					7
8	104	91	78	75	68	63	57	56	54	50				8
9	109	96	81	77	70	65	59	57	55	52				9
10	113	100	84	80	72	67	60	59	57	54	50			10
11	118	104	86	82	74	69	62	61	59	55	52			11
12	122	109	89	84	76	70	64	62	60	56	53			12
13	127	113	92	87	79	72	66	64	62	58	55	50		13
14	131	117	95	89	81	74	67	66	63	60	56	52	51	14
15	136	122	97	91	83	76	69	67	65	61	58	54	53	15
16	140	126	100	94	85	78	71	69	66	63	59	55	54	16
17	145	130	103	96	87	80	73	70	68	64	61	57	56	17
18	149	134	106	98	89	82	75	72	70	66	63	58	57	18
19	154	139	108	101	91	84	76	74	71	68	64	60	59	19
20	158	143	111	103	93	86	78	75	73	69	66	62	61	20
21	163	147	114	105	95	87	80	77	74	71	67	63	62	21
22	168	152	117	108	97	89	82	79	76	72	69	65	64	22
23	172	156	119	110	99	91	84	80	78	74	70	66	65	23
24		160	122	112	102	93	85	82	79	75	72	68	67	24
25		164	125	115	104	95	87	84	81	77	73	70	69	25
26		169	128	117	106	97	89	85	82	78	75	71	70	26
27		173	131	119	108	99	91	87	84	80	77	73	72	27
28		177	133	122	110	101	93	89	85	82	78	74	74	28
29			136	124	112	103	94	90	87	83	80	76	75	29
30			139	126	114	104	96	92	89	85	81	78	77	30
31			142	129	116	106	98	93	90	86	83	79	78	31
32			144	131	118	108	100	95	92	88	84	81	80	32
33				133	120	110	102	97	93	89	86	82	82	33
34				136	122	112	103	98	95	91	88	84	83	34
35				138	125	114	105	100	96	93	89	86	85	35

* These values have been calculated from samples which are not as representative as the age samples from 5 through 15 years. They are likely to be a little high for unselected or more adequately representative samples. They are offered as tentative guides for use with preschool groups.

TABLE 34 *(continued)*

RAW SCORE	CHRONOLOGICAL AGE IN YEARS													RAW SCORE
	3	4	5	6	7	8	9	10	11	12	13	14	15	
36				140	127	116	107	102	98	94	91	87	86	36
37				143	129	118	109	103	100	96	92	89	88	37
38				145	131	120	110	105	101	97	94	90	90	38
39					133	121	112	107	103	99	95	92	91	39
40					135	123	114	108	104	100	97	94	93	40
41					137	125	116	110	106	102	98	95	94	41
42					139	127	118	111	107	103	100	97	96	42
43					141	129	119	113	109	105	102	98	98	43
44					143	131	121	115	111	107	103	100	99	44
45					145	133	123	116	112	108	105	101	101	45
46					148	135	125	118	114	110	106	103	103	46
47					150	137	127	120	115	111	108	105	104	47
48						139	128	121	117	113	109	106	106	48
49						140	130	123	118	114	111	108	107	49
50						142	132	125	120	116	112	109	109	50
51						144	134	126	122	117	114	111	111	51
52						146	136	128	123	119	116	113	112	52
53						148	137	129	125	121	117	114	114	53
54						150	139	131	126	122	119	116	115	54
55							141	133	128	124	120	117	117	55
56							143	134	129	125	122	119	119	56
57							145	136	131	127	123	121	120	57
58							146	138	133	128	125	122	122	58
59							148	139	134	130	127	124	123	59
60							150	141	136	132	128	125	125	60
61								143	137	133	130	127	127	61
62								144	139	135	131	129	128	62
63								146	140	136	133	130	130	63
64								148	142	138	134	132	132	64
65								149	144	139	136	133	133	65
66								151	145	141	137	135	135	66
67									147	142	139	137	136	67
68									148	144	141	138	138	68
69									150	146	142	140	140	69
70										147	144	141	141	70
71										149	145	143	143	71

TABLE 35 | Table for Converting Raw Scores to Standard Scores

Drawing of a Woman, by Girls

RAW SCORE	3*	4*	5	6	7	8	9	10	11	12	13	14	15	RAW SCORE
0	62	55	52	52	49									0
1	66	59	54	54	50	48								1
2	70	63	57	56	52	50								2
3	74	67	59	58	54	51								3
4	78	70	62	60	56	53								4
5	83	74	64	62	58	55	48							5
6	87	78	67	64	60	56	50							6
7	91	81	69	66	62	58	52							7
8	96	85	72	69	64	60	54	49						8
9	100	89	74	70	66	62	55	51						9
10	104	92	77	73	68	63	57	53						10
11	109	96	79	75	70	65	59	54						11
12	113	100	82	77	71	67	60	56	50					12
13	117	104	84	79	73	68	62	57	52					13
14	121	108	87	81	75	70	64	59	53	50				14
15	126	111	89	83	77	72	65	61	55	52				15
16	130	115	92	86	79	74	67	62	56	53	50			16
17	134	119	94	88	81	75	69	64	58	55	51	48		17
18	139	122	97	90	83	77	71	65	60	56	53	50		18
19	143	126	99	92	85	79	72	67	61	58	55	51		19
20	147	130	102	94	87	81	74	69	63	60	56	53	50	20
21	151	134	104	96	89	82	76	70	64	61	58	55	52	21
22	156	137	107	98	90	84	77	72	66	63	59	56	54	22
23	160	141	109	100	92	86	79	73	68	64	61	58	56	23
24	164	145	112	103	94	87	81	75	69	66	63	60	57	24
25	169	149	114	105	96	89	82	77	71	67	64	61	59	25
26	173	152	117	107	98	91	84	78	72	69	66	63	61	26
27	177	156	119	109	100	93	86	80	74	71	67	65	63	27
28		160	122	111	102	94	88	81	76	72	69	66	64	28
29		164	124	113	104	96	89	83	77	74	71	68	66	29
30		168	126	115	106	97	91	85	79	75	72	70	68	30
31		171	129	117	108	99	93	86	80	77	74	71	70	31
32		175	131	119	109	101	94	88	82	78	75	73	71	32
33			134	122	111	103	96	89	84	80	77	75	73	33
34			136	124	113	105	98	91	85	82	79	76	75	34
35			139	126	115	106	100	93	87	83	80	78	77	35

* These values have been calculated from samples which are not as representative as the age samples from 5 through 15 years. They are likely to be a little high for unselected or more adequately representative samples. They are offered as tentative guides for use with preschool groups.

TABLE 35 (*continued*)

RAW SCORE	CHRONOLOGICAL AGE IN YEARS													RAW SCORE
	3	4	5	6	7	8	9	10	11	12	13	14	15	
36			141	128	117	108	101	94	88	85	82	80	78	36
37			144	130	119	110	103	96	90	86	83	81	80	37
38			146	132	121	111	105	97	91	88	85	83	82	38
39			149	134	123	113	106	99	93	89	87	85	84	39
40				136	125	115	108	101	95	91	88	86	86	40
41				139	127	117	110	102	96	92	90	88	87	41
42				141	129	118	111	104	98	94	91	90	89	42
43				143	130	120	113	105	99	96	93	91	91	43
44				145	132	122	115	107	101	97	95	93	93	44
45				147	134	123	117	109	103	99	96	95	94	45
46				149	136	125	118	110	104	100	98	96	96	46
47					138	127	120	112	106	102	99	98	98	47
48					110	129	122	113	107	103	101	100	100	48
49					142	130	123	115	109	105	103	101	101	49
50					144	132	125	117	111	107	104	103	103	50
51					146	134	127	118	112	108	106	105	105	51
52					148	136	128	120	114	110	107	106	107	52
53					149	137	130	121	115	111	109	108	109	53
54					151	139	132	123	117	113	111	110	110	54
55						141	134	124	119	114	112	111	112	55
56						142	135	126	120	116	114	113	114	56
57						144	137	128	122	118	115	115	116	57
58						146	139	129	123	119	117	116	117	58
59						148	140	131	125	121	119	118	119	59
60						149	142	132	126	122	120	120	121	60
61						151	144	134	128	124	122	121	123	61
62							146	136	130	125	123	123	124	62
63							147	137	131	127	125	125	126	63
64							149	139	133	128	127	126	128	64
65							151	140	134	130	128	128	130	65
66								142	136	132	130	130	132	66
67								144	138	133	131	131	133	67
68								145	139	135	133	133	135	68
69								147	141	136	135	135	137	69
70								148	142	138	136	136	139	70
71								150	144	139	138	138	140	71

Instruction for Using the Quality Scales

The Quality scales, described fully in Chapter VII, permit a much more rapid evaluation of drawings than the Point scales, but results are not so precise. When a rough estimate of the child's level of maturity will suffice, these scales are useful.

Arrange the plates of each scale before you, one sex at a time, or pin them in order on the wall in front of your desk. Each drawing in the scale represents a level of maturity; from 1.0, representing the least mature drawing, to 12.0, representing the most mature drawing.

First study the scale for a few minutes. Look at each drawing in turn. Notice that there is a progression in accuracy of detail and proportion from the first drawing to the last.

Take each drawing to be scored and compare it with the sample pictures in the scale. When you decide which drawing in the scale is most like the one you are judging, give the value of the scale example to the drawing you have before you. Enter the value on the face sheet of the test booklet under Quality scale for Man or Woman, as the case may be.

If there are many drawings to be scored, place them in groups on the table before you, according to the values assigned. Thus you will have several stacks of drawings with all those rated 2.0 placed together, all those rated 3.0 placed together, etc. When you have assigned values to all the drawings, take each stack in turn and go through it, to make sure that the drawings in that group are more or less equal in scale value. Change the value given any drawing until you have placed it in the category most representative of its maturity.

No Quality scale has been constructed for the Self drawing, and it seems inappropriate to use the plates for the Man and Woman scales to judge it. Children above seven or eight years include many juvenile features in their self-portraits—items of clothing, accessories, and the like—which may influence the global impression of the drawing, essentially the basis of the Quality scale method. The effect of these juvenile features on the judgment of such drawings has not been studied, but may be considerable.

The Quality scale plates are reproduced on the pages that follow; M–1 through M–12 for the Man scale, and W–1 through W–12 for the Woman scale.

M-1

M-2

M-3

M-4

M-5

M-6

M-7

M-8

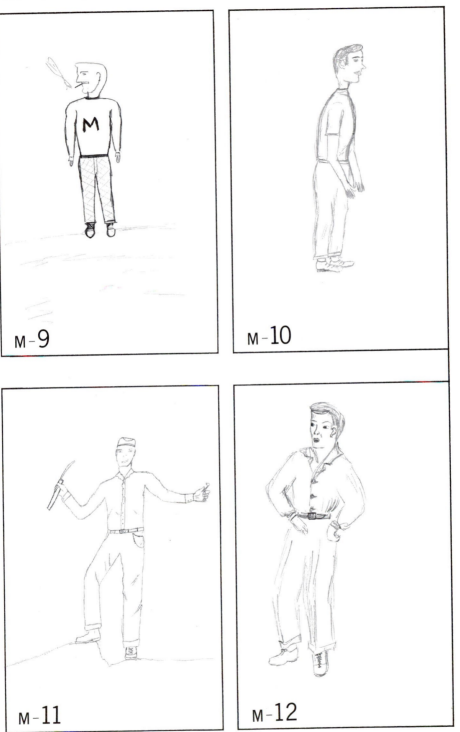

M-9

M-10

M-11

M-12

w-5

w-6

w-7

w-8

W-9

W-10

W-11

W-12

Instructions for Converting Quality Scale Scores to Standard Scores

Standard score equivalents for Quality scale values are listed in Tables 36 through 39. These tables are used as described on page 293 in reference to Tables 32-35. The standard score obtained from a Quality scale score is comparable to the standard score obtained from a Point scale raw score.

TABLE 36 | *Standard Score Equivalents for Quality Scale Scores*

Drawing of a Man, by Boys

QUALITY SCALE SCORE	5	6	7	8	9	10	11	12	13	14	15	QUALITY SCALE SCORE
						AGE						
1	76	71	64	61	59	58	57	56	56	53	51	1
2	92	84	76	71	68	67	65	64	64	61	60	2
3	108	97	88	81	78	75	73	72	72	70	69	3
4	124	110	100	02	87	84	82	81	80	79	78	4
5	140	123	112	102	96	93	90	89	88	87	87	5
6	156	136	124	112	106	102	98	97	96	96	96	6
7		149	136	123	115	111	107	105	104	104	105	7
8		162	148	133	124	119	115	113	113	113	114	8
9			160	143	134	128	123	121	121	121	123	9
10				154	143	137	132	129	129	130	132	10
11					153	146	140	137	137	139	141	11
12						155	148	145	145	147	150	12

TABLE 37 | *Standard Score Equivalents for Quality Scale Scores*

Drawing of a Man, by Girls

QUALITY SCALE SCORE	5	6	7	8	9	10	11	12	13	14	15	QUALITY SCALE SCORE
						AGE						
1	74	68	61	59	56	56	53	52	52	49	48	1
2	88	80	73	69	65	65	61	60	60	58	57	2
3	101	92	85	79	75	74	70	69	68	66	66	3
4	115	105	97	90	85	82	78	77	77	75	74	4
5	128	118	109	100	94	91	87	85	85	83	83	5
6	142	130	121	110	104	100	96	94	93	92	92	6
7	156	142	133	121	114	109	104	102	102	100	101	7
8		155	145	131	123	118	113	110	110	109	110	8
9			157	141	133	126	121	119	118	118	119	9
10			169	152	143	135	130	127	127	126	127	10
11				162	152	144	138	135	135	135	136	11
12					162	153	147	144	143	143	145	12

TABLE
38

Standard Score Equivalents for Quality Scale Scores

Drawing of a Woman, by Boys

QUALITY SCALE SCORE	AGE											QUALITY SCALE SCORE
	5	6	7	8	9	10	11	12	13	14	15	
1	75	70	64	59	58	56	55	55	53	48	44	1
2	92	84	76	70	68	65	64	64	62	58	55	2
3	108	99	88	81	78	75	73	73	71	68	66	3
4	125	113	100	92	88	84	82	81	80	78	76	4
5	142	127	112	103	98	93	91	90	90	88	87	5
6	158	141	124	114	108	103	100	99	99	98	98	6
7		156	136	126	118	112	110	108	108	108	108	7
8			148	137	128	122	119	117	117	118	119	8
9			160	148	138	131	128	126	126	128	130	9
10				159	148	140	137	134	135	138	141	10
11					158	150	146	143	144	148	151	11
12						159	155	152	153	158	162	12

TABLE
39

Standard Score Equivalents for Quality Scale Scores

Drawing of a Woman, by Girls

QUALITY SCALE SCORE	AGE											QUALITY SCALE SCORE
	5	6	7	8	9	10	11	12	13	14	15	
1	70	65	60	56	53	50	49	46	42	39	35	1
2	85	78	71	66	62	59	58	55	51	48	45	2
3	100	90	82	76	72	68	66	63	60	58	55	3
4	115	102	93	86	81	77	75	72	69	67	65	4
5	130	115	104	96	91	86	84	80	78	76	75	5
6	145	128	116	106	100	95	92	89	87	86	85	6
7	160	140	127	116	109	104	101	97	96	95	95	7
8		152	138	126	119	114	109	106	105	105	105	8
9			149	136	128	123	118	115	114	114	115	9
10			160	146	138	132	126	123	124	123	125	10
11				156	147	141	135	132	133	133	135	11
12					156	150	144	140	142	142	145	12

Instructions for Converting Standard Scores to Percentile Ranks

Teachers who use the Drawing Test may prefer to interpret raw scores in terms of percentiles rather than standard scores. The percentile rank shows the relative standing of a child in a theoretical group of 100, representing a particular population. A percentile rank of 65 on the Drawing Test means that a child ranks 65th from the bottom of a theoretical group of 100 children representative of all American children his age.

Actually, the standard score has an advantage in that it can be averaged, a procedure not appropriate for percentile ranks. The percentile, however, is more readily understood and is at present more widely used in school testing.

Table 40 provides the percentile rank for each standard score. Enter the table with the standard score obtained either from the Point or Quality scales. Because there is a constant relationship between standard scores and percentile ranks, this one table suffices for the Man and Woman Point scales and Quality scales as well as for both boys and girls. The face sheet of the booklet has a space for entering the percentile rank for each drawing.

TABLE 40 | *Percentile Rank Equivalents for Standard Scores*

STD. SC.	P.R.	STD. SC.	P.R.	STD. SC.	P.R.
133+	99	110	75	87	19
132	98	109	73	86	18
131	98	108	71	85	16
130	98	107	68	84	14
129	97	106	66	83	13
128	97	105	63	82	12
127	96	104	61	81	10
126	96	103	58	80	9
125	95	102	55	79	8
124	95	101	53	78	7
123	94	100	50	77	6
122	93	99	47	76	5
121	92	98	45	75	5
120	91	97	42	74	4
119	90	96	39	73	4
118	88	95	37	72	3
117	87	94	34	71	3
116	86	93	32	70	2
115	84	92	29	69	2
114	82	91	27	68	2
113	81	90	25	67 —	1
112	79	89	23		
111	77	88	21		

Completed Test Booklet

A completed test booklet is reproduced on the following four pages to illustrate its use. Although these particular drawings are superior, the same method of completing the booklet would apply to any drawings.

Goodenough-Harris Drawing Test

By Florence L. Goodenough and Dale B. Harris

Name **Karen Smith**   Boy____ (Girl)

School **Parkway school**   Date of Drawing **May 8, 1963**

Grade **Second**   Age **8**   Birth Date **May 3, 1955**

Father's Occupation **Herdsman at University Farm**

Examiner's Notes

Summary

	Raw Score	Standard Score	Percentile Rank
Point Scale			
Man	37	118	98
Woman	40	115	94
Average		116	
Self	42	118	88
Quality Scale			
Man	7	121	92
Woman	7	116	86
Average		118	

Make Your First Drawing Here

Draw a picture of a man. Make the very best picture you can. Be sure to make the whole man, not just his head and shoulders.

1. +   41. O
2. T   42. O
3. T   43. O
4. +   44. T
5. +   45. T

6. T   46. +
7. +   47. +
8. O   48. O
9. +   49. O
10. O   50. O

11. T   51. O
12. O   52. O
13. O   53. O
14. +   54. +
15. O   55. +

16. O   56. +
17. O   57. O
18. +   58. +
19. O   59. O
20. O   60. O

21. O   61. O
22. +   62. +
23. +   63. +
24. +   64. +
25. O   65. O

26. +   66. O
27. O   67. +
28. +   68. +
29. +   69. O
30. +   70. O

31. +   71. O
32. O   72. O
33. +   73. O
34. O
35. +

36. +
37. O
38. O
39. +
40. +

Raw Score   37

Make Your Second Drawing Here

Draw a picture of a woman. Make the very best picture you can. Be sure to make
the whole woman, not just her head and shoulders.

1. +	41. +
2. +	42. +
3. +	43. +
4. +	44. +
5. +	45. +
6. +	46. +
7. +	47. +
8. O	48. +
9. +	49. O
10. O	50. O
11. O	51. O
12. +	52. +
13. +	53. +
14. O	54. O
15. O	55. +
16. O	56. +
17. +	57. O
18. +	58. O
19. +	59. +
20. +	60. +
21. O	61. O
22. O	62. +
23. O	63. +
24. +	64. +
25. +	65. O
26. +	66. O
27. O	67. O
28. +	68. O
29. O	69. O
30. +	70. O
31. O	71. O
32. O	
33. +	
34. O	
35. +	
36. +	
37. O	
38. O	
39. O	
40. +	

Raw Score   _40_

Make Your Third Drawing Here

Draw a picture of yourself. Make the very best picture you can. Be sure to make
your whole self, not just your head and shoulders.

1. +	41. +		
2. +	42. +		
3. +	43. +		
4. +	44. +		
5. +	45. +		
6. +	46. +		
7. +	47. +		
8. 0	48. +		
9. 0	49. 0		
10. 0	50. 0		
11. 0	51. +		
12. 0	52. +		
13. +	53. +		
14. 0	54. +		
15. 0	55. +		
16. 0	56. +		
17. +	57. 0		
18. 0	58. +		
19. +	59. +		
20. +	60. +		
21. +	61. 0		
22. +	62. +		
23. 0	63. +		
24. +	64. +		
25. +	65. 0		
26. +	66. 0		
27. 0	67. 0		
28. +	68. 0		
29. 0	69. 0		
30. +	70. 0		
31. 0	71. 0		
32. 0	72.		
33. +	73.		
34. 0			
35. +			
36. +			
37. 0			
38. 0			
39. 0			
40. +			

Raw Score 42

Appendix

Instructions to Judges Used in Preparing Quality Scales

You are asked to judge a number of drawings (120) made by children of different ages. We are concerned with the ideas portrayed in the drawings rather than with the technical skill of the drawings. Thus, we are NOT interested in evaluating artistic skill as such.

Inclusion and accuracy of detail, and proportion are important as they reveal the level of MATURITY of the drawings. It is this maturity which we wish to evaluate. Please try to rate all the drawings at one sitting, since ratings done in several periods may have an error introduced.

Before you there are 13 cards numbered from 0 to 12 and a stack of drawings in a predetermined random order, indicated by the numbers in the lower right hand corner.

Look through a few of the drawings in order to get an idea of the *range* of the ideas represented in them.

Distribute the drawings in front of cards 1 through 11, according to the criteria described above.

Make eleven groups of drawings such that each group is *EQUALLY SEPARATED* from the next. Group 1 would be of least excellence, group 6 of median excellence, group 11 of greatest excellence. Thus, in going from groups 1 through 11, each succeeding group exceeds the next lower group by about the same "amount" of excellence. Categories 0 and 12 have been included so that drawings of OUTSTANDINGLY poor quality and drawings of OUTSTANDINGLY good quality may be set apart, when the judge feels that they deviate enough to place them one unit above or below *all* the rest. You need not use these categories unless you feel there are one or two which are *outstandingly* poor or *outstandingly* good.

Make your first judgments quickly. After you have sorted all of them into 11 piles, go through each pile separately, shifting any drawings up or down the row of piles until you are satisfied with the arrangement.

Then take a record sheet and opposite the number of each drawing on the record sheet put the number of the pile (given by the card) in which you placed it. It will be convenient to work pile by pile, locating the number of each drawing on the record sheet.

When all your judgments are recorded, sign and date the sheet and re-arrange the drawings in numerical order, as you found them. Your work will be speeded if you sort first by tens—all those below 10, those 10 to 19, the twenties, the thirties, etc.—and then rearrange each group of ten so the final stack runs from 1 to 120.

Thank you very much.

DALE B. HARRIS, Professor

Statistical Data on Quality Scale Plates

(Values determined by method described in Chapter VII. Drawings were se-lected to give evenly spaced median values with the smallest possible dispersions of judgments.)

MAN SCALE (28 judges)					WOMAN SCALE (19 judges)				
PLATE (Score value)	Q_3	Md.	Q_1	Q	PLATE (Score value)	Q_3	Md.	Q_1	Q
1.0	1.52	1.1	.56	.48	1.0	1.50	1.0	.55	.48
2.0	2.56	2.0	1.36	.60	2.0	2.50	2.0	1.50	.50
3.0	3.70	3.0	2.30	.70	3.0	3.83	3.0	2.38	.73
4.0	5.00	4.0	3.22	.89	4.0	4.67	3.9	3.25	.71
5.0	5.60	5.0	4.22	1.19	5.0	5.86	5.1	4.43	.72
6.0	7.66	6.0	5.12	1.27	6.0	6.71	6.0	5.29	.71
7.0	8.66	7.0	6.22	1.17	7.0	7.62	7.0	5.67	.78
8.0	9.20	7.9	6.66	1.27	8.0	9.00	8.0	7.17	.91
9.0	9.77	9.0	8.12	.82	9.0	10.50	9.0	8.17	1.16
10.0	10.87	10.0	9.00	.94	10.0	10.83	10.0	9.17	.83
11.0	11.66	11.0	10.14	.76	11.0	11.71	11.0	10.00	.85
12.0	12.30	11.7	11.21	.55	12.0	12.50	11.9	11.14	.68

Guide for Analysis of Self Drawing: An experimental form evolved for the study of Self drawing. (See Chapter VIII.)

The drawing of the Self may possibly reflect special personality features—interests, attitudes, and preoccupations—more readily than a child's drawing of the adult figure. This hypothesis, plausible though not empirically vali-dated, has appeared on several occasions in the literature summarized in Chapter III. The *Guide for Analysis of the Self Drawing*, which follows, resulted from several attempts to identify idiosyncratic aspects of the Self drawing. Four successive forms were developed and used extensively during the redesign of the Man Scale and the creation of the Woman Scale. The procedure finally adopted was to pose in succession several general questions requiring global judgments, and then to move to more specific questions and particular judgments. Thus, a rationale based on procedure exists for the arrangement of the present *Guide*.

The evaluator is asked first to look at the child's Self drawing, without reference to the other two drawings, to answer three general questions: (1) Does the figure appear to be complete? (2) Does it appear to be the figure of a child or adolescent rather than an adult? (3) Does it appear to suggest a specific individual rather than a generalized boy or girl? In the latter two questions, the evaluator is also asked to record such details as suggest an affirmative answer.

Preliminary studies have shown that increasingly with age children successfully portray both juvenile and individual traits or features in their drawings. These traits are at once apparent in the work of older children when they are included at all, and may even be present as early as age six or seven, in higher-scoring drawings. They are present in a large minority of drawings by nine- or ten-year-olds. Research should be conducted to discover what features of intellect or of personality, of concept formation or of special interests or attitude, characterize the child more successful in portraying juvenile and individual traits.

Having answered the three general questions listed above, the evaluator is directed to compare the Self drawing with the drawing of the same-sexed adult figure in order to establish the presence or absence of particular features. This check list of specific traits directs attention to the features most commonly shown by children, determined empirically from the author's unpublished tabulations. These items are arranged as a convenient check list, to show presence of features distinctively treated in either the adult or the Self drawing.

Having directed the evaluator's attention to certain features of the drawing, the *Guide* next asks again concerning the juvenile character of the Self drawing and goes on to other qualitative, global impressions which the evaluator now can, presumably, give more adequately.

The author attempted to develop a list of "maturity indicators" which children use to distinguish between the adult and the juvenile or Self figure. However, children show juvenile and individual features in many, many different ways. The author chose, therefore, to record the distinctive way a trait or feature was shown in a particular drawing when that drawing was compared with another one. The *Guide* permits the evaluator to check which of two drawings is distinctive and to record appropriate notes. To achieve quantification of a scale measuring "distinctiveness of treatment" would require an appropriate classificatory system. This check list may be considered an approach to such a scale.

Finally, the evaluator is asked to compare the *three* drawings in terms of general *style*. He is asked to specify his general judgment by making specific assessments of certain qualitative components which presumably led to his general judgment. These components have been based on both the clinical literature (see Chapter III) and on the author's empirical work.

Guide for Analysis of Self Drawing

NAME_____   SEX: M F   AGE_____

I. Examine figure of Self. Look first at the drawing on the last page of the test booklet.

   1. Figure complete (head, features, trunk, limbs, extremities) _____   NO   YES
     If NO, parts missing: _____
     _____

   2. Juvenile character indicated _____   NO   YES
     If YES, specify: _____
     _____

   3. Is a specific individual suggested?_____   NO   YES
     If YES, specify: _____
     _____

II. Compare two drawings. To complete question 1, inspect the Self figure and the adult figure of the same sex, checking presence of items in the following list, or noting any differences in portrayal. Return to the Self drawing to answer questions 2–7.

   1. Specific items

	ADULT	SELF			ADULT	SELF
Facial				*Activity*	___	___
freckles	___	___				
glasses	___	___		*Background or landscape*	___	___
cigarette or pipe	___	___				
mustache	___	___		*Size*	___	___
other _____	___	___				
_____	___	___		*Ornamentation*		
				symbol	___	___
Hair	___	___		design	___	___
				bizarre aspects	___	___
Garb						
hat	___	___		*"Glamor" or idealization*	___	___
cap	___	___				
jacket	___	___		*Indicators of maturity*		
trousers; skirt	___	___		*represented*	___	___
shoes	___	___				
accessories	___	___		*Equipment for work or*		
				play	___	___

   2. Does Self figure have a juvenile character?_____   NO   YES
     If YES, specify: _____
     _____

3. Does Self figure suggest traits which might be peculiar to an individual? _____ NO   YES
   If YES, specify: _____
   _____

4. Does Self figure contain features suggestive of a particular age group, or other indicators of maturity?_____ NO   YES
   If YES, specify: _____
   _____

5. Does Self figure suggest a "make-believe" or fantasy role? ____ NO   YES
   If YES, specify: _____
   _____

6. Does Self figure suggest a game or play activity?_____ NO   YES
   If YES, specify: _____
   _____

7. Quality of execution:
   Compared with adult figure of same sex, execution and detail of Self drawing are

   POORER   SAME   BETTER

   Compared with adult figure of opposite sex, execution and detail of Self drawing are

   POORER   SAME   BETTER

III. Compare three drawings.

1. In schema and general style, drawings are
   VERY SIMILAR   RATHER SIMILAR   SOMEWHAT DIFFERENT   VERY DIFFERENT

2. If "somewhat different" or "very different," check the drawing which is MOST:

	MAN	WOMAN	SELF	NO DIFF.
complete and detailed	_____	_____	_____	_____
incomplete	_____	_____	_____	_____
active, dynamic	_____	_____	_____	_____
stiff, wooden	_____	_____	_____	_____
realistic	_____	_____	_____	_____
"glamorized"	_____	_____	_____	_____
bizarre, odd	_____	_____	_____	_____
skillfully drawn	_____	_____	_____	_____
crude	_____	_____	_____	_____
erased or smudged	_____	_____	_____	_____
neatly drawn	_____	_____	_____	_____
large	_____	_____	_____	_____
small	_____	_____	_____	_____
other _____	_____	_____	_____	_____
_____	_____	_____	_____	_____
_____	_____	_____	_____	_____
_____	_____	_____	_____	_____

Scoring for Figures 9a–33, Chapter IV, pages 79–86

The scoring data below apply to Figures 9a through 33, which appear in Chapter IV to illustrate the development of female figure drawings. These drawings may be scored as practice exercises, and the results checked with the entries below.

FIG. 9a.   Man, by boy, 5-1. Raw Score 10; Standard Score 83; Percentile Rank 13

Items credited: 1, 4, 6, 8, 9, 11, 18, 30, 35, 54

FIG. 9b.   Woman, by same boy. Raw Score 11; Standard Score 86; Percentile Rank 18

Items credited: 1, 4, 6, 9, 13, 19, 20, 21, 24, 33, 63

Junctures of lines in this drawing are superior to those in the man figure drawn by the same boy.

FIG. 10.   Woman, by boy, 5-3. Raw Score 19; Standard Score 108; Percentile Rank 71

Items credited: 1, 4, 6, 9, 12, 13, 19, 24, 33, 35, 41, 43, 44, 55, 56, 59, 60, 63, 64

Simple cross line at wrist is sufficient to indicate Sleeve I (Item 44). Although junctures of lines (Item 63) are for the most part only fair, the item is a "marginal pass" on this drawing. Compare this drawing with Fig. 11, where Item 63 is clearly not credited.

FIG. 11.   Woman, by boy, 5-4. Raw Score 20; Standard Score 111; Percentile Rank 77

Items credited: 1, 4, 9, 13, 19, 24, 28, 32, 33, 35, 36, 41, 43, 44, 46, 47, 55, 56, 57, 59

FIG. 12.   Woman, by boy, 6-5. Raw Score 26; Standard Score 117; Percentile Rank 87

Items credited: 1, 2, 4, 9, 13, 17, 19, 24, 33, 35, 36, 41, 43, 44, 46, 48, 51, 52, 55, 56, 58, 59, 61, 62, 63, 64

Figure's right shoe is interpreted as a slip of the pencil, not as a transparency.

FIG. 13.   Woman, by boy, 6-8. Raw Score 24; Standard Score 112; Percentile Rank 79

Items credited: 1, 4, 9, 13, 17, 19, 20, 24, 33, 35, 36, 40, 41, 43, 48, 52, 55, 56, 57, 58, 59, 61, 62, 63

Item 64, Coordination: lines, is invalidated by the "coloring" technique which destroys the effect of firm lines.

Fɪɢ. 14. Woman, by boy, 6-10. Raw Score 28; Standard Score 122; Percentile Rank 93

Items credited: 1, 2, 4, 8, 9, 13, 17, 19, 20, 24, 25, 26, 28, 29, 33, 35, 36, 40, 41, 42, 43, 46, 52, 55, 56, 59, 60, 61

Item 17, Chin and forehead, is credited liberally in this case. Sleeve I (Item 44) is not credited, because no terminus is indicated at the wrist.

Fɪɢ. 15. Woman, by boy, 9-5. Raw Score 40; Standard Score 114; Percentile Rank 82

Items credited: 1, 2, 3, 4, 9, 10, 11, 13, 14, 16, 17, 19, 20, 24, 25, 26, 28, 33, 34, 35, 36, 38, 40, 41, 43, 44, 46, 48, 51, 52, 55, 56, 57, 58, 59, 61, 62, 63, 64, 66

Fɪɢ. 16. Woman, by boy, 10-2. Raw Score 39; Standard Score 107; Percentile Rank 68

Items credited: 1, 2, 3, 4, 5, 9, 10, 13, 18, 19, 20, 21, 24, 25, 26, 28, 29, 30, 32, 33, 35, 36, 41, 42, 43, 44, 46, 47, 51, 52, 53, 55, 56, 58, 59, 60, 61, 62, 64

Item 11, Bridge of nose, does not score; the nose fails to extend up to or between the eyes, and the bridge is as wide as the base.

Fɪɢ. 17. Woman, by boy, 10-9. Raw Score 37; Standard Score 103; Percentile Rank 58

Items credited: 1, 2, 4, 9, 10, 13, 19, 24, 25, 26, 27, 33, 34, 35, 40, 41, 42, 43, 44, 46, 48, 49, 50, 51, 52, 53, 55, 56, 57, 58, 59, 60, 61, 62, 63, 64, 68

In the orginal drawing the neck is faintly shown, apparently added after the head and trunk were formed of simple ellipses; therefore, Item 2, Neck present, was credited.

Fɪɢ. 18. Woman, by boy, 11-5. Raw Score 59; Standard Score 134; Percentile Rank 99

Items credited: 1, 2, 3, 4, 5, 6, 7, 8, 9, 10, 11, 13, 14, 15, 16, 17, 18, 19, 20, 21, 23, 24, 25, 26, 28, 30, 32, 33, 34, 35, 36, 38, 40, 41, 42, 43, 44, 45, 46, 47, 48, 49, 51, 52, 53, 54, 55, 56, 57, 58, 59, 60, 61, 62, 63, 64, 67, 70, 71

This drawing shows crude attempts to "sketch," a technique more common among adolescents than among younger children. Treatment of fingers, legs and sleeves shows this feature particularly well.

FIG. 19. Woman, by boy, 13-0. Raw Score 47; Standard Score 108; Percentile Rank 71

Items credited: 1, 2, 3, 4, 5, 7, 9, 10, 13, 19, 20, 24, 25, 26, 28, 29, 30, 32, 33, 34, 35, 36, 38, 40, 41, 42, 43, 44, 45, 46, 48, 51, 52, 55, 56, 57, 59, 60, 61, 62, 63, 64, 65, 66, 67, 69, 71

In this figure, Item 18, Line of jaw, is equivocal; it does not extend toward the ear and was thus scored strictly. Shoes were liberally interpreted as "feminine" (Item 38).

FIG. 20. Woman, by boy, 13-2. Raw Score 65; Standard Score 136; Percentile Rank 99

Items credited: 1, 2, 3, 4, 5, 6, 7, 8, 9, 10, 11, 12, 13, 14, 15, 16, 17, 19, 20, 21, 22, 24, 25, 26, 27, 28, 29, 30, 31, 32, 33, 34, 35, 36, 38, 40, 41, 42, 43, 44, 45, 46, 47, 48, 49, 51, 52, 53, 54, 55, 56, 57, 58, 59, 60, 61, 63, 64, 65, 66, 67, 68, 69, 70, 71

FIG. 21. Woman, by boy, 15-3. Raw Score 36; Standard Score 86; Percentile Rank 18

Items credited: 1, 2, 3, 4, 9, 10, 11, 13, 17, 19, 20, 23, 25, 33, 34, 35, 36, 38, 40, 43, 48, 49, 51, 52, 55, 56, 57, 58, 61, 62, 63, 64, 66, 67, 68, 70

This drawing, done with a sharp-pointed pencil and light pressure, was difficult to score. Eye detail items were scored strictly. The forehead (Item 17), though covered by hair, was scored liberally, as was Item 40 (one foot in profile may count for two). This drawing illustrates the sometimes incomplete and perhaps reluctantly drawn figures done by adolescents who, more than children, are aware of the complexity of the task and of their own limitations to produce visually accurate examples.

FIG. 22a. Man, by girl, 5-0. Raw Score 16; Standard Score 96; Percentile Rank 39

Items credited: 1, 2, 3, 4, 5, 9, 11, 14, 18, 22, 30, 35, 44, 46, 47, 54

FIG. 22b. Woman, by same girl. Raw Score 17; Standard Score 94; Percentile Rank 34

Items credited: 1, 2, 4, 5, 9, 13, 19, 20, 24, 28, 29, 30, 33, 41, 55, 56, 59

FIG. 23. Woman, by girl, 5-0. Raw Score 15; Standard Score 89; Percentile Rank 23

Items credited: 1, 4, 8, 9, 13, 19, 24, 33, 35, 41, 43, 44, 55, 56, 59

Hands present (Item 32) is not credited since there are no fingers and no mitt is apparently intended. Feminine garb (Item 52) is not credited, since the body does not appear in *two* segments.

FIG. 24. Woman, by girl, 7-0. Raw Score 33; Standard Score 111; Percentile Rank 77

Items credited: 1, 4, 5, 6, 9, 13, 19, 20, 24, 25, 26, 28, 30, 33, 35, 36, 40, 41, 42, 43, 44, 48, 49, 51, 52, 55, 56, 57, 59, 61, 62, 63, 64

This figure appears to reveal a crude attempt at perspective in the feet; therefore, Feet II (Item 36) and Placement of feet appropriate to figure (Item 40) are credited.

FIG. 25. Woman, by girl, 7-2. Raw Score 23; Standard Score 92; Percentile Rank 29

Items credited: 1, 2, 4, 5, 6, 9, 13, 19, 20, 23, 24, 25, 28, 29, 33, 35, 41, 43, 48, 52, 55, 56, 62

Note the interesting treatment of the neck; the child managed to get the angle correct on the figure's right side, but failed to reverse the corresponding angle on the figure's left side. A lack of co-ordination also appears in the treatment of line junctures and firmness of lines (Items 63 and 64).

FIG. 26. Woman, by girl, 9-8. Raw Score 44; Standard Score 115; Percentile Rank 84

Items credited: 1, 2, 3, 4, 5, 9, 10, 12, 13, 14, 16, 17, 19, 20, 21, 23, 24, 25, 26, 27, 33, 35, 38, 40, 41, 43, 44, 46, 48, 49, 51, 52, 55, 56, 58, 59, 60, 61, 62, 63, 64, 66, 67, 71

This drawing shows "feminine" features—small feet and attention to facial details. The drawing probably shows both necklace and neckline. Since the sleeve is indicated by a cuff, Item 44 is credited. However, Item 45 is not credited because no hand protrudes; admittedly a narrow interpretation of this item.

FIG. 27. Woman, by girl, 9-9. Raw Score 40; Standard Score 108; Percentile Rank 71

Items credited: 1, 2, 3, 4, 5, 9, 12, 13, 14, 15, 19, 20, 21, 23, 24, 25, 26, 28, 33, 35, 36, 41, 42, 43, 44, 45, 46, 47, 48, 49, 50, 51, 52, 55, 56, 58, 59, 62, 63, 64

The waistline, although crude, is better than a single horizontal line. Relative proportions of dress area (Item 62) is credited because it is assumed the child intended a formal or "party" dress.

FIG. 28. Woman, by girl, 9-11. Raw Score 52; Standard Score 128; Percentile Rank 97

Items credited: 1, 2, 3, 4, 5, 6, 7, 9, 10, 12, 13, 14, 15, 16, 17, 18, 19, 20, 21, 24, 25, 26, 33, 35, 36, 37, 38, 39, 40, 41, 42, 43, 44, 46, 47, 48, 49, 51, 52, 53, 54, 55, 56, 57, 59, 60, 61, 62, 63, 64, 65, 71

The treatment of hands shown here is typical of the method used by adolescents who wish to escape drawing a difficult item.

FIG. 29.   Woman, by girl, 10-10. Raw Score 52; Standard Score 120; Percentile Rank 91

Items credited: 1, 2, 3, 4, 5, 9, 10, 11, 13, 17, 19, 20, 21, 23, 24, 25, 26, 28, 29, 30, 33, 35, 36, 38, 39, 40, 41, 42, 43, 44, 45, 46, 47, 48, 49, 50, 51, 52, 53, 54, 55, 56, 58, 59, 60, 61, 62, 63, 64, 66, 68, 69

This drawing exhibits attempts to use a "sketching" technique; therefore, number and detail of fingers (Items 29 and 30) are credited. Coordination: lines (Item 64) is likewise liberally scored. The Hand (Item 32), being a general form, is scored more strictly. Bridge of the nose (Item 11) is credited, although it could equally well be considered a "button" or snub nose and not credited. This is a "feminine" drawing, showing small feet, jewelry, and dress detail.

FIG. 30.   Woman, by girl, 11-3. Raw Score 61; Standard Score 128; Percentile Rank 97

Items credited: 1, 2, 3, 4, 5, 6, 7, 8, 9, 10, 11, 13, 15, 17, 18, 19, 20, 21, 22, 23, 24, 25, 26, 27, 33, 34, 35, 36, 37, 38, 39, 40, 41, 42, 43, 44, 45, 46, 47, 48, 49, 50, 51, 52, 53, 54, 55, 56, 58, 59, 60, 61, 62, 63, 64, 65, 66, 67, 68, 69, 71

Another "feminine" drawing, including much facial detail. Hip and breast (Items 34 and 67) are only suggested by general contours and pencil strokes; however, both items are credited liberally.

FIG. 31.   Woman, by girl, 13-3. Raw Score 38; Standard Score 85; Percentile Rank 16

Items credited: 1, 2, 4, 5, 7, 8, 9, 10, 13, 14, 16, 19, 20, 24, 25, 26, 33, 34, 35, 36, 40, 41, 42, 43, 44, 48, 49, 52, 55, 56, 57, 58, 59, 60, 61, 62, 67, 68

Note the crude treatment of the neck as a pillar between head and trunk. Neckline is that of the trunk, and is not formed by the dress. Child has apparently tried to construct the figure from a series of oval forms, like the artist's lay figure. This effect may be the result of instruction in a particular technique of drawing.

FIG. 32.   Woman, by girl, 13-3. Raw Score 63; Standard Score 125; Percentile Rank 95

Items credited: 1, 2, 3, 4, 5, 6, 7, 8, 9, 13, 14, 15, 17, 18, 19, 20, 21, 22, 23, 24, 25, 26, 27, 28, 30, 32, 33, 34, 35, 36, 38, 39, 40, 41, 42, 43, 44, 45, 46, 47, 48, 49, 50, 51, 52, 53, 54, 55, 56, 58, 59, 60, 61, 62, 63, 64, 65, 66, 67, 68, 69, 70, 71

This drawing, executed with considerable technical skill, was difficult to score. Most items were scored rather liberally, except for the nose, since it was barely suggested in the sketch.

FIG. 33. Woman, by girl, 15-2. Raw Score 49; Standard Score 101; Percentile Rank 53

Items credited: 1, 2, 3, 4, 5, 6, 9, 10, 11, 12, 13, 15, 17, 18, 19, 20, 21, 23, 24, 25, 27, 33, 35, 40, 41, 42, 43, 44, 45, 46, 47, 48, 49, 51, 52, 55, 56, 57, 58, 59, 60, 61, 62, 63, 64, 65, 66, 69, 71

Not so well executed as the previous figure; this drawing shows many attempts to adopt a "sketching" technique, and is therefore scored somewhat liberally. For example, Superior motor coordination (Item 65) is credited.

Scoring for Figures 34a–45b, Chapter VIII, pages 135–138

Since these drawings were made by children not represented in the standardization population, Standard Scores and Percentile Ranks are not recorded.

FIG. 34a. Man, by girl, 5-10. Raw Score 19

Items credited: 1, 2, 3, 4, 5, 9, 11, 24, 30, 31, 35, 39, 40, 44, 46, 47, 54, 55, 64

Item 18 was not scored as *hair* but as a parka hood.

FIG. 34b. Woman, by same girl. Raw Score 19

Items credited: 1, 4, 5, 9, 10, 13, 24, 28, 33, 35, 36, 41, 42, 43, 54, 55, 56, 57, 59

Item 54 was scored very liberally.

FIG. 35. Woman, by girl, 9-5. Raw Score 48

Items credited: 1, 2, 3, 4, 5, 7, 9, 12, 13, 14, 18, 19, 20, 21, 22, 24, 25, 26, 28, 29, 30, 31, 32, 33, 35, 36, 41, 42, 43, 44, 45, 46, 47, 48, 49, 51, 52, 53, 55, 56, 57, 59, 61, 62, 63, 64, 69, 71

Item 31 was scored liberally.

FIG. 36. Woman, by boy, 10-2. Raw Score 38

Items credited: 1, 2, 3, 4, 5, 6, 7, 9, 10, 13, 17, 19, 20, 24, 25, 26, 27, 33, 35, 36, 40, 41, 42, 43, 44, 45, 46, 48, 51, 52, 55, 56, 58, 59, 60, 61, 62, 66

FIG. 37.   Man, by boy, 10-3. Raw Score 54

Items credited: 1, 2, 3, 4, 5, 9, 10, 11, 14, 15, 16, 17, 18, 19, 20, 22, 23, 24, 25, 26, 27, 28, 29, 30, 31, 32, 33, 35, 36, 37, 39, 40, 41, 42, 43, 44, 45, 46, 47, 48, 50, 53, 54, 55, 56, 57, 58, 59, 63, 64, 66, 67, 68, 69

FIG. 38.   Man, by boy, 10-5. Raw Score 47

Items credited: 1, 2, 3, 4, 5, 6, 8, 9, 10, 11, 14, 15, 16, 17, 22, 23, 24, 26, 27, 30, 31, 32, 33, 35, 36, 37, 39, 40, 41, 43, 44, 45, 46, 47, 48, 49, 53, 54, 55, 56, 57, 58, 59, 63, 64, 67, 68

Belt at bottom of the jacket is not considered an incongruity. Items 67 and 68 are credited, although they are very marginal in character.

FIG. 39.   Man, by boy, 10-9. Raw Score 60

Items credited: 1, 2, 3, 4, 5, 6, 7, 9, 10, 11, 14, 15, 16, 17, 18, 19, 20, 22, 23, 27, 28, 29, 30, 31, 32, 33, 34, 35, 36, 37, 39, 40, 42, 43, 44, 45, 46, 47, 48, 49, 50, 51, 52, 53, 54, 55, 56, 57, 58, 59, 62, 63, 64, 66, 67, 68, 69, 70, 71, 72

Item 3 credited because of direction line takes from figure's right shoulder. Liberal scoring granted because of parka. Items 12 and 13 were scored strictly. Lines at corners of mouth and below mouth might be taken to suggest lips in two dimensions.

FIG. 40.   Man, by boy, 10-11. Raw Score 48

Items credited: 1, 2, 3, 4, 6, 7, 9, 10, 11, 14, 17, 18, 19, 24, 26, 27, 28, 29, 30, 31, 32, 33, 35, 36, 37, 39, 40, 43, 44, 45, 46, 47, 50, 51, 53, 54, 55, 56, 58, 59, 60, 63, 64, 66, 67, 69, 70, 72

Item 14 was credited although obscured by beard and hair; Items 15 and 16 were scored strictly. Item 37 scored liberally in this case.

FIG. 41.   Man, by girl, 12-1. Raw Score 40

Items credited: 1, 2, 27, 28, 29, 30, 31, 32, 35, 36, 37, 38, 39, 40, 41, 43, 44, 45, 46, 47, 48, 49, 51, 53, 54, 55, 56, 57, 58, 59, 60, 61, 63, 64, 65, 67, 68, 70, 72, 73

Item 2 was scored liberally, since the child's intention was obvious. Items 37, 38, 57, and 65 were also scored somewhat liberally.

FIG. 42.   Woman, by boy, 13-0. Raw Score 50

Items credited: 1, 2, 3, 4, 5, 9, 10, 11, 13, 17, 19, 20, 21, 22, 24, 25, 26, 28, 29, 30, 31, 33, 34, 35, 36, 38, 39, 40, 41, 42, 43, 46, 48, 52, 55, 56, 57, 58, 59, 60, 61, 62, 63, 64, 66, 67, 68, 69, 70, 71

Item 31 was scored liberally.

FIG. 43a. Man, by boy, 13-10. Raw Score 59

> Items credited: 1, 4, 5, 6, 7, 9, 10, 11, 12, 13, 14, 15, 16, 17, 18, 19, 20, 21, 22, 23, 30, 31, 32, 33, 34, 35, 36, 37, 39, 40, 41, 42, 43, 44, 45, 46, 47, 48, 49, 50, 51, 52, 53, 54, 55, 56, 57, 58, 59, 62, 63, 64, 65, 66, 67, 68, 69, 70, 72

> Strict scoring denies Items 2 and 3, which the quality of the drawing as a whole might warrant.

FIG. 43b. Woman, by same boy. Raw Score 59

> Items credited: 1, 2, 3, 4, 5, 6, 7, 9, 10, 11, 13, 15, 17, 18, 19, 20, 21, 22, 24, 25, 26, 27, 28, 29, 30, 31, 32, 33, 34, 35, 36, 37, 40, 41, 42, 43, 44, 45, 46, 47, 48, 50, 51, 52, 53, 54, 55, 56, 57, 58, 59, 60, 61, 62, 63, 64, 66, 69, 71

FIG. 44. Man, by boy, 15-10. Raw Score 63

> Items credited: 1, 2, 3, 4, 9, 10, 11, 12, 13, 14, 15, 17, 18, 19, 20, 22, 23, 24, 25, 26, 27, 28, 29, 30, 31, 32, 33, 34, 35, 36, 37, 38, 39, 40, 44, 45, 46, 47, 48, 49, 50, 51, 52, 53, 54, 55, 56, 57, 58, 59, 60, 61, 63, 64, 65, 66, 67, 68, 69, 70, 71, 72, 73

> This type of drawing occurs occasionally among young adolescents, especially those who have been given sketching instruction or have learned techniques from studying published sketches. Items 12, 13, 17, 25, and 64 are scored somewhat liberally, because of the sketching technique employed.

FIG. 45a. Man, by girl, 15-11. Raw Score 56

> Items credited: 1, 2, 4, 5, 6, 7, 9, 10, 11, 12, 13, 14, 15, 17, 24, 25, 28, 29, 30, 31, 32, 33, 35, 36, 37, 38, 39, 40, 43, 44, 45, 46, 47, 48, 49, 50, 51, 52, 53, 54, 55, 56, 57, 58, 59, 60, 61, 63, 64, 65, 66, 67, 68, 69, 70, 73

> Items 2 and 50 were scored liberally.

FIG. 45b. Woman, by same girl. Raw Score 54

> Items credited: 1, 2, 3, 4, 5, 6 , 7, 9, 10, 11, 12, 13, 14, 15, 16, 17, 19, 20, 21, 22, 24, 25, 26, 33, 34, 35, 36, 37, 40, 41, 42, 43, 44, 45, 46, 47, 48, 49, 50, 51, 52, 53, 54, 55, 56, 57, 59, 60, 63, 64, 65, 66, 69, 71

Bibliography

The numbers in **bold face** following each reference give the text page or pages on which the reference is cited.

ADAM, L. *Primitive art.* (3rd ed.) Baltimore: Penguin Books, 1954. **204**

AIMEN, JUNE E. Comparison of children's easel painting after successful and unsuccessful completion of an experimental task. Unpublished master's thesis, Univer. of Wisconsin, 1954. **60**

ALBEE, G. W., & HAMLIN, R. M. An investigation of the reliability and validity of judgments of adjustment inferred from drawings. *J. clin. Psychol.*, 1949, 5, 389–392. **59**

ALBEE, G. W., & HAMLIN, R. M. Judgment of adjustment from drawings: the applicability of rating scale methods. *J. clin. Psychol.*, 1950, 6, 363–365. **59**

ALBERTI, LEONE BATTISTA. De Statua. In Janitschek, H. (Ed.), *Kleinere kunstheoretische Schriften, Quellenschriften für Kunstgeschichte*, II, Vienna, 1877. **196–197**

ALBIEN, G. Der Anteil der nachkonstruierenden Tätigkeit des Auges und der Apperception an dem Behalten und der Wiedergabe einfacher Formen. (The construction activity of the eye and apperception in remembering and reproducing simple form.) *Zeitschr. f. exp. Päd*, 1907, 5, 133–156; 1908, 6, 1–48. **168**

ALPER, THELMA & BLANE, H. T. Reactions of middle and lower class nursery school children to finger paints and crayons as a function of early habit training patterns. *Amer. Psychologist*, 1951, 6, 306. (Abstract) **60**

ALSCHULER, ROSE H. & HATTWICK, LA BERTA WEISS. *Painting and personality. A study of young children.* Chicago: Univer. of Chicago Press, 1947, Vols. I, II. **40, 52, 56**

AMES, LOUISE B. The Gesell Incomplete Man Test as a differential indicator of average and superior behavior in preschool children. *J. genet. Psychol.*, 1943, 62, 217–274. **22**

AMES, LOUISE B. Free drawing and completion drawing: a comparative study of preschool children. *J. genet. Psychol.*, 1945, 66, 161–165. **22**

AMES, LOUISE B. & HELLERSBERG, ELIZABETH. The Horn-Hellersberg Test: responses of three to eleven year old children. *Rorschach Res. Exch.*, 1949, 13, 415–432. **51**

AMES, LOUISE B., LEARNED, JANET, METRAUX, RUTH AND WALKER, R. Development of perception in the young child as observed in responses to the Rorschach test blots. *J. genet. Psychol.*, 1953, 82, 183–204. **188**

ANASTASI, ANNE & FOLEY, J. P., JR. A study of animal drawings by Indian children of the north Pacific coast. *J. soc. Psychol.*, 1938, 9, 363–374. **14**

ANASTASI, ANNE & FOLEY, J. P., JR. An experimental study of the drawing behavior of adult psychotics in comparison with that of a normal control group. *J. exp. Psychol.*, 1944, 34, 169–194. **28**

ANSBACHER, H. L. The Goodenough Draw-A-Man Test and primary mental abilities. *J. consult. Psychol.*, 1952, 16, 176–180. **35, 96, 97, 98**

APPEL, K. E. Drawings by children as aids in personality studies. *Amer. J. Orthopsychiat.*, 1931, 1, 129–144. **51**

ARNHEIM, R. *Art and visual perception.* Berkeley: Univer. of Calif. Press, 1954. **177–178, 202**

ATTNEAVE, F. Physical determinants of the judged complexity of shapes. *J. exp. Psychol.*, 1957, 53, 221–227. **187, 190, 205**

BALDWIN, J. M. *Mental development in the child and in the race.* New York: Macmillan, 1894. **12**

BALLARD, P. B. What London children like to draw. *J. exp. Ped.*, 1912, 1, 185–197. **13**

BALLARD, P. B. What children like to draw. *J. exp. Ped.*, 1913, 2, 127–129. **15**

BALLINGER, T. O. An investigation of the frequency of directional movement in the paintings and drawings of Indian children and adults. Unpublished manuscript, Univer. of New Mexico, 1951. **160**

BARCELLOS, FERNANDA. *Psico-diagnóstico através do desenho infatil.* (Psychodiagnostics through child drawing.) Araruama, Brasil: Author, 1952–3. (*Psychol. Abstr.*, 29:2425) **17**

BARNES, E. A study of children's drawings. *Ped. Sem.*, 1893, 2, 451–463. **12**

BARNHART, E. N. Developmental stages in compositional construction in children's drawings. *J. exp. Educ.*, 1942, 11, 156–184. **166**

BAUMSTEIN-HEISSLER, N. A propos du dessin: quelques opinions et travaux de psychologues sovietiques. (About drawing: some opinions and works of Soviet psychologists.) *Enfance*, 1955, 8, 377–399. **10 fn.**

BAYLEY, NANCY. A new look at the curve of intelligence. In *Proceedings, 1956 Invitational Conference on Testing Problems*, Educational Testing Service, Princeton, N. J., 1957. Pp. 11–23. **3**

BELART, W. Die sinnespsychologischen Grundlagen seiten- und hohenverkehrter Kinderzeichnungen. (The sensory basis of lateral and vertical inversions in children's drawings.) Z. *Kinderpsychiat.*, 1943, 10, 8–13. **161**

BELL, J. E. *Projective techniques.* New York: Longmans, 1948. **41, 55**

BELL, J. E. Perceptual development and the drawings of children. *Amer. J. Orthopsychiat.*, 1952, 22, 386–393. **165 fn. 195–196**

BELVES, P. Le portrait de'après nature. (Portrait from life.) *Enfance*, 1950, 3, 299–301. **161**

BENDER, LAURETTA. Gestalt principles in the sidewalk drawings and games of children. *J. genet. Psychol.*, 1932, 41, 192–210. **155, 162**

BENDER, LAURETTA. Art and therapy in the mental disturbances of children. *J. nerv. ment. Dis.*, 1937, 86, 249–263. **47, 48**

BENDER, LAURETTA. A visual motor gestalt test and its clinical use. *Resch. Monogr.* No. 3, Amer. Orthopsychiat. Ass., 1938. **47, 48, 155, 195**

BENDER, LAURETTA. The drawing of a man in chronic encephalitis in children. *J. nerv. ment. Dis.*, 1940, 41, 277–286. **26, 41, 47, 48, 55, 170, 195**

BENDER, LAURETTA & RAPOPORT, J. Animal drawings of children. *Amer. J. Orthopsychiat.*, 1944, 14, 521–527. **14**

BENDER, LAURETTA & SCHILDER, P. Form as a principle in the play of children. *J. genet. Psychol.*, 1936, 49, 254–261. **155**

BENDER, LAURETTA & SCHILDER, P. Graphic art as a special ability in children with a reading disability. *J. clin. exp. Psychopath.*, 1951, 12, 147–156. **48**

BENDER, LAURETTA & WOLFSON, W. Q. The nautical theme in the art and fantasy of children. *Amer. J. Orthopsychiat.*, 1943, 13, 462–467. **15**

BERDIE, R. F. Measurement of adult intelligence by drawings. *J. clin. Psychol.*, 1945, 1, 288–295. **20, 97**

BERMAN, S. & LAFFAL, J. Body type and figure drawing. *J. clin. Psychol.*, 1953, 9, 368–370. **45**

BERRIEN, F. K. A study of the drawings of abnormal children. *J. educ. Psychol.*, 1935, 26, 143–150. **26, 28, 47**

BIEHLER, ROBERT F. An analysis of free painting procedures as used with preschool children. Unpublished doctoral dissertation, Univer. of Minnesota, 1953. **57**

BIELIAUSKAS, V. J. Scorer's reliability in the quantitative scoring of the H–T–P technique. *J. clin. Psychol.*, 1956, 12, 366–369. **58**

BIELIAUSKAS, V. J. & KIRKHAM, SANDRA L. An evaluation of the "organic signs" in the H–T–P drawings. *J. clin. Psychol.*, 1958, 14, 50–54. **47**

BILLING, M. L. A report of a case of inverted writing and drawing. *Child Develpm.*, 1935, 6, 161–163, **161**

BIRCH, J. W. The Goodenough Drawing Test and older mentally retarded children. *Amer. J. ment. Defic.*, 1949, 54, 218–224. **20**

BLISS, M. & BERGER, A. Measurement of mental age as indicated by the male figure drawings of the mentally subnormal using Goodenough and Machover instructions. *Amer. J. ment. Defic.*, 1954, 59, 73–79. **42**

BLUM, LUCILLE H. & DRAGOSITZ, ANNA. Finger painting: the developmental aspects. *Child Develpm.*, 1947, 18, 88–105. **41**

BLUM, R. H. The validity of the Machover DAP techniques. *J. clin. Psychol.*, 1954, 10, 120–125. **62–63**

BOLIN, B. J., SCHNEPS, ANN, & THORNE, W. E. Further examination of the Tree-Scar-Trauma hypothesis. *J. clin. Psychol.*, 1956, 12, 395–397. **65**

BORING, E. G. *A history of experimental psychology.* (2nd ed.) New York: Appleton-Century-Crofts, 1950. **185**

BRIAN, CLARA R. & GOODENOUGH, FLORENCE L. The relative potency of color and form perception at various ages. *J. exp. Psychol.*, 1929, 12, 197–213. **186, 191**

BRIED, C. Le dessin de l'enfant; premières représéntations humaines. (The child's drawing; first human representations.) *Enfance*, 1950, 3, 261–275. **44**

BRILL, M. The reliability of the Goodenough Draw-a-man test and the validity and reliability of an abbreviated scoring method. *J. educ. Psychol.*, 1935, 26, 701–708. **21**

BRILL, M. A study of instability using the Goodenough drawing scale. *J. abnorm. soc. Psychol.*, 1937, 32, 288–302. **27, 28**

BRITSCH, G. *Theorie der bildenden Kunst.* (Theory of pictorial art.) Munich: F. Bruckmann, 1926. **175**

BROWN, D. D. *Notes on children's drawings.* Berkeley: Univer. of Calif. Publ., 1897. **12**

BROWN, D. G. & TOLOR, A. Human figure drawings as indicators of sexual identification and inversion. *Percept. mot. Skills*, 1957, 7, 199–211. **45**

BROWN, E. A. & GOITEIN, P. L. The significance of body image for personality assay.

J. nerv. ment. Dis., 1943, 97, 401–408. **51**

BROWN, R. *Words and things.* Glencoe, Ill.: Free Press, 1958. **191**

BUCK, J. N. The H–T–P test. *J. clin. Psychol.*, 1948, 4, 151–159. (a) **43**

BUCK, J. N. The H–T–P technique; a qualitative and quantitative scoring manual. *J. clin. Psychol.*, 1948, 4, 317–396. (b) **46, 47, 49, 55**

BÜHLER, CHARLOTTE, SMITTER, FAITH, & RICHARDSON, SYBIL. *Childhood problems and the teacher.* New York: Holt, 1952. **38**

BÜHLER, K. *The mental development of the child.* London: Routledge and Kegan Paul, Ltd., 1930. **173, 203**

BURKE, H. R. Raven's progressive matrices: a review and critical evaluation. *J. genet. Psychol.*, 1958, 93, 199–228. **98**

BURKHARDT, H. Über Verlagerung räumlicher Gestalten. (On the alteration of spatial form.) *Neue Psychol. Stud.*, 1933, 7, No. 3. **171**

BUROS, O. K. (Ed.) *Fourth mental measurements yearbook.* Highland Park, N. J.: Gryphon Press, 1953. **1, 72**

BURT, C. *Mental and scholastic tests.* London: P. S. King and Son, 1921. **11, 15, 17, 54, 109, 195**

BURT, C. *Mental and scholastic tests.* (3rd ed.) London: Staples Press, 1947. **195**

BURTON, A. & TUELLER, ROMA. Successive reproductions of visually perceived forms. *J. genet. Psychol.*, 1941, 58, 71–82. **170**

BUSEMANN, A. Die zeichnerische Reaktion des Kleinkindes auf Reizfiguren. (The drawing reaction of the small child to stimulus figures.) *Schweiz. Z. Psychol. Anwend.*, 1950, 9, 392–407. (*Psychol. Abstr.*, 25:6053) **158**

CALIGOR, L. *A new approach to figure drawing.* Springfield, Ill.: Charles C. Thomas, 1957. **51**

CAMPBELL, D. T. Personal communication. 1958. **162, 167, 168, 180, 184**

CAMPBELL, D. T. & GRUEN, W. Progression from simple to complex as a molar law of learning. *J. gen. Psychol.*, 1958, 59, 237–244. **168**

CARMICHAEL, L., HOGAN, H. P., & WALTER, A. A. An experimental study of the effect of language on the reproduction of visually perceived form. *J. exp. Psychol.*, 1932, 15, 73–86. **169**

CARP, FRANCES M. Psychological constriction on several projective tests. *J. consult. Psychol.*, 1950, 14, 268–275. **61**

CASSELL, R. H., JOHNSON, ANNA P., & BURNS, W. H. Examiner, ego defense, and the H–T–P test. *J. clin. Psychol.*, 1958, 14, 157–160. **57**

CHASE, JANE M. A study of the drawings of a male figure made by schizophrenic patients and normal subjects. *Charact. & Pers.*, 1941, 9, 208–217. **26**

CLAPARÉDE, E. Plan d'experiences collectives sur le dessin des enfants. (Plan for collective experiments on the drawing of children.) *Arch. de Psychol.*, 1907, 6, 276–278. **12**

CLARK, A. B. The child's attitude toward perspective problems. *Stanford Univer. Stud. in Educ.*, 1897, 1, 283–294. **193**

CLARK, J. S. Some observations on children's drawings. *Educ. Rev.*, 1897, 13, 76–82. **213**

CLARKE SCHOOL FOR THE DEAF. *Eighty-sixth Annual Report.* Northampton, Mass., 1953. **29**

COCKRELL, DURA-LOUISE. Design in the paintings of young children. *Sch. Arts. Mag.*, 1930, 30, 33–39; 112–119. **213–214**

COHEN, D. N. The Goodenough drawing scale applied to thirteen-year-old children. Unpublished master's thesis, Columbia Univer., 1933. **20, 102**

COHN, R. Role of "body image concept" in pattern of ipsilateral clinical extinction. *A.M.A. Arch. neurol. Psychiat.*, 1953, 70, 503–509. **47–48**

COOKE, E. Art teaching and child nature. *London J. of Educ.*, 1885. **10**

CORDEAU, T. Le nombre d'or dans le dessin enfantin. (The "golden section" in the drawings of children.) *Enfance*, 1953, 6, 147–151. **215**

CUTTER, F. Sexual differentiation in figure drawings and overt deviation. *J. clin. Psychol.*, 1956, 12, 369–372. **44**

DARKE, R. A. & GEIL, G. A. Homosexual activity: relation of degree and role to the Goodenough test and to the Cornell Selectee Index. *J. nerv. ment. Dis.*, 1948, 108, 217–240. **27**

DARWIN, C. A biographical sketch of an infant. *Mind*, 1877, 2, 285–294. **189**

DENNIS, W. Handwriting conventions as determinants of human figure drawings. *J. consult. Psychol.*, 1958, 22, 293–295. **161**

DES LAURIERS, A. & HALPERN, FLORENCE. Psychological tests in childhood schizophrenia. *Amer. J. Orthopsychiat.*, 1947, 17, 57–67. **26**

DESAI, KUNJLATA. Developmental stages in drawing a cow. Unpublished B.A. thesis, Baroda Univer., 1958. **14**

DESPERT, J. LOUISE. Technical approaches used in the study and treatment of emotional problems in children. Part III: Drawing. *Psychiat. Quart.*, 1937, 11, 267–295. **41**

DIXON, W. J. & MOOD, A. M. The statistical sign test. *J. Amer. Statis. Ass.*, 1946, 41, 557–566. **126**

DJUKIĆ, S. Evolucija pojedinih delova tela i lica u dečjem crtežu ljudske figure. (Evolution of certain parts of human body and face in children's drawings.) *Savremena škola*, 1953, 8, 450–458. (*Psychol. Abstr.*, 29:3714) **55**

DOPPELT, J. E. The organization of mental abilities in the age range 13 to 17. *Teach. Coll. Contr. Educ.*, No. 962, New York: Columbia Univer. Press, 1950. **153**

DREVER, J. A *dictionary of psychology*. Baltimore: Penguin Books, 1952. **215 fn.**

DUBOIS, P. H. A test standardized on Pueblo Indian children. *Psychol. Bull.*, 1939, 36, 523. (Abstract) **14**

DUNN, M. B. Global evaluation of children's drawings of "person" and "self." Unpublished doctoral dissertation, Columbia Univer., 1954. **109**

DUNNETT, RUTH. *Art and child personality.* London: Methuen & Co., 1948. **221**

DYETT, E. G. The Goodenough drawing scale applied to college students. Unpublished master's thesis, Columbia Univer., 1931. **20**

EARL, E. J. C. The human figure drawings of adult defectives. *J. Ment. Sci.*, 1933, 79, 305–328. **21**

EGGERS, MIRIAM M. Comparison of Army Alpha and Goodenough drawings in delinquent women. Unpublished master's thesis, Columbia Univer., 1931. **20, 102**

ELKISCH, PAULA. Children's drawings in a projective technique. *Psychol. Monogr.*, 1945, 58, No. 1. **50, 56**

ELKISCH, PAULA. The emotional significance of children's art work. *Childh. Educ.*, 1947, 23, 236–241. **50**

ELLIS, RACHEL. Comparison of scores on Goodenough Draw-a-man, Revised Stanford-Binet, and Wechsler Intelligence Scale for Children, obtained from a group of children seen in a psychiatric clinic. Unpublished master's colloquium paper, Univer. of Minnesota, 1953. **95, 96, 97**

ELLSWORTH, FRANCES F. Elements of form in the free paintings of twenty nursery school children. *J. gen. Psychol.*, 1939, 20, 487–501. **213**

ENG, HELGA. *The psychology of children's drawings.* London: Routledge and Kegan Paul, 1931. **203**

ENG, HELGA. *The psychology of child and youth drawing.* New York: Humanities Press, 1957. **203**

ENGEL, P. Über die teilinhaltliche Beachtung von Farbe und Form. Untersuchung an 800 Schulkindern. (On the proportionate interest in color and form. Experiment with 800 pupils.) *Z. päd. Psychol.*, 1935, 36, 202–214; 241–251. **186**

ENGERTH, G. Zeichenstöringen bei Patienten met Autotopagnosie. (Disorders of drawing in patients with autotopagnosia.) *Zsch. ges. Neurol. Psychiat.*, 1933, 143, 381–402. **47**

ENGLAND, A. O. A psychological study of children's drawings. *Amer. J. Orthopsychiat.*, 1943, 13, 525–531. **39**

FANTZ, R. L. Pattern vision in young infants. *Psychol. Rec.*, 1958, 8, 43–47. **185**

FAY, H. M. Une méthode pour le dépistage des arriérés dans les grandes collectivities d'enfants d'âge scolaire. (A method for locating the retarded in large populations of school age children.) *Bull. de la Ligue d'Hygiène Mentale*, Juill–Oct., 1923. **20 fn.**

FAY, H. M. *L'intelligence et le caractére; leurs anomalies chez l'enfant.* (Intelligence and personality: their abnormalities in the child.) Paris: Foyer Central d'Hygiène, 1934. **20 fn.**

FELDMAN, M. J. & HUNT, R. G. The relation of difficulty in drawing to ratings of adjustment based on human figure drawings. *J. consult. Psychol.*, 1958, 22, 217–219. **63**

FINGERT, H. H., KAGEN, JULIA R., & SCHILDER, P. The Goodenough test in insulin and metrazol treatment of schizophrenia. *J. gen. Psychol.*, 1939, 21, 349–365. **47**

FISHER, S. & FISHER, RHODA. Test of certain assumptions regarding figure drawing analysis. *J. abnorm. soc. Psychol.*, 1950, 45, 727–732. **63**

FISHER, S. & FISHER, RHODA. Style of sexual adjustment in disturbed women and its expression in figure drawings. *J. Psychol.*, 1952, 34, 169–179. **58**

FONTES, V., LEITE DA COSTA, M. I., & FERREIRA, A. Contribuição para o estudo do teste de Fay aplicado em crianças portuguesas. (Contribution to the study of the Fay test as used with Portuguese children.) *Criança portug.*, 1944, 3, 13–34. (*Psychol. Abstr.*, 19:1057) **20 fn.**

FORTIER, R. H. The response to color and ego functions. *Psychol. Bull.*, 1953, 50, 41–63. **56 fn.**

FOWLER, R. D. The relationship of social acceptance to discrepancies between the IQ scores on the Stanford-Binet intelligence scale and the Goodenough Draw-a-man test. Unpublished master's thesis, Univer. of Ala., 1953. **27**

FRANK, L. K. Tactile communication. *Genet. psychol. Monogr.*, 1957, 56, 209–255. **164**

FRANK, L. K., HARRISON, R., HELLERSBERG, ELISABETH, MACHOVER, KAREN, & STEINER, META. Personality development in adolescent girls. *Monogr. Soc. Res. Child Develpm.*, 1953, 16, No. 53. **49, 62**

FRANKIEL, RITA V. A quality scale for the Goodenough draw-a-man test. Unpublished master's thesis, Univer. of Minnesota, 1957. **110, 114**

FREED, H. & PASTOR, JOYCE T. Evaluation of the "Draw-a-Person" test (modified) in thalamotomy with particular reference to the body image. *J. nerv. ment. Dis.*, 1951, 114, 106–120. **47**

FREEMAN, F. N. & FLORY, C. D. Growth in intellectual ability as measured by re-
    peated tests. *Monogr. Soc. Res. Child Develpm.*, 1937, 2, No. 2, **3**

FRENCH, J. E. Children's preferences for pictures of varied complexity of pictorial
    pattern. *Elem. Sch. J.*, 1952, 53, 90–95. **162, 180**

GARRETT, H. E. A developmental theory of intelligence. *Amer. Psychologist*, 1946,
    I, 372–378. **3, 98, 99, 153**

GASQREK, KATHRYN ALBERT. A study of the consistency and the reliability of cer-
    tain of the formal and structural characteristics of children's drawings. Unpub-
    lished doctoral dissertation, Columbia Univer., 1951. **59**

GECK, F. J. The effectiveness of adding kinesthetic to visual and auditory percep-
    tion in the teaching of drawing. *J. educ. Res.*, 1947, 41, 97–101. **165**

GERALD, H. J. P. Inverted position in children's drawings: report of two cases.
    J. nerv. ment. Dis., 1928, 68, 449–455. **161**

GESELL, A. & AMES, LOUISE B. The development of directionality in drawing.
    J. genet. Psychol., 1946, 68, 45–61. **159**

GHENT, LILA. Perception of overlapping and embedded figures by children of dif-
    ferent ages. *Amer. J. Psychol.*, 1956, 69, 575–587. **187**

GIBSON, ELEANOR. Association and differentiation in perceptual learning. Paper
    read at Soc. Resch. Child Develpm., University Park, Pa., March, 1961. **190,
    205, 208, 209**

GIBSON, J. J. The reproduction of visually perceived forms. *J. exp. Psychol.*, 1929,
    12, 1–39. **169, 187**

GITLITZ, H. B. The Goodenough drawing scale applied to fourteen-year-old chil-
    dren. Unpublished master's thesis, Columbia Univer., 1933. **20**

GLOWATSKY, E. The verbal element in the intelligence scores of congenitally deaf
    and hard of hearing children. *Amer. Ann. Deaf*, 1953, 98, 328–335. **29**

GOLDWORTH, S. A comparative study of the drawings of a man and a woman done
    by normal, neurotic, schizophrenic, and brain-damaged individuals. Unpub-
    lished doctoral dissertation, Univer. of Pittsburgh, 1950. **46, 66**

GOLLIN, EUGENE S. Observations on method in child psychology. *Merrill-Palmer
    quart. of Behav. and Develpm.*, 1960, 6, 250–260. **167, 187**

GOMBRICH, E. H. *Art and illusion.* New York: Pantheon Books, 1960. **197, 202, 204**

GOODENOUGH, FLORENCE L. *Measurement of intelligence by drawings.* New York:
    Harcourt, Brace & World, 1926. **10 fn., 11, 14, 20, 23–24, 26, 30–31, 32, 35,
    37, 41, 42, 54, 70–72, 77 fn., 93, 95, 98, 103, 106, 126, 168, 189, 190, 193–
    195, 197, 200–201, 202**

GOODENOUGH, FLORENCE L. Studies in the psychology of children's drawings.
    Psychol. Bull., 1928, 25, 272–283. **10 fn.**

GOODENOUGH, FLORENCE L. Children's drawings. In Murchison, C. (Ed.), *A hand-
    book of child psychology.* (1st ed.) Worcester, Mass.: Clark Univer. Press, 1931.
    10 fn.

GOODENOUGH, FLORENCE & HARRIS, D. B. Studies in the psychology of children's
    drawings: II. 1928–1949. *Psychol. Bull.*, 1950, 47, 369–433. **10 fn., 133**

GÖTZE, K. *Das Kind als Künstler.* (The child as artist.) Hamburg, 1898. **12**

GRAEWE, H. *Untersuchung der Entwickelung des Zeichnens.* (A Study of the de-
    velopment of drawing.) Halle: Schroedel, 1932, **168**

GRAEWE, H. Das Tierzeichnen der Kinder. (Animal drawings of children.) *Zsch.
    päd. Psychol.*, 1935, 36, 251–256; 291–300. **14, 161**

GRAEWE, H. Geschichtlicher Überblick über die Psychologie des kindlichen Zeichnens. (Historical review of the psychology of children's drawing.) *Arch. ges. Psychol.*, 1936, 96, 103–220. **10 fn.**

GRAHAM, FRANCES K., BERMAN, PHYLLIS W., & ERNHART, CLAIRE B. Development in preschool children of the ability to copy forms. *Child Develpm.*, 1960, 31, 339–359. **184, 187, 205**

GRAHAM, S. R. A study of reliability in human figure drawings. *J. proj. Tech.*, 1956, 20, 385–386. **58**

GRAMS, A. & RINDER, L. Signs of homosexuality in human figure drawings. *J. consult. Psychol.*, 1958, 22, 394. **58**

GRANICK, S. & SMITH, L. J. Sex sequence in the Draw-a-Person test and its relation to the MMPI Masculinity-Femininity scale. *J. consult. Psychol.*, 1953, 17, 71–73. **45**

GRIDLEY, PEARL F. Graphic representation of a man by four-year-old children in nine prescribed drawing situations. *Genet. Psychol. Monogr.*, 1938, 20, 183–350. **23**

GUILFORD, J. P. *Psychometric methods.* (2nd ed.) New York: McGraw-Hill, 1954. **110**

GUILFORD, J. P. Three faces of intellect. *Amer. Psychologist*, 1959, 14, 469–479. **2**

GUNZBURG, H. C. The significance of various aspects in drawings by educationally subnormal children. *J. ment. Sci.*, 1950, 96, 951–975. **65**

GUNZBURG, H. C. Scope and limitations of the Goodenough drawing test method in clinical work with mental defectives. *J. clin. Psychol.*, 1955, 11, 8–15. **26, 35, 97**

HAMMER, E. F. Frustration-aggression hypothesis extended to socio-racial areas: comparison of Negro and white children's H–T–P's. *Psychiat. quart.*, 1953, 27, 597–607. **65**

HAMMER, E. F. Guide for qualitative research with the H–T–P. *J. gen. Psychol.*, 1954, 51, 41–60. **49**

HANVIK, L. J. The Goodenough test as a measure of intelligence in child psychiatric patients. *J. clin. Psychol.*, 1953, 9, 71–72. **26, 35, 97**

HARE, A. P. & HARE, RACHEL T. The draw-a-group test. *J. genet. Psychol.*, 1956, 89, 51–59. **51**

HARLOW, H. The formation of learning sets. *Psychol. Rev.*, 1949, 56, 51–65. **157, 207**

HARMS, E. Child art as an aid in the diagnosis of juvenile neuroses. *Amer. J. Orthopsychiat.*, 1941, 11, 191–20. **38**

HARMS, E. The psychology of formal creativeness: I. Six fundamental types of formal expression. *J. genet. Psychol.*, 1946, 69, 97–120. **38**

HARRIS, D. B. Intra-individual vs. inter-individual consistency in children's drawings of a man. *Amer. Psychologist*, 1950, 5, 293. (Abstract) **60, 172**

HARRIS, D. B. A note on some ability correlates of the Raven Progressive Matrices (1947) in the kindergarten. *J. educ. Psychol.*, 1959, 50, 228–229. **93–94, 97, 98**

HAVIGHURST, R. J., GUNTHER, MINNA K., & PRATT, INEZ E. Environment and the Draw-a-Man test: the performance of Indian children. *J. abnorm. soc. Psychol.*, 1946, 41, 50–63. **98**

HAVIGHURST, R. J. & JANKE, LEOTA LONG. Relations between ability and social status in a midwestern community. I: Ten-year-old children. *J. educ. Psychol.*, 1944, 35, 357–368. **35, 96, 97**

HEBB, D. O. *Organization of behavior*. New York: Wiley, 1949. **205, 206, 207, 208**

HELLERSBERG, ELISABETH F. The Horn-Hellersberg test and adjustment to reality. *Amer. J. Orthopsychiat.*, 1945, 15, 690–710. **51**

HELLERSBERG, ELISABETH F. *The individual's relation to reality in our culture*. Springfield, Ill.: Charles C. Thomas, 1950. **51**

HELSON, H. *Psychiatric screening of flying personnel: perception and personality. A critique of recent experimental literature*. Project No. 21–0202–0007, Report No. 1. Randolph Field, Texas: USAF School of Aviation Medicine, 1953. **187**

HEMMENDINGER, L. Perceptual organization and development as reflected in the structure of Rorschach test responses. *J. proj. Tech.*, 1953, 17, 162–170. **188**

HERRICK, MARY A. Children's drawings. *Ped. Sem.*, 1893, 3, 338–339. **12**

HEVNER, KATE. Experimental studies of the affective value of colors and lines. *J. appl. Psychol.*, 1935, 19, 385–398. **39**

HILDRETH, GERTRUDE. Developmental sequences in name writing. *Child Develpm.*, 1936, 7, 291–303. **159**

HILDRETH, GERTRUDE. *The child mind in evolution: a study of developmental sequence in drawing*. New York: King's Crown Press, 1941. **160**

HILDRETH, GERTRUDE. The simplification tendency in reproducing designs. *J. genet. Psychol.*, 1944, 64, 329–333. **171**

HINRICHS, W. E. The Goodenough drawing test in relation to delinquency and problem behavior. *Arch. Psychol.*, N. Y., 1935, No. 175. **27, 72**

HOFSTAETTER, P. R. The changing composition of "intelligence": a study of T-technique. *J. genet. Psychol.*, 1954, 85, 159–164. **3**

HOLTZMAN, W. H. The examiner as a variable in the Draw-a-Person test. *J. consult. Psychol.*, 1952, 16, 145–148. **58**

HOMMA, T. (The law of Pragnanz in the process of drawing figures.) *Jap. J. Psychol.*, 1937, 12, 112–153. (*Psychol. Abstr.*, 11:4462) **171**

HUNTON, VERA D. The recognition of inverted pictures by children. *J. genet. Psychol.*, 1955, 86, 281–288. **186**

HURLOCK, ELIZABETH B. The spontaneous drawings of adolescents. *J. genet. Psychol.*, 1943, 63, 141–156. **14, 28**

IGNAT'EV, E. I. Voprosy psikhologicheskogo analiza protsessa risovaniia. (Problems in the psychological analysis of the process of drawing.) *Izv. Akad. pedag. Nauk RSFSR*, 1950, No. 25, 71–116. (*Psychol. Abstr.*, 25:3729) **165**

IINUMA, R. & WATANABE, K. (Observations on moving objects drawn by children. Orientation & motion of railway trains.) *Jap. J. Psychol.*, 1937, 12, 393–408. (*Psychol. Abstr.*, 12:977) **160**

ISRAELITE, JUDITH. A comparison of the difficulty of items for intellectually normal children and mental defectives on the Goodenough drawing test. *Amer. J. Orthopsychiat.*, 1936, 6, 494–503. **21**

IVANOFF, E. Recherches expérimentales sur le dessin des écoliers de la Suisse Romande: correlation entre l'aptitude au dessin et les autres aptitudes. (Experiments on the drawing of Swiss school children: the correlation between drawing aptitude and other capacities.) *Arch. Psychol.*, 1909, 8, 97–156. **13**

JANITSCHEK, H. (Ed.) *Kleinere kunstheoretische Schriften. Quellenschriften für Kunstgeschichte*, II, Vienna, 1877. Contains Leone Battista Alberti's *De Statua*. **196–197**

JEFFREY, W. E. The effects of verbal and nonverbal responses in mediating an instrumental act. *J. exp. Psychol.*, 1953, 45, 327–333. **186**

JENSEN, B. T. Left–right orientation in profile drawing. *Amer. J. Psychol.*, 1952, 65, 80–83. (a) **160**

JENSEN, B. T. Reading habits and left–right orientation in profile drawings by Japanese children. *Amer. J. Psychol.*, 1952, 65, 306–307. (b) **161**

JOHNSON, A. P., ELLERD, A. A. & LAHEY, T. H. The Goodenough test as an aid to interpretation of children's school behavior. *Amer. J. ment. Def.*, 1950, 54, 516–520. **65, 96**

JOLLES, I. A *catalogue for the qualitative interpretation of the H–T–P.* Beverly Hills, Calif.: west. Psychol Ser., 1952. (a) **47, 49, 65**

JOLLES, I. A study of the validity of some hypotheses for the qualitative interpretation of the H–T–P for children of elementary school age: I. Sexual identification. *J. clin. Psychol.*, 1952, 8, 113–118. (b) **45, 65**

JOLLES, I. A study of the validity of some hypotheses for the qualitative interpretation of the H–T–P for children of elementary school age: II. The "phallic tree" as an indicator of psycho-sexual conflict. *J. clin. Psychol.*, 1952, 8, 245–255. (c) **54, 65**

JOLLES, I. & BECK, H. S. A study of the validity of some hypotheses for the qualitative interpretation of the H–T–P for children of elementary school age: III. Horizontal placement. *J. clin. Psychol.*, 1953, 9, 161–164. (a) **65**

JOLLES, I. & BECK, H. S. A study of the validity of some hypotheses for the qualitative interpretation of the H–T–P for children of elementary school age: IV. Vertical placement. *J. clin. Psychol.*, 1953, 9, 164–167. (b) **65**

JONES, A. W. & RICH, T. A. The Goodenough Draw-a-Man test as a measure of intelligence in aged adults. *J. consult. Psychol.*, 1957, 21, 235–238. **27**

JUNG, C. G. *Gestaltungen des Unbewussten.* (Creative forms of the unconscious.) Zurich: Rascher & Cie, 1950. **54**

KATO, M. (A genetic study of children's drawings of man.) *Jap. J. exp. Psychol.*, 1936, 3, 175–185. (*Psychol. Abstr.*, 11:3000) **165**

KATZAROFF, M. D. Qu'est ce que les enfants dessinent? (What do children draw?) *Arch. de Psychol.*, 1910, 9, 125. **13**

KELLOGG, RHODA. *What children scribble and why.* 570 Union St., San Francisco: Author, 1955. **156**

KENT, G. H. & ROSANOFF, A. J. A study of association in insanity. *Amer. J. of Insanity*, 1910, 67, 37–96; 317–390. **24**

KERR, MADELINE. Children's drawings of houses. *Brit. J. med. Psychol.*, 1937, 16, 206–218, **15, 109**

KERSCHENSTEINER, D. G. *Die Entwickelung der zeichnerischen Begabung.* (The development of drawing talent.) Munich: Gerber, 1905. **15, 108, 213**

KLINE, L. W. The Kline-Carey measuring scale for free-hand drawing. (Part I, Representation.) *Johns Hopkins Univer. Stud. in Educ.*, No. 5a. Baltimore: Johns Hopkins Press, 1922. (a) **108**

KLINE, L. W. & CAREY, GERTRUDE L. A measuring scale for free-hand drawing. *Johns Hopkins Univer. Stud. in Educ.*, No. 5. Baltimore: Johns Hopkins Press, 1922. (b) **108**

KNOPF, I. J. & RICHARDS, T. W. The child's differentiation of sex as reflected in drawings of the human figure. *J. genet. Psychol.*, 1952, 81, 99–112. **44**

KOBAYASHI, S. (A study on a variation of facsimiles drawn by children.) *Jap. J. Psychol.*, 1937, 12, 375–392. (*Psychol. Abstr.*, 12:979) **165**

KORNER, IJA N. & WESTWOOD, D. Inter-rater agreement in judging student adjustment from projective tests. *J. clin. Psychol.*, 1955, 11, 167–170. **58**

KOTKOV, B. & GOODMAN, M. The Draw-A-Person tests of obese women. *J. clin. Psychol.*, 1953, 9, 362–364. **45**

KRAUSS, R. Über graphischen Ausdruck. Eine experimentelle Untersuchung über das Erzeugen und Ausdeuten von gegenstandfreien Linien. (Concerning graphic expression. An experimental investigation of the production and interpretation of objectless lines.) *Beih. Z. angew. Psychol.*, No. 48, 1930. **39**

KRÖBER, W. Über des Aufzeichnen von Formen aus dem Gedächtnis. (The drawing of forms from memory.) *Z. angew. Psychol.*, 1938, 54, 273–327. **169**

KROUT, JOHANNA. Symbol Elaboration Test (S.E.T.): the reliability and validity of a new projective technique. *Psychol. Monogr.*, 1950, 64, No. 4. **51**

LAKIN, M. Certain formal characteristics of human figure drawings by institutionalized aged and by normal children. *J. consult. Psychol.*, 1956, 20, 471–474. **48**

LAMPRECHT, K. Les dessins d'enfants comme source historique. (Children's drawings as an historical source.) *Bull. de l'Academie Royale de Belgique, Classe des Lettres*, 1906, Nos. 9–10, 457–469. **12**

LANDISBURG, SELMA. A study of the H–T–P test. *Tr. Sch. Bull.*, 1947, 44, 140–152. **50**

LANTZ, BEATRICE. *Easel age scale.* Los Angeles: Calif. Test Bur., 1955. **110**

LARK-HOROWITZ, BETTY. Interlinkage of sensory memories in relation to training in drawing. *J. genet. Psychol.*, 1936, 49, 69–89. **169**

LARK-HOROWITZ, BETTY, BARNHART, E. N. & SILLS, ESTHER M. *Graphic work sample diagnosis.* Cleveland: The Cleveland Museum of Art, 1939. **109**

LARK-HOROWITZ, BETTY & NORTON, J. Children's art abilities: the interrelations and factorial structure of ten characteristics. *Child Develpm.*, 1960, 31, 453–462. **210, 216–217**

LEGRÜN, A. Zur Deutung von Kinderkritzelein. (On the significance of children's scribbling.) *Z. Kinderforsch.*, 1938, 47, 236–249. **158**

LEHNER, G. F. J. & GUNDERSON, E. K. Reliability of graphic indices in a projective test (the Draw-a-Person). *J. clin. Psychol.*, 1952, 8, 125–128. **57**

LEMBKE, W. Über Zeichnungen von "frechen" und "schuchternen" Schulkindern. (The significance of drawings by "bold" and "shy" pupils.) *Z. f. päd. Psychol.*, 1930, (Oct.) 459–469. (*Psychol. Abstr.*, 5:1657) **37**

LEROY, ALICE. Représentations de la perspective dans les dessins d'enfants. (Representation of perspective in the drawings of children.) *Enfance*, 1951, 4, 286–307. **213**

LEUBA, C. Children's reactions to elements of simple geometric patterns. *Amer. J. Psychol.*, 1940, 53, 575–578. **187**

LEVINE, M. & GALANTER, E. H. A note on the "tree and trauma" interpretation in the H–T–P. *J. consult. Psychol.*, 1953, 17, 74–75. **65**

LEVINSTEIN, S. *Kinderzeichnunger bis zum 14 Lebensjahre. Mit Parallelen aus der Urgeschichte, Kulturgeschichte, und Völkerkunde.* (Children's drawings to age fourteen. With parallels to the earliest history, the history of civilization, and folklore.) Leipzig: Voigtländer, 1905. **12.**

LEVY, LYDIA R. The function of the Goodenough drawing scale in the study of high school freshmen. Unpublished master's thesis, Columbia Univer., 1931. **20, 102**

LEVY, S. Figure drawing as a projective test. In L. E. Abt and L. Bellak (Eds.), *Projective psychology.* New York: Knopf, 1950. Pp. 257–297. **44**

LEWIN, K. A *dynamic theory of personality.* New York: McGraw-Hill, 1935. **170**

LEWIS, M. M. *Infant speech.* New York: Humanities Press, 1951. **181**

LINE, W. The growth of visual perception in children. *Brit. J. Psych. Mon. Suppl.* XV. Cambridge, Engl., 1931. **179, 188**

LISS, E. The graphic arts. *Amer. J. Orthopsychiat.,* 1938, 8, 95–99. **54**

LIVSON, N. & KRECH, D. Dynamic systems, perceptual differentiation, and intelligence. *J. Pers.,* 1956, 25, 46–58. **186**

LOBSIEN, M. Kinderzeichnung und Kunstkanon. *Z. f. päd. Psychol.,* 1905, 7, 393–404. **13**

LORD, E. & WOOD, L. Diagnostic values in a visuo-motor test. *Amer. J. Orthopsychiat.,* 1942, 12, 414–428. **47**

LORGE, I., TUCKMAN, J., & DUNN, M. B. Human figure drawings by younger and older adults. *J. clin. Psychol.,* 1958, 14, 54–56. **48**

LOUTTIT, C. M., & BROWNE C. G. The use of psychometric instruments in psychological clinics. *J. consult. Psychol.,* 1947, 11, 49–54. **72**

LOWENFELD, V. *The nature of creative activity.* New York: Harcourt, Brace & World, 1939. **29, 46, 164, 182–183, 203**

LOWENFELD, V. Tests for visual and haptical aptitudes. *Amer. J. Psychol.,* 1945, 58, 100–111. **30, 46, 182–183**

LOWENFELD, V. *Creative and mental growth.* New York: Macmillan, 1947. (Rev. ed., New York: Macmillan, 1952.) **30, 38, 154, 183**

LOWENFELD, V. *Creative and mental growth* (3rd ed.). New York: Macmillan, 1957. **30, 154, 166, 183, 202**

LÖWY, E. *Die Naturwiedergabe in der älteren griechischen Kunst.* (*The rendering of nature in early Greek art.*) London: Duckworth & Co., 1907. **204**

LUKENS, H. A study of children's drawings in the early years. *Ped. Sem.,* 1896, 4, 79–110. **12, 13**

LUNDHOLM, H. The affective tone of lines: experimental researches. *Psychol. Rev.,* 1921, 28, 43–60. **39**

LUQUET, G. H. *Les dessins d'un enfant.* (*The drawings of a child.*) Paris: F. Alcan, 1913. **12, 13, 193, 200**

LUQUET, G. H. Le réalisme intellectuel dans l'art primitif: I. Figuration de l'invisible. (Intellectual realism in primitive art. I. Representation of the invisible.) *J. de Psychol.,* 1927, 24, 765–797. (a) **37**

LUQUET, G. H. Le réalisme intellectuel dans l'art primitif: II. Le rendu de visible. (Intellectual realism in primitive art. II. The expression of the visible.) *J. de Psychol.,* 1927, 24, 888–927. (b) **37**

LUQUET, G. H. L'evolution du dessin enfantin. (The development of childish drawing.) *Bull. Soc. Binet,* 1929, 29, 145–163. **37**

MC CARTHY, DOROTHEA. A study of the reliability of the Goodenough drawing test of intelligence. *J. Psychol.,* 1944, 18, 201–206. **21**

MC CARTY, STELLA A. *Children's drawings.* Baltimore: Williams & Wilkins, 1924. **13, 108, 128, 129, 212–213**

MC CURDY, H. G. Group and individual variability on the Goodenough Draw-a-man test. *J. educ. Psychol.,* 1947, 38, 428–436. **21, 91**

MC ELWEE, EDNA W. The reliability of the Goodenough intelligence test used with sub-normal children fourteen years of age. *J. appl. Psychol.*, 1932, 16, 217–218. **35, 96**

MC ELWEE, EDNA W. Profile drawings of normal and sub-normal children. *J. appl. Psychol.*, 1934, 18, 599–603. **21**

MC FEE, JUNE K. *Preparation for art.* San Francisco: Wadsworth, 1961. **198–199, 205**

MACHOVER, KAREN. *Personality projection in the drawing of the human figure.* Springfield, Ill.: Charles C. Thomas, 1949. **28, 43, 44, 55**

MACHOVER, KAREN. Drawing of the human figure: a method of personality investigation. In H. H. Anderson & Gladys L. Anderson (Eds.), *An introduction to projective techniques.* New York: Prentice-Hall, 1951. Pp. 341–369. **44**

MACHOVER, KAREN. Human figure drawings of children. *J. proj. Tech.*, 1953, 17, 85–91. **44, 49**

MC HUGH, G. Changes in Goodenough IQ at the public school kindergarten level. *J. educ. Psychol.*, 1945, 36, 17–30. (a) **22, 96**

MC HUGH, G. Relationship between the Goodenough Drawing a Man test and the 1937 revision of the Stanford-Binet test. *J. educ. Psychol.*, 1945, 36, 119–124. (b) **22**

MC NEMAR, Q. *Psychological statistics.* New York: Wiley, 1949. **106**

MAINORD, FLORENCE B. A note on the use of figure drawings in the diagnosis of sexual inversion. *J. clin. Psychol.*, 1953, 9, 188–189. **45**

MAITLAND, LOUISE. What children draw to please themselves. *Inland Educator*, 1895, 1, 87. **12, 13**

MALRIEU, P. Observations sur quelques dessins libres chez l'enfant. (Observations on some free drawings of the child.) *J. Psychol. norm. path.*, 1950, 43, 239–244. **37, 213**

MANSON, J. B. The drawings of Pamela Bianca. *International Studio*, 1919, 68, 119–125. **30**

MARINO, DIVO. O desenho infantil e a sexualidade. (Infantile drawings and sexuality.) *Bol. Inst. int. amer. Prot. Infanc.*, Montevideo, 1956, 30, 10–18. (*Psychol. Abstr.*, 31:678) **17**

MARKEY, J. F. *The symbolic process.* London: Kegan Paul, Trench, Trubner, 1928. **181**

MARKHAM, SYLVIA. An item analysis of children's drawings of a house. *J. clin. Psychol.*, 1954, 10, 185–187. **15**

MARTIN, H. *Stile und Stilwandlungsgesetze der Kinderzeichnung.* (Styles and laws of change in style in children's drawings.) *Vjsch. f. Jugendk.*, 1932, 2, 211–226. (*Psychol. Abstr.*, 7:2086) **165**

MARTIN, MILDRED H. Some reactions of pre-school children to discipline. *Nerv. Child*, 1951, 9, 125–130. **61**

MARTIN, W. E. Identifying the insecure child: III. The use of children's drawings. *J. genet. Psychol.*, 1955, 86, 327–338. **54, 61**

MARTIN, W. E. & DAMRIN, DORA E. An analysis of the reliability and factorial composition of ratings of children's drawings. *Child Develpm.*, 1951, 22, 133–144. **56, 216**

MARTORANA, ANNA A. A comparison of the personal, emotional, and family adjustment of crippled and normal children. Unpublished doctoral dissertation, Univer. of Minnesota, 1954. **46**

MATEER, FLORENCE. *The unstable child.* New York: D. Appleton & Co., 1924. **24**

MEIER, N. C. (Ed.). Studies in the psychology of art. *Psychol. Monogr.*, 1933, 45, No. 1. **214–215**

MEILI-DWORETZKI, GERTRUD. *Das Bild Des Menchen in der Vorstellung und Darstellung des Kleinkindes.* (The image of men in the conception and representation of children.) Bern: Verlag Hans Huber, 1957. **162, 163, 164, 165, 180, 197, 201 fn.**

MICHAL-SMITH, H. The identification of pathological cerebral function through the H–T–P technique. *J. clin. Psychol.*, 1953, 9, 293–295. **47**

MILLER, MARY D. & RUTTER, FLORENCE. *Child artists of the Australian bush.* London: Harrap. 1952. **220**

MIRA, E. Myokinetic psychodiagnosis: a new technique for exploring the conative trends of personality. *Proc. roy. Soc. Med.*, 1940, 33, 173–194. **47, 51, 165**

MODELL, A. H. Changes in human figure drawings by patients who recover from regressed states. *Amer. J. Orthophychiat.*, 1951, 21, 584–596. **48**

MORRIS, D. Primate's esthetics. *Natural Hist.*, 1961, 70, 22–29. **158**

MORRIS, D. *The biology of art.* New York: Knopf, 1962. **158, 182**

MOTT, SINA M. The development of concepts: a study of children's drawings. *Child Develpm.*, 1936, 7, 144–148. (a) **23**

MOTT, SINA M. The development of concepts. *J. genet. Psychol.*, 1936, 48, 199–214. (b) **23**

MOTT, SINA M. The growth of an abstract concept. *Child Develpm.*, 1939, 10, 21–25. **23, 200**

MOTT, SINA M. Muscular activity an aid in concept formation. *Child Develpm.*, 1945, 16, 97–109. **23, 93, 94, 165, 172**

MOTT, SINA M. Concept of mother: a study of four and five year old children. *Child Develpm.*, 1954, 25, 99–106. **44**

MUNROE, RUTH, LEVINSON, THEA, & WAEHNER, TRUDE. A comparison of three projective techniques. *Charact. & Pers.*, 1944, 13, 1–21. **51**

MURPHY, MARY MARTHA. A Goodenough scale of evaluation of human figure drawings of three non-psychotic groups of adults. *J. clin. Psychol.*, 1956, 12, 397–399. **26**

MURPHY, MARY MARTHA. Sexual differentiation of male and female job applicants on the Draw-a-Person. *J. clin. Psychol.*, 1957, 13, 87–88. **44**

MURSELL, J. L. How children learn esthetic responses. In *The 49th Yearb. Nat. Soc. Stud. Educ., Part I: learning and instruction.* Chicago: Univer. of Chicago Press, 1950. Pp. 183–191. **235**

MYKLEBUST, H. R. & BRUTTEN, M. A study of the visual perception of deaf children. *Acta oto-laryng.* Stockh., 1953, Suppl. 105. **29**

NAGY, MARIA H. Children's conception of some bodily functions. *J. genet. Psychol.*, 1953, 83, 199–216. (a) **192**

NAGY, MARIA H. The representation of "germs" by children. *J. genet. Psychol.*, 1953, 83, 227–240. (b) **192**

NAPOLI, P. J. Finger painting and personality diagnosis. *Genet. Psychol. Monogr.*, 1946, 34, 129–231. **41, 56**

NAPOLI, P. J. Interpretive aspects of finger painting. *J. Psychol.*, 1947, 23, 93–132. **41, 56**

NAUMBERG, MARGARET. Studies of the "free" art expression of behavior problem children and adolescents as a means of diagnosis and therapy. *Nerv. ment. Dis. Monogr.*, No. 71, New York: Coolidge Foundation, 1947. **52**

NAVILLE, P. Correction d'un test de dessin par trois correcteurs différents. (Scoring of a drawing test by three different scorers.) *J. Psychol. norm. Path.*, 1948, 41, 241–259. **21**

NAVILLE, P. Éléments d'une bibliographie critique relative au graphisme enfantin jusqu'en 1949. (Elements of a critical bibliography of children's drawings up to 1949.) *Enfance*, 1950, 3, 310–403. (a) **10 fn.**

NAVILLE, P. Note sur les origines de la fonction graphique; de la tache au trait. (Note on the origins of the graphic function; from daub to line.) *Enfance*, 1950, 3, 189–203. (b) **161**

NEUBAUER, V. Zur Entwickelung der dekorativen Zeichnung. (The development of decorative drawing.) *Z. angew. Psychol.*, 1931, 39, 273–325. **167**

NISSON, H. W., MACHOVER, S. & KINDER, ELAINE F. A study of performance tests given to a group of native African Negro children. *Brit. J. Psychol.*, 1935, 25, 308–355. **189, 207**

NORCROSS, KATHRYN J. & SPIKER, C. C. The effects of type of stimulus pre-training on discrimination performance in preschool children. *Child Develpm.*, 1957, 28, 79–84. **186**

OAKLEY, C. A. Drawings of a man by adolescents. *Brit. J. Psychol.*, 1940, 31, 37–60. **20, 102**

OCHS, ELEANOR. Changes in Goodenough drawings associated with changes in social adjustment. *J. clin. Psychol.*, 1950, 6, 282–284. **25**

O'GRADY, R. M. A study of selected aspects of finger paintings by special class children. *J. genet. Psychol.*, 1954, 84, 27–38. **61**

ORNE, M. T. The mechanisms of hypnotic age regression: an experimental study. *J. abnorm. soc. Psychol.*, 1951, 46, 213–225. **48**

O'SHEA, M. V. Some aspects of drawing. *Educ. Rev.*, 1897, 14, 263–284. **12**

O'SHEA, M. V. Children's expression through drawing. *Proc. Nat'l. Educ. Ass.*, 1894, 1015–1023. **12**

OSTERREITH, P. A. Le test de copie d'une figure complexe; contribution à l'étude de la perception et de la mémoire. (Test of copying a complex figure; contribution to the study of perception and memory.) *Arch. Psychol., Genève*, 1944, 30, 206–356. (*Psychol. Abstr.*, 20:2126) **167**

ØSTLYNGEN, E. On the direction of drawings. *Studia Psychol. Paedagog., Lund.*, 1948, 2, 206–210. (*Psychol. Abstr.*, 22:4322) **160**

OWEN, MARGARET. Perception of simultaneous tactile stimuli in emotionally disturbed children and its relation to their body image concept. *J. nerv. ment. Dis.*, 1955, 121, 397–409. **47**

PALMER, H. R. The relationship of differences between Stanford-Binet and Goodenough IQ's to personal adjustment as indicated by the California test of personality. Unpublished master's thesis, Univer. of Ala., 1953. **27**

PAULSSON, G. The creative element in art. *Scand. Sci. Rev.*, 1923, 2, 11–173. **168**

PEARSON, G. H. J. Inverted position in children's drawings: report of two cases. *J. nerv. ment. Dis.*, 1928, 68, 449–455. **161**

PECHOUX, R., KOHLER, M. & GIRARD, V. Réflexions sur l'évaluation de l'intelligence chez les enfants irréguliers. (Reflections on the evaluation of intelligence in abnormal children.) *J. Méd. Lyon*, 1947, 28, 337–343. (*Psychol. Abstr.*,

21:4370) **35, 96**

PEREZ, M. B. *L'art et la poesie chez l'enfant.* (*Art and poetry of the child.*) Paris: F. Alcan, 1888. **12, 189**

PETERS, G. A. & MERRIFIELD, P. R. Graphic representation of emotional feelings. *J. clin. Psychol.,* 1958, 14, 375–378. **39**

PETERSON, E. G. & WILLIAMS, J. M. Intelligence of deaf children as measured by drawings. *Amer. Ann. Deaf,* 1930, 75, 273–290. **29**

PHATAK, PRAMILA. A study of the revised Goodenough scale with reference to artistic and non-artistic drawings. Unpublished, mimeo. Author, Univer. of Baroda, India, 1959. **93**

PHILLIPS, E. & STROMBERG, E. A comparative study of finger painting performance in detention home and high school pupils. *J. Psychol.,* 1948, 26, 507–516. **61**

PIAGET, J. *The psychology of intelligence.* London: Routledge and Kegan Paul, 1950. **3**

PIAGET, J. *The origin of intelligence in the child.* London: Routledge and Kegan Paul, 1953. **3, 190**

PIAGET, J. & STETTLER-VON ALBERTINI, BARBARA. Observations sur la perception des bonnes formes chez enfant par actualisation des lignes virtuelles. (Observations on the perception of "good Gestalten" in the child through realization of "virtual lines.") *Arch. Psychol., Genève,* 1954, 34, 203–242. **187**

PINTNER, R. Artistic appreciation among deaf children. *Amer. Ann. Deaf,* 1941, 86, 218–224. **29**

PLAUT, ERIKA & CRANNELL, C. W. The ability of clinical psychologists to discriminate between drawings by deteriorated schizophrenics and drawings by normal subjects. *Psychol. Rep.,* 1955, 1, 153–158. **63**

POFFENBERGER, A. T. & BARROW, B. E. The feeling value of lines. *J. appl. Psychol.,* 1924, 8, 187–205. **39**

PORTOCARRERO-DE LINARES, CRACUELA-VERA. El desarrollo del dibujo imitativo en la poblacion femenina de Lima. (The development of imitative drawing in the feminine population of Lima.) *Boletin del Institute Psicopedagogico Nacional,* 1948, 7, 47–148. **171**

PRECKER, J. A. Painting and drawing in personality assessment. *J. proj. Tech.,* 1950, 14, 262–286. **54**

PRUDHOMMEAU, M. *Le dessin de l'enfant.* (*The child's drawing.*) Paris: Presses Univer. de France, 1947. **172**

PRUDHOMMEAU, M. Dessin et écriture chez l'enfant. (Drawing and writing in the child.) *Enfance,* 1948, 1, 117–125. **159**

RABELLO, S. Caracteristicas do desenho infantil. (Characteristics of children's drawings.) *Bol. Deretoria Tecn. de Educ.,* 1932, 2, 15–78. (*Psychol. Abstr.,* 8:1247) **17**

RAWN, M. L. Degree of disturbance in figure drawings as related to mode of approach to problem solving. *J. genet. Psychol.,* 1957, 91, 191–196. **54**

RAVEN, J. C. *Controlled projection for children.* (2nd ed.) London: H. K. Lewis, 1951. **55**

READ, H. *Education through art.* (2nd ed.) New York: Pantheon Books, 1945. **156, 178, 183, 202, 203**

REICHENBERG-HACKETT, W. Changes in Goodenough drawings after a gratifying experience. *Amer. J. Orthopsychiat.,* 1953, 23, 501–517. **25, 60**

REITMAN, F. *Psychotic art*. New York: International Univer. Press, 1951. **48, 66, 176–177**

RENSHAW, S., WHERRY, R. J., & NEWLIN, J. C. Cutaneous localization in congenitally blind versus seeing children and adults. *J. genet. Psychol.*, 1930, 38, 239–248. **165**

REVESZ, G. *Psychology and art of the blind*. New York: Longmans, Green, 1950. **30, 164**

REY, A. Épreuves de dessin témoins du développement mental: I. (The use of drawings as measures of mental development.) *Arch. Psychol., Genève*, 1946, 31, 369–380. **20 fn., 102**

REY, A. Épreuves de dessin témoins du développement mental: II. (The use of drawings as measures of mental development.) *Arch. Psychol., Genève*, 1947, 32, 145–159. **166**

REY, A. Les conditions sensori-motrices du dessin. (The sensori-motor conditions in drawing.) *Schweiz Z. Psychol. Anwend.*, 1950, 9, 381–392. **161**

REZNIKOFF, M. & REZNIKOFF, HELGA R. The family drawing test: a comparative study of children's drawings. *J. clin. Psychol.*, 1956, 12, 167–169. **51**

REZNIKOFF, M. & TOMBLEN, D. The use of human figure drawings in the diagnosis of organic pathology. *J. consult. Psychol.*, 1956, 20, 467–470. **47**

RICCI, C. L'arte dei bambini. (Art of children.) Bologna: 1887. (Tr. by Maitland in *Pedag. Sem.*, 1894, 3, 302–307.) **10 fn.**

RICE, CHARLOTTE. Excellence of production and type of movements in drawing. *Child Develpm.*, 1930, 1, 1–14. (a) **159**

RICE, CHARLOTTE. The orientation of plane figures as a factor in their perception by children. *Child Develpm.*, 1930, 1, 111–143. (b) **186**

RIOUX, M. G. *Dessin et structure mentale. Contribution à l'étude psycho-sociale des milieux nord-Africains*. (Drawing and intellectual structure. A contribution to the psychosocial study of the north African habitats.) *Publications de la faculte des lettres d'Alger*. IIᵉ Série, Tome XIX. Presses Univer. de France, 1951. **10 fn.**

ROGERS, C. R. *Counseling and psychotherapy*. Boston: Houghton-Mifflin, 1942. **43**

ROSTOHAR, M. *Studie z vyvojové psychologie*, Dil. I. (Studies in developmental psychology.) Brn o: Opera Facult. Philosoph. Universit. Masarykian. Brunensis, Cisto 25, 1928. (*Psychol. Abstr.*, 4:805) **170, 189**

ROTTERSMAN, L. A comparison of the IQ scores on the new revised Stanford-Binet, Form L, the Wechsler Intelligence Scale for Children, and the Goodenough "Draw-a-man" test at the six year age level. Unpublished master's thesis, Univer. of Nebraska, 1950. **35, 96, 97**

ROUMA, G. Un cas de mythomanie. (A case of mythomania.) *Arch. de Psychol.*, 1908, 7, 258–282. **24**

ROUMA, G. *Le langage graphique de l'enfant*. (The child's graphic language.) Paris: Misch. et Thron, 1913. **13 fn., 16, 54, 161**

RUBIN, H. A quantitative study of the H–T–P and its relationship to the Wechsler-Bellevue scale. *J. clin. Psychol.*, 1954, 10, 35–38. **50, 65**

RUSH, GRACE PREYER. Visual grouping in relation to age. *Arch. Psychol., N. Y.*, 31, No. 217, 1937. **186**

SCHAEFER-SIMMERN, H. *The unfolding of artistic activity*. Berkeley: Univer. of Calif. Press, 1948. **175–176, 222**

SCHAPIRO, M. Style. In A. L. Kroeber (Ed.), *Anthropology today*. Chicago: Univer. of Chicago Press, 1953. Pp. 287–312. **204**

SCHEERER, M. & LYONS, J. Line drawing and matching responses to words. *J. Pers.*, 1947, 25, 251–273. **39**

SCHILDER, P. *Image and appearance of the human body*. London: Kegan Paul, 1935. **42**

SCHILDER, P. & LEVINE, E. L. Abstract art as an expression of human problems. *J. nerv. ment. Dis.*, 1942, 95, 1–10. **50, 54**

SCHILLER, P. H. Figural preferences in the drawings of a chimpanzee. *J. comp. physiol. Psychol.*, 1951, 44, 101–111. **157, 187**

SCHILLER, P. H. Innate motor action as a basis of learning (1949). In Claire H. Schiller (Ed.), *Instinctive behavior*. New York: Int. Univer. Press, 1957. Pp. 264–287. **157**

SCHLIEBE, G. Erlebnismotorik und zeichnerischer (physiognomischer) Ausdruck bei Kindern und Jugendlichen. (Empirical-motor and graphic-physiognomic expression in children and youth.) Z. *Kinderforsch.*, 1934, 43, 49–76. (*Psychol. Abstr.*, 9:3954) **38**

SCHRINGER, W. Der Goodenough-Test. (The Goodenough Draw-a-Man test.) *Psychol. Forsch.*, 1957, 25, 155–237. **10 fn.**

SCHUBERT, H. J. & WAGONER, MAZIE E. Sex differences in figure drawings by normal late adolescents. *Amer. Psychologist*, 1954, 9, 467. (Abstract) **45**

SCHUYTEN, M. C. Het oorspronkelijk teekenen als bijdrage tot kinderanalyse. (Early drawing as a contribution to child analysis.) *Paedologisch Jaarboek*, 1901, 2, 112–126. **13**

SCHUYTEN, M. C. De oorspronkelijke 'ventjes' der Antwerpsche schoolkindern. (The early "little men" of Antwerp school children.) *Paedologisch Jaarboek*, 1904, 5, 1–87. **13**

SCHUYTEN, M. C. Note pedagogique sur le dessins des enfants. (An educational note on children's drawings.) *Arch. de Psychol.*, 1907, 6, 389–391. **13**

SCHWARTZ, A. A. & ROSENBERG, I. H. Observations on the significance of animal drawings. *Amer. J. Orthopsychiat.*, 1955, 25, 729–746. **14**

SEASHORE, H. G. & BAVELAS, A. A study of frustration in children. *J. genet. Psychol.*, 1942, 61, 279–314. **52, 171**

SEEMAN, ERNEST. Development of the pictorial aptitude in children. *Charact. & Pers.*, 1934, 2, 209–221. **156**

SHAPIRO, D. S. Perceptions of significant family and environmental relationships in aggressive and withdrawn children. *J. consult. Psychol.*, 1957, 21, 381–385. **60**

SHARP, AGNES A. Diagnostic significance of a visual memory drawing test. *J. abnorm. soc. Psychol.*, 1949, 44, 517–527. **46, 47**

SHERIF, M. A study of some social factors in perception. *Arch. Psychol.*, N. Y., 1935, No. 187. **197**

SHERIF, M. *The psychology of social norms*. New York: Harper, 1936. **197**

SHERMAN, LEWIS J. Sexual differentiation or artistic ability? *J. clin. Psychol.*, 1958, 14, 170–171. **45, 63**

SHINN, MILICENT W. Notes on the development of a child. *Univer. of Calif. Stud.*, Vol. I. Berkeley, Calif.: Univer. of Calif., 1893. **12**

SHIRLEY, MARY & GOODENOUGH, FLORENCE L. A survey of the intelligence of deaf children in Minnesota schools. *Amer. Ann. Deaf*, 1932, 77, 238–247. **29, 173**

SILVER, A. A. Diagnostic value of three drawing tests for children. *J. Pediat.*, 1950, 37, 129–143. **44, 46**

SILVERSTEIN, A. B. & ROBINSON, H. A. The representation of orthopedic disability in children's figure drawings. *J. consult. Psychol.*, 1956, 20, 333–341. **46**

SKEELS, H. M. A study of some factors in form board accomplishments of preschool children. *Univer. Iowa Stud.: Stud. Child Welfare*, 1933, 7, No. 2. **186**

SLOAN, W. & GUERTIN, W. H. A comparison of H–T–P and Wechsler-Bellevue IQ's in mental defectives. *J. clin. Psychol.*, 1948, 4, 424–426. **65**

SLOCHOWER, MURIEL Z. Experiments on dimensional and figural problems in the clay and pencil reproductions of line figures by young children: I. Dimension. *J. genet. Psychol.*, 1946, 69, 57–75. (a) **170**

SLOCHOWER, MURIEL Z. Experiments on dimensional and figural problems in the clay and pencil reproductions of line figures by young children: II. Shape. *J. genet. Psychol.*, 1946, 69, 77–95. (b) **170**

SMITH, F. O. What the Goodenough intelligence test measures. *Psychol. Bull.*, 1937, 34, 760–761. (Abstract) **21, 35**

SNYGG, D. & COMBS, A. W. *Individual behavior; a new frame of reference for psychology.* New York: Harper, 1949. **43**

SOLOMON, P., KUBZANSKY, P. E., LEIDERMAN, P. H., MENDELSON, J. H., TRUMBULL, R. & WEXLER, D. (Eds.) *Sensory deprivation.* Cambridge, Mass.: Harvard Univer. Press, 1961. **164**

SORGE, S. Neue versuche über die Wiedergabe abstraktes optischer Gebilde. (A new experiment on the reproduction of abstract visual forms.) *Arch. ges. Psychol.*, 1940, 106, 1–89. **171**

SPEARMAN. C. *The abilities of man.* London: Macmillan, 1927. **2**

SPIELREIN, S. Kinderzeichnungen bei offenen und geschlossenen Augen: Untersuchnungen über die unterschwelligen kinästhetischen Vorstellungen. (Children's drawings with eyes open and shut.) *Imago*, 1931, 17, 359–391. (*Psychol. Abstr.*, 6:2966) **51**

SPIKER, C. C. & TERRELL, G. Factors associated with transpositional behavior of preschool children. *J. genet. Psychol.*, 1955, 86, 143–158. **186**

SPOERL, DOROTHY T. Personality and drawing in retarded children. *Charact. & Pers.*, 1940, 8, 227–239. (a) **21, 97**

SPOERL, DOROTHY T. The drawing ability of mentally retarded children. *J. genet. Psychol.*, 1940, 57, 259–277. (b) **21, 97**

SPRINGER, N. N. A comparative study of the intelligence of deaf and hearing children. *Amer. Ann. Deaf*, 1938, 83, 138–152. **29**

SPRINGER, N. N. A study of drawings of maladjusted and adjusted children. *J. genet. Psychol.*, 1941, 58, 131–138. **25, 28**

STARKE, P. An attempt to differentiate delinquents from non-delinquents by tests of dominance behavior, dominance feeling and the Goodenough drawing of a man. Unpublished master's thesis, Univer. of Minn., 1950. **27, 28**

STERN, CLARA & STERN, W. Die zeichnerische Entwickelung einer Knaben von 4 bis 7 Jahre. (The drawing development of a boy from 4 to 7 years.) *Z. f. angew. Psychol.*, 1910, 3, 1–31. **16**

STERN, W. Spezielle Beschreibung der Ausstellung freier Kinderzeichnungen aus Breslau. (Description of the exhibition of children's free drawings from Breslau.) *Bericht über den Kongress für Kinderforschung und Jugendfursorge in Berlin*, 1907, 411–417. **16**

STERN, W. Die Entwickelung der Raumwahrnehmung in der ersten Kindheit. (The development of space perception in early childhood.) Z. f. angew. Psychol., 1909, 2, 412. **16, 166**

STERN, W. Psychologie der frühen Kindheit. (The psychology of early childhood.) Leipzig: Quelle & Meyer, 1914. **16**

STERN, W., KOHLER, W., & VERWORN, M. Sammlungen freier Kinderzeichnungen. (Collections of children's free drawings.) Z. f. angew. Psychol., 1908, 1, 179–187; 472–476. **16**

STEVENSON, H. W. & MC BEE, G. The learning of object and pattern discriminations by children. J. comp. physiol. Psychol., 1958, 51, 752–754. **186**

STEWART, LOUIS H. The expression of personality in drawings and paintings. Genet. Psychol. Monogr., 1955, 51, 45–103. **56, 198, 210, 217–219**

STEWART, NAOMI in E. K. Buros (Ed.), Fourth mental measurements yearbook. Highland Park, N. J.: Gryphon Press, 1953. **1**

STONE, P. M. A study of objectively scored drawings of human figures in relation to the emotional adjustment of 6th grade pupils. Unpublished doctoral dissertation, Yeshiva Univer., 1952. **63–64**

STOTIJN-EGGE, SOLVEIG. Onderzoek over de ontwikkeling van het tekenen bij laagstaande oligophrenen. (Investigation of the drawing ability of low-grade oligophrenics.) Leiden: "Luctor et Emergo," 1952. **158, 172**

STREET, R. F. A gestalt completion test. New York: Teachers College, Columbia Univer., 1931. **186**

SULLY, J. Studies of childhood. (Rev. ed.) New York: D. Appleton, 1903. **200, 202**

SULLY, J. Children's ways. New York: D. Appleton, 1907. **12**

SULLY, J. Studies of childhood. New York: D. Appleton, 1908. **12**

SWENSEN, C. H. & NEWTON, K. R. The development of sexual differentiation on the Draw-A-Person test. J. clin. Psychol., 1955, 11, 417–419. **44**

SWENSEN, C. H. Sexual differentiation on the Draw-A-Person test. J. clin. Psychol., 1955, 11, 37–41. **44**

SWENSEN, C. H. Empirical evaluations of human figure drawings. Psychol. Bull., 1957, 54, 431–466. **58 fn., 62, 63**

SWINEFORD, FRANCES. Growth in the general and verbal bi-factors from grade VII to grade IX. J. educ. Psychol., 1947, 38, 257–272. **153**

THIEL, G. Eine Untersuchung von Kinderzeichnungen taubstummer Schuler. (An investigation of the drawings of deaf and dumb children.) Z. Kinderforsch., 1927, 33, 138–176. **29**

THOMAS, R. M. Effects of frustration on children's paintings. Child Develpm., 1951, 22, 123–132. **60**

THOMPSON, G. G. The effect of chronological age on aesthetic preferences for rectangles of different proportions. J. exp. Psychol., 1946, 36, 50–58. **215**

THORNDIKE, E. L. The measurement of achievement in drawing. Teach. Coll. Rec., 1913, 14, No. 5. **108**

THORNDIKE, E. L. The measurement of intelligence. New York: Bur. Publ., Teachers College, Columbia Univer., 1926. **3**

THURSTONE, L. L. Primary mental abilities. Psychometr. Monogr., No. 1, 1938. **2**

TIEBOUT, CAROLYN. The measurement of quality in children's paintings by the scale method. Psychol. Monogr., 1936, 48, 85–94. **109**

TOLOR, A. Teachers' judgments of the popularity of children from their human figure drawings. *J. clin. Psychol.*, 1955, 11, 158–162. **63**

TOLOR, A. & TOLOR, BELLE. Judgment of children's popularity from their human figure drawings. *J. proj. Tech.*, 1955, 19, 170–175. **63**

TOLOR, A. The stability of tree drawings as related to several Rorschach signs of rigidity. *J. clin. Psychol.*, 1957, 13, 162–164. **65**

TOWNSEND, E. A. A study of copying ability in children. *Genet. Psychol. Monogr.*, 1951, 43, 3–51. **166, 167**

VAN DER HORST, L. Affect, expression, and symbolic function in the drawing of children. In M. L. Reymert (Ed.), *Feelings and emotions*. New York: McGraw-Hill, 1950. Pp. 398–417. **182**

VEDDER, R. Over het copieren van eenvoudige geometrische figuren door oligophrenen en jonge kinderen. (The copying of geometric figures by feebleminded and young children.) Amsterdam: N. V. Noord-Hollandsche Uitgevers Maatschappi, 1939. **47**

VERNIER, CLAIRE M. *Projective test productions. I. Projective drawings*. New York: Grune & Stratton, 1952. **49, 53, 66**

VERNON, P. E. *The structure of human abilities*. London: Methuen, 1950. **2**

VERWORN, M. Kinderkunst und Urgeschichte. (Child art and earliest history.) *Korrespondenz der deutscher anthropologische Gesellschaft*, 1907, 27, 42–46. **15**

VINACKE, W. E. The investigation of concept formation. *Psychol. Bull.*, 1951, 48, 1–31. **179, 191**

VINACKE, W. E. *The psychology of thinking*. New York: McGraw-Hill, 1952. **233**

VINACKE, W. E. Concept formation in children of school ages. *Educ.*, 1954, 74, 527–534. **179, 191**

VOGELSANG, H. Aus der Ideenwelt jugendlicher Rechtsbrecher. (From the young delinquent's world of ideas.) *Zsch. f. Jugendk.*, 1934, 4, 120–125. **28**

VOLKELT, H. Fortschritte der experimentellen Kinderpsychologie. (Progress in experimental child psychology.) Pp. 80–135 in *IX Kongr. f. exp. Psychol.*, Jena: Verlag von G. Fischer, 1926. **164, 180**

WAEHNER, TRUDE. Interpretation of spontaneous drawings and paintings. *Genet. Psychol. Monogr.*, 1946, 33, 3–70. **50, 55**

WAGNER, MAZIE E. & SCHUBERT, H. J. P. *D.A.P. quality scale*. Kenmore, New York: Delaware Letter Shop, 3055 Delaware Ave., 1955. **109**

WALTON, W. E. Empathic responses in children. *Psychol. Monogr.*, 1936, 48, 40–67. **39**

WARREN, H. C. *Dictionary of psychology*. New York: Houghton Mifflin, 1934. **6 fn.**

WARTEGG, E. Gestaltung und Charakter. (Organization and character.) *Beih. Z. angew. Psychol.*, 1939, No. 84. **51**

WAWRZASZEK, F., JOHNSON, O. G., & SCIERA, J. L. A comparison of H–T–P responses of handicapped and non-handicapped children. *J. clin. Psychol.*, 1958, 14, 160–162. **46**

WECHSLER, D. *The measurement of adult intelligence*. Baltimore: Williams and Wilkins, 1939. **88**

WEIDER, A. & NOLLER, P. A. Objective studies of children's drawings of human figures. I. Sex awareness and socio-economic level. *J. clin. Psychol.*, 1950, 6, 319–325. **45**

WEIDER, A. & NOLLER, P. A. Objective studies of children's drawings of human figures. II. Sex, age, intelligence. *J. clin. Psychol.*, 1953, 9, 20–23. **45**

WEIL, P. G. Caractéristiques du développement du dessin par groupes d'âges, selon divers auteurs. (Characteristics of the development of drawing by age groups according to various authors.) *Enfance*, 1950, 3, 221–226. (a) **20 fn.**

WEIL, P. G. Le test de dessin d'un bonhomme comme contrôle periodique simple et rapide de la croissance mentale. (The test of drawing a man as a simple and rapid periodic check of the mental growth.) *Enfance*, 1950, 3, 227–243. (b) **20 fn.**

WELLMAN, BETH L. Motor achievements of preschool children. *Childh. Educ.*, 1937, 13, 311–316. **3**

WERNER, H. *Comparative psychology of mental development.* Chicago: Follett, 1948. **179, 180, 181, 182**

WHITMYRE, J. W. The significance of artistic excellence in the judgment of adjustment inferred from human figure drawings. *J. consult. Psychol.*, 1953, 17, 421–424. **63**

WILLIAMS, J. H. Validity and reliability of the Goodenough intelligence test. *Sch. & Soc.*, 1935, 41, 653–656. **21, 35, 96**

WILLIAMS, J. N. Interpretation of drawings made by maladjusted children. *Virginia med. Monogr.*, 1940, 67, 533–538. **39**

WILLIAMS, MARION L. The growth of intelligence as measured by the Goodenough drawing test. *J. appl. Psychol.*, 1930, 14, 239–256. **22**

WINDSOR, RUTH S. An experimental study of easel painting as a projective technique with nursery school children. *J. genet. Psychol.*, 1949, 75, 73–83. **41, 55–56, 60**

WINTSCH, J. Le dessin comme témoin du développement mental: I. (Drawing as an index of mental development.) *Z. Kinderpsychiat.*, 1935, 2, 33–44. **20 fn., 102**

WITKIN, H. A. et al. *Personality through perception.* New York: Harper, 1954. **198**

WOLFF, W. Projective methods for personality analysis of expressive behavior in preschool children. *Charact. & Pers.*, 1942, 10, 309–330. **51**

WOLFF, W. The personality of the preschool child: The child's search for his self. New York: Grune & Stratton, 1946. **50, 51, 55, 61, 95**

WOOD, L. & SHULMAN, E. The Ellis visual designs test. *J. educ. Psychol.*, 1940, 31, 591–602. **47**

WOODS, W. A. & COOK, W. E. Proficiency in drawing and placement of hands in drawings of the human figure. *J. consult. Psychol.*, 1954, 18, 119–121. **63**

YEPSEN, L. N. The reliability of the Goodenough drawing test with feebleminded subjects. *J. educ. Psychol.*, 1929, 20, 448–451. **21, 35, 96**

ZAZZO, RÉNÉ. Première contribution des psychologues scolaires a la psychologie différentielle des sexes. (A first contribution of school psychologists to the differential psychology of the sexes.) *Enfance*, 1948, 1, 168–175. **129**

ZAZZO, RÉNÉ. Le geste graphique et la structuration de l'espace. (The act of drawing and the structuration of space.) *Enfance*, 1950, 3, 204–220. **160**

ZESBAUGH, H. A. *Children's drawings of the human figure.* Chicago: Univer. of Chicago Press, 1934. **160**

ZILAHI-BEKE, A. Zusammenhänge zwischen Kunst- und Charakterentwickelung. (Relationships between artistic development and personality development.) *Int. Zsch. f. Indiv. psychol.*, 1931, 9, 51–60. **40**

Name Index

Subject Index

McQuarrie Test for Mechanical Ability, correlated with Goodenough, 35, 97
Maladjusted children, drawings of, 27, 28, 40
Maladjustment, drawings as indicator of, 27, 28
Male figure, as subject for Goodenough scale, 69
Manual for Goodenough-Harris Drawing Test, 239–311
Marston Scale of Introversion-Extroversion, and drawings, 23
Masculine traits and drawing. See Sex difference
Mass, use of, 213, 214
Maturity, factor in drawing, 216, 224
  on HTP test, 50
  measures of, 5, 8
Meaning, as component in drawing, 173
Medium used and schema, 202
Memory, drawing from, 168–171
Memory image and drawing, 204
Mental ability, as academic ability, 5
  factorial composition of, 3
  growth of, 2–3
Mental age, limitations of concept, 4
  and ability to copy models, 167
  new indices for, 4
Mental age scale, limitations of, 88
Mental content, in organismic theory, 179
Mental defectives. See Mentally retarded
Mental development, transitions in, 3, 4. See also Mental ability
  uneven, and drawings, 24
Mental growth in drawings, scaled, 22
Mentally retarded, drawings of, 15, 16–17, 21, 25, 26, 79, 158, 172–173, 194, 195, 222
  examples of drawings, 266–269, 270–274
  finger paintings of, 61
  and HTP test, 65–66
  and perception of relationships, 194
  preschool, drawings of, 244–245
  thought processes in, 193–194
Methods tried to score items, 70–72
Michelangelo, study of, 40
MMPI Test, 45
Minnesota Paper Formboard Test, and Goodenough, 36, 97
Minnesota Scale for Paternal Occupations, 73, 112
Mixed profile in drawings, 16, 21
Modeling or shading, in female figure, 77, 78
Modification of copied design, classification for, 171. See Distortions in drawings
Motifs (assigned objects), and drawings, 59
Motion factor, in drawing, 217
Motivation, and drawings, 38, 227–228
Motor abilities of children, and age, 3

Motor components, in cognition, 165
  in drawing, 129, 161, 162, 169, 175, 182, 210
Motor control in drawing and painting, 155–157, 161–162
Motor coordination items, sex difference, 127, 128, 129
Motor skill, and copying from a model, 167
Mouth, treatment of, in female figure, 78
Movement, represented in drawings, 33, 71, 77, 218
  related to artistic merit, 93
  sex differences, 128, 218
Myokinetic Psychodiagnosis, 47

Naming of drawings by young children, 161
Nativist view in psychology, and drawing, 174
Naturalism, factor in drawing, 218
Naturalistic drawings. See Representative drawings
Negro-white differences on HTP, 65
Neural processes in brain, 175, 178, 196
Neurological damage, effects on drawings, 26, 28, 46–48, 66
Neurological functioning, and body image, 47–48
Neuro-Psychologic theory of perception applied to drawing, 205–209
Nomothetic vs. idiographic approach to personality, 25
Norms for tests, changes in, 1
Norwegian children, drawings of, 160
Nose, treatment of, 127. See also Sex differences

Object, concept of, 191
Object recognition and drawing, 189–191
Observation in art training, importance of, 199, 220, 221, 222
Observation of drawing behavior, importance of, 153, 183
Observer's role in perception, 197
Occupational types drawn, 23
Organismic theory of drawing, 179–181
  evaluated, 227, 231
  experimental evaluation of, 184–185
  phenomenological character of, 179
Organization, in cognition, 179
  in drawings, 162–163, 165–166
  in representative drawing, 163–166
Orientation of drawings on page, 160–161
Ornamentation, in Eskimo drawings, 132–133
Outline, use of, in drawing, 166, 213. See also Formal element

Paintings, scale for evaluating, 110
Part-to-whole procedure in drawing behavior, 166, 170